Introducing ZBrush®

THIRD EDITION

Introducing ZBrush®

THIRD EDITION

ERIC KELLER

John Wiley & Sons, Inc.

Acquisitions Editor: Mariann Barsolo
Development Editor: Lisa Bishop
Technical Editor: Louie Tucci
Production Editor: Eric Charbonneau
Copy Editor: Linda Recktenwald
Editorial Manager: Pete Gaughan
Production Manager: Tim Tate
Vice President and Executive Group Publisher: Richard Swadley
Vice President and Publisher: Neil Edde
Supervising Producer: Rich Graves
Media Associate Producer: Doug Kuhn
Media Quality Assurance: Marilyn Hummel
Book Designer: Caryl Gorska
Compositors: Chris Gillespie, Kate Kaminski, and Maureen Forys, Happenstance Type-O-Rama
Proofreaders: Jen Larsen and Louise Watson, Word One New York
Indexer: Jack Lewis
Project Coordinator, Cover: Katherine Crocker
Cover Designer: Ryan Sneed
Cover Image: Eric Keller

Copyright © 2012 by John Wiley & Sons, Inc., Indianapolis, Indiana

Published simultaneously in Canada

ISBN: 978-1-118-24482-1

ISBN: 978-1-118-33329-7 (ebk.)

ISBN: 978-1-118-33046-3 (ebk.)

ISBN: 978-1-118-33113-2 (ebk.)

For general information on our other products and services or to obtain technical support, please contact our Customer Care Department within the U.S. at (877) 762-2974, outside the U.S. at (317) 572-3993 or fax (317) 572-4002.

Wiley publishes in a variety of print and electronic formats and by print-on-demand. Some material included with standard print versions of this book may not be included in e-books or in print-on-demand. If this book refers to media such as a CD or DVD that is not included in the version you purchased, you may download this material at http://booksupport.wiley.com. For more information about Wiley products, visit www.wiley.com.

Library of Congress Control Number: 2012936418

10 9 8 7 6 5 4 3 2 1

Dear Reader,

Thank you for choosing *Introducing ZBrush, Third Edition*. This book is part of a family of premium-quality Sybex books, all of which are written by outstanding authors who combine practical experience with a gift for teaching.

Sybex was founded in 1976. More than 30 years later, we're still committed to producing consistently exceptional books. With each of our titles, we're working hard to set a new standard for the industry. From the paper we print on to the authors we work with, our goal is to bring you the best books available.

I hope you see all that reflected in these pages. I'd be very interested to hear your comments and get your feedback on how we're doing. Feel free to let me know what you think about this or any other Sybex book by sending me an email at nedde@wiley.com. If you think you've found a technical error in this book, please visit http://sybex.custhelp.com. Customer feedback is critical to our efforts at Sybex.

Best regards,

Neil Edde
Vice President and Publisher
Sybex, an Imprint of Wiley

For my best friend, Travis

Acknowledgments

I'd like to thank all the people who worked so hard on this project, most especially the editors, Lisa Bishop, Eric Charbonneau, Louie Tucci, and Linda Recktenwald. I'd also like to thank Mariann Barsolo and Pete Gaughan. I really want to thank all the folks at Pixologic, including Jaime Labelle, Ofer Alon, Louie Tucci, Melissa Zalinksi, Solomon Blair, Ernest Lee, and of course, Paul Gaboury. The folks at Pixologic welcomed me into the exclusive ZBrush 4 beta programs and went out of their way to help me create the best ZBrush book possible.

I want to thank my students, teachers, and friends who provided the images for the color inserts, including Scott Spencer, Mark Dedecker, Louie Tucci, Jared Krichevsky, Padhia Avocado, Sabra Haskell, Jamin Joseph Lackie, and Ara Kermanikian.

I'd like to thank the following artists, teachers, and authors for their inspiration over the years: Gael McGill, Alex Alavarez, Mark Dedecker, Scott Spencer, Dariush Derakhshani, Kevin Llewellyn, John Brown, Drew Berry, Diana Zeng, Max Dayan, John Mahoney, and everyone at the Gnomon School of Visual Effects.

Naturally, all the programmers and designers who work so hard to develop this software deserve special recognition for their hard work. They are the true artists who allow the rest of us to create such fantastic things.

Extra special thanks go my wife, Zoe, for tolerating my nonstop talk of subtools, ShadowBox, and unified skins, as well as my pals Daisy and Joe, who force me to go outside. And as always, special thanks to little Blue, whose hungry ghost still haunts the kitchen.

About the Author

Eric Keller is a freelance visual effects artist working in Hollywood. He divides his time between the entertainment industry and scientific visualization. He teaches the Introducing Digital Sculpting class at the Gnomon School of Visual Effects in Hollywood and has authored numerous animation and visualization tutorials for the Harvard Medical School course *Maya for Molecular Biologists*, taught by Gael McGill. Eric was hired by Pixologic to create over 20 video tutorials demonstrating the new features of ZBrush 4, and participated in the beta programs for version 3.5, version 4, and version 4 R2, R3.

Eric started out as an animator at the Howard Hughes Medical Institute, where he created animations for science education for seven years. In 2005, he and his wife moved to Los Angeles, where he could study and learn from the masters of visual effects. His goal is to bring the artistry and technology of Hollywood computer graphics to the field of scientific research in the hope that it can inspire and inform the scientific community and the general public.

Eric has worked at some of the best design studios in Los Angeles, including Prologue Films, Imaginary Forces, Yu and Company, BLT and Associates, and The Syndicate. Projects include feature film title animations for *The Invasion*, *Enchanted*, *Sympathy for Lady Vengeance*, and *Dragon Wars*. He has also contributed to numerous commercials, television shows, and design projects. Currently, Eric is the visual effects supervisor for E. O. Wilson's *Life on Earth* project for the iPad.

Other books by Eric Keller include *Maya Visual Effects: The Innovator's Guide*, *Introducing ZBrush* (first and second editions), *Mastering Maya 2009*, and *Mastering Maya 2011*, all published by Sybex. He was a contributing author to *Mastering Maya 7* and *Mastering Maya 2012*. He has authored the video series *Essential ZBrush 3.1* for Lynda.com as well as numerous tutorials and articles for *3D World* magazine. Many of his tutorials are available online at www.bloopatone.com and www.molecularmovies.org.

CONTENTS AT A GLANCE

Contents

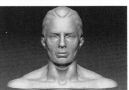

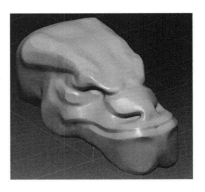

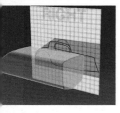

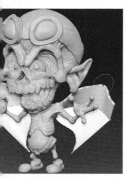

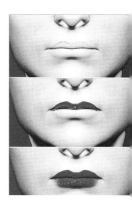

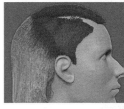

Foreword

Here we are at the third edition of *Introducing ZBrush* by Eric Keller. Let me first say it is an honor to be asked by Eric to write the foreword to his exceptional book. I have had the pleasure of knowing Eric for several years now. We first met at the Gnomon School of Visual Effects in Hollywood, where Eric has run several successful courses. I have learned much from his experience, and if it were not for his recommendation, I never would have had the opportunity to write my own ZBrush books. Based on Eric's previous titles and his experience as a teacher, I am confident you are in the best of hands with Eric as your guide to this amazing program.

It is amazing to realize that we have already come to the third edition of this landmark ZBrush book. In a relatively short period of time, so many new and exciting things have changed with the program. It seems to me the minds behind ZBrush are continually pressing the accelerator on innovation. Each new point update seems packed to the rafters with groundbreaking features and improvements on various tools. It has come to the point that we seem to expect Pixologic to revolutionize some aspect of the program with each release. If you are new to ZBrush, you are about to experience one of the most unique and liberating programs for artists on the market. If you have worked with previous versions, be prepared to see an entire arsenal of new tools and possibilities!

ZBrush is merely 12 years old, and in just over half that time it has gone from a unique painting program to the industry-standard digital sculpting software. It has changed how we create character models, from initial design to final paint and detailing. Not only has Pixologic defined high-resolution brush-based sculpting for the film and game industries, but ZBrush has opened up entirely new applications for digital sculpting tools. In the last five years, manufacturing has seen ZBrush enter the scene to be used as a highly effective medium for creating sculptures. Creators of fine art have begun to integrate ZBrush into their creative process. In just the past year, I have used ZBrush to create everything from prosthetic bodies to fine art public sculpture and collectible action figures. Anyone who seeks to become proficient as a sculptor in ZBrush will find they have a staggering number of opportunities to find an application for their skill set!

ZBrush has even gained a foothold in the world of concept design. Many directors are now eager to see their creatures and characters designed in three dimensions rather than on paper. This allows a new level of freedom because they can interactively see the character in 3D space and make changes on the fly. This level of freedom is always appealing to directors who want to know they have explored every possibility in the design process. It also allows talented sculptors to take part in the initial conceptual phases of the project rather than replicating a completed design from a set of drawings.

This is truly an exciting time to be learning ZBrush, and I can think of no better guide than Eric to lead you into the world of digital sculpting. Eric's many years of experience as a working production artist have made him sensitive to the need for reliable and efficient workflows. He is also an accomplished artist with pixels and pencils. For this reason, Eric's instruction will go beyond how to use the program into how to approach ZBrush with an artist's sensibility. That's what makes each of you reading this book unique. You are all artists, and the vision, experience, and education you each bring to the program is what makes the work shine. ZBrush is a tool to liberate your creative power from the limits of technology. I have taken up too much of your time already—carry on with the path to learning this unique and powerful artist's tool. Enjoy the journey!

—SCOTT SPENCER, character designer and sculptor

Introduction

In 2010, Pixologic celebrated the tenth anniversary of the debut of ZBrush. ZBrush was introduced to the world as an experimental art application with a unique technology that allowed users to create illustrations in two and a half dimensions. I remember seeing the Pixologic booth at a Macworld in New York in the summer of 2000. The booth was small but the presentation was remarkable. I grabbed a demo copy, installed it on my Mac laptop, and played with it on the train ride home from New York. At the time I was primarily interested in 3D modeling and animation, so after Macworld, my focus returned to LightWave and Autodesk® Maya®, and the demo copy of ZBrush collected dust on my shelf.

I remember reading an article in 2003 in *Cinefex* magazine on the making of *The Return of the King*. The author of the article mentioned that the ghostly character of the King of the Dead, who confronts Aragorn, was created in ZBrush. Within seconds of reading that I was downloading the newer version of ZBrush and working my way through the tutorials. I could not believe that the little 2.5 dimensional painting program I had played with only a few years earlier could have created such an amazingly detailed and realistic character. From that point on I became a ZBrush user. Because much of my work at the time involved creating organic surfaces for animations in the fields of cell biology and medicine, ZBrush seemed to be the perfect solution. For many years before ZBrush, a number of 3D applications promised "digital sculpting"—an interface in which the modeling tools used to create virtual surfaces were so intuitive that it felt like working with clay. ZBrush was the first application to actually deliver this technology.

I was not alone in my realization of the potential of ZBrush. Over the years many other CG artists have discovered that ZBrush is the key to realizing their fantastic visions. Each update to ZBrush has included not only tools but technological innovations that are designed to make computer graphics less technical and more accessible to artists. In version 2 we had ZSpheres, which allowed us to create virtual armatures that could be converted into polygons and sculpted into organic shapes. Version 3 introduced subtools, which made the task of creating sculptures with multiple, independent parts easy, and the sculpting brushes, which can be used to intuitively sculpt details into the surface. Version 3.5 introduced ZSketching, a process where strips of virtual clay are painted onto an armature and smoothed and sculpted into organic forms.

Version 4 introduced ShadowBox, a volumetric sculpting interface that generates a mesh at the center of a cube based on the profiles that you paint on the sides of the cube. In early 2012 Pixologic released a series of updates that greatly expanded the modeling and rendering capabilities of ZBrush. The new features in version 4 R3 introduced Dynamesh, which is a dynamic sculpting mesh that can be updated in real time, allowing you unlimited sculpting freedom. Version 4 R3 also introduces FiberMesh, which is a hair sculpting system, and LightCap, which is an advanced lighting tool.

ZBrush version 4 R3 has doubled the capabilities of the previous version, giving you a wide variety of approaches that you can apply to any sculpture that you can imagine. ZBrush 4 R3 is a virtual sculpting studio. And this advanced and experimental technology is intended for artists. The tools are so new and so powerful that I had to completely rewrite this book (and I was happy to do so). The original version of this book, published in 2008, was written for beginners, even artists who had never touched computer graphics software before. It was a pretty good overview of the basics of illustrating and sculpting in ZBrush. This edition has also been written with the absolute beginner in mind. This book focuses primarily on the digital sculpting aspects of ZBrush, with less emphasis on 2.5 dimensional painting techniques. This is because digital sculpting has become the most popular use of ZBrush.

The types of artists using ZBrush have changed in the past year or so. I have noticed that the students who take my *Introduction to Digital Sculpting* class at the Gnomon School of Visual Effects in Hollywood are not just interested in using ZBrush to design characters for feature films, broadcast, and video games. Recently, jewelry designers, toy sculptors, visual effects and environment designers, matte painters, illustrators, and fine art artists have all been joining the ranks of the growing army of ZBrush artists. I have tried to write this book so that the widest possible audience can adopt ZBrush into whatever discipline they currently practice.

This book is about getting you up to speed as quickly as possible so that you feel comfortable using the software. Hopefully, after reading this book you'll be eager to move on to more advanced instruction, such as the books recently written by my friend and mentor Scott Spencer. These include *ZBrush Creature Design: Creating Dynamic Concept Imagery for Film and Games* and *ZBrush Digital Sculpting Human Anatomy*. Pixologic's own Paul Gaboury has also released a book, *ZBrush Professional Tips and Techniques,* with detailed tutorials from Paul and some of the leading artists in the industry. These books are all available from Sybex.

In this book, a variety of tools and techniques are described and demonstrated using simple subjects such as fantasy dragons and a cartoon car. As you go through the exercises in this book, you should start to see that there are many ways to approach a particular problem. Over time you'll discover the approaches that you like the best, and by adopting them and perfecting them, you'll develop your own style of ZBrush art.

Who Should Buy This Book

This book is written for users who are new to ZBrush as well as new to digital sculpting. If you've never used ZBrush before, this book is meant for you. If you have used older versions of the software, you will find that this book brings you up to date with the newest developments. ZBrush has changed a lot in recent years and continues to do so. You'll find that even if you feel somewhat experienced as a user of older versions, there's a lot of new stuff in this edition. If you are a user of similar software, such as Autodesk® Mudbox™, this book will help you easily make the transition to ZBrush.

If you've never used digital art software before, you should still be OK with this book. However, you do need to be comfortable using a computer. This book can't help you solve problems that exist outside the software itself. You should be comfortable working in your operating system. You need to be familiar with opening and saving files and the like. It is helpful to understand something about other image editing and painting programs, such as Adobe Photoshop and Corel Painter.

The bonus chapters on the DVD that come with this book deal with working with other 3D applications, such as Autodesk® Maya®. However, if you don't intend to use ZBrush with other applications, you can skip these sections.

This book assumes that you are using a digital tablet and stylus while working in ZBrush. It's not absolutely necessary to have a tablet when using ZBrush, but it will make your life a lot easier. Using ZBrush with a mouse is like sculpting clay while wearing mittens.

At the time of this writing Pixologic was furiously releasing updates and introducing new tools. Pixologic's own Louie Tucci tech-edited the book, ensuring that all information is accurate and up to date. That being said, I can only expect that new editions of the software will be released after this book hits the shelves. This may lead to some inconsistencies with the images in the book and the location of various controls within the current ZBrush interface. My apologies if this occurs; please make a note of which version of the software you are using and check the Pixologic website for detailed information on what has changed in your version.

What's Inside

Most of the lessons in each chapter are accompanied by example scenes from the DVD included with the book. In addition, bonus movies are included to help illustrate some aspects of the examples in the text of the book.

Chapter 1: Digital Art Basics An overview of the fundamental concepts of working with computer graphics. Concepts such as resolution, color depth, compression, and anti-aliasing are explained. Also, some of the history behind ZBrush, as well as special ZBrush technology like the pixol, are introduced.

Chapter 2: Understanding the ZBrush Interface A tour of the ZBrush interface. This chapter is very important for understanding how to get around in ZBrush. Even if you have used older versions of ZBrush, it's a good idea to read this chapter so that you understand the changes that have been made as well as how to find the controls for newer features.

Chapter 3: Basic Digital Sculpting This chapter is meant to get you started with your first basic digital sculpt. The subject for the first exercises is a simple fantasy dragon's head. You'll learn about working with dynamic levels of subdivision, as well as ZBrush's unique Dynamesh technology.

Chapter 4: Polymesh Editing This chapter introduces the concept of subtools, which allow you to create complex sculptures that use multiple independent parts. Polygroups and the Slice brush are introduced as ways to manage complex surfaces. The chapter also demonstrates how to create a simple dragon using ZBrush's unique ZSphere tool. Finally, you'll learn how to use the extremely intuitive ZSketching brushes to create complex organic sculpts quickly and easily.

Chapter 5: ShadowBox and Clip Brushes ShadowBox is a brand-new ZBrush innovation that is perfect for creating hard-surface models. In this chapter, the exercises demonstrate how to use ShadowBox to create the body of a hot rod. The clip brushes are another new feature that can be used to create hard edges on a surface. In this chapter, you'll see how to use clip brushes to clean up the surface of the hot rod body. Also you'll learn how the Insert Mesh brushes can be used to shape a surface.

Chapter 6: Advanced ZSphere Techniques In this chapter, you'll learn how the ZSphere tool is the Swiss army knife of ZBrush. The tutorials demonstrate how to rearrange the surface of a character using ZSphere retopology. You'll learn about projection, ZSphere rigging, ZSphere deformations, mannequin projects, and the curve brushes.

Chapter 7: Advanced Brush Techniques This chapter takes a detailed look at how the sculpting brushes in ZBrush work. You'll learn how to design your own custom brushes to accomplish specific tasks and effects. You'll learn how to save the brushes for use on future projects.

Chapter 8: Polypainting and SpotLight Polypainting is used to apply color detail to surfaces. In this chapter, you'll learn techniques for painting realistic color on a dragon's head. The SpotLight image-editing and projection interface is introduced as well.

Chapter 9: FiberMesh, Materials, and Rendering In this chapter you'll learn how to create and style a character's hair using FiberMesh. You'll learn how to create dramatic lighting and realistic materials that can be applied to your sculpture. You'll learn about the new BPR LightCap lighting and rendering technology, which can be used to add effects such as transparency, ambient occlusion, and subsurface scattering. These all make your models look spectacular.

Chapter 10: Surface Noise, Layers, and the ZBrush Timeline ZBrush 4 R3 introduces an advanced tool for creating detailed noise on the surface of your model. The Timeline enables animation within ZBrush. In this chapter, you'll learn how these features can help you test models designed for animation in ZBrush, store and animate camera views, record your ZBrush sessions, and create animated turntable movies. You'll see how layers can be used to create variations of your model's shape and color.

The following material is available in PDF format on the book's companion DVD:

Bonus Content 1: GoZ GoZ is a ZBrush plug-in designed to make it easier to send models from ZBrush to other animation programs such as Autodesk® Maya® and 3ds Max®, Luxology's modo, and Maxon's Cinema 4D. You'll also learn how to create texture, normal, and displacement maps for your ZBrush models.

Bonus Content 2: ZScripts and ZPlugins ZBrush has a number of free plug-ins available that can automate common ZBrush techniques and extend the capabilities of existing ZBrush tools. This chapter demonstrates how to install the free plug-ins and includes descriptions of the more commonly used plug-ins.

The companion DVD is home to all the demo files, samples, and bonus resources mentioned in the book. See the Appendix for more details on the contents and how to access them.

How to Contact the Author

I enjoy hearing from the readers of my books. Feedback helps me to continually improve my skills as an author. You can contact me through my website, www.bloopatone.com, as well as see examples of my own artwork there.

Sybex strives to keep you supplied with the latest tools and information you need for your work. Please check the book's website at www.sybex.com/go/introducingzbrush3e, where Sybex will post additional content and updates that supplement this book, should the need arise. If you are using the eBook version of the text, you can contact Sybex through their website to find out how to download the support materials found on the DVD.

CHAPTER 1

Digital Art Basics

Any experienced artist knows that the composition of the tools they use—the chemistry of the paint, the ingredients of the clay—affects the quality of a finished work of art. When you are learning to become an artist, you spend a great deal of time studying how the tools behave. It is the same with digital art. This chapter reviews the fundamentals of digital art. Just as an oil painter needs to learn how the mixture of pigments and oils works with the canvas, a digital artist needs to learn how color depth, channels, file formats, and other elements factor into the quality of a digital masterpiece.

This chapter includes the following topics:

- **An introduction to ZBrush**
- **Understanding digital images**
- **Understanding 3D space**
- **Being a digital artist**

An Introduction to ZBrush

Imagine walking into a fully stocked artist's studio. Inside you find cabinets and drawers full of paints and brushes, a large canvas, a closet full of every type of sculpting medium imaginable, a lighting rig, a camera, a light box, a projector, a kiln, armatures for maquettes, and a seemingly infinite array of carving and cutting tools. On top of this everything has been neatly arranged for optimal use while working. This is ZBrush, a self-contained studio where you can digitally create paintings and sculptures—and even combinations of the two. Furthermore, you are not limited to what you find in ZBrush. Digital 3D models and 2D textures can easily be imported from other applications and used as tools within ZBrush. ZBrush can function as a self-contained digital art workspace or as an integral part of a production pipeline for video games, films, or even toy manufacturing.

A few years ago, the most common use of ZBrush was for creating and editing digital models that are then animated and rendered in other 3D packages, such as Autodesk® Maya® and 3ds Max® software, Maxon's Cinema 4D, and Luxology's modo. This is still true, but ZBrush is finding its way into many other industries.

When creating models for film, artists choose to create models in ZBrush because the unique technology behind ZBrush allows them to work with very dense models (literally millions of polygons). ZBrush artists can create a stunningly rich level of detail on organic surfaces in a way that traditional 3D packages just can't. Fine wrinkles, fleshy folds, pores, bumps, scales, scars, and scratches can be easily sculpted into the model and then exported either as part of the geometry or as bump and displacement textures that can enhance the geometry of a model when the model is rendered in another package. The result is often an amazing level of detail and realism built into a virtual object (see Figure 1.1). Colors can also be painted directly on the model in ZBrush in an intuitive fashion and then exported as texture maps for use in shaders applied to the same model in other 3D packages. Production pipelines at studios such as ILM, Gentle Giant, Weta, and Sony Pictures Imageworks have used ZBrush in this way to create many of the characters, monsters, and set pieces seen in such films as *The Lord of the Rings*, *Pirates of the Caribbean*, and *Sky Captain and the World of Tomorrow*.

More recently, ZBrush has been adapted for use in areas beyond animation and effects. These days artists are using ZBrush as a tool in the production of toys, game characters and environments, medical and scientific visualization; in jewelry design and concept design; and even to help in the creation of physical sculpture.

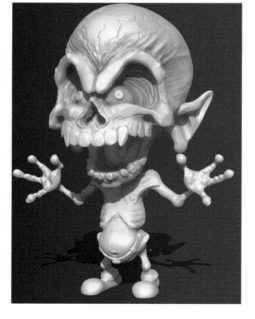

Figure 1.1

A highly detailed model created in ZBrush

Artists are using ZBrush to design models on computers and then translating them into physical versions via 3D printing technology (see Figure 1.2). As the 3D printing process becomes more common and less expensive, one can imagine how ZBrush can easily be integrated into a desktop fabrication pipeline in the near future.

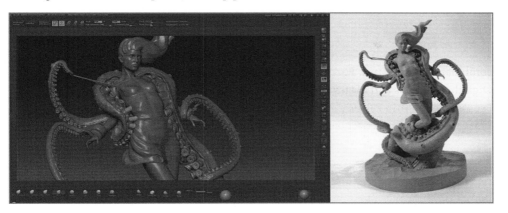

Figure 1.2

A physical model that was sculpted by Chris Bostjanick in ZBrush and printed using a 3D printer.

ZBrush can also be used for the creation of digital illustrations: The program has digital sculpting and painting tools as well as its own unique rendering technology. Within ZBrush, artists can create custom virtual materials, which can simulate very realistic surfaces or create a very stylized look. These materials can be applied to an artistic composition and, when rendered, react to virtual lights and shadows. Many artists have taken advantage of the flexible workspace and powerful tools to create amazing ZBrush compositions. In addition, ZBrush works very well with other 2D paint programs, such as Adobe Photoshop and Corel Painter. Digital 3D models and 2D images can be exported and imported freely between these programs, so there is no limit to what can be achieved when ZBrush is incorporated into the digital artist's toolbox.

Understanding Digital Images

Now let's take a brief look at several ways digital imagery can be created on a computer and displayed on a monitor. Computers display digital images using colored squares known as *pixels*. This section reviews the basics of working with pixels and related issues.

Anatomy of a Pixel

A pixel is a colored square that appears on the screen at a specified position—pretty simple, at least to begin with. A raster graphic is an image made up of thousands of pixels. A pixel is imbued with a certain amount of color and position information that is stored in memory. If you load a rasterized graphic into a digital viewing program and then scale the image up (or zoom in), you can actually see how the image is composed of these pixels (see Figure 1.3).

Figure 1.3

Raster images are composed of tiny colored squares called pixels, which are visible when you enlarge the image.

A digital image file stores the positional information of these pixels in terms of x- and y-coordinates. The y-coordinate is the vertical position and the x-coordinate is the horizontal position. It may seem obvious, but it's important to note that when you zoom in or scroll around on a digital image in the software, the position and size of each pixel change relative to the screen. However, the software still needs to remember the position and size of each pixel relative to the digital image that is being viewed. You should be aware of this fact, but don't spend too much time thinking about it now; that's your computer's job.

Creating Smooth Images with Anti-Aliasing

Aliasing refers to the situation in which a curving line or shape displayed on a computer screen appears jagged. This is because the image is composed of tiny squares. To correct this problem, graphic software employs *anti-aliasing*, which smoothes the edges of curving shapes by blending the color of the pixels along the edges with other pixels of similar hue but varying degrees of lightness. This fools the eye into perceiving the edges as being smooth.

Figure 1.4

The letters in the word jagged are aliased. The letters in the word smooth are anti-aliased.

In Figure 1.4, the letters in the word *jagged* appear jagged because the square pixels are visible along the curving edges of the letters; this image is *aliased*. The letters in the word *smooth* appear smooth because of the blending technique that mixes pixels of varying lightness along the curving edges of the letters. The image is *anti-aliased*.

Channels and Color Depth

Along with positional data, the pixel stores information about how to display colors. A computer screen creates color by mixing red, green, and blue light. If a pixel is 100 percent red mixed with 0 percent blue and 0 percent green, it looks red. If a pixel is composed of 50 percent red with 50 percent blue and 0 percent green values, the pixel will look purple. When all three values are 0 percent, the pixel is black, and when all three are 100 percent, the pixel is white.

Color depth refers to how much color information is stored for each pixel in the image. A grayscale image discards all color information except for black, white, and the range of gray in between; this usually comes out to 256 shades of gray. The result is a black-and-white image. Since color information is limited to the 256 shades of gray, the image file has less information that needs to be stored.

If you have studied painting, you may have learned that the primary colors are defined as red, yellow, and blue. The secondary color green, for example, is created when blue is mixed with yellow. This is true for paint but not so for colors created by a lighted computer screen. As far as computers are concerned, red, green, and blue are the primary colors. Red and green mixed together produce the secondary color yellow.

An RGB image stores red, green, and blue information. The information is divided into three channels (red, green, and blue) and each channel stores the values (or percentage) of red, green, and blue for each pixel. To see a demonstration of how this works, follow these instructions to view the RGB values of various colors using ZBrush's color chooser:

1. Start ZBrush.

2. Click Color on the menu bar to open the Color palette.

3. Drag your cursor around in the color selector area (see Figure 1.5).

4. Observe the changing R, G, and B numeric values below the color area. These values change depending on the mixture required to create the selected color. Notice that the highest value possible for each channel is 255 and the lowest is 0 (see Figure 1.5).

5. Click the R, G, and B sliders to select them and type in numeric values. Set R to **255**, G to **0**, and B to **255**. The resulting color is a bright fuchsia.

An image in an RGBA format has an additional, fourth channel known as the *alpha channel*. The alpha channel stores information on the opacity of individual pixels. This allows for an image to have regions of transparency. The left side of Figure 1.6 shows a basic scene rendered in a 3D program; the floating spheres are transparent. The right side of Figure 1.6

Figure 1.5

The numbers in the R (red), G (green), and B (blue) fields indicate the values for the red, green, and blue channels.

shows the alpha channel. White areas are 100 percent opaque and black areas are 100 percent transparent. The gray areas show the amount of transparency.

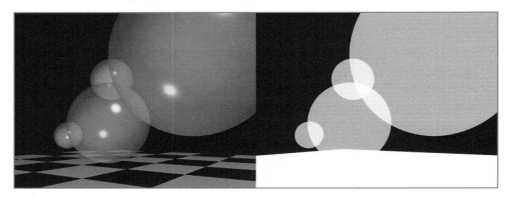

Color depth refers to how much information is used for each of these color channels. Computers use bits to store information. A bit is a series of 1s and 0s (known as binary because there are only two options, 1 and 0). A 24-bit RGB image uses 8 bits of information for each channel (3 × 8 = 24). Each 8-bit channel stores a range of 256 shades of color, allowing an image to have a total of 16 million colors. A 32-bit RGBA image uses an additional 8 bits for the alpha channel.

The more bits you have, the more information you can store, and with more bits, the image can be displayed using a wider range of color. More memory is required to store and work with higher-bit images. An image that uses 16 bits per channel (48 bits total for an RGB image, 64 bits for RGBA) can be confusingly referred to as a 16-bit image (as in a 16-bit TIFF or 16-bit SGI).

Beware. This is not the same as a 16-bit or high-color image that uses about 5 bits for each channel. Welcome to the confusing world of computer terminology. You will get used to these kinds of terminology conflicts with some experience. Although computers are strictly logical, the humans that create and use them are not always so! If you are working as an artist in television or film production, you will be using 16-bit (per channel) images much more often than 16-bit (5 bits per channel) high-color images.

Image Formats

A digital image can be stored in a number of ways, known as formats. A format is simply the arrangement of information in a file. Typical image formats include Tagged Image File Format (TIFF), Joint Photographic Experts Group (JPEG), and Graphics Interchange Format (GIF).

Many programs have their own native document format. Photoshop can read many file formats but also has its own Photoshop Document (PSD) format. Likewise, Corel's Painter stores special information in a format called Resource Interchange File Format (RIFF). ZBrush has its own ZBR document format.

An image format can be compressed to conserve storage space. Some image formats have compression built in (such as JPEG and GIF), and some can exist with or without compression (such as SGI, or Silicon Graphics Image). Compression usually affects the quality of the image. If you look closely at a JPEG image from a typical website using a browser, you may notice that it is blurry or grainy or that the colors are not quite right. Image quality has been sacrificed to allow faster download for viewing images over the Internet.

When the quality of an image is diminished by the compression, it is said to be a *lossy* compression format. There are also *lossless* compressions that can reduce the size of an image without significantly affecting quality. These formats, such as Portable Network Graphics (PNG), result in file sizes that are larger than those for which lossy compression is used. Compression applied to sequences of images is also used for video.

In Figure 1.7, the image on the left is uncompressed and the image on the right is compressed. Look closely and you can see the distortion, known as *artifacts,* in the image on the right. This distortion is especially apparent in the details on the cactus and the edges of the plants.

Figure 1.7

The image on the left is uncompressed; the image on the right is compressed.

Understanding file formats and compression will become important as you work with computer graphics, not only with respect to images you create and share in ZBrush, but also with textures and alphas created in ZBrush and used on 3D models in other programs. If you use a compressed image as the source for a texture used to color a model or as a tool for sculpting, the resulting model can suffer because of low image quality. In addition, some 3D applications and rendering engines will prefer some formats more than others, which is important to understand when you export images created in ZBrush for use in other software packages. These aspects of working with images in ZBrush will be covered in more depth later in this book.

Vector Images

As stated earlier, computers can also use vectors to create digital images. A vector graphic is created from formulas and mathematical calculations performed by the computer and its software. The results of these calculations are smooth lines and shapes that are often filled with colors. Vector graphics are continually drawn and updated when the image is scaled, moved, or rotated, so the graphic is always of the same quality no matter what its size and position.

Adobe Illustrator and Adobe Flash are popular vector graphic programs. Vectors are used in a modeling interface to represent 3D objects in 3D packages such as Maya and 3ds Max, and these packages have special rendering engines that can create vector graphics as final output as well. You can't create vector images in ZBrush, so I'll end the discussion of vectors for now.

Understanding Resolution

It is hard to overstate the importance of understanding resolution when working with ZBrush. Unfortunately, computer resolution is kind of a tricky concept. There's a lot of confusing terminology as well as different types of resolution and different ways to measure and calculate resolution. This is a topic that I will revisit often throughout this book, so don't panic if you haven't mastered completely the concept of resolution by the end of this section.

Simply put, *resolution* refers to the density of information within a given area. Most often in computer graphics, resolution is applied to the number of pixels that can be squeezed into a portion of the screen. However, it can also refer to the number of polygons or points squeezed into part of a 3D model. The resolution of your computer screen can determine how the resolution of your images is displayed and created. In addition, when you apply a 2D image texture to a 3D model, the pixel resolution of the 2D image and the polygon resolution of the 3D model must be taken into account or the results achieved may be somewhat disappointing. You do this kind of work a lot in ZBrush, thus resolution is something you must always keep in mind.

Screen Resolution

Let's start with screen resolution. The computer you use to create your ZBrush images and models no doubt has a computer monitor attached to it. The monitor displays text and images on the screen. Screen resolution refers to the number of square-sized pixels that appear on the screen, and this is measured horizontally and vertically. The physical size of the screen itself is usually described in diagonal terms. A 22-inch monitor refers to a screen size that measures 22 inches from one corner diagonally to the opposite corner.

Your particular screen should be able to display text and images in a number of different resolutions. The current resolution is set in the operating system's control panel or system preferences. Screen resolution is described in the number of pixels available horizontally times the number of pixels available vertically. Some typical resolutions include 640x480, which used to be the common standard in the old days when monitors were smaller; 720x486, which is the standard for broadcast television in the United States; and 1920x1080, which is used for high-definition television (HDTV).

Screen resolution will affect how ZBrush looks on your screen. When you have your screen set to a low resolution, less space is available to display both the ZBrush interface and the documents. This is one reason why computer graphics artists will invest a great deal of money on the largest computer monitor they can afford or even use two monitors connected to the same computer.

Document Resolution

Next, let's look at document resolution. In the earlier discussion on pixels, I mentioned that when you zoom in on a digital image using a graphics program, you can see the individual pixels that make up the image. Now, the actual pixels that display the image on the screen do not get any larger or smaller, and you do not affect the resolution settings in your computer's hardware. Rather, the graphics program allows you to see a visual representation of the image at a higher magnification than the document's native resolution.

If you take a document that is 320×240 in size and set the magnification to 200 percent, the document is now shown at 640×480 and each pixel on the document is using four times as many computer monitor pixels. Thus, it looks blocky. Likewise, when you zoom out, or shrink the document, half the number of pixels is displayed. Zooming in and out of a document is a useful feature for graphics programs. It can allow you to work on the fine details of an image. But of course, here is where things get tricky: Because of the ability of computer software to zoom in and out of an image, document resolution can be different than screen resolution. When working with computer images, you must always keep in mind the resolution of your document regardless of how it appears on the screen.

Dots per inch (dpi) is typically used to describe document resolution (sometimes referred to as ppi, or pixels per inch), even in countries such as France that have long used the metric system. An image that is displayed on a computer monitor at 100 percent of its resolution is usually 72 dpi. An image destined for the printed page needs to be at a higher resolution, at least 300 dpi and often between 600 and 1200 dpi for commercial printing.

Image Resolution

When speaking with 3D texture artists, you'll often hear terms like *2K texture map* thrown around. What they mean is an image that is 2048 pixels×2048 pixels. The term *2K* means two thousand to normal people, but to computer graphics artists, 2K = 2048. This is because most texture images are set to a resolution that is a power of 2. Thus 1K = 1024 (210), 4K= 4096 (212), and 512 (29) means, well, 512×512.

Images of these sizes are always square, as long as you're talking to texture artists. However, if you walk into a production facility and they ask you to render an animation at 2K and you give them a square 2048×2048 image sequence, they may quickly toss you out the door. Why? Because to production people, 2K actually means 2048 pixels×1556 pixels, which is not really 2K at all (or even square for that matter). In this context, 2K is short-hand for *2K Academy*, which is a standardized resolution for film. Again, not terribly logical or consistent terminology, but it all comes down to context. Since this book is focused on ZBrush, I'll be talking the language of texture artists. So 2K means 2048×2048. If and when you move to animation software such as Maya, you may need to be aware that 2K means different things to different people, depending on the context. The safest bet is to get the people you're talking with to be specific about what they want. Geeks love jargon, but it's more often a hindrance than a help.

> Some computer professionals use K as shorthand for kilobyte, or KB, which refers to the actual storage size of a file on disk—yet another level of confusion.

Aspect Ratio

Aspect ratio refers to the dimensions of the image size as a ratio. When you create an image at 320×240 or 640×480, the aspect ratio is 4:3. If the aspect ratio is 16:9 or 1.85:1, the image size is widescreen. A typical 16:9 resolution is 1280×720. This is something you may be more concerned with when rendering an animation for final output from an animation package such as Maya. In ZBrush, aspect ratio may enter the conversation only when you're creating a composition that could be used as a matte painting in an animation or for another purpose.

Polygon Resolution

Finally, resolution can also be used to describe the number of points or polygons that make up a 3D model. I'll discuss polygons in more detail later on in this chapter, but for now you should understand that the surface of a 3D model is composed of geometric shapes defined by three or more points (polygons in ZBrush are restricted to three or four points, but in other modeling programs polygons can have more points). The polygons of a model can be subdivided, which increases its smooth appearance and allows for a higher level of detail to be sculpted into the surface.

In ZBrush, a model can consist of millions and millions of polygons, as you can see in Figure 1.8. Because of the special way ZBrush handles memory, these high-resolution models can easily be edited with much less of a performance slowdown than would be experienced using other 3D applications. Furthermore, ZBrush stores many levels of subdivision resolution within a single model file, so you can raise and lower the resolution of the 3D geometry while you are working as well as export the same model at several different resolutions for use in another 3D animation package.

Figure 1.8

A high-resolution model in ZBrush. The lines on the surface show how the model consists of thousands of square polygons.

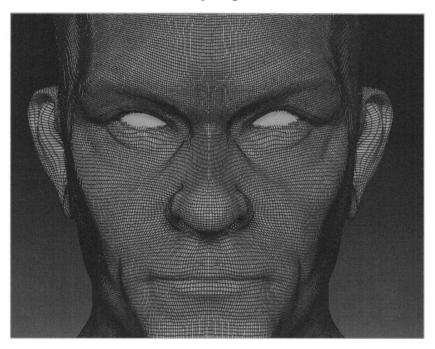

This ends our introduction to the concept of resolution. Rest assured that this topic will be popping up again throughout this book!

Understanding 3D Space

In a typical 3D software package such as Maya, 3D space is defined in terms of x-, y-, and z-coordinates. The horizontal dimension is usually described by the x-axis, vertical space is usually defined by the y-coordinates, and depth is usually defined by the z-coordinates (some packages reverse the meaning of the y- and z-axes). In Maya, the virtual world contains a grid. It's also crucial to understand that a point in 3D space, such as an individual vertex on a piece of 3D geometry, has an absolute position in the 3D world. The absolute position of a vertex in 3D space is defined using "world space" coordinates. It also has a position relative to the object it is part of; the relative position of a vertex in 3D space is defined using its "local space," or "object space" coordinates.

Think of it this way: You are wearing a pointy party hat. The point at the very tip of the hat exists in the world at the top of your head; the world space y-coordinates of this point are very high relative to the points that make up the rest of you. At the same time, the object space y-coordinates of the tip of the hat are also very high relative to the rest of you. However, if you decided to hang upside down while wearing the party hat, the world space coordinates of the tip of the hat would now be lower than the world space coordinates that make up the rest of you. Yet, in terms of object space, we understand that the tip of the hat is still the very top of the object, even when the hat is upside down. This is based on how we understand the object and its purpose in the world. If you were to model that hat using 3D modeling software, you would understand that the tip of the hat is the top, even when you rotate the hat upside down. The 3D software also keeps track of these ideas using the two sets of coordinates—world and object (see Figure 1.9).

Figure 1.9

A typical 3D modeling environment: The grid and the 3D compass help the artist keep track of x-, y-, and z-coordinates in virtual 3D space.

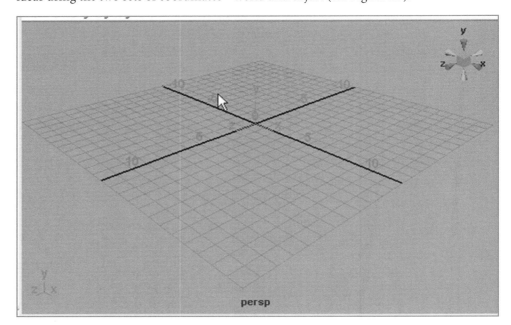

Anatomy of a Polygon

There really is no such thing as a 3D object in computer graphics. Unless you are working with rapid prototyping machines that can fabricate a physical object based on data stored in a virtual 3D file, you will always be working with two-dimensional representations of three-dimensional objects on a computer screen.

When we speak of 3D, we are using shorthand that assumes we are talking about a 3D virtual object that exists on a 2D screen. A typical digital painting program such as Photoshop plots pixels horizontally and vertically, along the x- and y-axis respectively. A

3D program stores information with additional coordinates along the z-axis, which gives the virtual image depth. A virtual object existing in the 3D space of the software is made of polygons. The polygons give the object a surface that can be deformed, translated, and animated.

A polygon is a geometric shape defined by three or more points (points are also referred to as vertices); examples of polygons are shown in Figure 1.10.

> ZBrush restricts the polygons to three or four points, but other software packages can have polygons with any number of vertices. This is important to remember when importing objects from another package into ZBrush. ZBrush will automatically split an n-sided (more than 4-point) polygon into 3- and 4-point polygons (or quadrilaterals) when it is imported.

In other programs you may encounter other types of 3D geometry, such as NURBS (which stands for non-uniform rational basis spline) and subdivision surfaces. These are converted at render time to triangle-shaped polygons by the rendering engine; thus polygons are the standard currency of 3D software. When it comes to 3D models, ZBrush works only with polygon geometry.

As was discussed in the section titled "Understanding Resolution," the number of polygons an object has will affect how smooth the surface appears and how much detail can be modeled into that surface. The resolution of a 3D object is also referred to as its *density*. ZBrush is programmed in such a way that a 3D object can have millions of polygons and an astonishing level of detail while still maintaining a high level of response on the computer during the sculpting and editing process. This is what allows the ZBrush artist to feel as if they are sculpting digital clay in a very intuitive and artistic fashion.

Figure 1.10

An image of 3-point, 4-point, and n-sided polygons as displayed in Autodesk Maya.

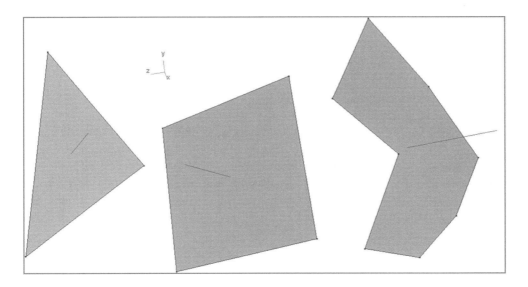

ZBrush does not actually use the Open Graphics Library (OpenGL) specification when it displays 3D objects on the screen. Pixologic has developed its own protocols for 2D and 3D images based on the *pixol*. This means that ZBrush is free from the polygon limits imposed by the OpenGL standard. It also means that ZBrush is not dependent on the power of your machine's graphics card. Instead, ZBrush requires a fair amount of RAM (a gigabyte or more) and lots of free hard disk space. For this reason ZBrush runs quite well even on a decent laptop.

A polygon appears in ZBrush as a shaded shape with three or four vertices. A virtual 3D object is made up of adjacent polygons that form the surface. (In ZBrush, the term *3D tool* is used to refer to a 3D object; the reason for this is explained in Chapter 2, "Understanding the ZBrush Interface.") The surface of a polygon has an inside and an outside. The information regarding which side of a polygon faces out and which side faces in is known as the polygon's *normal*. A 3D tool made up of millions of polygons has millions of normals that describe how the surface appears when it reacts to virtual light and shadow (see Figure 1.11).

Figure 1.11

An image of a model in ZBrush with its normals visible. The normal is displayed as a line that shows which side of the polygon is pointing "out."

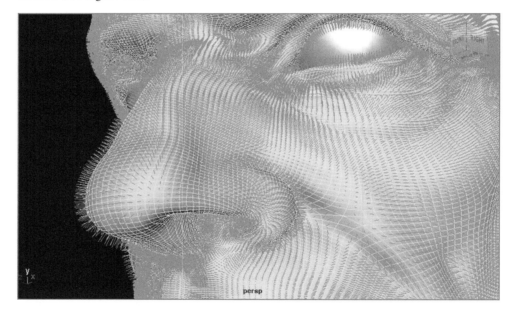

Normals are an important aspect of working with polygon geometry. Information about the direction of normals on a dense object can be stored in a special texture known as a *normal map*. Rendering engines for 3D software and video games can make a lower-density version of the same model appear to have more detail than its geometry will allow by using a normal map to help shade the object.

Pixols versus Pixels

As was stated earlier, an image created in a typical digital painting program is usually composed of thousands of pixels. A pixel is a square that contains information about color, transparency, and its location along the x- and y-axes. The unique innovation of ZBrush is the pixol, which is like a pixel with added information about its location along the z-axis. In other words, a pixol contains depth information as well as color, transparency, and x and y positional data (see Figure 1.12). Furthermore, the pixol also stores information on the material applied to it. This means each pixol knows how to react to the lighting, shading, and the environment of a ZBrush composition when it is rendered.

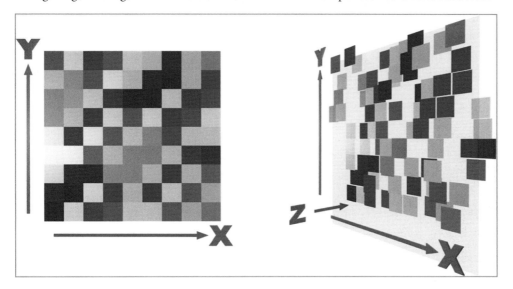

Figure 1.12

The left side of the diagram shows how standard pixels work using x and y information; the right side shows how pixols also store z-depth information.

When Pixologic first introduced ZBrush, it began as a paint program that could create images in two and a half dimensions (known as 2.5D). A brush stroke in ZBrush is painted on the canvas and can then be rotated, scaled, and positioned anywhere on the canvas. This explains why the ZBrush interface does not use the typical 3D world with separate cameras and lights like you'll find in other 3D programs. Everything exists on a canvas. ZBrush added 3D objects that could be incorporated into 2.5 dimensional compositions as well as materials and lights that added shadow and reflections. Subsequent versions of ZBrush refined the sculpting tools and improved the portability of 3D objects with animation projects, which led to the overwhelming popularity of ZBrush as a digital sculpting program.

If you're mostly concerned with sculpting 3D models, you may not worry too much about pixols, but it's good to have an awareness of what this term refers to, and it will help you understand the behavior of a model on the ZBrush canvas. If you'd like to create digital illustrations in ZBrush, then an understanding of pixols can become a powerful tool.

Being a Digital Artist

There is nothing inherent in the computer or the software that will turn you into a great artist. Becoming a good artist still must be achieved the old-fashioned way—through hard work, practice, and study. Nine times out of ten, when you see some jaw-dropping, amazing piece of digital art in an Internet forum or as part of a film, the artist who created it has spent a fair amount of time studying traditional art. Even if the artist has never held a real paintbrush, they still have studied what it takes to make a great work.

This book is concerned with making you feel comfortable using ZBrush. There will not be much discussion on the fundamentals of art or sculpting. That said, you should understand that composition, balance, positive and negative space, lighting, anatomy, form, and silhouette are just a few of the concepts a real artist (digital or traditional) must master. I strongly encourage you step away from the computer monitor, pick up a pencil or a brush, and attend some life drawing classes. Likewise, working with digital clay is much more meaningful if you've spent time sculpting with actual clay. Your digital artwork will reveal much about who you are as well as how much time you have taken to study and explore traditional art techniques and the natural world.

Resources

This book is just the beginning. While working through the exercises in this book on your way to mastering the ZBrush interface and its tools, you should also take the time to explore more using the resources on this list. In addition, *ZBrush Character Creation, Second Edition*, by Scott Spencer (Sybex, 2011) picks up where this book leaves off. His book will incorporate a deep level of understanding of the art of digital sculpture and the concepts behind creating great artwork into more advanced ZBrush topics and lessons.

The two most valuable sources for information regarding ZBrush are Pixologic's website (www.pixologic.com) and ZBrushCentral (www.zbrushcentral.com). You can check out www.pixologic.com for the latest information on updates, plug-ins, and new features for ZBrush as well as artist interviews and free video tutorials in the ZClassroom section (www.pixologic.com/zclassroom/homeroom/).

ZBrush users gather at ZBrushCentral to post their work, critique the work of fellow artists, ask questions, solve problems, and share their enthusiasm for ZBrush. Feel free to visit the site, create a free account, and post examples of your work. The members of ZBrushCentral come from all over the world and represent all ages and skill levels (see Figure 1.13).

Here is a list of useful websites:

www.pixologic.com

www.pixologic.com/zclassroom/homeroom/

Figure 1.13
ZBrushCentral is an online community for ZBrush users of all skill levels.

www.zbrushcentral.com

www.zbrushworkshops.com

www.cgchannel.com

www.gnomon3d.com

www.scottspencer.com

www.3d.sk

www.conceptart.org

www.figuresandfocus.com

I recommend the following books:

- *ZBrush Character Creation, Second Edition*, by Scott Spencer (Sybex, 2011)
- *ZBrush Digital Sculpting Human Anatomy*, by Scott Spencer (Sybex, 2011)
- *ZBrush Creature Design: Creating Dynamic Concept Imagery for Film and Games* by Scott Spencer (Sybex, 2012)
- *The Artist's Complete Guide to Facial Expressions* by Gary Faigin (Watson-Guptill, 1990)
- *Constructive Anatomy* by George Bridgman (Dover, 1973)
- *Bridgman's Life Drawing* by George Bridgman (Dover, 1971)
- *Artistic Anatomy* by Dr. Paul Richer (Winston-Guptill, 1971)
- *Anatomy for the Artist* by Sarah Simblet (DK Publishing, 2001)

And finally, the Gnomon workshop has a large number of DVDs devoted to ZBrush as well as an excellent series of clay maquette sculpture DVDs by John Brown. These can be ordered online at www.thegnomonworkshop.com.

CHAPTER 2

Understanding the ZBrush Interface

From the moment the ZBrush interface appears, its creative potential is obvious. Few other digital art packages boast such an elegant working environment. The ZBrush interface may seem a little intimidating, but once you grasp the philosophy behind the design, you'll find that it is a comfortable place for digital sculpting and painting.

This chapter walks you through the ZBrush interface; it's much like a tour of an artist's studio.

In this particular tour, I will try to strike a balance between explaining where the ZBrush tools are and explaining what they do. The rest of the book will provide deeper explanations about the tools and interface features. To get the most out of this chapter, you should have ZBrush open on a nearby computer. Included in this tour are a few exercises to help you make sense of the interface.

We will cover the following topics:

- **The ZBrush canvas**

- **The organization of shelves**

- **Palettes**

- **Using trays**

The Zen of ZBrush

If you've never done any 3D modeling or animation, you might actually be able to approach ZBrush with a slight advantage over someone who has spent a lot of time in programs such as Autodesk® Maya®, Autodesk® 3ds Max®, or XSI. This is because the tools in ZBrush are very different from what you find in typical 3D modeling and animation programs. If you are an experienced 3D modeler, you may panic a little bit at the fact that ZBrush does not use a typical 3D space environment. Either way, the best thing to do when you first open ZBrush is to shed your preconceived ideas of how a 3D program is *supposed* to work. In fact, don't think of ZBrush as a 3D modeling program, a paint program, or even a texturing program. Instead, step back for a moment and accept the essence of ZBrush. It is a digital sculpting and painting workshop.

Figure 2.1 shows the ZBrush interface in all its glory. Our tour of the interface will start at the center and move outward, from left to right in a clockwise fashion.

Figure 2.1

The ZBrush Interface

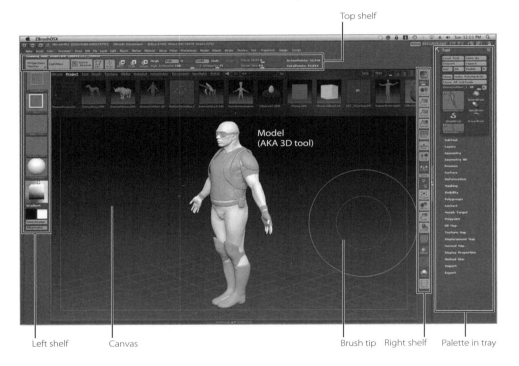

The ZBrush Canvas

Let's start with the center of the interface; the canvas, and then work our way outward. Breaking the interface down like this will help to make it more accessible. The canvas is shown in Figure 2.2.

The canvas is the square that dominates the center of the program. It is where you create your art, whether it is a digital painting or a three-dimensional digital sculpture or any combination of paint strokes and sculpture. The canvas has some special properties that are part of what makes ZBrush so different. It's quite obvious from the outset that the canvas has height and width, which we refer to as the y- and x-axes. The ZBrush canvas also has a depth axis, or a z-axis. Hence the name, ZBrush. When you use a tool to paint a brush stroke on the canvas, you can move it backward and forward in space, placing it in front of or behind other brush strokes. The default gradient you see on the canvas is meant to suggest the depth dimension in the canvas.

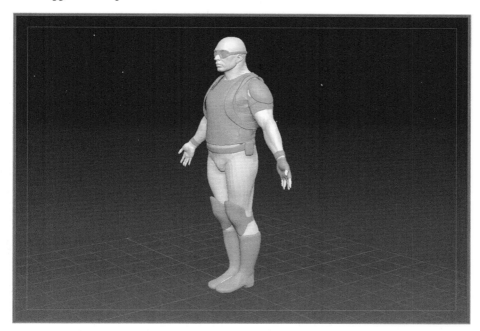

Figure 2.2

The ZBrush canvas is where you create your digital paintings and sculptures.

The canvas can be thought of as a place to create digital illustrations using digital brush strokes, or it can be thought of as a virtual sculpting stand where you can mold a lump of digital clay into anything you can imagine. And, in fact, the canvas can also be used to integrate your sculptures into your illustrations.

An illustration created on the canvas is referred to as a ZBrush document. Documents can be saved in the special ZBR format or exported in a number of other formats, such as the Adobe Photoshop format. A digital sculpture created on the canvas is referred to as a mesh or a 3D tool. You can save sculptures in the special ZTL format or export them in a number of 3D model formats, such as OBJ or Maya ASCII (.ma). You can save your document, tool, and many other elements all in a single file called a ZProject. ZProjects use the ZPR file format. ZProjects are a lot like scenes in other 3D animation packages. When you save a ZProject, ZBrush tracks the current state of your tools, lighting, materials, and other elements so that the next time you load the project, you can pick up exactly where you left off. As we continue the tour, I'll point out how to save documents, 3D tools, and ZProjects.

INTERFACE LAYOUT AND COLOR PRESETS

ZBrush ships with a number of interface layout and color presets. These allow you to change the look of the interface and rearrange the tools to fit your working style. You can change the colors and the layouts by clicking the buttons in the upper-right portion of the interface (shown below). To keep things simple, for this book I'm using the default interface layout, which is how ZBrush looks when you start the program. To make the images easier to see in the black-and-white figures of this book, one of the lighter interface color presets has been selected.

Light Box

Light Box is a special pop-up browser that appears at the top of the canvas when you start ZBrush (Figure 2.3). To show or hide Light Box, press the comma (",") key on your keyboard. The name Light Box is meant to suggest the light tables that photographers use when examining collections of their photographic negatives.

Light Box is a visual display of the files within the Pixologic directory structure of your computer's hard drive. The purpose of Light Box is to allow you to easily load the files you need to work on your ZBrush creations without having to navigate through your

Figure 2.3

The Light Box interface appears as a strip of images at the top of the canvas when you start ZBrush.

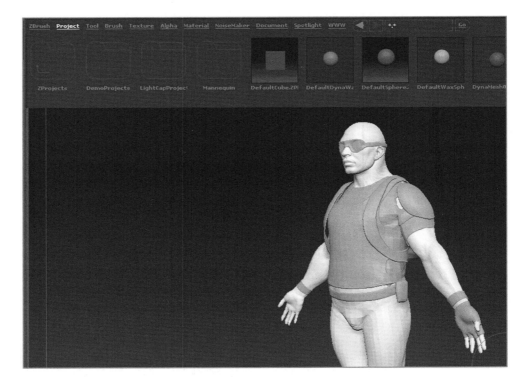

operating system's browsers. Light Box keeps all the files you need at your fingertips, whether they are the sample files that ship with ZBrush or your own creations.

The menu at the top of Light Box is a link to the directories within the Pixologic folder on your computer's hard drive (in Windows, this folder is inside the `Program Files\ Pixologic\ZBrush 4R3` directory; in Mac OS, this folder is in the `Applications/ZBrush 4R3` folder). The headings within Light Box link to the ZBrushes, ZTools, ZAlphas, ZMaterials, ZTextures, and ZProjects folders.

If you click the Project link, you'll see an icon that represents each of the files within the ZProjects folder. If you save your own file to this folder, you'll see it appear in this strip under the Project heading the next time you bring up Light Box. Likewise, saving a file to the ZTools folder will make it appear under the Tool heading in ZBrush. You can drag the icons on the strip left or right to see all of the files in the Project folder. To do this, click the space between two tool icons and drag to the left.

To load a file, double-click (or quickly double-tap your stylus on your digital tablet) an icon. Follow these steps to load the DemoSoldier.ZPR project from Light Box:

1. Press the comma hotkey to open Light Box if it's not already visible.

2. Click the Project header in the list above the icons. You'll see a number of different-colored spheres as well as some folders.

3. Double-click the DemoProjects folder (top of Figure 2.4).

4. Find the DemoSoldier.ZPR project (fourth icon from the left) and double-click it (bottom of Figure 2.4).

5. You'll get a message asking if you want to save the current project before loading the DemoSoldier.ZPR project. Click No; after a few seconds the DemoSoldier appears on the canvas ready for action.

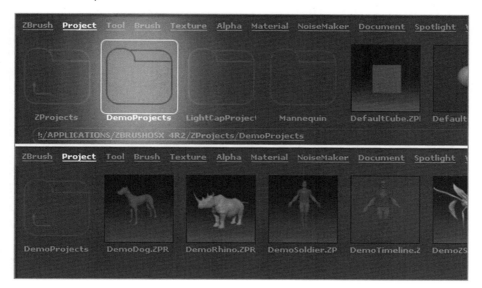

Figure 2.4

In the Projects section of Light Box double-click the DemoProjects folder (top). Then double-click the DemoSoldier.ZPR project icon to load it.

This is how you use Light Box to load a file. A project is a self-contained ZBrush scene, so each time you load a project it will close any files you currently have open (hence, the warning). When you load other types of files such as tools, materials, or brushes from Light Box, the new files will simply be added to your current ZBrush session. You'll get plenty of practice using Light Box in this book, so don't worry if this is not completely clear just yet.

If you'd like to search the contents of the folder displayed in Light Box, type a search term in the field at the top, next to the menu bar in the Light Box interface. Try typing in **Default***. Adding the asterisk will tell ZBrush to search for all files in the Project folder that start with Default (see Figure 2.5). Click the Go button or press the Enter/Return key to start the search.

Figure 2.5
You can search for files within Light Box by typing text in the search field.

You can change the height of the Light Box display by clicking one of the four stack icons at the far right of the Light Box menu. The icons within Light Box will automatically rearrange themselves to fit the new height. This is useful when you have a lot of files in the folder.

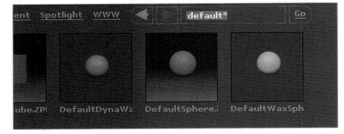

The New button at the far right lets you stack an additional Light Box strip on top of the current one. Using this feature, you can have a number of Light Box strips open, each one displaying the contents of a different folder. Try clicking the New button and then switch to the Tool folder. Add a third strip and open the Brush folder (see Figure 2.6).

To remove a strip, just click the Close button.

Figure 2.6
Additional Light Box strips can be added by clicking the New button. Each strip can display the contents of a different folder.

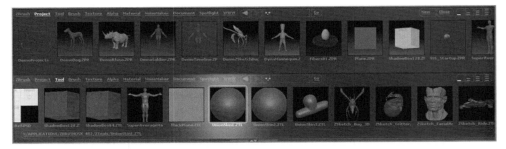

ADD FOLDERS TO LIGHT BOX

To add a folder to Light Box, you can create a shortcut for one of your own folders anywhere on your hard drive and then place the shortcut within the Pixologic folder. This works on Windows but not on Macintosh.

The ZBrush Shelves

On the top and either side of the canvas are *shelves* that hold the ZBrush buttons and controls (see Figure 2.7). We'll explore these shelves by moving from left to right around the canvas.

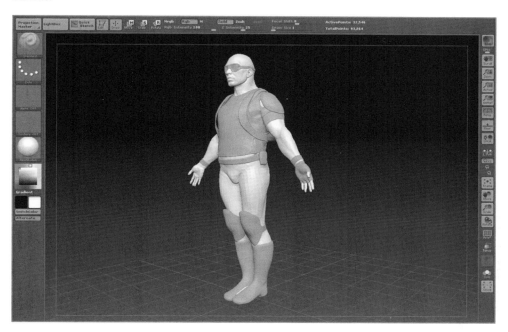

Figure 2.7

Shelves with various buttons and settings surround the ZBrush canvas on the left, top, and right.

The Shelf on the Left

The left shelf has buttons that open fly-out libraries of items that you will access often in a typical ZBrush editing session. The fly-out libraries (from the top of the left shelf, moving down) consist of the sculpting brushes, the stroke types, the alphas, the textures, the material shaders, the color picker, and the color 1 and color 2 swatches.

> **INLINE HELP**
>
> If you forget what a button or control in ZBrush does, you can hold the Ctrl key down while your mouse pointer hovers over the button in question. A little text box will appear with some explanatory notes about what the button does.

The sculpting brushes are a used for editing 3D meshes. To use these brushes, the mesh must be in Edit mode; otherwise, the icon for the sculpting brushes is grayed out and the fly-out library of brushes is inaccessible. We'll go into detail about how to activate

Edit mode and what it means to be in Edit mode later in this chapter. For now, follow these steps so that you can see the contents of the sculpting brush library:

1. Press the comma key on your keyboard to open Light Box.

2. Click the Project header.

3. Double-click the DefaultSphere.ZPR icon.

   This loads the DefaultSphere mesh onto the canvas. The mesh is in Edit mode already, so the Sculpting brush icon on the left shelf should be available.

4. Click the brush icon to open the sculpting brush fly-out library (see Figure 2.8).

Figure 2.8

The fly-out library of sculpting brushes

As you can see, there are a lot of sculpting brushes. The fly-out library is filled with the presets that come with ZBrush. These are used to shape, pose, and detail your meshes. In Chapter 3, "Basic Digital Sculpting," you'll learn the basics of using the brush presets, and throughout the book you'll gain insight into how you can make and save your own custom brush presets.

As you hold the mouse pointer over one of the icons, you'll see an enlarged view of the icon below the fly-out sculpting brush library. The name of the brush will appear along with information about its base type. Each preset is a variation of a few base brush types.

You can reduce the list of brushes in the fly-out library by typing the first letter of a brush name while the fly-out is open. Try typing **C**. All of the icons in the Brush palette will be dimmed except the ones that start with the letter C. As you learn the names of your favorite brush types, you can take advantage of this method of searching the fly-out brush library to quickly switch brushes. You'll notice that many brushes have two capital letters, such as ClayLine. If you type **C** and then **B** while the brush fly-out is open, the fly-out library will close and the brush icon on the left shelf will switch to the ClayBuildup brush. This is the only brush that has *C* and *B* capitalized in the name.

LIGHT BOX BRUSH LIBRARY

You probably noticed that there is a link called Brush in the Light Box interface. This is a link to even more brush presets! The presets are organized into subfolders. The name of each subfolder gives you an idea of the type of brushes it contains, so the Flatten folder contains a number of brushes that can be used to flatten a surface.

These extra brushes are presets that Pixologic created and then decided could not fit into the fly-out library but included with ZBrush nonetheless. To load one of these extra brushes, just double-click its icon in Light Box, and it will then appear in the brush library and remain there until you quit ZBrush.

To continue with our tour of the left shelf, underneath the brush library you'll find the stroke type fly-out library.

The icon displayed for stroke type will be different depending on the current active sculpting brush. This is because the stroke type modifies the behavior of the current brush. If the Standard brush is loaded as the current active brush, the dots icon will appear as the current stroke type. Hover the pointer above the button to see an enlarged view of the current stroke type, and click the button to open the fly-out library (see Figure 2.9). There are a few different stroke types available. The sliders at the bottom of the stroke type library change depending on the currently selected stroke type. The stroke type can be changed for the current brush by choosing one of the other stroke type icons. As you'll see in Chapter 3, you can greatly affect the way in which a brush behaves by choosing a different stroke type.

Figure 2.9

The fly-out library of stroke types

On the left shelf, the icon below stroke type is the icon for the alpha fly-out library. Hold the mouse pointer over the icon to see an enlarged view of the alpha. Click the icon to open the fly-out alpha library (see Figure 2.10). Alphas are grayscale images loaded into ZBrush. They can be used for many purposes, but most often they are used to add effects to sculpting brushes.

Think of the different nozzles added to cake decorating tools to change the shape of frosting as it's applied to the top of a cake. This is the basic concept behind alphas. At the bottom of the alpha fly-out library you'll see buttons that, among other things, enable you to import and export your own, custom alphas. To select a different alpha for the current brush, just click one of the icons in the library. I'll be discussing the many uses of alphas as well as how they work in great detail through the book.

Below the alphas fly-out button you'll see the textures fly-out library. When the Standard brush is selected as the active brush, you'll see no image and the label Texture Off, meaning no texture is applied to the current brush. Textures, like alphas, are simply

Figure 2.10

The fly-out library of alphas

two-dimensional image files, but unlike alphas, textures are color images. Hover the mouse over the texture icon to see an enlarged view, and click the textures button to see the inventory of texture presets that come with ZBrush. When the fly-out library is open, you can hover the pointer over a texture to see an enlarged view appear above the library (see Figure 2.11). Clicking the icon again changes the active texture.

Textures have many uses. For instance, you can apply a texture to a sculpting brush and use the colors of the texture to paint on your models. You can also convert the colors of a 3D model into a texture, which can then be exported for use in other 3D software packages. At the bottom of the library you'll find buttons for importing and exporting textures as well as for other specific functions. Just as with alphas, we'll be revisiting the many uses of textures throughout the book. I'll go into detail about working with textures in Chapter 8, "Polypainting and Spotlight."

At this point you're probably getting a good idea of how the buttons on the left shelf work; they all give you easy access to commonly used libraries. The last fly-out library is the material presets. Hover the mouse pointer over the materials icon to see a preview of the material as it looks on the current 3D mesh. Click this to see the materials fly-out library (see Figure 2.12).

Figure 2.11

The fly-out library of textures

Figure 2.12

The fly-out library of materials

Materials determine the surface quality of the objects on the canvas. For example, a material might affect the shininess or the roughness of a surface or how the surface reacts to light effects on the canvas. Some materials add color to objects as well. As you hover the mouse over each of the icons in the materials fly-out library, you'll see a preview of the current 3D object in each of the materials. Click one of the icons to switch materials. Materials can be applied to the entire object at once or painted on specific areas using the current sculpting brush. Materials are explained in detail in Chapter 9, "Rendering, Lighting, and Materials."

On the left shelf, below the materials library button, you'll find the color picker. This is not a fly-out library; instead, it's a mini-interface that allows you to choose different colors for a variety of uses in ZBrush. As you hold the mouse over the color picker, you'll see text that displays the RGB (red, green, and blue) values for the currently selected color (Figure 2.13).

Figure 2.13

The color picker

The color picker has one square within another. You select the value and saturation of the current color from the inner square, and you select the current hue with the outer square. Below the picker are two swatches for holding the main and secondary colors in memory. The color picker has many functions in ZBrush. We'll use this interface throughout the book. We'll look at advanced uses of the color picker in Chapter 8.

COLOR SELECTION

If you want to select a color from the objects on the canvas, hold the brush cursor over the color you'd like to sample and press the C hotkey. This is like using the eye dropper tool in Photoshop.

The Shelf at the Top

The top shelf appears above the canvas and contains a number of buttons. From left to right you can divide the buttons into four sections. The first section contains buttons for launching some special plug-ins. These buttons are labeled Projection Master, Light Box, and Quick Sketch (see Figure 2.14). The Quick Sketch and Projection Master plug-ins won't make much sense until you've learned a few more things about ZBrush. Plug-ins such as these are covered in detail in the "Bonus Content 2: ZScripts and ZPlugins" chapter found on the DVD. The Light Box button toggles the visibility of Light Box.

The second section of the top shelf contains a series of five important buttons (see Figure 2.15). These buttons are labeled Edit, Draw, Move, Scale, and Rotate.

The Edit mode button enables the sculpting brushes so that you can alter a mesh on the canvas. If Edit mode is off, then ZBrush is in Paint mode, and drawing on the canvas simply places copies of your meshes on it. This is useful when you want to use ZBrush to create illustrations but can be confusing when you are trying to sculpt a model.

Next to the Edit button on the top shelf you'll see the Draw, Move, Scale, and Rotate buttons. When the Draw button is on, the current brush either draws a stroke on the canvas or, when editing a 3D model, lets you use the sculpting brushes to shape a model.

The way in which the Move, Scale, and Rotate buttons behave is different depending on whether you're working on a 3D mesh in Edit mode or adding strokes to an illustration. We'll be using these buttons a lot throughout the book, so you'll get a clear understanding of the different way these functions can be used. For the moment, just think of them as ways to position objects drawn on the canvas. The hotkeys for these functions are W for Move, E for Scale, and R for Rotate.

The third section of the top shelf is a series of buttons and sliders (see Figure 2.16). If these buttons are grayed out, make sure that the Draw button on the top shelf is on. The buttons are labeled Mrgb, Rgb, and M. The *M* stands for *material* and the *Rgb* stands for *red green blue*, which to a computer is the same thing as saying *color*. So these buttons choose between painting modes. You can paint material and color (Mrgb), just color (Rgb), or just material (M). The slider below these three buttons controls the intensity of the color contribution of the current brush. If none of these buttons are activated, the brush will affect the canvas only according to the settings applied by the next set of buttons.

Figure 2.14

The three buttons on the top shelf for launching plug-ins

Figure 2.15

Five buttons on the top shelf are used to change the mode of the canvas and manipulate objects placed on the canvas.

Figure 2.16

The third section of controls on the top shelf includes a series of sliders and buttons that control the size and behavior of the current brush.

UNDERSTANDING EDIT MODE

ZBrush actually started as more of an illustration software package rather than a digital sculpting tool. The unique thing about ZBrush, when it first appeared back in 2000, is that it was the only software that allowed you to paint in two and a half dimensions. This meant that you could paint a stroke on the canvas and then move the canvas up and down as well as back and forth—something that can't be done in other digital paint programs. In addition to paint strokes, the original version of ZBrush included simple 3D shapes that could be incorporated into the illustrations painted on the canvas. The idea was that switching to Edit mode allowed you to make changes to the shape of the 3D primitives, and then you could switch out of Edit mode to place the altered primitives in your illustration. Over time, ZBrush added much more sophisticated sculpting tools and was quickly adopted as the standard for digital sculpting. In fact, ZBrush revolutionized the way digital artists model 3D objects. But the 2.5D illustration capabilities are still at the heart of ZBrush. And therefore, you have to remember that the paradigm of using Edit mode to alter 3D objects is still a big part of sculpting in ZBrush. To see how this works, try this simple exercise:

1. Open Light Box by holding the cursor at the bottom of the screen. When it appears, click the Project link, and then click the DemoProjects folder.

2. Double-click the DemoDog.ZPR project. If a dialog box appears asking you to save the current project, choose No. The dog will appear on the canvas along with a grid representing the floor of the 3D scene. Notice that the Edit button is activated on the top shelf.

3. In the color picker on the left shelf, select a white color so that the model is easier to see.

4. Drag the pointer on a blank part of the canvas. (If you're using a mouse, hold the left mouse button while dragging; if you're using a digital tablet, simply drag the stylus on the tablet.) You'll see the dog and the 3D grid rotate in 3D dimensions. This is the typical behavior of a 3D mesh in Edit mode.

5. Click the Edit mode button on the top shelf (or press the T hotkey) to turn off Edit mode. The grid disappears.

continued

6. Drag on a blank part of the canvas again. Now you'll see another dog appear; the first dog remains frozen. Drag several more dogs on the canvas.

This is the typical behavior of ZBrush when Edit mode is off. In this case, you're essentially creating an illustration using the dog mesh. Beginners usually feel as though something has gone wrong with ZBrush when they experience this behavior, but it's simply a result of Edit mode being disabled. ZBrush is doing exactly what it's supposed to do.

7. On the left shelf, click the DragRect button to open the stroke type fly-out library. Set the stroke type to Freehand.

8. Drag on the canvas; now you'll see a series of dogs appear.

continues

continued

Hopefully a light bulb is going off in your head. What's going on is that you've altered the dog tool so that now you're painting with dogs. Each brush stroke is made up of dog models. This is what Paint mode is all about in ZBrush.

9. Use the stroke type library on the left shelf to switch the stroke type back to DragRect. Drag on the canvas to add another dog to the illustration.

10. Turn Edit mode back on using the button on the top shelf (or press the T hotkey again). The grid reappears under the last dog drawn on the canvas.

    As you drag on the canvas, the last dog added to the canvas rotates, but the other dogs remain frozen. You're back in Edit mode, so now you can sculpt on the dog, thus editing the dog mesh.

11. To clear the other dogs off the canvas, press Ctrl+N. To center the dog mesh in the canvas view, press the F hotkey.

12. Drag on the surface of the dog to make some changes using the Standard brush. Make the changes fairly obvious, such as a gross swelling in the poor dog's head.

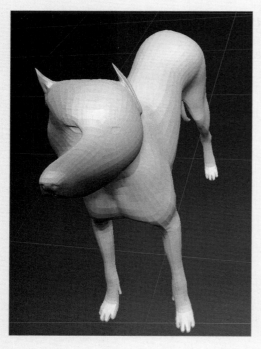

13. Switch out of Edit mode and drag on the canvas again. Now you'll see that the changes you made while in Edit mode are applied to every new dog added to the canvas.

continued

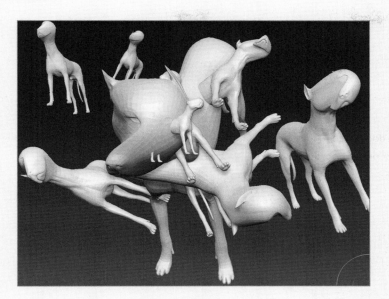

As you switch in and out of Edit mode, you can continue to change the dog model, but the changes will appear only in subsequent dogs painted on the canvas when Edit mode is off. You are editing the dog tool, hence the term *Edit mode*.

It can be easy to switch out of Edit mode by accident when sculpting a 3D mesh. When this happens, don't panic; just press Ctrl+N to clear the canvas of any unwanted copies of the model. Drag on the canvas to create a new copy of the model and turn on the Edit mode button on the top shelf (hotkey = T).

A similar triad of buttons follows. These buttons are labeled Zadd, Zsub, and Zcut, and they control whether or not a sculpting brush raises the surface of a 3D tool (Zadd) or pushes it down (Zsub); ZCut is only used for strokes or models that have been "dropped" onto the canvas (meaning that you have switched out of Edit mode and the model has been converted to a 2.5D illustration), not for sculpting. The Z intensity slider controls how much each stroke of the brush raises, lowers, or cuts into the surface of the 3D tool. If none of these buttons are activated, the brush may simply be set to paint color, material, or both without changing the 3D tool. These also affect how paint strokes behave when you're creating an illustration on the canvas.

Finishing off the third section of the top shelf are the sliders that control the focal shift and the size of the brush. The brush appears on the canvas as a circle within a circle

Figure 2.17

The Focal Shift slider controls the distance between the center circle and the outer circle in the brush display. This region is the intensity falloff of the brush.

Figure 2.18

The last section of the top shelf reveals statistics about the number of points in the 3D mesh on the canvas.

Figure 2.19

The buttons at the top of the right shelf control the display of the canvas in ZBrush.

(Figure 2.17). The Draw Size slider controls the diameter of both circles as a group, which in turn controls how much of the canvas or tool is affected by the brush. The Focal Shift slider controls the softness or falloff of the edge of the brush. Moving this slider back and forth will cause the inner circle to grow and shrink. If both circles are the same size, the brush will have a hard edge; if there is a large gap between the size of the outer circle and the inner circle, there will be a sizable falloff from the center to the edge of the area affected by the brush.

The final section of the top shelf is a numerical display that informs you as to how many points make up the current 3D mesh (Figure 2.18). Points (or vertices) appear at the corner of each polygon in the mesh. If a 3D mesh has many separate pieces, you can choose which piece of the mesh you want to edit. This number of points in the part of the mesh you're editing is displayed as ActivePoints. The total number of all the points of all the parts of the mesh is displayed as TotalPoints. For example, if you have the DemoSoldier in Edit mode on the canvas, the soldier's body is made up of 32,546 points, and this number is displayed as ActivePoints. If you add all the points of his body to all of the points for each part of his clothing, the total is 93,064, which is displayed as TotalPoints.

USE THE SPACEBAR TO ACCESS SHELF BUTTONS

The spacebar is used as a shortcut for calling up the major shelf buttons around the canvas. If you get tired of hunting around for commonly used buttons on the shelves, try holding the spacebar to get quick access. The pop-up menu appears right next to the brush icon.

The Shelf on the Right

The right shelf contains controls that are meant to help you navigate the canvas. From top to bottom this shelf can be divided into four sections.

The first section at the top of the shelf contains six buttons that manipulate the display of the canvas (see Figure 2.19).

The button at the very top activates Best Preview Render (BPR) mode, which is one of the five render options available in ZBrush. When you activate BPR, the objects on the screen appear at a higher quality than they do in the default Preview mode. Your image will include shadows, higher-quality anti-aliasing, and effects such as ambient occlusion, transparency, and subsurface scattering. Creating a BPR render takes more time than creating a render in the default Preview render mode. The other render modes are Flat, Fast, Preview, and Best. These are all discussed at length in Chapter 9.

The SPix slider below the BPR button controls the anti-aliasing quality of the render created in Best Preview Render mode.

The Scroll and Zoom controls move the canvas around. When you use the Zoom tool to move into the canvas, you'll see the edges of the strokes on the canvas become jagged. It's just like zooming into an image in a paint program such as Photoshop.

The Actual and AAHalf buttons snap the canvas to 100 percent and 50 percent in size, respectively. This helps improve the look of the model on the canvas and when rendering by making the anti-aliasing along the edges smooth.

The next section on the right shelf is made up of three buttons that control the display of objects on the canvas (see Figure 2.20). These are options that can be used as aids while you work on editing a 3D mesh. The Persp button turns on perspective distortion (hotkey = P). By default, 3D meshes are displayed in isometric view, meaning that the natural lines of perspective are ignored. This can be useful for aligning a 3D mesh with a 2D drawing. The perspective button augments the appearance of the mesh, which can make the appearance of the mesh more natural (see Figure 2.21).

Figure 2.20

The Persp, Floor, and Local buttons affect the behavior of the canvas while you're editing a 3D tool.

Figure 2.21

The image at the top shows a 3D mesh with the Persp button off; the image on the bottom shows the same mesh with the Persp button on.

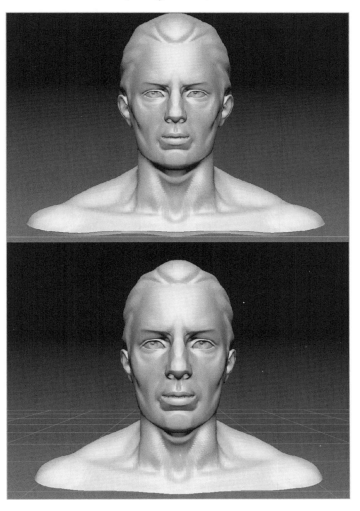

The Floor button activates a 3D grid that is aligned with the 3D tool (hotkey = Shift+P). If you're used to working in other 3D programs, using this option may make you feel more comfortable because it gives you a better understanding of the 3D tool's position in 3D space. At the top of the button are the letters *X*, *Y*, and *Z*. Turning on any one of these buttons turns on the display of the grid along the corresponding axis. By default, the y-axis is activated (see Figure 2.22).

Figure 2.22

The Floor button activates the display of a grid for each axis. In this image, the x- and y-axes are displayed.

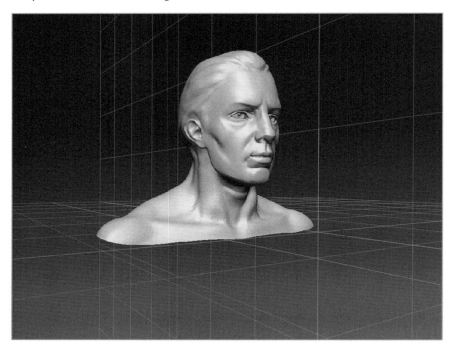

The Local pivot button will make the last area of an edited 3D tool become the center of rotation during editing. This is a very useful function and helps keep you from getting lost on your 3D tool as you spin it around.

The third section of buttons on the right shelf includes the L.Sym and rotation axes controls (see Figure 2.23). To understand how these buttons work, imagine that when you are editing a 3D mesh, the canvas acts as a virtual sculpting stand. These buttons affect the relationship of the mesh to the stand as well as how to rotate the view of the mesh on the stand.

Figure 2.23

The L.Sym and rotation axes buttons make up the third section of buttons on the right shelf.

The L.Sym button controls how symmetry is calculated while editing a 3D tool. L.Sym is short for Local Symmetry. When it's off, symmetry is calculated in world space. In other words, symmetry is calculated based on the center of the virtual sculpting stand. When L.Sym is on, symmetry is calculated based on the center of the mesh, even if the mesh is not at the center of the stand.

The three buttons below L.Sym control the axis of rotation as you change the view of the mesh. Think of these buttons as a way to control the rotation of the virtual sculpting stand. When the XYZ button is on, rotation of the view is not restricted to any particular axis when you drag left or right. When the Z button is activated, rotation of the view is restricted to the z-axis when you drag left or right on the canvas. When Y is active, the rotation of the view is restricted to the y-axis when you drag left or right on the canvas.

The fourth section of buttons on the right shelf controls the display of 3D meshes on the canvas (see Figure 2.24). The Frame button centers the view of the 3D object in the canvas.

Navigating the ZBrush Canvas

The Move, Scale, and Rotate buttons on the right shelf can be a bit confusing at first because there are also Move, Scale, and Rotate buttons on the top shelf. They do not do the same thing. The buttons on the right shelf are for use on 3D tools in Edit mode. They help you manipulate the view of a 3D tool while working. Think of them as controls for manipulating the virtual sculpture stand. When you use these buttons, you don't change the model, just what you're able to see on the model while working.

Try this short exercise to understand how to navigate the ZBrush canvas using these buttons or the navigation hotkeys.

1. Press the comma hotkey to open Light Box (or click the Light Box button on the top shelf).

2. Click the Projects link; within Projects, double-click the DemoProjects folder. Double-click the DemoSoldier.ZPR button to load the DemoSoldier project.

3. On the left shelf, drag up to the left corner of the color picker to choose a white color. This will make it easier to see what is going on with the model.

4. On the right shelf, move the mouse pointer over the Move button and drag. You'll see the soldier model move around. Remember that you're actually moving the view of the soldier model, not the model itself.

5. Now hold the Alt key and the right mouse button (or, if you're using a digital tablet, hold the button on your stylus) and drag on a blank part of the canvas. This is another way to move the view.

6. On the right shelf, move the pointer over the Scale button and drag. The view of the DemoSoldier shrinks when you drag up or left and enlarges when you drag down or right. This is just like using the Zoom feature on a camera.

7. Hold the right mouse button and the Ctrl key, and drag on the canvas. The soldier zooms in and out again. This is the same as dragging over the Scale button on the right shelf.

Figure 2.24

The fourth section of buttons on the right shelf controls the display of the 3D mesh on the canvas.

8. On the right shelf, move the pointer over the Rotate button and drag. The view of the soldier rotates.

9. Hold the right mouse button and drag on the canvas without holding any keys, and you'll see the same behavior; this rotates the view of the soldier model.

As mentioned earlier, the axis of rotation buttons on the right shelf change the way the Rotate feature works. Switching to Z or Y restricts the rotation to that axis when you drag left or right.

Mesh View Options

The PolyF button turns on a wireframe display on the current 3D mesh. When PolyF is on, you can clearly see the individual polygons that make up the mesh. If the mesh is made up of multiple objects, the wireframe is visible for the current active object. To get a better sense of what this means, try this while the DemoSoldier project is still loaded:

1. Turn on the PolyF button. You'll see the wireframe display of the mesh's polygons. The wireframe display is divided into colored regions denoting polygroups. We'll get into polygroups in Chapter 3.

2. Rotate the view by dragging on a blank part of the canvas so that you can see the soldier's backpack.

3. Alt+click the backpack. The view changes so that now you can see the wireframe of the backpack (see Figure 2.25).

Figure 2.25

The PolyF button displays the wireframe of the active parts of the mesh. Alt+click the soldier's backpack to make it the active part of the mesh.

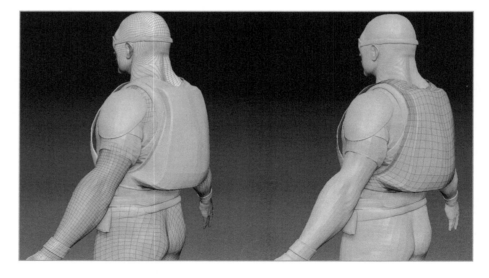

TOOLS AND SUBTOOLS

As I mentioned at the start of the chapter, a 3D mesh is also known as a 3D tool. A 3D tool that is made up of different parts can be split into subtools. This is the case with the DemoSoldier. His body is the main tool and his backpack is a subtool, as are his goggles, gloves, shirt, and so on. Working with subtools is covered in detail in Chapter 4, "Polymesh Editing." By Alt+clicking different parts of the model, you're changing the active subtool. Once a subtool is active, it can be edited without affecting the other subtools of the mesh.

The Transp button activates Transparency, allowing you to see the active subtool through the other subtools (as long as the mesh has been divided into subtools). Transparency has two modes: Ghost and Standard transparency. Ghost is on by default, and you can toggle between the two transparency modes by turning the Ghost button on or off:

1. With the DemoSoldier still on the canvas, turn off PolyF to turn off the display of the polyframe.

2. Turn on the Transp button. Rotate the view. You can see the backpack through the other parts of the model.

3. Turn off Ghost to see how the Standard transparency mode behaves (see Figure 2.26).

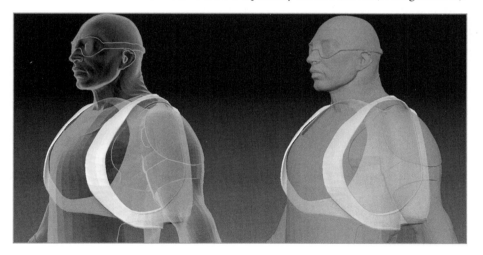

Figure 2.26

Transparency allows you to see a subtool through the other parts of a 3D mesh. The left image shows the Ghost mode of transparency; the right image shows the Standard mode of transparency.

The Solo button instantly hides all subtools except the current active subtool. This comes in very handy when working on a complex mesh that has been divided into many subtools.

The Xpose button temporarily moves all of the subtools out of the way while still leaving them visible. This way you can focus on editing a single subtool without having the others obscure your view. It's also a great way to get a sense of how a 3D mesh has been organized into subtools (see Figure 2.27).

Figure 2.27

The Xpose button moves all the other subtools out of the way while you're working on the active subtool.

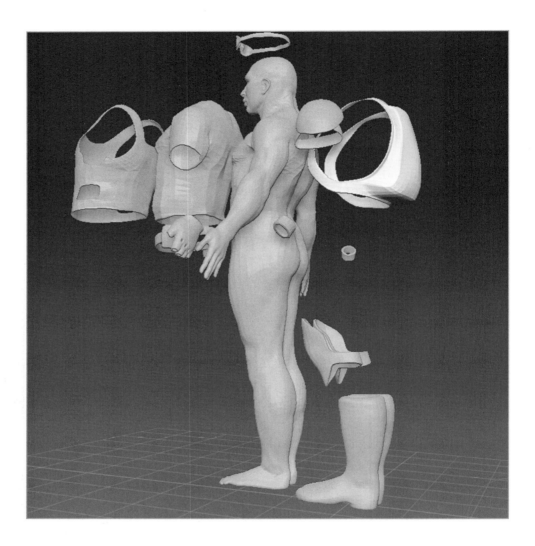

Figure 2.27

The Xpose button moves all the other subtools out of the way while you're working on the active subtool.

Trays and Palettes

We'll continue working our way outward from the canvas to another level. This takes us to the trays. On the right side of the canvas you'll see a section labeled Tool within a large area (see Figure 2.28). The large area is a tray. If you click the divider between the right shelf and the tray, the tray collapses, expanding the work area. Click the divider again and it reappears. The tray is analogous to a drawer in an artist's toolbox. Trays exist on the right and the left sides of the canvas as well as below the canvas.

The palettes are sets of controls that are organized under the headings at the top of the interface. For example, the Document palette contains a number of settings that control the appearance and behavior of the canvas as well as buttons for saving, importing, and exporting images to and from the canvas. To see the settings in the Document palette, click the Document button at the top of the interface (see Figure 2.29).

The palettes are organized at the top of the interface alphabetically, starting with the Alpha menu at the upper left and ending with the ZScript menu on the upper right. You'll find that some palettes are accessed constantly during a ZBrush session, and some you use only once in a while. This is where the trays come in. In the right tray, click the circular icon at the upper-right corner of the Tool palette (see Figure 2.30). The palette disappears from the tray.

Click the word *Tool* in the bar at the top of the interface. Now the palette appears beneath the Tool heading like a menu in more conventional software packages. Click the circular icon again, and it pops back over to the right tray. The palette will stay in the tray regardless of whether the tray is open or closed.

Make sure the Tool palette is in the tray and expand the Transform palette. Click its circular icon in the upper right. The Transform palette pops over to the right tray above the Tool palette. You can load the tray with all of your favorite palettes and remove them by clicking their circular icons. This action becomes very quick and natural after a little practice. Clicking the title bar of a palette while it's in the tray will col-lapse the palette, freeing more room in the tray for other palettes while keeping the palette available in the tray (see Figure 2.31).

Figure 2.28

A tray on the right side of the ZBrush interface contains a set of buttons and controls under the heading Tool. Click the divider to collapse or expand the tray

Figure 2.29

Clicking the Document button at the top of the interface reveals the con-tents of the Document palette.

Figure 2.30

Click the circular icon in the upper right of a palette to move it out of a tray.

The palettes load up the tray from top to bottom in the order in which you add them. By default, the palettes will automatically place themselves in the tray on the right of the screen when you click the circular button. If you decide you prefer a palette to be in the tray on the left side, you can grab the handle with your cursor and drag the entire palette to the tray. The cursor will turn into a crosshair when it's over the handle, indicating that you can drag the palette by the handle.

You can also drag palettes to different locations on the tray to rearrange them. It's easiest to do this by dragging from the top menu to a blank spot below the last palette in a tray. To remove a palette from a tray, drag its circular handle icon off the tray or click it. Notice that a palette temporarily disappears from a tray when you click its label in the top menu. This keeps you from being able to load multiple copies of the palette into a tray, which would be confusing for both you and ZBrush.

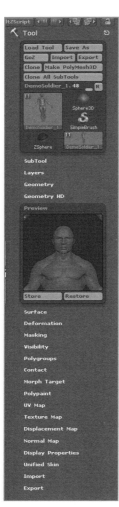

Make sure the Tool palette is in the tray on the right side of the canvas and that it is expanded so that you can see the contents. Click the large tool icon in the upper left of the palette to expand the tool inventory. Choose a 3D tool such as the Gear tool. The Tool palette has a large number of subpalettes. Subpalettes are groups of controls within rounded boxes that appear depending on what has been chosen as the current tool; some are collapsed by default to keep the palette from getting too long. You can expand them—try clicking the word *Preview* in the Tool palette, and you'll see the Preview settings expand in their own subpalette (see Figure 2.32).

If you expand a number of subpalettes, you'll see that the Tool palette gets so long that all of its contents can't fit on the screen. No problem; you can click the side of the Tool palette and drag up and down. The palette scrolls up and down, giving you access to all the different settings.

Throughout this book I will describe the location of specific controls in relation to the subpalette of a particular palette. So for example, if I say "find the SDiv slider in the Geometry subpalette of the Tool palette," then I mean that you should expand the Tool palette and then expand the Geometry subpalette within the Tool palette to find the SDiv slider. It's important to understand this because there are some subpalettes that use the same name as a palette. For example there is a Texture palette and there is a Texture Map subpalette in the Tool palette.

Now that you have some idea of how palettes and trays work, let's look at the settings available in each palette. These descriptions will be very brief. More detailed explanations will be found in the exercises of this book.

Alpha Earlier in this chapter you were introduced to alphas, which are grayscale image files used for a variety of purposes in ZBrush. If you recall, the alpha icon on the left shelf opens the alpha fly-out library. The Alpha palette (shown in Figure 2.33) interface has a large number of controls that are arranged in subpalettes and can be used for fine-tuning the appearance and behavior of the alphas you use in ZBrush. Clicking the image of the alpha in the upper left of the Alpha palette is another way to access the library of alphas.

Figure 2.31

The Transform palette has been added to the tray on the right of the interface. The Tool palette at the bottom of the tray has been collapsed to save room.

Figure 2.32

The Tool palette contains a large number of subpalettes. These can be expanded by clicking their labels. In this image, the Preview subpalette has been expanded.

Brush The Brush palette has a very large number of controls that are arranged in subpalettes and can be used to modify the behavior of the sculpting brushes (see Figure 2.34). You can save the modifications you make to the brushes as your own custom presets, which can be used in future ZBrush sessions. Chapter 7, "Advanced Brush Techniques," explains how to use the controls in this palette and how to save your own brush presets. Clicking the brush icon in the upper left of the palette is another way to access the brush fly-out library.

Color The Color palette has a copy of the color picker you see on the left shelf. It also has numerous additional pickers and controls found in the Modifiers subpalette (see Figure 2.35).

Figure 2.33

The Alpha palette contains controls and settings to adjust the alpha images you use in ZBrush.

Figure 2.34

The Brush palette contains settings for changing the way in which brushes behave. You can use the controls in this palette to create and save your own custom brush presets.

Figure 2.35

The Color palette provides a number of different ways to set the current color.

Document The Document palette is where you load and save ZBrush documents. You can also import and export Photoshop files and other supported formats, such as BMP, JPEG, and TIFF (see Figure 2.36).

ZBRUSH SUPPORT OF PHOTOSHOP FILES

ZBrush and Photoshop work extremely well together; however, ZBrush will not import Photoshop layers or export layers in a single file. Using the ZAppLink plug-in, Photoshop and ZBrush can be used interchangeably to paint colors directly on the surface of the model. For more about these techniques read the section on ZAppLink in the bonus content chapter: "Zscripts and Plug-Ins," found on the DVD.

Figure 2.36

The Document palette has controls for setting the size and the background of the canvas.

The Document palette also has controls for setting the background gradient colors, the border colors, and, most important, the size of the document. The Pro button constrains the proportions of the document, maintaining the current aspect ratio. Set the document size when you are first starting a document. You can't resize the image while in the midst of creating a composition without dropping all the tools onto the canvas.

Draw The Draw palette has controls that duplicate the brush controls in the top shelf as well as some of the buttons on the right shelf. These are size, focal shift, and the material and color settings as well as the brush depth controls (Zadd, Zsub, and Zcut). Below these controls is a subpalette that offers a preview of the brush stroke as well as more advanced controls. This subpalette is used for the 2.5D brush strokes created in Paint mode and not so much the brushes used to alter a 3D model in Edit mode.

The preview shows how the tip of the brush looks to the ZBrush canvas. You can rotate the image to see a 3D view. The width, height, and depth of the brush tip can be adjusted as well as how the brush stroke is embedded into previously existing strokes on the canvas. These settings will affect all of the brushes you use in a ZBrush session; they are global controls for how the strokes are drawn on the canvas.

The Draw palette also has a Persp button and a FocalLength slider (see Figure 2.37). The Persp and Floor buttons do the same thing as the Persp and Floor buttons on the right shelf, but there are some additional controls. The FocalLength slider controls the amount of perspective distortion applied to the object when the Persp button is on. The Align To Object button keeps the perspective distortion of the 3D tool relative to its location on the canvas. There are also controls for setting the position and colors of the grid display that is activated when the Floor button is on.

Figure 2.37

The Draw palette has controls for changing the way strokes and 3D tools are drawn on the canvas.

CHANGE THE BACKGROUND COLOR OF THE CANVAS

Here's a quick demonstration on how to change the background color of the canvas:

1. Open the Document palette, and click the circular icon in the upper left to move the palette into a tray. This will keep the palette from closing while you adjust the controls.

2. Click the button labeled Back, and drag all the way across the canvas to the color picker. As you drag, you may notice the color of the canvas change.

    The label Back in the Document palette is short for *background*. While you drag, ZBrush is setting the background color to match whatever color is directly below the mouse pointer. By dragging over the color picker on the left shelf, you can choose any color visible in the picker.

3. Select a light gray by dragging over the left side of the inner square of the color picker. Let go when you have a nice gray color selected.

4. In the Document palette, click and drag on the slider below the Range heading. Drag to the left to set Range to 0. Setting Range to 0 removes the gradient.

    If you'd like to store this gray background as the default setting whenever ZBrush starts, click the Save As Startup Doc button at the bottom of the palette.

Edit This palette offers access to the Undo and Redo buttons as well as a running tab of how many undos are available in the queue. The undo hotkeys, as in many programs, are Ctrl+Z for undo and Ctrl+Shift+Z for redo. You can change the number of undos that ZBrush stores in memory using the sliders in the Mem subpalette of the Preferences palette. If you have a lot of RAM, you can increase the Tool Undo slider so that more undos are available while sculpting. By default the slider is set to 4. The Preferences palette is discussed in more detail later in this section.

File The File palette contains buttons for saving elements of your ZBrush session. You can choose to save a ZBrush project using the Save As button at the top of the palette (see Figure 2.38). Projects are saved in the ZPR format. This format contains the current active 3D mesh and its position on the canvas. The project file remembers if the tool is in Edit mode, the materials on the tool, and even the background color of the canvas. The Load button loads saved ZBrush projects, and Revert sets the current project back to the last saved state.

Figure 2.38

The File palette has a number of buttons that allow you to save the various elements of a ZBrush session.

There are also buttons in the File palette that duplicate the Save buttons found in other palettes. For example, the Save button under Canvas duplicates the Save button found in the Document palette—in other words, it saves strokes drawn on the canvas but not the current 3D mesh. The Save button under Tool Mesh saves the current 3D tool (as long as Edit mode is on) but not any strokes drawn on the canvas.

It can be a little confusing when you're first learning ZBrush to remember what to save or load. The safest bet is to use the Save button at the top of the File palette to save the current ZBrush project. This ensures that the next time you start ZBrush, you can open the project (using the Open button at the top of the File palette) and pick up right where you left off.

If you save the project in the ZProjects folder within the Pixologic folder, you'll find your saved files listed under the Projects setting in Light Box.

Layer ZBrush can create layers in a document, similar to layers in a paint program such as Photoshop. However, remember that ZBrush has depth, so unlike layers in a typical 2D paint program, where one layer obscures all layers below it, ZBrush layers respect the depth of all strokes in all the layers equally.

Layers are used most often when ZBrush is used as an illustration program.

Light The Light palette is where you adjust the settings for the current light, create additional lights, and adjust shadows and shadow type.

You can reposition a light by dragging the cursor over the material preview sphere (see Figure 2.39). The sphere will update to show the lighting position in the scene. The ability to easily change the lighting while you work in ZBrush is an important feature. Sculptors in the real world continually change the angle of the light while they work on a sculpture. Seeing the sculpture in a new light can reveal problems or open up areas of artistic exploration.

Lighting and ZBrush have become much more sophisticated in recent versions, and now it's entirely possible to create photorealistic lighting within ZBrush. Lights and their settings will be explored more in Chapter 9.

Macro The Macro palette offers controls for recording and loading macros. A macro is simply a list of commands that tell ZBrush to do something. Let's say you find yourself constantly resetting the document size to a specific resolution. You can record a macro that performs this specific action, and then it will appear in the Macro palette as a button. Click the button and everything you did while recording the macro will happen again; your document will be resized to your stored specifications.

Figure 2.39

Use the controls in the Light palette to change the position of the lights. This will affect the appearance of 3D meshes and strokes placed on the canvas.

NOT ALL MATERIALS RESPOND TO LIGHT

Some materials, such as the Red Wax material, have the lighting effects built into the material itself so the model will not react to a change in lighting position if it has this material applied. If you click the material icon on the left shelf to open the material fly-out library, you'll notice that the materials are arranged into two major categories below the Quick Pick section. The materials listed under MatCap will not react to changes in lighting in the scene. The materials in the Standard Materials section, such as the Basic material, will react to changes in lighting.

If you adjust the controls in the Light palette and you don't see any change, open the material fly-out library and choose a standard material from the lower portion of the material inventory, such as the Basic material. The difference between standard and MatCap material is explained in Chapter 9.

Marker You use markers to store information about a 3D tool's position on the canvas before it has been dropped. This way you can redraw the tool if you need to recall it later on after changes have been made to the composition. The buttons on the Marker palette determine what information is to be stored on the canvas. The markers themselves are hot spots on the canvas. Using the Multi-marker tool, you can create groups of 3D tools that can be stored as a single tool. However, the introduction of subtools in ZBrush 3 replaced most of the usefulness of this feature.

Material In ZBrush, *material* refers to the quality of a surface and how it reacts to light, shadow, and other strokes in the scene. Materials come in two main types: *MatCap*, which are materials that have lighting and shading built in, and standard materials.

Creating and using materials in ZBrush is a pretty big topic that will be fully explored in Chapter 9. For now, it's enough to say that the Material palette is where you can edit, load, save, and clone the materials you use in a scene. The controls listed under the Modifiers subpalette allow you to edit existing material presets to make your own custom materials. You can save these presets for use in other ZBrush projects (see Figure 2.40).

Movie The Movie palette contains controls for recording movies from the canvas (Figure 2.41). You can make movies that show off your work or explain specific techniques, or you can use movies as a means to present ideas to a client or director. The movies you record can be exported in the QuickTime format for easy sharing, and you can use the controls in the Movie palette to create turntable animations, which are useful for showing off your work from all angles.

Figure 2.40

The Material palette and material inventory show the many materials that can be applied to ZBrush strokes. The settings in the Modifiers subpalette of the Material palette allow you to create and save your own custom materials.

One of the most exciting features of the Movie palette is the TimeLine feature. It is enabled by expanding the TimeLine subpalette and clicking the Show button. The TimeLine interface then appears as a strip beneath the top shelf (see Figure 2.42). Using the TimeLine, you can animate the display, the movement, the color, and many other aspects of 3D meshes on the canvas. The TimeLine is covered extensively in Chapter 10, "Layers and the TimeLine."

Picker The controls in the Picker palette determine how brushes sample information as they interact with strokes and 3D meshes on the canvas. This has a big impact on how sculpting brushes behave. The Picker palette is fairly advanced and will be covered in more detail in Chapter 7.

Preferences The Preferences palette is where you set the overall behavior of ZBrush. It contains settings for everything from customizing the interface to how 3D models behave when they are imported. We'll revisit this palette throughout the book to help you understand more about how the controls here can improve your interaction with ZBrush.

Render The Render palette is where you access the controls for the lighting, shading, anti-aliasing, and other qualities of your ZBrush composition. The controls in this palette are used in conjunction with the controls in the Light palette and Material palette. Rendering in ZBrush occurs right on the canvas as opposed to in a separate interface as with many other 3D programs. Depending on the settings, a render can take anywhere from a few seconds to a few minutes. You can choose between several render quality settings (see Figure 2.43).

- Preview is the default quality setting. It shows basic color and texture information with simple real-time shadowing.

- The Fast setting removes material and shadow information from the scene to improve performance.

- Flat displays only the color of the strokes and 3D meshes on the screen.

- Best is the most computationally expensive. A number of settings in the Render palette affect how Best quality is calculated. Best quality renders the lighting, texturing, shadow, and materials of the strokes on the canvas and takes into account how they interact with each other in terms of reflection and light occlusion.

Figure 2.42

When you enable the visibility of the TimeLine in the Movie palette, it appears below the top shelf.

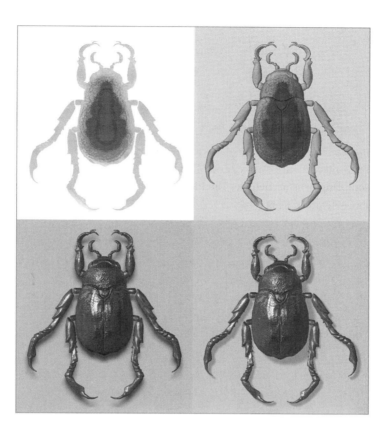

Figure 2.43
A 3D model rendered in the four different render qualities—Flat, Fast, Preview, and Best (clockwise from upper left)—using the Reflected Map material.

ZBrush 4 added Best Preview Render (BPR) mode, which has many special features such as ambient occlusion shadowing, subsurface scattering, and subtool transparency. A BPR render is activated using the BPR button at the top of the Render palette or using the button on the right shelf (hotkey = Shift+R). The Render palette contains a number of settings for tuning a BPR render (see Figure 2.44). BPR has become the render mode of choice for most ZBrush artists. Many of the exercises in this book will use BPR.

None of these render settings will affect a model exported from ZBrush. They only control how the model appears while it's displayed on the ZBrush canvas. The settings on the Render palette will be discussed further in Chapter 9.

Stencil　The Stencil palette is related to the controls in the Alpha palette. A stencil masks out areas on the canvas where paint strokes will appear. Figure 2.45 shows how a stencil, created from an alpha, can be used to protect areas of a 3D mesh from changes made by a sculpting brush. A stencil can be created from an alpha and then moved about the screen as you work, allowing for some interesting texturing possibilities. The controls in the Stencil palette change the way the stencil behaves and how it is displayed.

Figure 2.44
Controls for tuning effects such as sub-surface scattering (Sss) in a BPR render are found in the Render palette.

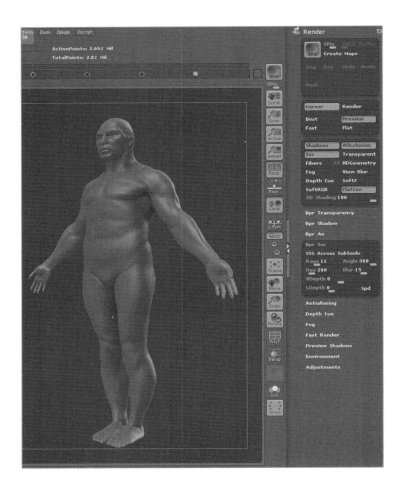

To create a stencil, select an alpha from the alpha library, open the Alpha palette, and click the Make St button. The screen turns gray, and you can see the alpha in black. You can edit the stencil using the options in the Stencil palette. To move the stencil around, hold the spacebar and drag the coin controller to position the stencil.

Much of the functionality of stencils has been replaced by ZBrush's Spotlight, which offers a more intuitive interface and more options. Spotlight is covered in Chapter 8.

Stroke The Stroke palette allows access to the stroke inventory as well as a variety of settings for customizing the strokes (see Figure 2.46). Strokes affect how a brush stroke draws on the canvas. For example, the FreeHand stroke causes the brush to paint like a normal paintbrush would. If the FreeHand stroke is used with a 3D model tool, the copies of the model will flow out of the brush in a line. Other stroke types, such as DragRect, allow for precise positioning of a stroke on the canvas. As you drag, the stroke will appear, scale, and rotate depending on how you move the cursor before releasing pressure on the digital tablet or letting go of the left mouse button. Additional settings such as LazyMouse, Curve Mode, and Backtrack help you precisely control how brush strokes are applied to a 3D mesh. These features are explored in Chapters 6 and 7.

Texture   The Texture palette is similar to the Alpha palette in that the controls here allow you to load, save, and adjust textures. Textures are 2D color images that can be created in ZBrush or in other paint programs and used for a variety of purposes (see Figure 2.47). Textures can be used to paint 3D tools. You can also create a texture based on the colors applied to a painted 3D tool. The texture can be exported for use in a 3D animation and rendering program as a texture map in a shader. Textures are discussed in detail in Chapter 8.

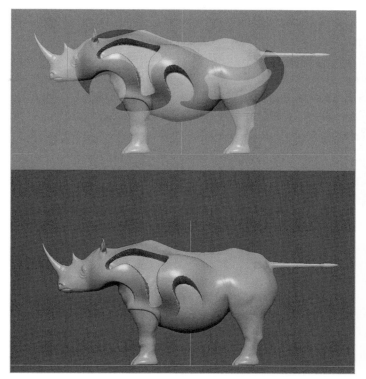

Figure 2.45

A stencil is used to protect areas of a 3D mesh from changes made with a sculpting brush.

Figure 2.46

The Stroke palette settings control how brush strokes behave on the canvas. These settings affect both the tools and the sculpting brushes.

Figure 2.47

The Texture palette contains controls for changing the look of the 2D color images used within ZBrush.

In addition to loading and saving textures, the controls in the Texture palette allow you to do the following:

- Flip a texture horizontally and vertically
- Invert the colors of a texture
- Adjust the colors using a gradient based on the main and secondary color buttons
- Resize and clone a texture
- Make an alpha based on a texture
- Fill the background using a texture
- Create a texture based on the current state of the canvas

Tool   The Tool palette is the most essential palette in ZBrush; it is at the heart of digital sculpting and painting. Tools are what ZBrush uses to paint on the canvas. Some paintbrushes found in the Tool palette are tools, but so are 3D meshes. This is because you can use a mesh as a type of paintbrush that paints copies of the mesh on the canvas.

In the Tool palette, you'll find an inventory of the tools available for the current ZBrush session. Click the large icon in the upper left of the Tool palette to open the inventory (see Figure 2.48). The window is divided into three sections: Quick Pick, 3D Meshes, and 2.5D Brushes.

The Quick Pick section stores recently used tools for easy access.

The 3D Meshes section contains the models you have loaded into ZBrush as well as some 3D primitives and ZSpheres, which are a very special type of 3D tool discussed in Chapter 4.

The 2.5D brushes are primarily used for illustrating. They are used to make marks on the canvas or alter what is already drawn on the canvas.

Figure 2.48

The inventory of tools in the Tool palette

The Tool palette has hundreds of controls and sliders. Using the controls found here, you can import and export 3D meshes for use in other 3D software, add additional parts to your meshes, paint colors onto your meshes, animate your meshes, create UV texture coordinates, extract normal and displacement maps, and duplicate, mirror, deform, and add surface noise. And the list goes on. As you'll see starting in Chapter 3, the Tool palette will quickly become your home in ZBrush. Figure 2.49 shows how complex the Tool palette can become when a working on a mesh in Edit mode.

MAKING 2.5D BRUSH STROKES

The idea behind 2.5D brushes is that they combine the natural feel of digital painting with the ability to position strokes in three dimensions. Try this short exercise to get a sense of what this means:

1. Make sure ZBrush is open. Choose Preferences → Init ZBrush. This will clear the canvas and reset all tools (always make sure you save your work before using this feature!).

2. When you click the Init ZBrush button, a dialog box opens. It asks if you want to initialize ZBrush. Choose Yes.

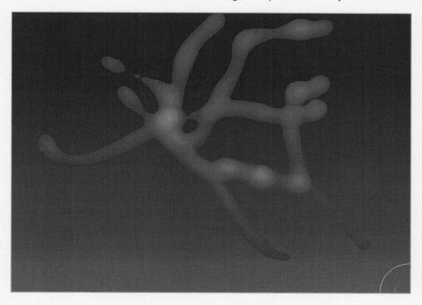

3. Make sure the Tool palette is in the tray on the right side of the screen.

4. In the Tool palette, click the large brush icon labeled SimpleBrush to open the tool inventory. From the 2.5D Brushes section at the bottom of the inventory, choose SphereBrush.

continues

continued

5. Drag across the canvas to make a mark with the SphereBrush. Make a few marks (see the following image).

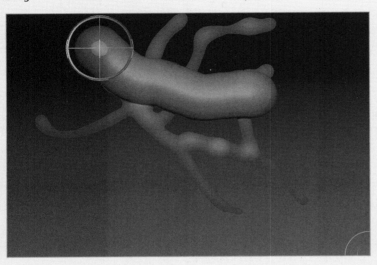

6. On the top shelf, click the Move button or press the W hotkey.

    The last stroke you created disappears. Don't worry; it's not gone. It has just moved behind the canvas.

7. Drag downward on a blank part of the canvas; this may take a few downward strokes. You'll see the stroke appear, but now it has moved above the other strokes, so you can clearly see the spheres that make up the stroke (as shown in the following image).

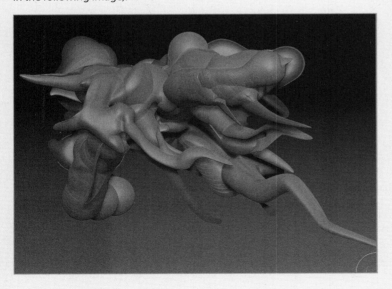

continued

8. Drag on the edge of the Transform Gyro to move the stroke to a new position. Drag up or down on a blank part of the canvas to move the stroke back and forth.

9. Click the Rotate button on the top shelf or press the R hotkey. Drag on the Transform Gyro to rotate the stroke.

10. Click the Draw button on the top of the shelf or press the Q hotkey. Draw some more strokes with the SphereBrush.

11. Switch back to Move mode to activate the Transform Gyro (hotkey = W). Drag on the Gyro to move the last stroke.

Unless you hold the Ctrl key while painting strokes, you can only move the last stroke placed on the canvas. If you do hold the Ctrl key while painting on the canvas, the Transform Gyro will let you move all the strokes you painted while holding the Ctrl key as a single stroke. The strokes that can no longer be moved have been "dropped" onto the canvas, so now they have been embedded. This is the nature of 2.5D painting in ZBrush. It's not really like 3D modeling in a program such as Maya. Painting in 2.5D is more like painting in a digital paint program that lets you move strokes around on the canvas, up and down as well as back and forth.

Experiment with some of the other 2.5D brush tools and see how they add strokes to the canvas and how they affect strokes already placed on the canvas.

Try using the Smudge brush to smear the strokes created with the SphereBrush. You can smudge the canvas and then switch to Move mode to move the smudging effect around the canvas.

Use the SnakeHook brush to pull parts of the image toward you. Some of the brush strokes, such as those created by the SnakeHook brush, can't be moved or rotated. It doesn't take long before you are able to make a mess on the canvas.

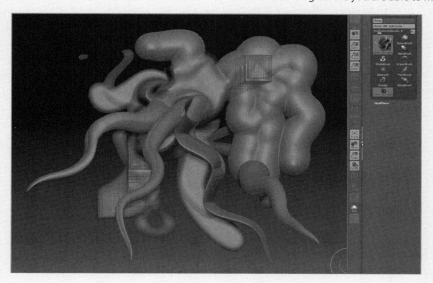

The 2.5D brushes can be very powerful. They are most often used when creating 2.5D illustrations on the ZBrush canvas. When you are creating digital sculptures using 3D meshes, they are not used nearly as much. The one exception is when using the Projection Master plug-in. The Projection Master plug-in is described in detail in the chapter, "Zscripts and Plug-Ins," that is found on the DVD.

Transform The Transform palette contains a number of buttons that exist on the shelves as well. These include the Draw and Edit buttons and the Move, Scale, and Rotate buttons found on the top shelf as well as the buttons located on the right shelf.

The most important feature of the Transform palette is the symmetry settings (see Figure 2.50). The symmetry feature is used when editing a 3D mesh. It can be used to speed up the sculpting process by allowing you to work on both sides of a 3D mesh at the same time. You'll learn how to use symmetry starting in Chapter 3. The X hotkey can be used to toggle symmetry on and off while you are sculpting.

Zplugin The Zplugin palette is where you can access plug-ins for ZBrush as well as links to important ZBrush-related sites. There is also an access point for editing your ZBrush license as well as a link to the help files. ZPlugins are covered in the bonus chapter on the DVD; be sure to check it out because a large number of extra features are available through Zplugins.

ZScript ZBrush has a built-in scripting language called ZScript. ZScripts can be simple macros, or they can be functional plug-ins with their own interface. ZScripts can be recorded through the interface using the controls on this palette or by typing commands into a text file.

The Title Bar

The final stop on our interface tour is the title bar. Here you will find useful bits of information on the upper-left side of the screen. These include the title of the document, the name of the person or company to whom this copy of ZBrush has been registered, and information regarding memory usage and time spent in the current session.

On the right side of the title bar are some useful buttons. Moving from left to right, the first button, labeled Menus, is a toggle for hiding the menus. The second button is the DefaultZScript button, which can be used to load custom zscripts.

Figure 2.49

The Tool palette gets very complex when a mesh is in the process of being edited.

Figure 2.50

The Transform palette contains the symmetry settings.

Summary

In this chapter, I took you on a quick tour of the ZBrush interface. The goal of this tour was to get you comfortable enough with locating tools and settings in ZBrush that you can easily work through the exercises in the rest of the book. Now that you have an idea of where everything is, you'll start learning about how the interface is a big part of the power of ZBrush.

Complete descriptions of all the tools and palettes can be found in the ZBrush documentation. The palettes are described in detail in the Palette Reference.

CHAPTER 3

Basic Digital Sculpting

Digital sculpting refers to a brush-based approach to creating three-dimensional models on a computer. ZBrush revolutionized the computer game and entertainment industry as well as digital art by introducing its unique digital sculpting technology about 12 years ago. Since then, the older methods of pushing and pulling individual polygon vertices and faces have largely been replaced with digital sculpting. Digital sculpting in ZBrush offers a much more intuitive and artistic way to create models. This is what has made ZBrush so attractive to artists who are less interested in the technical aspects of computer software and more concerned with creating great artwork.

In this chapter, you'll be introduced to the basics of digital sculpting in ZBrush. We will cover the following topics:

- **Understanding digital clay**

- **Loading and saving ZBrush projects**

- **Using sculpting brushes**

- **Working with dynamic levels of subdivision**

- **Using Dynamesh to create a sculpting topology**

- **Applying masks to your surface**

- **Using parametric 3D objects**

- **Using deformations**

- **Moving parts using Transpose**

Digital Clay

Digital clay is a term affectionately applied to a polygon mesh in ZBrush. This type of mesh is a surface made up of connected polygon faces. Each face shares vertices and edges with neighboring polygon faces (see Figure 3.1). ZBrush allows the polygon faces to be made up of three- or four-sided polygons. These meshes are called digital clay because of the way in which they are shaped by the sculpting brushes. Shaping polygon meshes with the brushes feels so intuitive that it's a lot like working with clay.

Figure 3.1

Digital clay is a polygon mesh made up of three- or four-sided polygons.

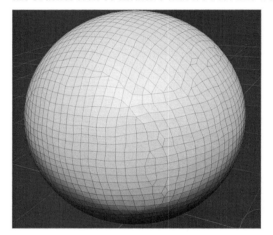

Many terms are used interchangeably in ZBrush. *Digital clay*, *polygon mesh*, *3D model*, and *3D tool* all mean pretty much the same thing. You create your models by shaping the surface on the canvas using the sculpting brushes. In order to use the brushes, you must activate Edit mode on the top shelf. Think of Edit mode as Sculpt mode.

The digital clay you use to start your model can be generated a number of different ways. You can use one of the 3D primitive presets or one of the premade models that comes with ZBrush, or you can import a polygon model created in another software package such as modo, Autodesk® 3ds Max®, Cinema 4D, or Autodesk® Maya®. In addition to working with conventional meshes, ZBrush has a number of unique tools that allow you to generate digital clay that can then be sculpted into any shape you wish.

EDIT MODE

Edit mode has been known to trip up many new ZBrush users, and it can cause some frustration at first. Often, you'll find that you accidentally moved out of Edit mode (perhaps by inadvertently pressing the T hotkey), and when you try to sculpt on the surface of a model, a new copy of the model appears instead. And as you continue to draw strokes, more copies of the model appear. To stop this behavior, just remember these simple steps:

1. Press Ctrl+N to clear the canvas.

2. Drag on the canvas to add a copy of the model on the canvas.

3. Press the T hotkey to switch to Edit mode.

4. Continue working on your model.

continued

> What is the deal with Edit mode anyway? It makes more sense when you learn that ZBrush began as an innovative illustration tool. The 3D tools are special paintbrushes designed to paint copies of 3D objects on the canvas. Edit mode is used to change the shape of the 3D objects painted on the canvas. While in Edit mode, ZBrush stores the changes made to the 3D tool, keeping an update while you work. When you turn off Edit mode and paint on the canvas, the edited version of the object appears.
>
> As a digital sculptor, you may not be interested in painting pictures with your edited 3D objects. In this case, you're going to be working in Edit mode most of the time. But it's important to understand what Edit mode is in case you encounter a type of behavior you don't understand. When working with ZBrush keep in mind the motto "It isn't broken; it's just weird." The more comfortable you become with ZBrush, the less weird it will seem, but try to be patient at first!

In this chapter, you'll learn the basics by starting with a simple lump of digital clay that you'll shape with the sculpting brushes. As you go, you'll learn new tools and techniques, and in later chapters you'll learn even more ways to start and sculpt a model.

Using the Sculpting Brushes to Create a Dragon's Head

The easiest way to learn your way around ZBrush is to start with a clearly defined goal. In this case, I've chosen a dragon's head as the subject because, well, everyone loves dragons; they are simple, familiar, culturally universal, and fun.

Regardless of how you generate your initial mesh, you will almost always use the sculpting brushes to shape your lump into something more exciting. Once you understand how to use the brushes, all the other elements of the ZBrush interface will make sense. The following demonstrates the fastest and easiest way to start sculpting.

1. Start ZBrush if it's not open already.

2. Open the Light Box browser and choose the Project tab. Double-click the DefaultSphere.ZPR project (Figure 3.2). If you already have a model loaded on the canvas, ZBrush will ask if you want to save your work. If you do want to save it, click the Save button in the File palette. Once the work has been saved, a sphere will appear on the canvas.

DRAGON REFERENCE

A quick search on the Internet will pull up thousands of reference images for dragons. I also recommend the book *Dracopedia* by William O'Connor (David and Charles Ltd., 2009) as well as *Fantasy Art Workshop* and *Forging Dragons* by John Howe (David and Charles Ltd., 2008, 2009). I've included some images of real Komodo dragons that I took at the Los Angeles Zoo. Of course, you can also just try sculpting with your own vision; you might not end up with a masterpiece on your first try, but the goal of this chapter is just to have fun playing around in ZBrush so that you get the hang of how it works.

Light Box is a quick and easy browsing interface used to load projects, digital sculptures, textures, and other resources onto the ZBrush canvas. If you are not familiar with using Light Box, consult Chapter 2.

Figure 3.2

Choose the DefaultSphere.ZPR project from the Project section of Light Box.

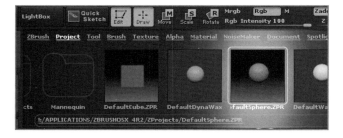

SAVING ZBRUSH FILES

When you're first learning ZBrush, you'll want to save your files as a ZBrush project. This ensures that the next time you load the project file, you can pick up where you left off and nothing is lost. Later on, you'll learn how to save individual elements such as 3D tools, textures, brushes, and more. To save a ZBrush project, click the Save As button in the File palette at the top of the screen. The project is saved in the special ZPR format. You can save the project anywhere you like on your hard drive. If you'd like the project to appear in the Project section of Light Box, save it in the ZBrush R3\ZProjects directory. On Windows, this is located in the Program Files directory. On the Mac, it is found in the Applications directory. Be aware that projects save a lot of information, and therefore the files can get quite large. It never hurts to save multiple versions as you work just in case a file gets corrupted. This is true for all software. If your model disappears when you save your project just drag on the canvas and it will reappear; this is an odd display bug which can be a little unnerving especially when you are using the software for the first time!

The DefaultSphere that appears on the canvas is known in ZBrush terminology as the *PolySphere*. What is a PolySphere? It is a rounded cube and not a typical spherical mesh. A typical spherical mesh has poles—areas on the surface where a large number of triangular faces share a single vertex. These poles can cause pinching and distortion in your sculpt. The advantage of the PolySphere is that it does not have poles, so it is much easier to work with. I use the PolySphere all the time for this reason (see Figure 3.3).

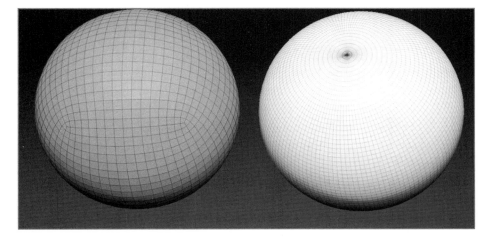

Figure 3.3

The PolySphere on the left is easier to sculpt because it does not have poles like the Sphere3D on the right.

If you're not sure whether you're using a PolySphere or a typical spherical mesh, click the PolyF button on the right shelf, and you'll see the wireframe display on the mesh. The PolySphere should look like the sphere on the left in Figure 3.3 and *not* the sphere on the right.

3. Move the cursor so that the tip of your sculpting brush appears above the mesh, and you'll see two red dots above the surface. When you load the DefaultSphere project, symmetry along the x-axis is automatically turned on. This is great because it makes it easy to sculpt a simple head since most heads are symmetrical along the x-axis.

You can turn symmetry on or off by pressing the X hotkey. For now let's leave it on. Later in this chapter you'll learn about more advanced symmetry options. If you run into a situation where symmetry has been activated but you see only a single dot, you may need to rotate the model until you're facing the correct axis, at which point the two dots should appear. Basic navigation is covered in Chapter 2, "Understanding the ZBrush Interface."

When I start a sculpt, I like to use the BasicMaterial2 shader, which you will find in the material fly-out library on the left shelf. Simply open the library by clicking the Material icon, and choose BasicMaterial2. How to use the material library is covered in Chapter 2. The BasicMaterial2 shader is not as exciting as some of the others, but it gives you the best sense of the shape of your sculpt as you work. It's good to change materials occasionally while you work.

4. Now let's start shaping the head using the Move brush. Open the sculpting brush fly-out library in the upper left of the ZBrush canvas and find the Move brush.

SEARCHING THE BRUSH LIBRARY

The brush fly-out library contains a large number of brush presets. If you know the name of the brush you are looking for, you can speed up your search by typing the first letter of the brush's name while the fly-out is open. For example, if you are looking for the Move brush, open the sculpting brush library and then type M. You'll see all the brush icons become grayed out except those that start with *M*. This makes it easier to spot the Move brush.

You'll also notice that each brush has a letter in the upper-left corner of its icon. If you type this letter while the brush fly-out library is open, ZBrush will set the brush preset as the currently active brush. For example, typing M and then B while the brush fly-out library is open will automatically set the current brush to the Move brush preset. Typing C and then B while the brush fly-out library is open sets the current brush to the ClayBuildup brush preset.

5. Let's start by getting a general sense of the dragon head shape. To do this we'll push and pull on the PolySphere using a large brush size. Increase the brush size slider until there is a large red circle for the brush tip; then drag on the surface of the PolySphere. Notice that changes are made to both sides of the PolySphere at the same time.

6. Push, pull, drag, and shape until you have something slightly dragon-like (see Figure 3.4). Pull out the front to create a snout, and then push in areas for the eyes. Don't be afraid to adjust your draw size while you work. In fact, if you hold the S hotkey, the Brush Size slider will appear on the canvas, saving you a trip to the top shelf.

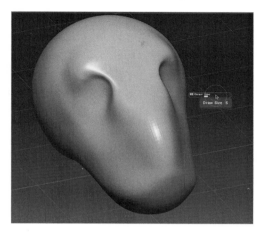

Figure 3.4

Use the Move brush to start shaping the PolySphere into something that looks like a dragon's head.

TIPS ON USING THE MOVE BRUSH

- Increase the Z intensity if you want to have a stronger influence on the surface. Sometimes I like to have a strong intensity with a small brush size for precise changes and a low Z intensity with a large brush size to make more general changes.

- Hold the Alt key while dragging on the surface to move the surface along the surface normal (surface normals are defined in Chapter 1, "Digital Art Basics"). Drag left while holding the Alt key to push in; drag right while holding the Alt key to push out.

- Change the Focal Shift slider to adjust the brush falloff. A low focal shift will give the brush a hard edge; a high focal shift will create a smooth falloff.

- Other variations of the Move brush are available in both the sculpting brush library and the Brush/Move section of Light Box. These variations can create some really interesting effects.

7. Open the sculpting brush library and select the Move Elastic brush. Try using the Move Elastic brush while shaping your head model. This brush has a very rubbery feel to it (Figure 3.5). I find that by moving the surface back and forth very gently, I can create some interesting shapes in the surface. It does take a little practice.

The Move Elastic brush works best on meshes with 24,000 polygons or less. If you use it on a dense mesh (meaning a mesh with a lot of polygons), it will slow down performance significantly. This is because ZBrush is updating the model as you work, which takes some calculations. As you work through the examples in this book, you'll learn about other Move brush variations, such as the Move Topological and Move Parts brushes. Switching brushes while working is a great way to explore new ideas and forms.

8. Try the Nudge brush, which is similar to the Move brush but with a slightly more precise feel. Once you have something you like, click the Save button in the File palette and save the model to your local disk using a unique name such as dragon_ 01.ZPR. The basic dragon's head is shown in Figure 3.6.

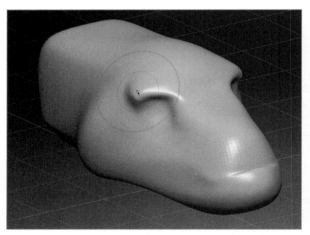

Figure 3.5

Try using the Move Elastic brush to shape the head; compare how the surface reacts to the Move Elastic brush versus the Move brush.

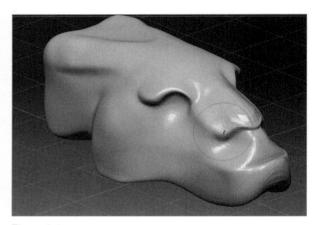

Figure 3.6

A basic dragon's head is shaped using the Move, Move Elastic, and Nudge brushes.

Using the Smooth Brush

As you shape your model, you'll no doubt get some stretching in the surface. One way to deal with this is to use the Smooth brush. Hold down the Shift key and drag over the model. The Smooth brush evens out the surface and reduces the stretching.

The shape of the surface seems to shrink and melt away as you brush over it while holding down the Shift key. The Smooth brush averages the distance between the vertices on the surface. If the changes are too extreme, you can lower the Z intensity of the Smooth brush.

1. Increase the draw size of the brush and smooth the parts of the surface that appear stretched. The smooth effect is stronger with a larger brush size because a larger area

of the surface is being sampled as you brush. You can quickly call up the brush size controls by holding the spacebar while the brush is over the canvas.

2. Hold down the Shift key and adjust the Z intensity.

3. Paint over the stretched areas of the surface while holding the Shift key to smooth the surface. Note that the brush icon turns blue when you are holding the Shift key, indicating that you are in Smooth mode.

4. Release the Shift key, and pull on the model to continue shaping with the Move brush.

5. Sometimes gently tapping the surface using the digital tablet is the best approach; it can keep you from obliterating your work. Digital clay is flexible enough that you can test a large number of ideas while you work. When I start sculpting a model from a PolySphere, I spend a lot of time using just the Move and Smooth brushes while focusing on the form (see Figure 3.7).

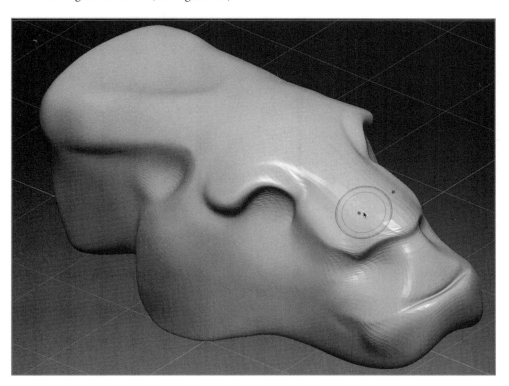

Figure 3.7

Alternate using the Move and Smooth brushes while creating the basic shape of the dragon's head.

6. Don't forget to save the file frequently as you work! Click the Save As button in the File menu to save the ZBrush project.

TIPS ON USING THE SMOOTH BRUSH

- The Z intensity of the Smooth brush is independent of the current brush, meaning that the value changes when you switch to the Smooth brush. ZBrush remembers the Z intensity of the Smooth brush even when you release the Shift key and switch to another brush. This is also true of the Focal Shift setting but not Draw Size.

- A high Z intensity, such as the default setting of 100, can quickly obliterate details sculpted into the mesh. It's good practice to set the Z intensity of the Smooth brush to somewhere between 20 and 40 while working.

- A number of other smoothing brushes are available in the brush fly-out library and in the Brush section of Light Box. If you choose one of these brushes, you'll get a message letting you know that the chosen smoothing brush will be active only while you are holding down the Shift key. The other smoothing brushes have unique properties that will make more sense once you've learned more about ZBrush.

- The Brush palette contains a set of controls that are dedicated to the Smooth brush. These are found toward the bottom in the Smooth Brush Modifiers subpalette, as shown in the following image. This palette will be explained in more detail in Chapter 7, "Advanced Brush Techniques." For now it is useful to know that the Alt Brush Size slider adjusts the size of the Smooth brush. This value is a multiplier for the Draw Size setting. When you set Alt Brush Size to 2, every time you hold down the Shift key, the draw size of the Smooth brush will be twice the draw size of the current brush. A setting of 10 will make the Smooth brush 10 times the current brush size.

Defining Forms with the Standard and Clay Brushes

Once you have the basic dragon's head form established, you can start building basic detail using the standard band clay sculpting brushes. Of course, you can use the sculpting brushes in any order you wish and switch between the brushes at any time. I find it's easier to introduce the sculpting process to new students by working with just a few brushes at a time. Focus on large bony forms for now; at this point you should not worry about little details like scales and wrinkles.

The Standard brush causes the points of the mesh to be pushed outward based on an average of their normal direction. If you hold the Alt key while dragging across the surface, the brush is reversed so that the mesh gets pushed inward.

The Clay brush also causes the surface to be raised, but it generally fills in the recessed areas of the surface first, making the brush feel as though you're pressing clay into the surface. It's important to understand that none of the sculpting brushes actually add or remove points from the surface; they just move the existing points around based on their own specific algorithms.

Just like with the other brushes, the Z intensity increases the amount of influence the brush has on the surface, and the Focal Shift adjusts the falloff.

1. Open the sculpting brush library and press the S key and then the T key to select the Standard brush. Reduce the size of the brush so the changes you make aren't too extreme.

2. Brush over the surface of your shaped PolySphere to sculpt the bony forms above the eye for the dragon. Try making nostrils as well.

3. Experiment with adjusting the Z intensity, Draw Size, and Focal Shift while you work, and see what kind of shapes you can build into the head.

4. Hold the Alt key to dig into the surface. Remember to constantly rotate and examine the model as you work. Try to shape the whole surface, and don't get too caught up in overworking a single area.

5. Open the sculpting brush library and chose the Clay brush (press the C key and then the L key to select the Clay brush). Brush over the surface, and compare how the brush behaves to the Standard and Move brushes (see Figure 3.8).

6. Don't forget that any time you want to smooth the details on the surface, just press the Shift key.

7. Save your model when you have something that you like.

Figure 3.8

Use the Standard and Clay brushes to further define the forms of the head.

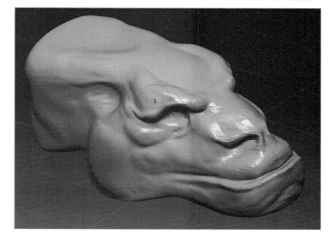

TIPS ON USING THE CLAY BRUSH

- Sometimes the Clay brush can cause problems when you're working on thin surfaces such as ears. While the part of the surface that is facing you may appear fine, the reverse side may become stretched, as shown in the following image below. To fix this, open the Brush palette, click the Auto Masking button, and activate the Backface Mask button. This is off by default simply because it may slow down performance on high-density meshes.

- There are many variations of the Clay brush. Try using the Clay Tubes and Clay Buildup brushes, and see how they behave when working on your model.

- Just like the Standard brush, the Clay brush will dig into the surface when you hold the Alt key.

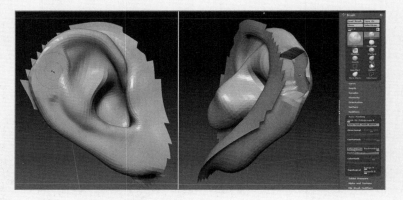

BRUSH ALGORITHMS

By now you've gotten a taste of the basics when working with sculpting brushes, but let's take a moment to contemplate the nature of these amazing tools.

Each sculpting brush is based on an algorithm, which is simply a recipe that tells ZBrush how a particular brush will affect the surface of the digital clay. As you brush across the surface of the model, imagine that a short conversation takes places between the brush tip and the surface of the clay. This conversation is known as *sampling*. While sampling, the brush determines the number of polygons within the Draw Size, the normal direction of the polygons, whether the surface is masked or painted (topics we'll discuss in detail a bit later), and other important bits of information. At the same time, ZBrush is paying attention to the algorithm of the current brush and how it moves the points on the surface. It's also keeping track of the brush's Z intensity, Draw Size, Focal Shift, how the brush is oriented relative to the surface, and how the brush should react to the amount of pressure you are applying to your digital tablet.

continued

You don't need to have a computer science degree to understand how to work with the algorithms. It's enough to know that the Standard brush moves the points of the surface outward based on an average of the normal direction of the surface. The algorithm of the Inflate brush, on the other hand, pushes the points out based on the normal direction of each point. The result is that the Standard brush and the Inflate brush behave in different ways when sculpting the surface.

ZBrush gives you a wide variety of controls that allow you to customize your brushes and even create your own variations. Most of these controls are found in the Brush palette. Many of these controls are discussed in more detail in Chapter 7. If you're dying to know how to make your own brushes, feel free to skip ahead to that chapter. For now, you should understand that the brush presets are based on a few base types. You can find out which base type the brush uses by holding your pointer over the icon in the Brush palette. At the bottom of the preview you'll see a little note that indicates the base type for the brush. Notice that the Clay, Clay Tubes, Clay Buildup, and Polish brushes all use the Clay base type. A description of the base types is found in Chapter 7 of this book.

Clay
Base Type: Clay

Clay Tubes
Base Type: Clay

Clay Buildup
Base Type: Clay

Working with Dynamic Levels of Subdivision

You may have seen many highly detailed ZBrush models on the Internet or in movies or video games. How do artists get all this detail into their ZBrush model? It's done by subdividing the mesh, which means that the number of polygons that make up the surface is multiplied, giving you more polygons to work with so the brushes can easily add more detail.

The great thing about ZBrush is that when you add more polygons to the surface by subdividing, you can easily go back to a lower number of polygons. In fact, you can go back and forth between a version of the model that has few polygons and less detail and a version of the model that has many polygons and a lot of detail. You can do this as often as you like while you shape your model. So at lower levels of subdivision (known as an SDiv level) you can shape the overall form, kind of like what you've already done with your dragon's head. Then you can subdivide, add more details like the nostrils and eye sockets, then subdivide a few more times to add scales and curling lips, and so on until the model is made up of millions of polygons and loads of realistic detail. But you can, at any time, go back to the lower SDiv level, make changes to the overall form, and ZBrush will remember and retain all of those crazy details, so that when you switch back to a high SDiv level, you still have your scales and wrinkles and curling dragon lips. This gives you an amazing amount of control as an artist, and it's something you really can't do in traditional media such as clay.

In this next section, we'll take the dragon's head you have been working with and add a few levels of subdivision to show how to use this to your advantage.

1. Use the File menu to open the most recent version of your dragon's head model.

2. Make sure the Edit button on the top shelf is on, indicating that you are in Edit mode.

3. Expand the Geometry subpalette of the Tool palette, and take a look at the SDiv slider.

The default PolySphere you used to start your model already has three SDiv levels, and you can easily add even more.

4. Drag the SDiv slider to the left to move to a lower SDiv level. You'll see that the model looks a little chunkier at lower levels of subdivision.

5. Turn on the PolyF button on the left shelf so you can see the wireframe. At lower SDiv levels there are fewer polygons and they appear larger (left image in Figure 3.9).

6. Move the SDiv slider all the way up to level 3. Click the Divide button in the Geometry subpalette to subdivide the model. This subdivides the model, which means that the number of polygons at SDiv 3 are multiplied by 4 (right image in Figure 3.9).

7. Look at the Total Points listed on the top shelf; the model now has 98,306 points. The SDiv slider now goes from 1 to 4, the highest level of subdivision.

Figure 3.9

Low subdivision levels have fewer polygons and less detail (left image). Add a fourth level of subdivision to increase the number of polygons available for sculpting (right image).

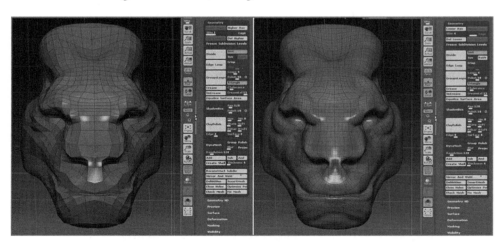

8. Click the Divide button again; now the model has five SDiv levels, and at SDiv 5 the total number of points is 393,218.

9. Experiment with moving to different SDiv levels, and make changes with the Move, Standard, Smooth, and Clay brushes. See how this affects details at higher subdivision levels. It's also easy to make major changes to the form at lower SDiv levels without destroying the details you sculpt at the higher levels (see Figure 3.10).

Figure 3.10

You can switch between higher and lower subdivision levels as you work to sculpt detail or make major changes to the form.

10. When you feel like you understand SDiv levels, use the File menu to save your model.

TIPS ON WORKING WITH SUBDIVISION LEVELS

- To add a level of subdivision, you must have the slider set to the highest SDiv level; otherwise, you'll get a warning message.

- You can delete the levels of subdivision by clicking the Delete Lower or Delete Higher Levels Of Subdivision button. Doing this will automatically renumber the SDiv levels, so if you are at level 3 and you delete lower levels of subdivision, what was level 3 now becomes level 1.

- When you subdivide the model, the surface will be smoothed automatically. If you want to keep the hard-edge look of the model when you subdivide, turn off the Smt button next to the Divide button in the Geometry subpalette.

- You can add a lower level of subdivision by setting the SDiv slider to the lowest level and clicking the Reconstruct Lower Subdivision button found in the Geometry sub-palette. Use this with caution because it can sometimes affect detail at the highest SDiv level. When in doubt, save the file before clicking this button! In some cases this won't work. If the mesh has triangles, ZBrush will not be able to add a lower level of subdivision.

- You can subdivide sections of a mesh if parts become overly stretched. To do this, move the SDiv slider to the lowest SDiv level and click the Equalize Surface button in the Geometry subpalette. You can also explicitly subdivide a section of the surface using masking. This will be discussed later in the chapter in the section on masks.

TOPOLOGY

In the world of digital 3D modeling, the term *topology* refers to how the polygon faces that make up a 3D mesh are arranged on the surface. There are different methods for creating topology. Some topologies are better suited for digital sculpting than others. To create the best possible motion for the creatures and characters they animate, animators working in 3D software have special requirements for the topology of the models they use. If you intend to create models for use in video games or in animation, you will need to become very conscious of topology. ZBrush even has tools that allow you to re-create the topology of a model after you have sculpted it.

These days it has become common practice to sculpt the model first using a sculpting-friendly topology. Then, once the model has been approved for animation or printing, you can "retopologize" the surface to create an animation-friendly or printer-friendly topology. The original model is always available as a source for generating any kind of topology you need.

The following image shows the same model. The version on the left has an animation-friendly topology; notice how the edges of the polygons form loops around the mouth and eyes. This kind of edge flow deforms well when animating facial expressions. The version on the right has an even distribution of polygons that are all about the same size. This kind of topology works well when sculpting shapes into the mesh. You can create, sculpt, and use both types of topologies in ZBrush. Which topology you use depends on what you want to do with the model and your preference as an artist. The makers of ZBrush are not interested in restricting you to one workflow over another. They are more interested in giving you as much creative freedom as you need to achieve your goals. And, of course, ZBrush allows you many ways to move between animation and sculpting topologies; you'll learn about these techniques throughout this book. The next section covers how to convert a model into a sculpting topology using Dynamesh.

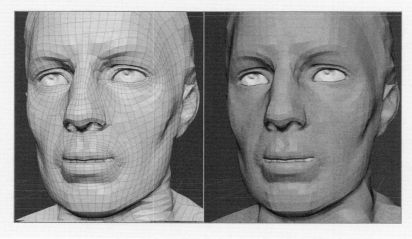

Creating a Sculpting Topology with Dynamesh

As you work over the surface with the sculpting brushes, the surface may appear stretched as the polygons of the mesh are pulled. This happens especially when you pull out the mouth of a dragon or try to make ears or horns. The Smooth brush can help alleviate this, but it can only take you so far, and too much smoothing results in kind of an amorphous blob. Subdividing the model also helps eliminate the stretching, but as you sculpt against the "grain" of the polygon, the surface still can look stretched unless you work on a mesh that has millions of polygons.

To eliminate these types of problems Pixologic has introduced a new technology known as Dynamesh. Dynamesh creates a sculpting-friendly topology dynamically as you work whenever you need it. Dynamesh is a special mode that, when activated, rebuilds the topology of your mesh to make it easier to sculpt. Let's try it out on the dragon's head you have been working on.

Z-SPEAK

The folks at Pixologic love inventing new terms almost as much as inventing new tools. *Dynamesh*, *ZSketch*, *ShadowBox*, and *FiberMesh* are just a few of the terms that will soon become a part of your vocabulary as you delve deeper into ZBrush. As you become fluent in Z-speak, you'll find it's a handy way to connect and communicate with other ZBrush users; however, you may get some strange looks from "regular" 3D artists. But who wants to be regular anyway?

Using Dynamesh on the Dragon's Head Model

1. Open the most recent version of the dragon's head model. Turn on the PolyF button on the left side of the canvas so you can see how the polygons on the surface are arranged; this will also make it clear which parts of the model may be badly stretched.

2. Set the SDiv to the highest level, and click the Delete Lower SDiv Level button to remove the lower SDiv levels. The SDiv slider will become grayed out, indicating that there are no longer any lower levels of subdivision.

3. Expand the Tool palette to the Geometry tab. Turn on the Dynamesh button. After a few seconds you'll see the model update (see Figure 3.11). The shape should look about the same, but notice that now, instead of stretched polygons of various sizes, the surface is made up of many square-shaped polygons plus a few small triangles. This type of topology is much easier to sculpt.

Figure 3.11

Dynamesh instantly retopologizes the surface of the model so it is easier to sculpt. The result is a surface made up of evenly distributed squares and triangles.

4. You may see stretch marks, but this is a result of the original shape being projected onto the new Dynamesh. Hold down the Shift key and drag over the stretch marks to remove them with the Smooth brush.

If you feel like you don't have enough polygons (or maybe too many), you can easily change the number dynamically (hence the term *Dynamesh*) by changing the Resolution slider below the Dynamesh button. The surface updates automatically. Lower values mean fewer and larger polygons.

5. Now to see how powerful Dynamesh is, it's time to go a little crazy. Make sure the Dynamesh button is still on while you work, and use the Move brush to push and pull, to drag out the parts of the dragon head to a crazy extreme, and to try pulling out some horns.

6. The stretch marks will appear again, but don't worry! Press Shift+A (or hold down the Ctrl key and drag on a blank part of the canvas and release). Dynamesh re-creates each time you do this, so you can work very quickly and eliminate the stretch marks instantly (see Figure 3.12).

Figure 3.12

Pull some horns out of the head using the Move brush. Hold down the Ctrl key and drag on the canvas to instantly retopologize the surface, eliminating stretching.

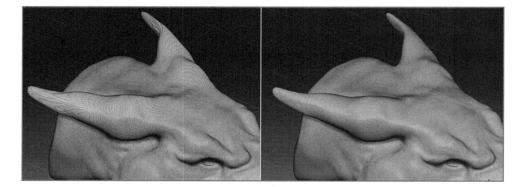

7. The power of Dynamesh is that it frees you from worrying about stretched polygons while you work. Turn off the PolyF button and experiment using the sculpting brushes to shape the horn. Every time you feel the surface is becoming too stretched,

just Ctrl+drag on the canvas to activate Dynamesh, and then use the Smooth brush to clean up the surface.

8. Try adding tendrils to the jaw or even some teeth popping out of the mouth using the Snakehook brush. Repeat the process of pulling geometry with the Move brush, updating the surface with Dynamesh, and then smoothing the surface with the Smooth brush.

Figure 3.13 shows the process I went through in shaping my dragon's head. Throughout this process I'm still experimenting with ideas, adjusting the anatomy and the personality of the dragon as I work. You'll find that this workflow turns ZBrush into a great tool for sketching out ideas.

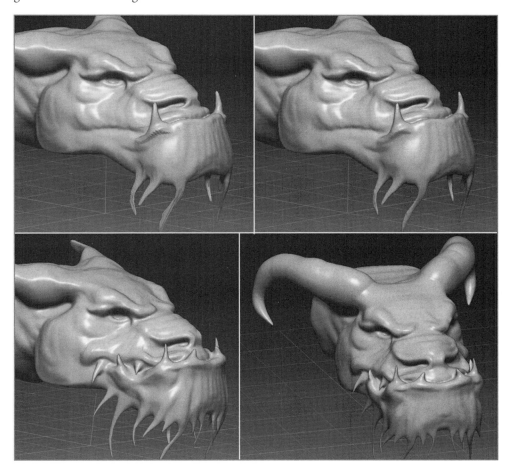

Figure 3.13

Using Dynamesh to update the topology of the surface as you work, you can easily pull clay out from the geometry of the head.

Editing Your Design

Using Dynamesh, you can feel free to experiment while sculpting. You're never stuck with what you make, and you can always easily make radical changes and then remove them at will if you change your mind. For example, I've decided that the horns on my dragon make him look too much like a ram. I want to get rid of them without starting over. Using the Dynamesh workflow, I can simply squish the horns back into the head and try something different.

To make this easier you can use the Move Topological brush to push the horns back into the head. The Move Topological brush samples the surface as you work to determine which parts of the mesh are connected. You can use this brush to move the horns close to the head without affecting the head itself. The brush may feel a little sticky because the mesh is fairly dense. Generally, it's best to use the brush on a lower-density mesh.

Figure 3.14

The Resolution slider is found below the Dynamesh button in the Geometry subpalette of the Tool palette.

Currently, my mesh has more than 150,000 points, but I deleted the lower levels of subdivision. So how can you create a mesh that's a little easier to work with? You can change the resolution of Dynamesh so there are fewer polygons to work with, making it easier to edit the overall form:

1. In the Geometry palette, make sure the Dynamesh button is still on. It should be a bright color. Set the Resolution slider to **64** and Ctrl+drag on the canvas (see Figure 3.14). The surface should update. If it does not, touch the surface with the brush to make a small change and then Ctrl+drag on the canvas again. Sometimes Dynamesh requires that you make a small change before updating.

2. The mesh should now be a lower resolution; after I did this, the number of points in my surface moved from 190,000 down to 49,800. In ZBrush terms, that's a medium-level resolution, which should work great with the Move Topological brush.

How did I come up with a setting of 64? I came to this value through experimentation. If the resolution you choose is not low or high enough for what you want, you can undo (Ctrl+Z), set a new value, and then try again until you get a resolution you like. The scale of the object will affect the resolution. A very small object requires a higher-resolution setting to get a decent number of polygons; a very large object can become extremely dense when you "dynamesh" at even a low-resolution setting.

3. Select the Move Topological brush and move the horns toward the head. No need to be overly careful; just drag them back as if the head was made of clay.

4. Use the Smooth brush as you work to smooth the surface.

5. Once the horns are close to the head, use the Inflate brush to pump up the area so that the horn and head geometry overlap.

6. Now Ctrl+drag on the canvas to "re-dynamesh." The horns are fused with the surface.

7. Use the Smooth, Move, and Clay brushes to clean up the area. Then Ctrl+drag on the surface to re-dynamesh as you go. Before you know it, those goofy horns are just a fading memory (see Figure 3.15).

8 Set the Resolution slider below the Dynamesh button back to **128** and Ctrl+drag on the canvas. Now you have a high resolution again, and you can continue to work.

I decided to get rid of the teeth and the tendrils using the same techniques (see Figure 3.16). You can continually model and shape with Dynamesh as you explore ideas.

Figure 3.15

Use the Move Topological and Inflate brushes to move the horns back toward the surface. Activate Dynamesh again, and the horns are fused to the surface. With a little cleanup, the horns are completely gone.

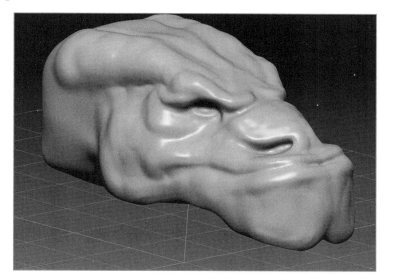

Figure 3.16

The tendrils on the chin have been removed by simply pushing them back into the surface and re-dynameshing the surface.

Refining the Surface with Polish Brushes

As you sculpt your digital clay, you may notice that the shape can become quite lumpy. You can reduce the lumpiness of the form as well as bring definition to the planes of the dragon's head using the polish brushes.

1. Open the most recent version of your dragon's head project. Make sure that the dragon's head is on the canvas and that Edit mode is active.

2. Open the sculpting brush library and press the H key on your keyboard. This switches the current brush to the hPolish (hard polish) brush (the only brush preset that starts with the letter *h*).

3. Use the brush to start defining the forms of the head; think about the bone structure of the dragon as you work. Again, no need to worry about fine details such as scales and wrinkles; at this point you just want to establish the final overall form of the head (see Figure 3.17).

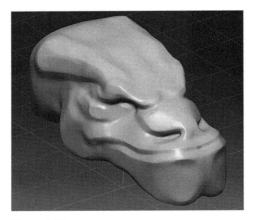

Figure 3.17
Use the hPolish brush to refine the forms of the dragon's head.

TIPS ON USING POLISH BRUSHES

- Just as with the other sculpting brushes I tend to smooth as I work by alternating holding and releasing the Shift key.

- The hPolish brush can be used to create sharp angles when it is used to polish adjacent forms.

- Several variations of the Polish brush are available in the brush library, including nPolish and sPolish, and even more in the Brush section of Light Box.

- The hPolish brush presses down the surface; if you want to use the brush to build out the surface, hold down the Alt key.

- The Trim Dynamic brush can also be used to refine the surface. It is similar to the hPolish brush but with some subtle differences. I use both while I am working. The Trim Dynamic brush is good at flattening sharp edges.

- If you activate the Polish option to the right of the Dynamesh button in the Geometry subpalette of the Tool palette, then every time you re-dynamesh the surface, it will add an overall polish to the surface. This can eliminate lumps as well as accentuate the contours of your design. It also keeps the dynameshed surface from becoming too "soft."

Masking

Masking protects a specified part of the mesh as you make changes. Masks give you more precise control over the mesh, and there are a number of ways to create masks. Masks are created using the Masking Pen brush. This brush is activated when you hold down the Ctrl key while the Draw button is active on the top shelf.

Using masks you can increase the level of precision you have when using the sculpting brushes. Also, a number of processes in ZBrush require that parts of the surface be masked in order to work properly. Let's start by discussing the basics of creating masks.

USING SCULPTING BRUSHES AND HOTKEYS

When you are using the sculpting brushes together with hotkeys, you can start to get tangled fingers and a little mixed up as to what hotkey does what. It does take some practice. Keep these general rules in mind when learning ZBrush hotkeys:

- Hold Shift to activate smoothing brushes.

- Hold Ctrl to activate masking function.

- Hold the Alt button to reverse the brush; this creates the opposite action in the brush. If the brush normally pushes out, then it will push in when you hold the Alt key. If the brush normally smoothes, then the Alt key will make it sharpen, and if the brush normally masks, holding Alt will make it unmask.

  By the end of the chapter I'll add a few more rules to this list. But first you should try using these options as you practice in the next few exercises.

Mask Controls

In this exercise you'll use masking to control which parts of the dragon's head model can be edited with the brushes.

1. Load the most recent version of your dragon's head model into ZBrush. We're going to look at how masks can be used to modify the lower lip of the dragon.

2. Open the sculpting brush fly-out library on the left shelf and press S and then T to choose the Standard brush.

3. Make sure symmetry is activated along the x-axis. If you rotate the view of the head to the top, front, or bottom, you should see two red dots as you hold the brush tip over the mesh. This means symmetry is on. If you don't see two dots, press the X hotkey to turn symmetry on.

4. Open the Material library on the left shelf and choose the SkinShade4 material (see Figure 3.18). This material will make it easier to see the masks you paint on the surface.

Figure 3.18

Open the Material
library on the left
shelf and select
the SkinShade4
material.

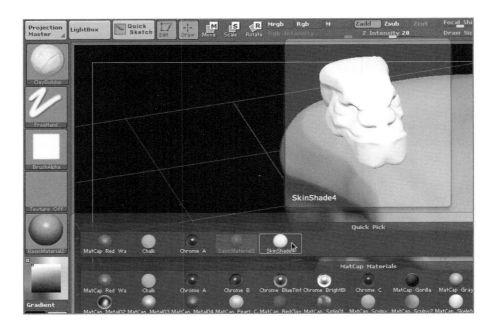

5. Hold down the Ctrl key and brush along the lip of the dragon. The masked area appears as a dark gray color on the surface (see the left image in Figure 3.19).

6. Release the Ctrl key and try painting on the dark area with the sculpting brush. Nothing happens. Try painting on the white areas, and you'll see that the surface is raised under the brush just as you would expect using the Standard brush. The darker areas are protected from the brush (see right image in Figure 3.19).

Figure 3.19

The mask on the
lower lip of the
dragon protects
the surface from
changes made with
the sculpting brush.

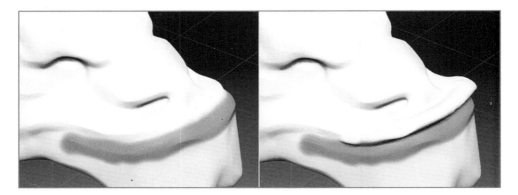

When you press and hold the Ctrl key while the Draw button is on in the top shelf, you activate the MaskPen brush. As you hold down the Ctrl key, note that the brush icon on the left shelf displays the MaskPen brush (see Figure 3.20).

Of course, the changes I just made on the surface are not what I want at all; in fact, I want the opposite. I want to pull out the lip to make room for some giant teeth jutting out of the lower jaw. So I need to undo the last few strokes, invert the mask, and then edit the lip while the rest of the head is masked.

Figure 3.20

While you hold down the Ctrl key, the brush switches to the MaskPen brush.

7. If you've made similar changes on your dragon, press Ctrl+Z to undo those brush strokes. You can undo several times by repeatedly pressing Ctrl+Z. Return the dragon to the point before you sculpted the unmasked areas. Try not to undo painting the mask though.

8. You should end up with a mask painted on the lip. Now you'll invert the mask so everything is masked except the lip. To do this you can either press Ctrl+I or hold Ctrl and tap on a blank part of the canvas. Either action inverts the mask painted on the surface. Now it should appear light colored while the rest of the dragon appears dark gray (see the left image in Figure 3.21).

9. Before sculpting the lower lip, you can blur the edges of the mask, which can help make the brushstrokes at the edge of the mask a little smoother. To do this, hold the Ctrl key and tap or click the masked part of the surface. The edges of the mask should look blurred. Each time you repeat this action, it will blur the mask a little more (see the right image in Figure 3.21).

Figure 3.21

The mask is inverted (left image); then the edges of the mask are blurred (right image).

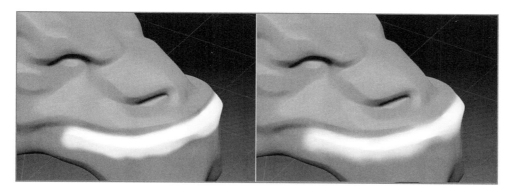

10. Now open the Brush palette and switch to the Move brush (press the M key and then the V key while the brush library is open). Use the Move brush to pull the lip up and out a little, as shown in the upper left of Figure 3.22.

Figure 3.22 shows how I used the Move, Inflate, Smooth, and hPolish brushes to form an exaggerated underbite in the dragon.

Figure 3.22

The Move, Inflate, Smooth, and hPolish brushes are used to pull out the lower lip of the dragon.

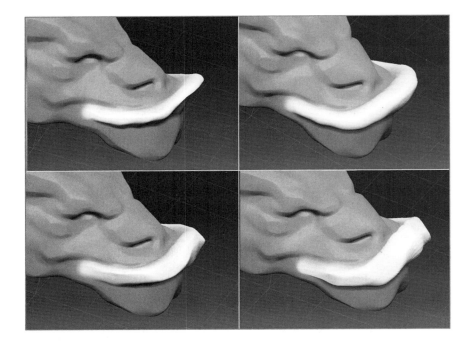

Editing the Mask

Masks are useful and extremely flexible. You can edit the mask using the masking brushes in order to precisely isolate areas for further sculpting, all while protecting the areas you don't want the brushes to affect. In this section, you'll use more masking features to edit the mask painted on the dragon's lip.

The big problem with the way the lip looks on my dragon is that it has too much of an overhang. I'm going to use the mask pen to expand the current mask and then use the ClayBuildup brush to create flesh below the lip so that it looks like the lip is stretched over large teeth coming out of the jaw. Here's how you can accomplish the same thing on your model:

1. Start by erasing part of the mask below the lower lip. Hold Ctrl+Alt at the same time and paint two oval areas below the lip. (Remember that the Ctrl key masks and the Alt key reverses, so by holding Ctrl and Alt together you create a reverse mask, which erases the mask wherever you paint. (See the top-left image in Figure 3.23.)

2. Now open the Sculpting Brush library on the left shelf and select the ClayBuildup brush (the hotkey for this brush is C and then B while the brush library is open). Use the brush to fill in the area below the lip, as shown in the upper right of Figure 3.23.

3. Use the Smooth and hPolish brushes to clean up the sculpted area (see the lower-left image in Figure 3.23).

At this point the surface is getting stretched, so you can dynamesh the surface to remove the stretching. To do this you need to first clear the mask and then dynamesh. Both actions use the Ctrl+drag gesture.

4. Hold Ctrl, drag on a blank part of the canvas, and release. This clears the mask.

5. Hold Ctrl, drag on a blank part of the canvas, and release again. It's the same action as in step 4, but this time, since Dynamesh is still active, the surface will be retopologized instantly (see the lower right in Figure 3.23).

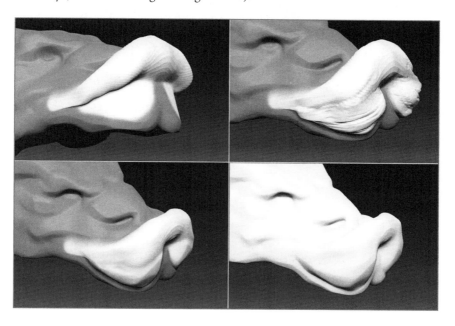

Figure 3.23

The MaskPen brush is used as an eraser to expand the mask (upper left). The ClayBuildup brush is used to fill in the area below the lip (upper right). The unmasked portion is refined using the Smooth and hPolish brushes (lower left). The surface is unmasked and dynameshed to remove stretching.

By using similar techniques you can continue to shape the dragon's head to get it ready for adding teeth and eyeballs. Figure 3.24 shows some of the steps I used to refine the surface. In addition to using the Standard, Clay Tubes, Smooth, Move, and hPolish brushes, I used the DamStandard brush (found in the brush library when you press the D key and then the S key) to create fine lines. Try this brush to start sketching lines on the surface to help separate the features. You'll find this brush absolutely indispensible for sculpting. I also frequently re-dynamesh the surface with the Polish option activated in the Geometry palette; this keeps the surface smooth and the edges refined. Make sure you save your project if you come up with something you like!

Figure 3.24

Using the MaskPen, Standard, Smooth, Inflate, Move, DamStandard, and hPolish brushes, the features are shaped and refined. Dynamesh is applied with the Polish feature enabled to keep the surface smooth and edges sharp.

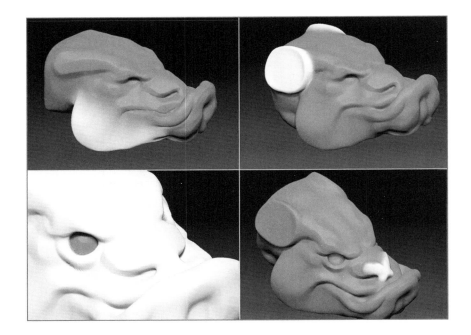

BASIC MASKING HOTKEYS AND FUNCTIONS

- ViewMask (hotkey = Ctrl+H) enables the visibility of the mask—the dark area on the surface. If this button is off, the mask will not be visible, but it will still prevent changes from being made to the masked area of the surface. Sometimes the dark area of the mask can be distracting while you work on the surface, so ZBrush gives you the option of turning mask visibility off. If you ever encounter a situation in which it seems as if a sculpting brush is not working properly, double-check to see if the ViewMask button is off. It may be that you have accidentally applied a mask that you can't see.

- Inverse (hotkey = Ctrl+I) swaps the masked and unmasked parts of the surface so that the masked parts become unmasked and the unmasked parts become masked. You can also invert the mask by holding the Ctrl key and clicking a blank part of the canvas.

- Clear (hotkey = Ctrl+Shift+A) removes all masks from the surface. You can also clear the mask by holding down the Ctrl key while dragging on a blank part of the canvas. When you release the brush, all masks will be cleared.

- MaskAll (hotkey = Ctrl+A) applies a mask to the whole surface. You can also hold down the Ctrl key and click a blank part of the canvas to mask everything, provided nothing is masked already.

continued

- BlurMask blurs the edges of the mask. The mask is still present but not as intense along the blurred edges. Another way to blur the mask is to Ctrl+tap on the masked area.

- SharpenMask sharpens the edges of the mask, making them more defined. Another way to sharpen the mask is to Ctrl+Alt+tap on the masked area.

- Hold the Ctrl+Alt keys together and paint on the surface to erase part of the mask.

- Toward the bottom of the Masking subpalette you'll see a slider labeled Intens, as shown in the following image. This controls the intensity of the mask. The value of this slider is applied to the next mask painted on the surface; it does not affect any masks currently applied to the surface. If you set this to 50, the next mask you create will be at half the normal strength. This means that the surface will still be affected by changes you make with the sculpting brushes but only at half strength.

- There are many advanced masking features in the Masking subpalette, including Mask Ambient Occlusion and Mask By Cavity. These features will be covered in the sections on advanced sculpting techniques later in this book.

Mask Pen Stroke Types

The MaskPen brush can use all of the stroke types that a regular sculpting brush uses and a few extra (Rectangle, Circle, Curve, and Lasso). To change the MaskPen brush's stroke type, hold down the Ctrl key, and then open the stroke type fly-out library and click one of the stroke type icons (see Figure 3.25).

Figure 3.25

The MaskPen brush can use the same stroke types that are available for sculpting brushes plus a few special stroke types.

TIPS ON USING STROKE TYPES WITH THE MASKPEN BRUSH

- You can select an alpha texture from the alpha fly-out library to change the shape of the mask based on a 2D image. The following image shows how the Star alpha has been applied to a mask brush.

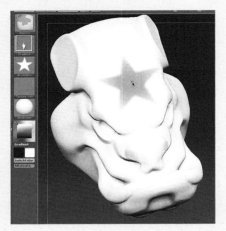

- When you choose the Rect stroke type for the masking brush, you can then use the MaskPen brush to define a rectangular-shaped area to be masked. As you hold the brush down and drag, you can set the size of the masked area. The center of the mask is indicated by a white plus sign.

continued

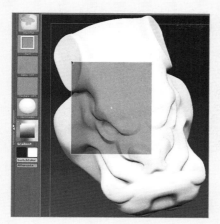

- Try not to confuse the Rect stroke type with the DragRect stroke type; they sound very similar but they behave very differently.

- If you want to reposition the rectangular mask (Rect stroke type) while using the Rect stroke type, let go of the Ctrl key and hold down the spacebar. Once your mask is in position, release pressure from the tablet to apply the mask.

- At the bottom of the stroke type fly-out library are two options: Square and Center. These buttons are shown in the following image. These options apply to the **Rect** and **Circle** stroke types. When the Square option is enabled, the masked area is always a perfect square. When the Center option is enabled, the center of the masked area is determined by wherever you initially click on the canvas. As you continue to drag, the mask is sized relative to the center. When Center is off, dragging out a corner of the rectangular area creates the mask.

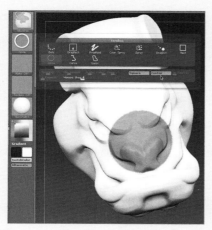

continues

continued

- A number of masking brush presets already have some of these features enabled. These are the MaskCircle, MaskCurve, MaskCurvePen, MaskLasso, MaskPen, and MaskRect brush presets. These are shown in the following image. To choose one of these presets you can hold the Ctrl key and open the brush fly-out library on the left shelf. When you switch to a masking pen, it is mapped to the Ctrl key.

- If you create a mask on a side of an object, the mask goes all the way through the surface and masks the opposite side as well.

- The Circle stroke type behaves just like the Rect stroke type except that the selected area is an oval and not a rectangle. If you activate the Square option in the modifiers, the masked area will always be a perfect circle.

- The Lasso stroke type lets you define a free-form area for the mask by drawing on the canvas while holding down the Ctrl key.

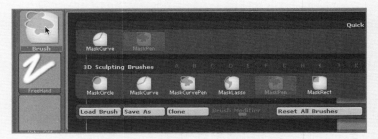

- The MaskCurvePen is a more advanced stroke type that will be discussed in Chapter 5, "ShadowBox and Clip Brushes."

Masking is a big part of working with ZBrush. Before you move on to the next section, make sure you spend some time practicing. Open the DefaultSphere.ZPR project in Light Box and experiment with using masks and brushes on a simple surface.

Insert Brushes

The MeshInsert brush allows you to add a presculpted mesh to your model with a brush stroke. It's a great way to add eyes, ears, teeth, and anything else you'd like to add to a surface. In this section, you'll use the brush to add eyes to the dragon.

To use this brush successfully, you'll need to understand the masking techniques of the previous section. You'll also be introduced to the Transpose brush and learn a new way to generate digital clay.

Using the InsertSphere Brush to Add Eyes

There are a wide variety of ways to add eyes to a creature or character in ZBrush. In this section, you'll use the InsertSphere brush to add two simple spheres to the dragon's head.

1. Open the most recent version of your dragon's head model.

2. Make sure that the Dynamesh button in the Geometry subpalette of the Tool palette is still activated.

3. Make sure symmetry along the x-axis is still active. This is toggled on or off by pressing the X hotkey.

4. Open the brush fly-out library on the left shelf. Press the I key and then the P key to switch to the InsertSphere brush (upper-left image in Figure 3.26).

5. Rotate the view of the model so that you can see in the eye socket.

6. Drag on the surface deep in the eye socket; as you drag, you'll see a sphere grow with the brush stroke. Don't let go of the brush just yet! As you drag, you can adjust the size of the sphere by dragging left or right (the upper-right image in Figure 3.26).

7. When you are happy with the size, let go of the brush. The sphere is now placed, but notice that the rest of the head is instantly masked. This is convenient because it allows you to continue easily making adjustments to the sphere after drawing it out without affecting the rest of the model (lower-left image in Figure 3.26).

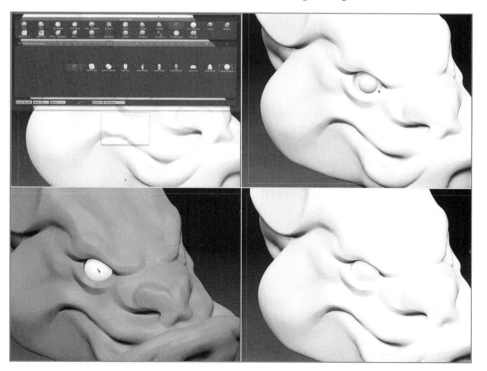

Figure 3.26

Select the InsertSphere brush from the brush library (upper left). Drag inside the eye socket to insert the sphere, and continue dragging to size (upper right). The model is automatically masked when you release the InsertSphere brush (lower left). After the sphere is inserted, it is fused with the rest of the surface using Dynamesh.

8. If you want to try that again, just press Ctrl+Z to undo, and try creating the eye again. I tried to scale mine so that there is just a slight gap between the eye socket and the sphere.

9. If you like the way the eye looks, Ctrl+drag on a blank part of the canvas once to clear the mask and then again to activate Dynamesh. Dynamesh fuses the eyeball sphere with the rest of the dragon's head surface (see the lower-right image in Figure 3.26).

10. After placing the eye, I used the sculpting and masking brushes as well as Dynamesh to create an eyelid. Figure 3.27 shows the result with the BasicMaterial2 shader applied to the surface.

Figure 3.27

The sculpting and masking brushes are used to create the eyelid around the inserted eye.

This time I increased the Resolution slider under the Dynamesh button in the Geometry subpalette of the Tool palette to 256. This allowed me to retain more of the sculpted eyelid detail each time I activated Dynamesh.

The real power of the InsertSphere brush is that you can use it to insert your own custom mesh objects into a surface. You can customize the InsertSphere brush so that you can use it to add lips, even a whole robot arm to any model you create. This is true for the insertHead, insertCube, and many of the other insert brush types. But keep in mind that these brushes work best while your model is in Dynamesh mode.

In the next section you'll see how you can use one of the parametric 3D primitives to create a nice sharp tooth and then see how you can use the insert brush to add the tooth to the model.

Creating Teeth Using Parametric 3D Objects

In this section you'll create a tooth using a parametric 3D object. The 3D parametric objects are all contained in the ZBrush tool library. They are called *parametric* because you shape them using numerical controls and not the sculpting brushes. Once you have a shape you like, you can convert it into a regular 3D mesh that can then be sculpted with the brushes. It sounds a little confusing at first, but we'll start simply with a basic tooth, which should make the idea clear.

1. Make sure the most recent version of your dragon's head project is loaded into ZBrush.

2. Open the tool library in the Tool palette and select the Cone3D brush (see Figure 3.28).

The dragon's head will disappear, and you'll see a cone on the canvas. Don't worry; the dragon is just fine. By selecting a different tool from the Tool library, you've essentially moved the dragon off your virtual sculpting stand and replaced it with an instance of the cone. You can switch back at any time by opening the tool library and selecting the dragon's head model. Most likely the model is still named PolySphere. We'll talk more about organizing and renaming tools in Chapter 4, "Polymesh Editing." For now let's keep focused on the basics.

Figure 3.28
Select the Cone3D object from the tool library.

3. Try to touch the cone with the sculpting brush. You'll get a warning telling you that you need to convert the primitive into a PolyMesh3D object (Figure 3.29). No need to do that just yet, but be aware that you get this warning whenever you try to sculpt a parametric object.

4. Click the canvas to make the warning go away. At this point you don't want to turn the model into a polymesh just yet. Before converting the cone into a polymesh, you will use the special sliders in the Initialize subpalette to shape the cone into a tooth.

5. Turn on the PolyF button on the right shelf so you can see the wireframe on the surface of the cone. This just makes it easier to see how the sliders in the Initialize subpalette affect the polygons of the mesh.

6. Select the Tool palette and expand the Initialize subpalette, which is located at the bottom of the Tool palette. Try adjusting the sliders; you'll see the surface update as you make changes.

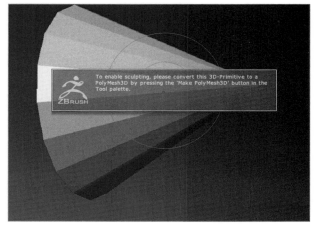

Figure 3.29
ZBrush displays a warning when you try to sculpt the cone.

Using these sliders, you can decide how many divisions you want in the cone and whether the bottom is closed or has a hole through it.

7. Use the following settings for the Initialize subpalette in the cone:

      X Size: **50**

      Y Size: **50**

      Z Size: **100**

      Inner Radius: **0**

      HDivide: **48**

      VDivide: **24**

      TaperTo: **100**

The result should be a nice pointy cone, as shown in Figure 3.30.

Figure 3.30

The cone is shaped using the sliders in the Initialize sub-palette of the Tool palette.

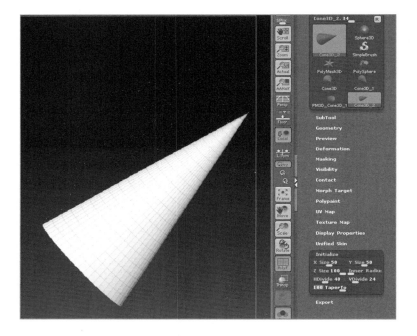

Now that the cone has been shaped parametrically, you can convert it into a sculptable mesh.

8. At the top of the Tool palette click the Make PolyMesh3D button (see Figure 3.31). You won't see much happen to the cone. If the PolyF button is on, it will change color (this color change will be explained in Chapter 4).

9. Turn off the PolyF button. Try touching the surface with a sculpting brush. Now the warning does not appear, and you can see that the brush is affecting the surface (see Figure 3.32).

10. Press Ctrl+Z to undo any of the changes in the cone.

Figure 3.31

The Cone3D object is converted into a sculptable poly-mesh object by clicking the Make PolyMesh3Dbutton in the Tool palette.

It's important to understand that when you click the Make PolyMesh3D button, ZBrush actually creates a mesh copy of the parametric tool you're working on. In fact, if you open up the sculpting library you'll see two cones, one labeled Cone3D and the other labeled PM3D_ Cone3D_1 (see Figure 3.33). Cone3D is the original cone and PM3D_ Cone3D_1 is the mesh copy. This is actually very convenient because you can switch back to the original Cone3D object, make more changes with the sliders in the Initialize sub-palette, and then make another copy with the Make PolyMesh3D button. Using this method you can quickly generate as many variations on the original cone as you like.

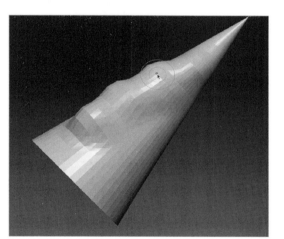

Figure 3.32

Once converted to a polymesh object, the cone can be sculpted with the sculpting brushes.

Figure 3.33

A polymesh copy of the parametric Cone3D tool is placed in the tool library when you click the Convert to PolyMesh3D button.

3D PARAMETRIC OBJECTS

The great benefit of using 3D parametric objects is that they allow you to quickly create shapes that would be very difficult to do using the sculpting objects alone. I use them all the time for creating mechanical parts, horns, teeth, and even sea shells. The sliders in the Initialize palette determine their shape. You can find out more information on what a slider does by holding the Ctrl key while the cursor is over the slider. Here's a description of each object and some tips on how you can use them:

Sphere3D This basic sphere has a pole at either end. Use the X Size, Y Size, and Z Size sliders in the Initialize subpalette of the Tool palette to shape the sphere into oblong spheroids. Use the Coverage slider to make the sphere a dome. The HDivide and VDivide sliders determine the horizontal and vertical divisions. In the following image you can see how a slice is removed from the Sphere3D by adjusting the Coverage slider.

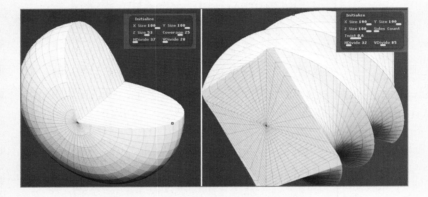

Cube3D At first this looks like a common cube, but it actually has a few surprises that you can discover when you play with the sliders in the Initialize subpalette. Like the Sphere3D, you can change the dimensions of the cube using the X Size, Y Size, and Z Size sliders. The Sides Count changes the number of sides around the z-axis, so you can change the cube into a hexagonal column or even a cylinder. The Twist slider twists the sides around the z-axis. This tool is great for fancy columns, drill bits, or modern architecture. In the image on the right of the previous graphic, the cube has been twisted around the z-axis.

Cylinder3D This object can be easily turned into a hollow pipe by adjusting the Inner Radius slider. You can also use the TaperTo slider to make one end narrower than the other.

Cone3D This object is essentially the same as the Cylinder but the TaperTo slider in the Initialize palette is preset to a value of 100, making it into a cone.

continued

Ring3D This is an indispensible tool for making donuts and horns, or even demonic donuts that have horns. Use the SRadius slider to determine the thickness of the ring; use Coverage to make the ring open or closed. Scale adds a taper to one end of the ring. The Twist slider rotates the polygons of the surface around the axis, adding a twist along the surface. In the following graphic, Ring3D is shown on the left.

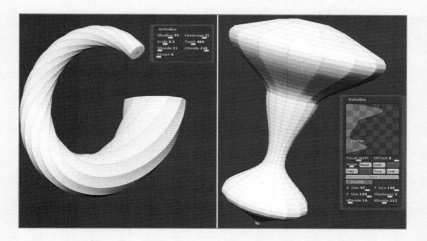

SweepProfile3D This versatile tool uses a curve editor to determine its shape. This type of editor is a curve on a two-dimensional graph. You add points to the curve and drag them to shape the curve, which, in turn, shapes the object. The best way to understand this is to play with the curve. The Sweep Profile uses the S Profile curve to determine the shape and the T Profile curve to determine the thickness. The T Profile curve works only when the Thickness slider is above or below 0. This object is a great way to start lamps, goblets, and other lathed-type shapes. In the previous graphic, you can see how the curve is used to shape the sweep profile in the image on the right.

Only one Edit Curve interface can be open at a time. To expand the Edit Curve, click the collapsed graph; to close it, either open another curve editor or click the Close bar below the graph.

Terrain3D Like the Sweep Profile, this surface is shaped with two curve editors. The V Profile curve shapes the vertical profile, and the H Profile shapes the horizontal profile. This tool works well as a starting place for flowing fabric or rolling hills.

Plane3D This is pretty much just a plane. You can determine the size using the H Radius and V Radius sliders.

continues

continued

Circle3D This object is a flat circle. The outside radius is set using the ORadius1 and ORadius2 sliders; the inside radius is set using the IRadius1 and IRadius2 sliders. Using these sliders you can create some interesting abstract designs.

Arrow3D This object is like the cylinder with a cone on top. The TipR and TipH sliders set the radius and height of the tip. The InnerR sets the inner radius and the InnerI sets the inner inset. The BaseR and BaseL sliders set the radius and inset of the base. The Double button mirrors the pointed end to the opposite side of the arrow. This object is a good starting place for spikes, simple trees, and weapons.

Spiral3D This object has slider controls very similar to the Ring3D object, but it has additional controls that allow you to offset the helical shape of the surface, which is perfect for creating horns for rams, curling snakes, or snail shells.

Helix3D This is very similar to the Spiral3D except that instead of using numerical sliders it uses edit curves to determine the shape. This means that you have more control over the look of the object, so there is more variety in the types of surfaces you can make.

Gear3D This is the perfect tool for creating mechanical parts. The Initialize palette for the Gear3D object has a mixture of sliders and edit curves. I often find myself playing with these settings for hours on end because of the amazing number of options available. The following image shows a model created using the Gear3D tool after about 5 minutes of noodling with the various curve editors in the Initialize subpalette.

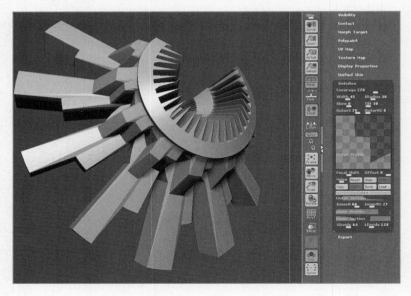

continued

When you use the curve editor to change the shape of a particular attribute, you can click on the curve to add a point, drag the point off the curve to remove it, adjust the circle around the point on the curve to edit its influence, and create a sharp angle in the curve by dragging a point off the curve editor and then back on again. As with many aspects of ZBrush, you should take some time to practice using the curve editor.

Sphereinder3D As the name suggests, this tool is a combination of the Sphere and the Cylinder. It's great for making capsules or cylinders with rounded edges.

The 3D parametric objects are a great source for creative exploration. As I noted before, the general workflow is to select one of the objects that most closely resembles what you want to create, then shape it using the sliders and curves in the Initialize subpalette, and when you're happy, click the Make PolyMesh 3D button at the top of the Tool palette. This makes a copy of the object, which you can now shape with the sculpting brushes.

It can be confusing when the tool library starts to fill up with copies of your objects. Keep in mind that only the parametric objects have an Initialize subpalette, and the poly-mesh copies start with the prefix PM3D_.

Bending the Tooth Using Deformations

Now let's put a slight bend in the tooth to make it more like a dragon's tooth. To do this, we'll use the Smooth Bend deformer in the Deformations subpalette of the Tool palette. The Deformation subpalette contains a large number of sliders, each of which can be used to deform your surface, allowing you to twist, mold, bend, and manipulate the overall shape of your object with numerical precision (see Figure 3.34).

1. Open the Deformation subpalette of the Tool palette. Find the SBend slider. You'll see very tiny letters (X, Y, and Z) to the right of the SBend slider. These letters establish the axial direction for the deformation. You can turn them on or off by clicking them. Click the letter so that only Y is highlighted and X and Z are grayed out.

2. Nudge the slider to the right; as you do this, you'll see the cone bend. You need to bend it only slightly. A value of about 15 should work fine. If you go too far, just press undo (Ctrl+Z) and try again (see Figure 3.35). The bent tooth is shown in Figure 3.36.

Figure 3.34

The deformers are a set of sliders found in the Deformation subpalette of the Tool palette.

Figure 3.35

Set the SBend axis to Y, and set the deformer value to 15.

Figure 3.36

The dragon's tooth is created by applying the SBend deformer to the polymesh cone.

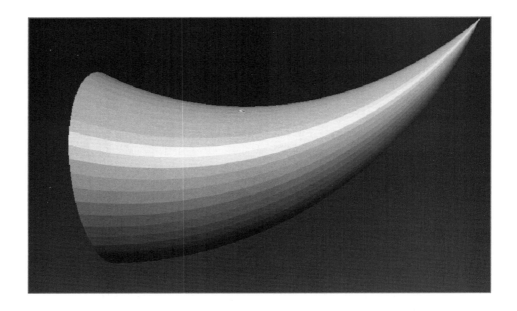

DEFORMATION SLIDER VALUES

Whenever you want to put an exact value into a slider such as a deformer, select the slider name; after a second you'll see the number 0 highlighted, and you can then type in the precise value of the slider. This can be a little easier than trying to move the slider to get an exact value.

The actions of the deformations are cumulative. In other words, if you set SBend to **20**, then the deformer bends the surface by a factor of 20. Type **20** again, and it bends it again by another factor of 20. To get the object to deform in the opposite direction, you can move the slider to the left or type in a negative number. You can always undo the action of a deformer. Sometimes it takes a few tries to get exactly what you want. To find out more about what each deformer does, hold the cursor over the slider and press the Ctrl key.

3. Once you have a nice-looking tooth, it's a good idea to save the project using the Save As button in the File menu. When you save a project, all of your tools are saved as well, including the dragon head and the tooth (both the original parametric tooth and the polymesh version).

Using the Insert Brush to Add the Tooth to the Dragon

Now that you have a tooth modeled, it's time to add it to the dragon. Just like with the eye, you'll use an insert brush to accomplish this. The first step is to edit one of the existing brushes so that it will allow you to add the tooth created in the previous sections by simply dragging on the model.

1. Open your most recent version of the dragon's head model by clicking the Open button in the File palette.

2. Open the sculpting brush library and choose the InsertSphere brush (or any of the other insert brushes).

3. Open the Brush palette at the top of the interface, and expand the Modifiers subpalette. I find it helpful to place the Brush palette in the tray on the right of the screen (as shown in Figure 3.37). You'll see a little window with a red sphere in it. Click this window to open the tool library. Select the PM3D_Cone_1 tool from the library. This is your dragon's tooth created in the previous sections (it's possible that your tool may have a slightly different name depending on how many cone tools you created in the previous exercise; just make sure it is the bent cone and you should be fine).

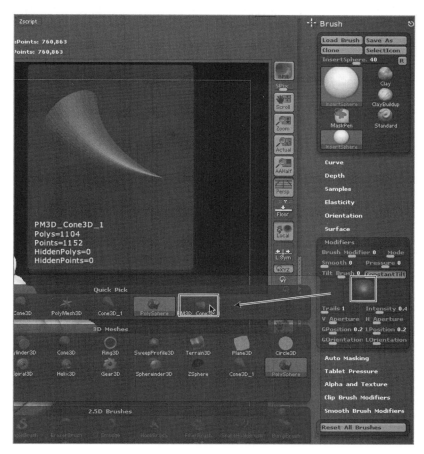

Figure 3.37

Use the Modifiers subpalette of the Brush palette to select the tooth from the tool library.

Figure 3.38

The icon for the InsertSphere brush changes automatically.

4. When you select the tooth model, notice that the icon for the brush in the palette also changes (see Figure 3.38). The brush is still named InsertSphere.

5. Now to insert the tooth, rotate the view of the dragon so you are looking at it from the top. See if you can find a good spot to place a tooth. Be sure symmetry is enabled (hotkey = X) and drag on the surface of the model. Symmetry will cause ZBrush to create a copy of the tooth on the other side of the dragon as well.

SAVING YOUR TOOTH BRUSH

You have just created your first custom brush! This brush can be used to insert the tooth as long as this session of ZBrush is open. But what if you want to use this brush again for future toothy monsters? You can simply click the Save button in the Brush palette to save the brush and reopen it later on. To do this, follow these steps:

1. Open the Brush palette and click the Save As button at the top of the palette.

2. Use the Save dialog box to save the brush as insertTooth.zbp. Save this file in the Pixologic/ZBrush 4 R3/ZBrushes/Insert folder. Then you can find it in Light Box in the Brushes/Insert folder. (Mac users note that this folder is found in Applications\ZBrush 4R3\ZBrushes\Insert.)

The tooth appears in the mouth, and as you drag it, the tooth continues to grow in size. If the dragon's head disappears while you are dragging, don't panic; once you let go, the head reappears.

6. Let go of the brush once you have a medium-size tooth (see Figure 3.39). You'll notice that the head become instantly masked when you let go (if this does not happen, double-check that the Auto Mask Mesh Insert button is enabled in the Auto Masking subpalette of the Brush palette).

7. Save your project by clicking the Save button in the File palette.

Figure 3.39

The tooth is placed in the dragon's mouth from above.

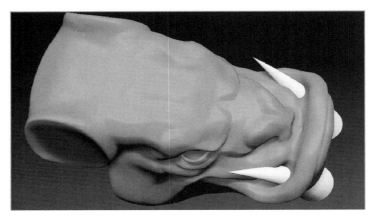

It's highly unlikely that the placement of the tooth was exactly what you want. You can undo and try again, but you might find yourself going crazy trying to get it perfect using the InsertTooth brush alone. This is why the dragon's head is instantly masked when you insert a mesh. It allows you to adjust the inserted mesh after you draw it into the object without affecting the original surface.

After you insert the mesh, you'll need to perform a few more steps to get it positioned perfectly. The first time you do this it may feel a bit overwhelming, but it actually becomes very intuitive and fast with a little practice. In the next section you'll learn how you can use the versatile Transpose brush to move, scale, and rotate the tooth.

Using the Transpose Brush to Position the Tooth

The Transpose brush is a special type of brush that lets you move, scale, and rotate your meshes. Generally it's used in conjunction with masking as a way to pose figures or move individual parts of an object. In this section, you'll learn the basics of using it as a way to position the tooth you've added to your dragon's head.

The Transpose brush is activated when you click the Move, Scale, or Rotate button on the top shelf while a mesh is in Edit mode, or you can select the Transpose brush from the sculpting brush library. When you select this brush, the brush cursor changes into a line with three pairs of concentric circles (see Figure 3.40). One pair of circles is at the center, and the other two are at either end of the line. The line that connects the three pairs of circles is known as the *action line*, and it determines the central axis of the control.

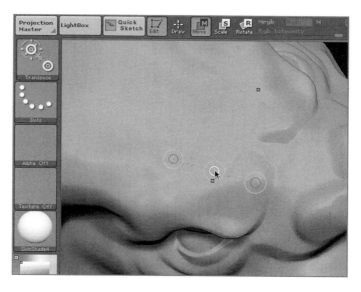

Figure 3.40

The Transpose control looks like a line connecting three pairs of concentric circles.

The three pairs of circles along the action line are the handles. The outside circle of each pair is used to position the control, and the inside circle of each pair is used to pose the mesh. It takes a little practice, but after some experimentation, you'll find that using the control becomes easy. I like to think of the Transpose brush as a virtual wrench. Any part of the surface that is not masked can be pulled, scaled, or twisted as you move around the handles of the brush.

The following demonstrates how to use the Transpose control to position the tooth you inserted into the mouth in the previous section:

1. Continue with the model from the previous section or click the Open button in the File palette to open the most recent version of your dragon's head. Make sure that the mask is still applied to the head and that the teeth remain unmasked.

2. Make sure the Persp button on the right shelf is off. This is not always necessary, but I find that it's easier to move parts of the object precisely when Perspective mode is off.

3. Rotate the view of the dragon's head so that you are looking at it from the side. Remember that as you rotate the view, you can hold the Shift key to snap it into place for a perfect side view (yes, it takes a little practice as well!).

4. Open the Sculpting Brush palette and press the T key for transpose and then R to select the brush. Alternatively, you can click on the Move button on the top shelf.

In the case of my dragon, the teeth are very large and stick out of the bottom of its jaw. I'm going to start by moving the teeth up, and then I will scale them down and finally rotate them. Since symmetry is activated, anything I do to one tooth will be mirrored to the tooth on the opposite side.

5. Click the bottom part of the tooth in the side view, and drag upward to a blank area on the canvas. As you do this, the Transpose brush draws out the line with the circular handles. No need to be overly precise when doing this, just a general position is fine (Figure 3.41, left image).

6. Hold the cursor over the center circle; you'll see a second white circle appear at the center or the handle; drag upward on the center circle to move the tooth up. Continue to drag on this until you have the tooth in a rough position, situated in the mouth but poking out from behind the lower lip (Figure 3.41, right image).

7. Now to scale the tooth down, click the Scale button on the top shelf or press the E hotkey. The Transpose brush looks the same, but you've just switched to Scale mode.

8. Drag again from the bottom of the tooth toward the top to create a new handle. Select the center of the circular handle at the top of the tool, and drag downward toward the opposite end of the handle. This scales the tooth down. Repeat this dragging action a few times until the tooth is a more reasonable, yet still fearsome size (Figure 3.42, left).

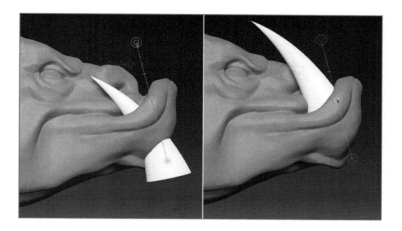

Figure 3.41

Draw the Transpose line from the bottom of the tooth to the space above the head (left image). Drag on the center circle to move the tooth into position (right image).

Keep the idea of a virtual wrench in mind; it's a good way to visualize how Transpose works. Basically, each handle on the Transpose brush works in a different way.

THE FUNDAMENTAL RULES OF TRANSPOSE

- The outer circle of each handle lets you position Transpose in 3D space. Drag on the outer circles at the end of the handle to position the ends.

- The inner circle of each handle deforms the unmasked parts of the mesh based on the current mode (Move, Scale, or Rotate) of Transpose.

- The circle on the opposite side of the Transpose handle sets the pivot point from the deformation.

- The hotkeys for each mode of the brush are Move = W, Scale = E, and Rotate = R.

- More advanced Transpose techniques are discussed in Chapter 4.

9. To rotate the tooth, click the Rotate button on the top shelf or press the R hotkey. Drag on the tooth again from the bottom toward the top, but this time drag into empty space above the tooth.

10. Just as in step 8, select the center of the circle in the top handle, and drag it left or right to rotate the tooth. Notice that the pivot point of rotation is the circle at the opposite end of the Transpose handle. You can change the pivot point by simply dragging on the outer circle of the handle at the opposite end (Figure 3.42, center image).

11. Rotate the view of the head so that you can see it from the top. Try dragging out a new handle and rotate the tooth again. You can see that because symmetry is active, the tooth on the opposite side is affected as well (Figure 3.42, right image).

Figure 3.42

The tooth is scaled and rotated using Transpose. Because symmetry is activated, changes on one tooth are mirrored to the tooth on the opposite side.

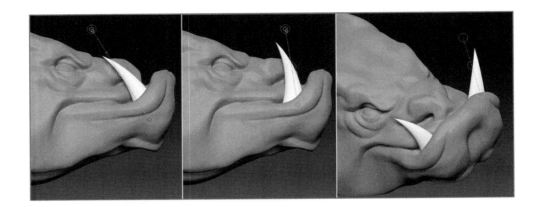

12. Spend some time practicing moving, scaling, and rotating the tooth until you like the way it is positioned. Be careful not to clear the mask on the surface. As long as the head is masked, you should be able to easily manipulate the tooth without affecting the work you've done on the head.

MASTERING TRANSPOSE

Many beginning students have a bad, if not allergic, reaction to the Transpose brush. It's not like anything you'll find in another 3D program, and I've had a number of students give up in frustration when they first encounter these techniques. The tool seems to defy all logic.

In reality it's an amazing feature, but it does take practice. If you spend 30 minutes transposing an object using this tool, you'll be on your way to mastering it. Patience is the key.

Before Transpose was introduced in version 3 of ZBrush, digital sculptors would often export their model, rig it in another program such as Maya, pose the rigged version, and then export and reimport it into ZBrush. That can take a few hours even for an experienced modeler.

With ZBrush you'll find that you can skip all the exporting and rigging and posing and focus on posing each part of the model at any stage of its development.

One thing that can trip you up is if two symmetrical surfaces, such as the dragon's teeth, overlap along the center line. If symmetry is enabled, you can find that the overlapping parts become all stretched and stuck together. The best way to avoid this is careful placement of the surfaces when you use the insert brush. Make sure that the surfaces are not too close together as you place them. This is why I suggested placing the teeth from a top view of the dragon.

13. Once you have your tooth scaled, rotated, and positioned, click the Save button in the File palette to save your work.

In the next section, you'll learn a great trick for quickly duplicating the teeth. And you'll finish the head of the dragon with some nice curling horns.

Duplicating the Teeth Using Transpose

In this section you'll learn a cool trick for duplicating objects using the Transpose brush. Using this technique you'll add a row of teeth to the dragon's head you've been developing throughout this chapter.

1. Click the Open button in the File palette to open the most recent version of your dragon's head. Make sure that the mask is still applied to the head and that the teeth remain unmasked.

2. Press the W hotkey to switch to the Move mode of Transpose.

3. Using the Transpose brush, drag an action line across the tooth. Again, you don't need to be overly careful, as long as you can clearly see the center circle of the tool.

4. Drag the center circle of the Transpose handle while holding the Ctrl key. This instantly duplicates the unmasked surface. The original tooth is now masked along with the rest of the head.

5. Use the Transpose brush to position the new tooth next to the original. Since symmetry is still enabled, a mirrored copy of the tooth has been duplicated on the other side (Figure 3.43, left image).

6. Press the E hotkey to switch to Scale mode, and scale down the duplicate tooth.

7. Press the R hotkey to switch to Rotate mode, and rotate the tooth into a better position. If the teeth are all perfectly aligned, the dragon will not look quite as fierce (Figure 3.43, right image).

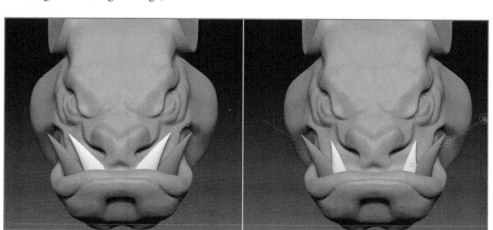

Figure 3.43

The tooth is duplicated and moved toward the center using the Transpose brush (left image). The duplicate tooth and its mirror copy are scaled and rotated using the Transpose brush (right image).

8. Repeat these steps to add a number of teeth that poke out between the lips. Make the teeth different sizes and rotate them in different directions. You can see how I have used this technique in Figure 3.44.

Figure 3.44

Multiple teeth are created by duplication with the Transpose brush. The teeth are scaled and rotated to create a gruesome array.

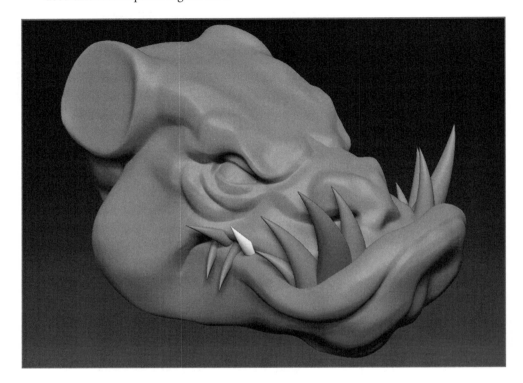

9. Once you feel like you have enough teeth, click the Save button in the File palette to save the project.

Adding Horns to the Dragon Head

You'll notice that in my version of the dragon I have two round, flat areas on either side of the head. I created these with the intention of adding horns to the surface. To add horns, I used the same techniques as I demonstrated with the teeth. Instead of using the Cone parametric tool to make the horns, I used the Spiral3D tool. I created my own InsertHorn brush from a polymesh version of the Helix3D tool and then inserted into the mesh. I then used Transpose to align the horns on the head correctly. Figure 3.45 shows stages in the process. I recommend trying these techniques on your own model as a way to review the techniques described in this chapter. ZBrush gets much easier with practice. I highly recommend going through these steps.

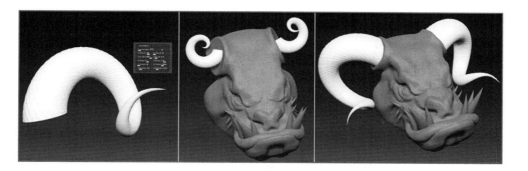

Figure 3.45

Horns of the dragon are created using the Spiral3D tool and then inserted using a customized insert brush. Using the Transpose brush they are moved, scaled, and rotated to match the head.

It may take a while to get the horns aligned. Remember that you can invert the mask (Ctrl+I) and use the Move brush to make the flesh of the dragon head meet the end of the horns. Just make sure that you don't clear the mask entirely!

Save the file when you are happy with the placement of the horns. Don't worry about detail just yet. In the next chapter you'll take this model even further as you learn about polygroups, subtools, and ZSpheres.

To see a version of the head that I created up to this point, open the `dragonHead_v01.ZPR` project from the Chapter 3 folder on the DVD that comes with this book. I also included my `insertTooth.zbp` brush and my `insertHorn.zbp` brush. You can load these brushes using the Load button in the Brush palette.

ZBRUSH PRACTICE

There is a common misconception that art generated on a computer is the product of simply pressing a few buttons. Many feel that if they can't create great-looking images instantly on their first try, then the problem lies with the software. This is simply not true.

Computer art is a medium, just like pencil, clay, and paint. You will only get better with practice. Some people take to ZBrush like a fish to water, just as some people seem to be able to play the piano perfectly from the first time they touch the keyboard. But trust me, I've had students who excel instantly and students who struggle (and I have struggled much over the years as well!). In the long run, it's only the students who practice who do well. The work of my students who struggled a year ago but kept practicing is indistinguishable from the work of students who seemed to be great from the first time they tried ZBrush. In fact, sometimes the work of those who struggle and persevere is even better! If this chapter has been a challenge, then just try it again. Keep it up until it clicks, and you'll be amazed at what you can create! It's a lot like skiing. The first day of skiing you get a lot of snow in your face, but at some point, after falling down enough times, everything suddenly makes sense and you're flying. Keep going until it works; trust me, it is worth it!

Summary

In this chapter you've taken your first steps into the world of digital sculpting with ZBrush. You've learned how to take a simple polymesh sphere and shape it into the form of a dragon's head using the sculpting brushes. You've learned how to use Dynamesh to create a sculpting-friendly topology and how to add parts using parametric 3D objects and Transpose.

In Chapter 4, "Polymesh Editing," you'll learn how to organize the mesh using polygroups, how to create a simple multi-object hierarchy using subtools, and how to work with ZSpheres to create an armature for your model.

Polymesh Editing

As you become more comfortable shaping your creations using the sculpting brushes, no doubt your projects will become more ambitious. ZBrush gives you a number of ways to edit your mesh so that your fantastic ideas are easier to realize. This chapter explores ways to edit, organize, and expand sculpts using selection brushes, polygroups, and subtools.

In addition to these techniques, this chapter introduces the ZSphere, ZBrush's unique armature tool, and ZSketching, which is a mesh-creation method that can be applied directly on a ZSphere armature or an existing mesh using special sculpting brushes.

This chapter includes the following topics:

- **Using selection brushes**

- **Working with polygroups**

- **Using the SliceCurve brush**

- **Appending subtools**

- **Using SubTool Master**

- **Working in the SubTool subpalette**

- **Creating an armature using ZSpheres**

- **Creating a ZSketch**

Selection Brushes

In Chapter 3 you learned how you can apply a mask to a surface in order to protect specific areas from changes. Selection brushes are an even more powerful way to accomplish this and can be used with masking techniques to focus on a specific part of the model.

As you've seen, ZBrush reserves a few hotkeys for specific brushes. The Shift key is reserved for smoothing brushes, the Ctrl key is reserved for masking brushes, and the Alt key is the "opposite" key, meaning that it inverts the action of the current brush. The selection brushes are mapped to the Ctrl+Shift key combination. So when you want to select specific polygons of a mesh, you hold the Ctrl and Shift keys together, which activates the brush in the Brush palette, and then while holding the keys you drag a selection marquee on the canvas and then let go. The polygons within the selected area remain visible while the unselected polygons are temporarily hidden. But of course there's more to it than that. This section goes into more detail about how to use the selection brushes and the many options available for customizing your selections.

Selecting Parts of the Dragon's Head

There are two selection brushes: SelectRect and SelectLasso. The main difference is the stroke type applied to the preset. You can modify the way the brushes behave by choosing additional stroke types.

Let's look at how these brushes work. For this exercise you can use the dragon model you created for the previous chapter, or you can open the Dragon_Chapter4.ZPR project found on the DVD that comes with this book.

1. Open the most recent version of your model or open the Dragon_Chapter4.ZPR project from the Chapter 4 folder of the DVD that comes with this book.

This model has been "dynameshed" into a single mesh (see Figure 4.1). As you can see, it has become a fairly complex shape considering it started as a sphere! Let's see how we can select just the front part of the muzzle.

Figure 4.1

The dynameshed dragon's head is a single surface.

2. Make sure the Persp button is off on the right shelf. It's much easier to make a precise selection if perspective distortion is deactivated.

3. Rotate the view of the model to the side; remember that if you hold the Shift key after you start rotating, the model will snap to the closest orthographic view.

4. Hold the Ctrl and Shift keys at the same time. Drag on a blank part of the canvas starting above and to the right of the end of the dragon's muzzle (Figure 4.2, left image).

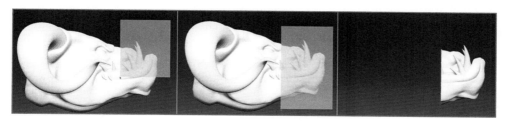

Figure 4.2

Hold Ctrl+Shift and drag the green rectangle over the area you want to select. Let go, and the unselected portion is hidden.

5. As you drag, you'll see a green rectangle appear. After you start dragging, you can let go of the Ctrl and Shift keys, but don't release the mouse button (or if you're using a tablet, don't release the pressure).

The green rectangle indicates the selection area. Place this over the area that you want to select (Figure 4.2, center).

6. While the selection area is active you can resize it by dragging the corner out. See if you can stretch the selection rectangle over the muzzle. Hold the spacebar and drag if you want to change the position of the entire selection.

7. Once the rectangle is over the muzzle, release the mouse button (or release the pressure on the pen if you're using a digital tablet).

The parts of the mesh that are outside the selection area disappear (Figure 4.2, right). Don't worry; they have not been deleted; they've just been hidden. The jagged edge of the visible part is caused by the fact that the polygons along the edge are still visible. This is easy to see when you zoom in on the edge and turn on the PolyF button to see the wireframe (see Figure 4.3).

8. Rotate the view of the model, and you'll see that the inside of the muzzle is invisible. Expand the Display sub-palette of the Tool palette and click the Double button. The polygon display now shows both sides of the polygon faces, as shown in Figure 4.4.

Figure 4.3

The jagged edge along the border of the selection is caused by the edges of the polygons that remain visible.

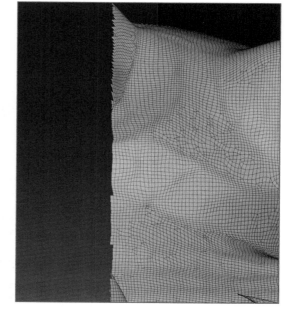

Figure 4.4

The back sides of the faces are invisible by default. Turn on the Double button in the Display subpalette of the Tool palette to see the opposite side.

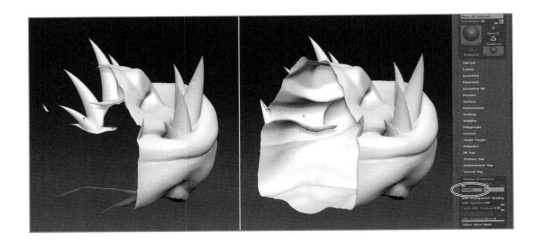

ZBrush hides the reverse side of polygon faces to make performance more efficient. Double is usually off by default. It's a good idea to turn Double on so that you can see both sides of the faces while you're working. If Double is off, you may not see parts of the model that are selected, and this can lead to mistakes down the road.

9. To bring the whole model back into view, hold the Ctrl+Shift keys and click on a blank part of the canvas. The model reappears.

TIPS ON USING THE SELECTION BRUSHES

- Selection brushes work with symmetry, so if symmetry is active, then the selection will be mirrored across the axis of symmetry.

- To switch to the SelectLasso brush, hold Ctrl+Shift and click the brush library on the left shelf. You'll see an abbreviated version of the library containing all the brushes that are mapped to the Ctrl+Shift keys, as shown in the following image.

continued

- The SelectLasso brush lets you make freeform selections, so you simply draw out a green area. Anything within the area is considered selected. This is useful for selecting areas that are a bit tough to select with just the rectangle.

- You can change the stroke type for the current select brush by holding Ctrl+Shift and clicking the Stroke Type library icon on the left shelf. You can change the stroke type to Circle, Curve, Rectangle, or Lasso (yes, this means that it's possible to assign the Lasso stroke type to the SelectRect brush and vice-versa. Try not to do that because you'll get confused very quickly). If you want to invert the selection so that everything inside the selected area is hidden, hold Ctrl+Shift and then hold the Alt key. The selection area now turns red, indicating that the selection will be hidden.

- You can toggle between selections by Ctrl+Shift-clicking on the visible part of the mesh. This inverts the visibility of the mesh so that the hidden part is revealed and the revealed part is now hidden.

- You can hide a single edge loop of the mesh by choosing the SelectLasso brush and Ctrl+Shift-clicking on a polygon edge, as shown in the image. This is easy to do by mistake. If rows of polygons disappear when you Ctrl+Shift-click on the model, just undo (Ctrl+Z) and try again. This takes a little practice to get the hang of it.

Masking Selections

How are selection brushes useful? You'll find going forward that there are a lot of ways in which the selection brushes can be used to edit a model, especially as the model becomes more complex. One way I find the brushes useful is to mask parts of the surface quickly.

In this example you'll see how the selection brush with the Circle stroke type can be used to create a mask for the eye area.

1. Continuing from the last section with the same model, make sure that the entire mesh is visible by Ctrl+Shift-clicking a blank part of the canvas.

2. Rotate the model to a side view, and zoom in on the area of the eye by holding the Ctrl key and the right mouse button and dragging on the canvas.

3. Hold Ctrl+Shift and select the SelectRect button from the brush library.

4. Hold the Ctrl+Shift keys and select the Circle stroke type from the stroke type library. While the library is open, turn on the Square and Center buttons (see Figure 4.5).

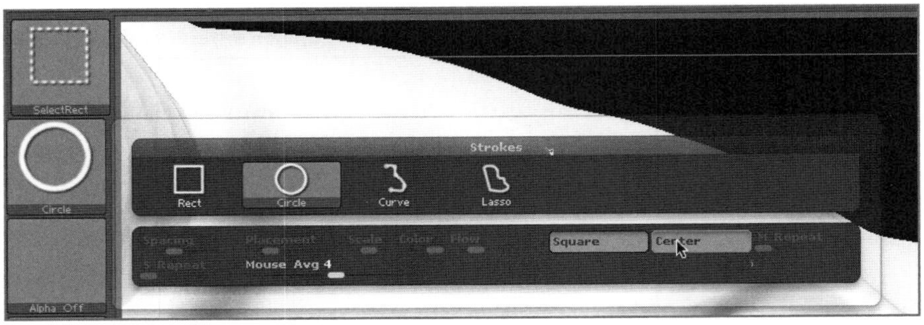

Figure 4.5

Choose the Circle stroke type for the SelectRect brush. Activate the Square and Center options.

Why would you want to switch to a circle and then turn on the Square button? That sounds like crazy talk. Well, the Square button in the stroke type library does not actually make a square. This just means that the stroke of the brush will have the same length and height. When this option is applied to the Rectangular stroke type, the result is a selection that is a perfect square. When the Square option is activated for the Circle stroke type, the result is a selection that is a perfect circle.

The Center option means that the stroke will start from the center of the brush tip as opposed to the corner. The Square and Center options can be used independently or together. I like to have them both on when I use the Circle stroke type.

5. Now you have set up the selection brush so that it can select a perfect circle. Hold Ctrl+Shift and drag a selection from the center of the eye in the side view (see Figure 4.6, left). If your selection is not exactly where you want it, remember that while the brush is still active you can hold the spacebar and move it into a better position.

6. Release the brush. You should have just a circular area around the eye remaining (see Figure 4.6, center). Rotate the view and you'll see that, since symmetry is activated, the eye on the other side is also still selected. But it's also possible that a few other bits in the middle of the head may still be visible (see Figure 4.6, right).

This is why it is important to make sure that the Double option in the Display palette is activated so that when you rotate the view after making the selection, you can see any the other polygons that may have been inadvertently selected.

7. Hold Ctrl+Shift and open the brush library. Select the SelectLasso brush.

Figure 4.6

Use the selection brush to select a perfect circle around the dragon's eye. Rotate the view to see if other parts were accidentally selected.

8. Hold Ctrl+Shift and drag a selection lasso over parts of the model that you want to hide. Before releasing the brush, hold the Alt key so that the selection turns red, and then release the brush (see Figure 4.7). Since symmetry is enabled, the polygons on the opposite side will also be hidden even if you did not explicitly select them with the brush.

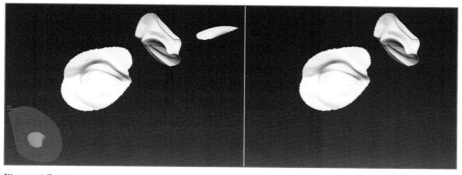

Figure 4.7

Choose the SelectLasso brush and hold Ctrl+Shift+Alt to create a red selection area over the parts you want to hide (left image). Release the brush to hide these parts (right image).

Yes, it seems a little complicated the first few times you do this. In reality, with a little practice, it actually becomes second nature.

9. Once you have pared down the selection to just the area around the eyes, press Ctrl+A to mask the visible area. You'll see the visible polygons turn gray.

10. Now Ctrl+Shift+click a blank part of the canvas. This reveals the entire mesh (see the left image in Figure 4.8). Note that the eyes are masked based on what was previously selected. The polygons that were hidden were not affected by Mask All.

11. Ctrl+click the canvas (or press Ctrl+I) to invert the selection. Now the mask is applied to everything but the eyes (see center image in Figure 4.8).

12. Ctrl+click the mesh itself. This blurs the edge of the mask, making a nice smooth transition between the eye area and the rest of the mesh (see Figure 4.8, right image).

Figure 4.8

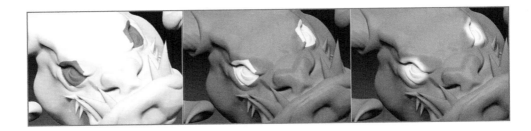

After masking the selected area, Ctrl+Shift-click the canvas to reveal the surface (left image), Ctrl+click a blank part of the canvas to invert the mask (center image), and then Ctrl+click the surface to blur the mask (right image).

Now you can use the sculpting tools to work on just the eyes.

Every ZBrush artist uses selection and masking in their own way. This particular method is mostly designed to show you how selection and masking can be used together, but you may find a more efficient workflow as you become more experienced. But what happens when you go to all this trouble to make a mask, then you clear the mask, and then later on decide that you want to remask the same area? Do you have to go through all these steps again? Luckily no, you don't. There is a way to save your selections for future masking and other tasks using polygroups.

Polygroups

The polygons of a mesh can be organized into groups known as *polygroups*. This is useful when you need to isolate a particular part of a surface area over and over again. Rather than creating the same mask every time you need to work on one part of your mesh,

Figure 4.9

The polygons of a mesh have been arranged into polygroups indicated by the colored regions.

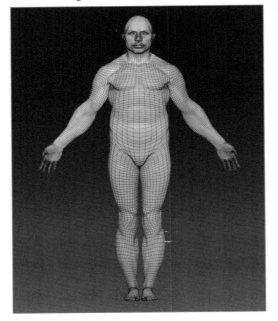

which can be very tricky on complex surfaces, you can create a polygroup, which is saved with the mesh. The grouped area of the mesh can be isolated for masking and other operations as often as you like for as long as you keep the polygroup.

Polygroups are displayed as colors applied to the polygons. You can see these colors only when the PolyF button is enabled on the right shelf (hotkey = Shift+F). The colors of the polygons do not affect any colors painted on the surface. They just provide a visual indication of how the polygons of the mesh have been arranged into groups (see Figure 4.9).

TIPS ON WORKING WITH POLYGROUPS

- An individual polygon can't be a member of more than one group at a time.
- Polygroups are saved as part of the mesh.
- You can rearrange the mesh into different polygroups as often as you like.
- You can create a polygroup when the mesh is at any subdivision level, but the results are more predictable when you create polygroups at the lowest subdivision.
- If you create a polygroup at a high subdivision level and then move the SDiv slider down to a lower level, the polygroups can get a little confused, which may alter the membership of the polygons in the polygroup.

Arranging a Face into Polygroups

In this example you'll see how you can organize a face into polygroups and then how the polygroups can be useful when sculpting.

1. Open the femaleHead.ZPR project from the Chapter 4 folder on the DVD. This project contains a simple female head sculpt. Sadly for her, she is bald at the moment. Let's start by creating a polygroup for the face. To do this you'll use the SelectLasso brush to hide everything but the face.

2. Rotate the model to a side view (remember to turn off the Persp button on the right shelf so that perspective distortion does not interfere with the selection).

3. On the right shelf, turn on PolyF so that you can see the wireframe on the model. The mesh will turn red (note that the eyes remain gray; we'll talk about that in the section on subtools later in the chapter). Symmetry should already be activated along the x-axis in this project.

4. Hold Ctrl+Shift and select the SelectLasso brush from the Brush palette.

5. Hold Ctrl+Shift and start dragging a selection area from the upper right of the face. Follow the topology of the face all the way down to the chin. Release the brush once you've made the selection (see Figure 4.10).

It's highly unlikely that the selection you created was perfect on the first try. That's OK; it rarely is. I always need to do a little cleanup after making an initial selection.

6. Rotate the model to examine your handiwork. In the Display subpalette of the Tool palette, activate the Double button so you can see the back side of the polygons.

7. To clean up the edges of the selection use the SelectLasso brush. Draw a selection around the edge of any polygons you want to hide; hold the Alt key to make the selection turn red and then let go. Since Symmetry is activated along the x-axis, the corresponding polygons on the opposite side should be hidden as well.

Figure 4.10

Use the SelectLasso brush to select just the polygons of the face.

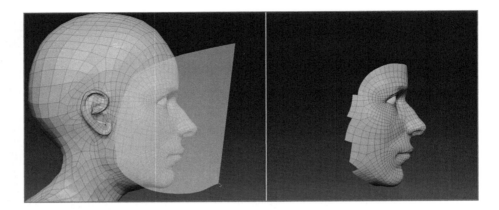

8. Continue to hide polygons along the edge until you are satisfied. No need to stress out if it's not absolutely perfect; the main idea is to understand the overall technique (see Figure 4.11).

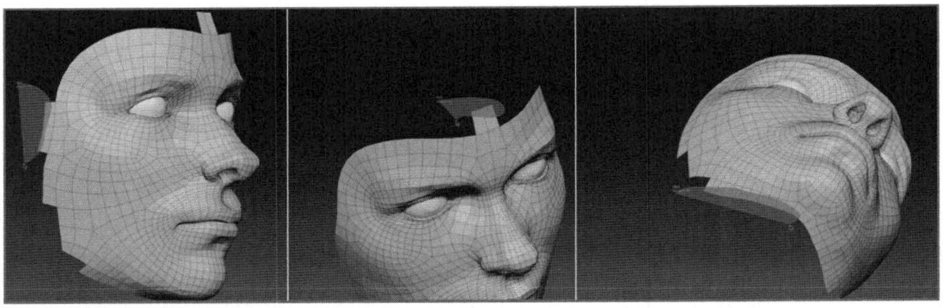

Figure 4.11

The SelectLasso brush is used to hide stray polygons.

9. Once you have just the face visible, expand the Polygroups subpalette of the Tool palette and click the Group Visible button (see Figure 4.12). The face turns a different color.

10. Hold Ctrl+Shift and click a blank part of the canvas to bring back the rest of the head. Note that the head and face are now two different colors (see Figure 4.13).

Figure 4.12

Click the Group Visible button to place the visible polygons into a new polygroup.

GROW OR SHRINK YOUR SELECTION

There's a little-known trick for fine-tuning your selection: you can click the Grow (hotkey = Ctrl+Shift+X) or Shrink (hotkey = Ctrl+Shift+S) button in the Visibility subpalette of the Tool palette to grow or shrink your selection by one row of polygons. The Outer Ring button hides everything except the row of polygons along the border of the selection.

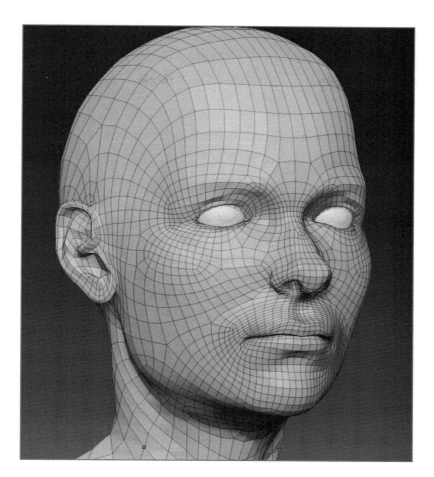

Figure 4.13

The polygroups are indicated by different colors. These colors are visible only when the PolyF button on the right shelf is activated.

TIPS ON WORKING WITH POLYGROUPS

- The colors indicate the polygroups. ZBrush chooses the colors randomly. Sometimes ZBrush chooses colors that are very similar, making it hard to see the grouping. If you don't like the color ZBrush chooses, just keep clicking the Group Visible button until you get a color you like.

- To hide everything outside the polygroup, Ctrl+Shift+click the center of a polygon within the group.

- To invert the visibility of the mesh, Ctrl+Shift+click again the center of one of the polygons within the polygroup.

continues

continued

- After inverting the visibility of a polygroup, when you Ctrl+Shift+click a polygon within a polygroup, that polygroup will become hidden.

- If you click a vertex shared by polygons in two or three adjacent polygroups, everything outside those polygroups will be hidden.

- If for some reason the polygroup is not created the way you want, you can press Ctrl+Z to undo and try again.

- You can convert a masked area into a polygroup by clicking the From Masking button in the Polygroup subpalette of the Tool palette.

- Polygroups exist regardless of whether the PolyF button is on or off. If PolyF is off (and the wireframe is not visible), the polygroups will still function the same way; you just can't see them.

Creating a Polygroup for the Eyelids

Now let's create a polygroup for the eyelids. Creating polygroups ahead of time for areas you frequently need to isolate is a common and useful ZBrush technique. This is going to be a bit of a challenge since the eyelids are very close together, but this process will teach you a few tricks that can help you out of a jam with your own models.

Figure 4.14

Turn on the Solo button to hide the eyes.

1. Continuing with the same head from the previous section, hold Ctrl+Shift and click one of the polygons in the face polygroup. The head should disappear, leaving just the face visible.

2. On the right shelf, click the Solo button. This will hide the eyes (see Figure 4.14).

3. Use the SelectLasso brush to isolate the area around one eye (see Figure 4.15). Since Symmetry is on, the selection should be mirrored to the other side.

4. Use the SelectLasso brush in Hide mode to hide any stray polygons and pare down the selection so that just the polygons bordering the upper and lower eyelids are visible (see Figure 4.15, right image).

Figure 4.15

Select the polygons around the eyes.

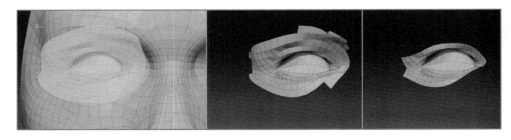

5. Click the Group Visible button to make a polygroup for the overall eye area.

6. The eyelids are a little trickier since it's a very small area. It's a good idea to have a separate polygroup for the upper and lower lids. Zoom in on the eye polygroup, and create a lasso selection around just the area of the upper eyelid.

7. Pare down the selection until only the polygons of the upper eye are visible. Then click the Group Visible button (see Figure 4.16, left).

8. Ctrl+Shift+click the canvas to reveal the whole head. You should have four polygroups: one each for the head, the face, the upper eyelid, and the lower eyelid (see Figure 4.16, right).

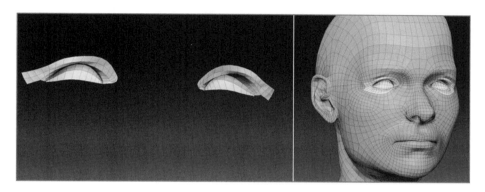

Figure 4.16

Create a polygroup by isolating the polygons of the upper eyelid.

9. Now let's say you want to mask everything but the upper eyelid. Ctrl+Shift+click the upper eyelid polygroup to hide everything except this area.

10. Press Ctrl+A to mask all. Then Ctrl+Shift+click a blank part of the canvas.

11. Ctrl+click a blank part of the canvas (or press Ctrl+I if you find that easier) to invert the mask. Voila! The upper eyelid is isolated for easy sculpting (see Figure 4.17).

Figure 4.17

The upper eyelid is easy to mask thanks to polygroups.

Using Morph Target to Create Polygroups

How do you create a polygroup for a truly tricky area, for example, the lips on this head? This is a challenge because the mouth is closed and the polygons of the lips overlap, making it very difficult to select with the SelectLasso brush. To get around this you can store a morph target.

A morph target stores the position of each vertex in the mesh in memory; it's like the ultimate backup plan. As long as you have a morph target stored, you can always go back to the original shape of the surface even if you've made a million changes. Morph targets do not store the polygroup info, which is good because it means you can smooth out an area, create a polygroup, and then use the morph target to jump back to the original shape. This is exactly what you'll do to make a polygroup for the lower lip on this model.

1. Continuing with the model from the previous section, make sure the head is visible and clear any masks applied to the surface.

2. Open the Morph Target subpalette of the Tool palette and click the StoreMT button (if this button is grayed out, click the DelMT button to delete any existing morph targets. You can store only one morph target at a time for a model). This is shown in Figure 4.18.

3. The StoreMT button will now become grayed out, indicating that a morph target is stored for the model. From the sculpting brush library, choose the Move Topological brush.

4. Use the brush to pull down the lower lip (upper-left image in Figure 4.19). No need to be overly careful; just open the lips so that you can see the inside of the mouth.

5. Hold the Shift key and brush over the area to smooth it (upper-right image in Figure 4.19).

6. Once the lips have been separated, use the SelectLasso brush to select the polygons of the lower lip. This should hide the rest of the head.

7. Rotate the model and make sure any stray polygons are also hidden.

8. Click the Group Visible button to create a polygroup for the lower lip (lower-left image in Figure 4.19).

Figure 4.18

Click the StoreMT button to store a morph target (left image). Once a morph target is stored, the button is grayed out and the other options become available (right image).

9. Ctrl+Shift+click the canvas to reveal the rest of the model.

10. In the Morph Target subpalette of the Tool palette, click the Switch button to go back to the original shape of the head, but notice that now the lip has its own polygroup (Figure 4.19, lower-right image).

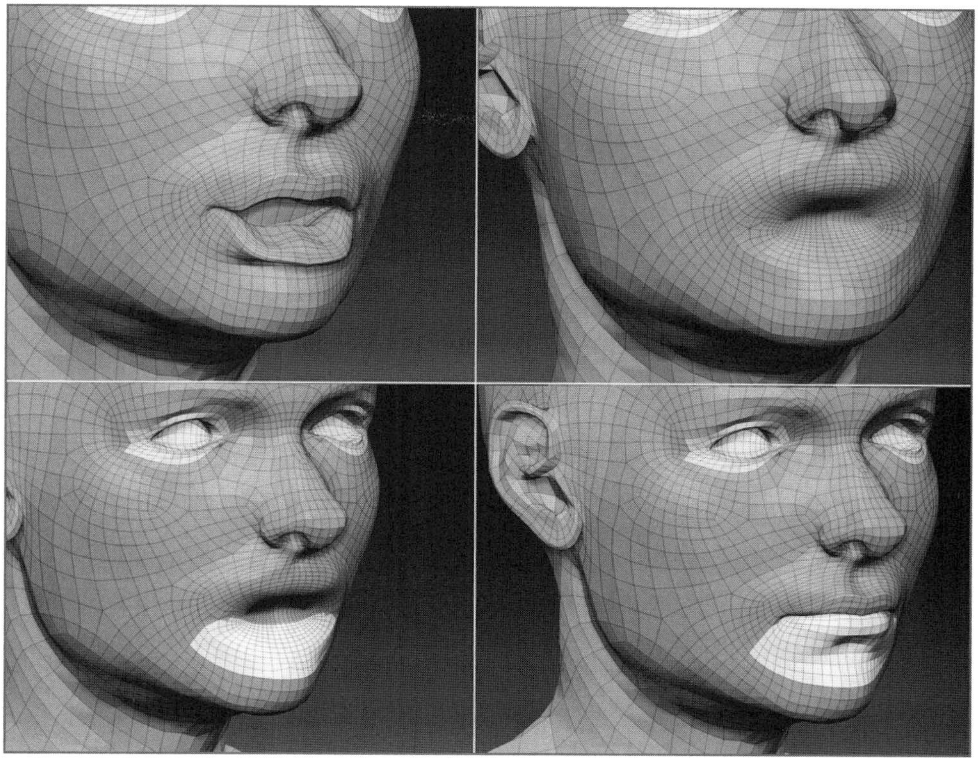

Figure 4.19

After storing a morph target, pull the lower lip down (upper-left image). Use the Smooth brush to smooth the area for easier selection (upper right). Create a polygroup for the lower lip (lower left). Click the Switch button in the Morph Target subpalette to switch back to the original head (lower right).

TIPS ON WORKING WITH MORPH TARGETS

- Morph targets are stored with the model when you save the project. As long as you don't delete the morph target, it will still be saved when you reload the model at a later time.

- Store the morph target before you hide any part of the model.

- You can store only one morph target per model and only on the SDiv level where you created it.

- You can use the Morph brush in the sculpting brush library to paint parts of the model back into the stored state. This acts as an undo brush, which is extremely useful.

- 3D layers are a similar to morph targets but are much more advanced; these are discussed in Chapter 10, "Surface Noise, Layers, and The ZBrush Timeline."

Polygroups and Dynamesh

You can create polygroups for parts of your surface while the model is in Dynamesh mode; however, once you "re-dynamesh" the surface, the polygroup disappears. This is because the surface is completely retopologized, meaning that the point order of the original surface is replaced by a new point order that obliterates the group information stored with the mesh. So how are polygroups useful when working in Dynamesh mode? Well, they offer a really great way to split the model into separate volumes and then stick them back together again. It's actually quite amazing. Let's take a look at how this works by returning to the dragon model.

Using the SliceCurve Brush to Create Polygroups

Let's say you're developing your dragon model, and you suddenly decide you don't like the placement of the horns. Seems like it would take a lot of work to chop them off and stick them somewhere else on the head. In fact, it's not a lot of work at all thanks to the SliceCurve brush. This brush lets you create polygroups by slicing through the mesh. The brush draws out a line, and anything on one side of the line becomes a new polygroup. It also divides the polygroups along the length of the line; this means that this brush is restricted to meshes that do not have multiple levels of subdivision.

1. Use the File menu to open the latest version of your dragon model or open the Dragon_Chapter4.ZPR project from the Chapter 4 folder on the DVD.

2. Make sure the Persp button is off so that perspective distortion does not interfere with your selection.

3. Rotate the model to a front view. Remember that you can hold the Shift key after you start rotating the view of the model, and it will snap to an orthographic view.

4. Hold the Ctrl+Shift keys and select the SliceCurve brush from the brush library (see Figure 4.20). Like the selection brushes, this brush is mapped to the Ctrl+Shift key combination.

Figure 4.20

Hold Ctrl+Shift and select the SliceCurve brush from the brush library

5. Hold Ctrl+Shift and start drawing a line starting from the lower left of the dragon's head just below the horn. As you draw the line, tap the Alt key to add a bend in the line. This pins the line down at the point where you tap the Alt key; you can bend the line after this point. You want to create a line that carefully winds its way between the head and the horn (Figure 4.21, left image).

6. The line should cross the horn at the root and run parallel to the angle where the horn emerges from the head. Everything on the shaded side of the line will be placed into a new polygroup.

7. Once you have the line drawn, release the brush.

   After a few seconds the line will disappear, and it will look like nothing has happened.

8. Turn on the PolyF button on the left shelf to see the result. The horn on the left side of the screen is colored differently than the rest of the head because it has been placed into its own polygroup (see Figure 4.21, right image). The mesh is very dense so it may be hard to see.

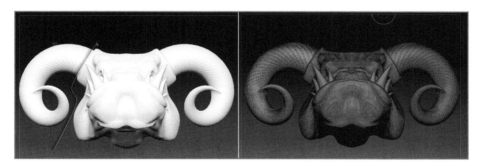

Figure 4.21

Draw the SliceCurve between the head and the horn. Turn on the PolyF button to see the newly created polygroups.

9. The SliceCurve brush does not work with symmetry. So how do you get the other horn into the same polygroup? If the surface is perfectly symmetrical, as in the case of this dragon, you can click the Mirror and Weld button in the Geometry subpalette of the Tool palette. Do this and you'll see the other horn change color to match the horn on the left side of the screen.

MIRROR AND WELD

When using Mirror and Weld it's important to understand that ZBrush always mirrors the positive side to the negative side. How can you tell which is the positive side? If the Floor button is on, you can rotate the view to see the grid from the top. The red axis line at the center of the grid points in the positive direction. If you want to mirror the negative side to the positive side, you must first click the Mirror button in the Deformation subpalette to flip the model and then click Mirror and Weld to make the change. The catch is that the model needs no levels of subdivision in order for Mirror to work.

Figure 4.22

Turn on the Groups button in the Dynamesh options of the Tool palette.

10. Now that you understand that the SliceCurve brush has created a different group for the horns, you can turn off the PolyF button on the right shelf. Since the mesh is very dense, the wireframe display can slow down the performance of ZBrush. The polygroups exist even when this button is off.

11. Now for the exciting part. To separate the horns from the head, turn on the Groups button in the Dynamesh options. This tells ZBrush to create separate volumes for each polygroup whenever the surface is re-dynameshed (see Figure 4.22).

12. Now Ctrl+drag on a blank part of the canvas to activate Dynamesh. After a few seconds the calculation will be complete. You won't see much of a difference except for a very thin gap between the horns and the head (see Figure 4.23).

Figure 4.23

When the head is re-dynameshed, the horn is separated from the head by a small gap.

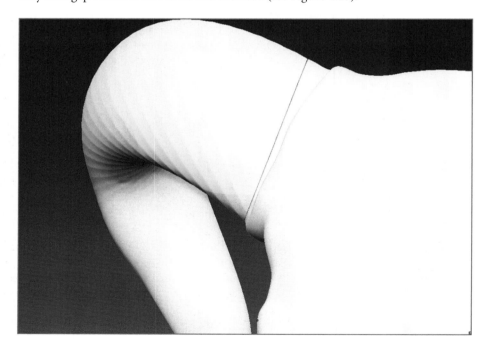

Masking by Polygroups

At this point you've cut the horns off the head. Now it would be nice to move them away from the head easily. You can do this thanks to the Mask By Polygroups feature found in the Brush palette. By activating this feature, the brushes will affect only the polygons of the surface that share the same polygroup at the point of brush contact. Like many things in ZBrush, the verbal explanation sounds more complicated than what it actually means. Go through the following steps and it should become clearer.

1. Open the Brush palette and find the Auto Masking subpalette. Expand the subpalette and set the Mask By Polygroups slider to **100** (meaning 100 percent strength). This is shown in Figure 4.24.

2. Switch to the Transpose brush in Move mode by clicking the Move button on the top shelf or by pressing the W hotkey. This activates the Transpose handle you learned about in Chapter 3.

3. Draw out the transpose line starting from the left horn. Click the horn and drag up into the empty space above the head (see Figure 4.25, upper left).

4. Click and drag the center circle of the Transpose handle to move the horn up. It might be a little slow because the mesh is dense, but the horns should move up and away from the head (both horns should move since Symmetry is activated; see Figure 4.25, upper right).

Figure 4.24

Set Mask By Polygroups to 100 in the Brush palette.

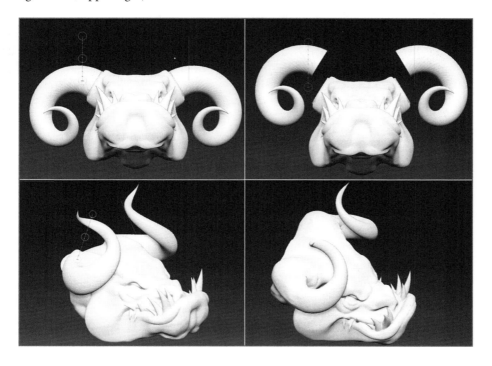

Figure 4.25

Thanks to the Mask By Polygroup feature, the horns can be moved away from the mesh, rotated, repositioned, and fused back into the surface using Dynamesh. The sculpting brushes are used to make the mesh seamless.

Notice that the end of the horn is closed off and there is no hole on the surface of the head; this is because Dynamesh created separate, closed volumes based on the polygrouping of the mesh.

5. Rotate the view of the head to a side view. Switch to Rotate mode of Transpose (hotkey = R) and rotate the horns. Try a different configuration. Switch between Move and Rotate and arrange the horns in a new way. Move the horns so that they intersect the surface (see the lower left in Figure 4.25).

6. Don't worry too much about how neatly the horns fit into the surface; you can clean this up using the sculpting brushes later on.

7. In the Dynamesh options, turn off the Group button. Ctrl+drag on the surface to re-dynamesh. Now the horns are fused back into the surface as a single volume.

8. Use the sculpting brushes (Clay Buildup, hPolish, and Smooth are good choices) to reshape the area where the horns meet the head (see Figure 4.25, lower right). As to whether or not the new arrangement is an improvement, it is for the dragon to decide.

It's hard to overstate the amount of freedom this technique gives you. Performing a similar action in a traditional polygon modeling software package would take hours of work. In this case it's like you're lopping of a lump of clay, slapping it back on in another position, and smoothing it with your fingers. You can easily chop off a character's head or arm and replace it with a different version as many times as you want.

Working with Subtools

Up to now you've done an awful lot with just a single mesh, but ZBrush does not limit you to single surfaces. You can actually build multisurface objects using subtools. Each subtool is an independent surface that can have its own levels of subdivision, its own polygroup arrangement, coloring, and so on. Furthermore, when you sculpt on one subtool, none of the other subtools are affected so that the other subtools are protected from accidental changes.

As you may recall from Chapter 2, a 3D mesh in ZBrush is also known as a 3D tool. This is because ZBrush considers tools to be anything that makes a mark on the canvas itself. For example, a 3D dragon tool can be used to paint copies of 3D dragons on the canvas. The term *subtool* is used to describe a 3D tool that has been parented to an initial 3D tool. There's no technical difference between the types of meshes that become subtools and the tools themselves. You can add hundreds of subtools to your initial mesh, making your sculptures as complex as you'd like. The DemoSoldier example tool that comes with ZBrush is an example of a model that is made up of many subtools. To load DemoSoldier, open the Tool section of Light Box and click the DemoSoldier.ZTL file (see Figure 4.26).

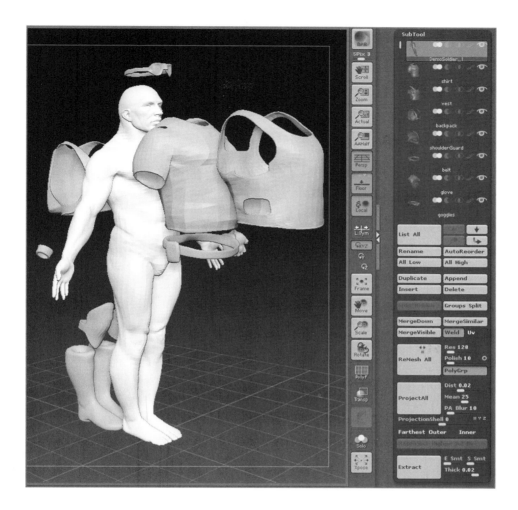

Figure 4.26

The DemoSoldier tool is made up of many subtools.

The relationship between tools and subtools is extremely simple. It is not meant to be a complex hierarchy like you might find in other 3D packages; a subtool is a 3D tool that is chosen and appended to a main tool, and that's pretty much all there is to it. Using the SubTool interface in the Tool palette, you can rearrange the order of subtools, control their visibility, and add, delete, and even merge subtools together into a single tool. If you've used Adobe Photoshop, you may find that the concept of the SubTool interface is reminiscent of Photoshop's Layers palette.

The SubTool Subpalette

The SubTool subpalette lists all the subtools associated with the main tool. To work with a subtool, it must be active. An active subtool is indicated by the coloring around the boxes listed in the SubTool subpalette; in the default color scheme, the active subtool is indicated by a dark outline. Other color scheme presets, such as the one used in this book, use a light-colored highlight to indicate the active subtool.

Only one subtool can be active at a time. To make a subtool active, you need to click its box in the SubTool subpalette or hold the Alt key while clicking on part of the object on the canvas.

On the canvas, the inactive subtools will be shaded in a slightly darker color than active subtools. If Transparency is enabled on the right shelf, all the subtools except the active subtool will appear transparent. The Ghost button changes the look of the transparent objects on the canvas.

On the right shelf, you can click the Solo button to temporarily hide all of the subtools except the active one. As you click different subtools in the SubTool subpalette, you'll see the visibility of the current subtool on the canvas change as well.

TIPS ON WORKING WITH THE SUBTOOL SUBPALETTE INTERFACE

This covers the basics. You'll learn more advanced features throughout the exercises in this book:

- The subtools are listed in the SubTool subpalette as a vertical stack. Each subtool has its own box with a preview icon, its name, and a number of other buttons.

- Hold your mouse over the subtool's box to reveal a pop-up window with information about the subtool, such as the number of polygons and points in the subtool at its current subdivision level.

- To the left of the stack of subtools is a scroll bar that becomes active when the list of subtools become too long to display in the SubTool subpalette.

- On the right side of the box for each subtool is an eyeball icon. This toggles the visibility of the subtool on the canvas. Click the eyeball icon of an inactive subtool to turn it off.

- The currently active subtool will remain visible regardless of whether or not the eyeball icon is on.

- To turn off the visibility of all the subtools except the currently active subtool, click the eyeball icon of the currently active subtool so that it turns off. This can also be achieved by clicking the Solo button on the right shelf.

- To turn on the visibility of all of the subtools at once, click the eyeball icon for the currently active subtool so that it turns on.

- To turn on the visibility of all of the subtools at once, click the eyeball icon for the currently active subtool so that it turns on.

continued

- To switch from one subtool to another, select the subtool's box in the SubTool subpalette.

- You can filter the display of the subtools in the List All pop-up box by typing the first letter of the subtool you are looking for. So, for example, if you want to quickly switch to a subtool named Goggles, just type **G**. If no other subtool start with *g*, the Goggles subtool will automatically become selected in the subtool stack. If more than one subtool starts with *g*, you'll see all the subtools that start with *g* in the List All pop-up. Other subtools will be grayed out. Type the second letter of the subtool to switch to that subtool. For example, type **G** and then **O** to switch to the Goggles subtool while the List All pop-up is open.

- Next to the List All button are four arrow buttons. The top two arrow buttons can be used to move up or down through the list of subtools in the stack. The bottom two arrows change the position of the active subtool in the stack. The bent-upward arrow moves the subtool up one position in the stack, and the bent-downward arrow moves the active subtool down one position in the stack.

- The Duplicate button makes a copy of the active subtool and adds it to the stack of subtools.

- The Append button adds a tool selected from the tools available in the tool fly-out inventory to the bottom of the subtool stack; the Insert button does the same thing, but the appended subtool is placed just below the active subtool in the subtool stack.

- The Delete button deletes the currently active subtool. When you click this button, a warning message appears letting you know that deleting a subtool is not undoable.

- The Split Hidden button splits a tool into subtools based on which parts of the mesh have been hidden.

- The Grp Split button separates a tool into subtools based on how the mesh has been arranged into polygroups.

Sculpting a Hair Mesh

ZBrush's subtool workflow is very flexible. You can append a raw lump of digital clay to an existing tool and sculpt it into shape, or you can append a fully sculpted object. In this example, you'll append a PolySphere and use it as a starting point for a simple hairdo.

1. Open the femaleHead.ZPR project from the Chapter 4 folder on the DVD.

Figure 4.27

The SubTool sub-palette shows that the femaleHead and Eyes are separate subtools.

This project has the same female head you got to know earlier in the chapter. It actually already has a simple subtool arrangement. The head is one tool and the eyes are a subtool.

2. Expand the SubTool subpalette of the Tool palette and take a look at how the subtools are arranged. Each slot in the SubTool subpalette holds a subtool. The female head is at the top of the list, and just below are the eyes (see Figure 4.27).

Now to create some hair you'll append a PolySphere as a third subtool. Before you can do this you must load the PolySphere into the current ZBrush session.

3. Open Light Box (hotkey = ,), switch to the Tool section, and drag the icons to the left until you see the `PolySphere.ZTL` tool. Double-click this tool to load it into the current session (see Figure 4.28).

When you load the PolySphere tool by double-clicking it, the female head disappears and is replaced by the PolySphere. Don't panic; all that has happened is that you've switched the tool you are currently working on. Think of it as swapping tools on the virtual sculpting stand.

4. Take a look at the tool library. You should see the femaleHead model icon with a little number 2 in the upper-left corner. The number 2 refers to the number of subtools this model contains. Click the femaleHead in the tool library to switch back to this model. If there are a lot of models loaded in the current session, you may need to open the tool library by clicking the large icon in the upper left of the tool library (see Figure 4.29).

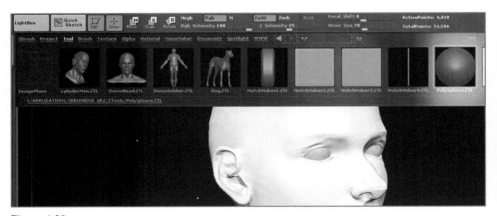

Figure 4.28

Select the PolySphere.ZTL file from the Tool section of Light Box.

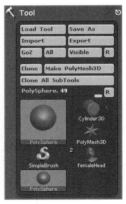

Figure 4.29

The femaleHead tool in the tool library has a number 2 in the corner indicating the number of subtools in the model.

5. Now to add the polySphere to the head. Click the Append button in the SubTool subpalette of the Tool palette. This opens a pop-up copy of the tool library. Select the PolySphere from the pop-up tool library (see Figure 4.30). This will add it to the model below the eyes.

Figure 4.30

Click the Append button to open the pop-up tool library; then select the PolySphere to add it to the femaleHead.

6. Make sure the appended PolySphere subtool is selected in the SubTool subpalette by clicking its slot. (Note that on the canvas the selected subtool is a lighter color than the unselected subtools. You can select only one subtool at a time.)

7. Click the Rename button in the SubTool subpalette and type **Hair** in the pop-up window (see Figure 4.31). Press Enter. The PolySphere has now been renamed Hair.

8. Now to position the hair subtool, rotate the view of the model to a side view. Make sure Persp is off on the right shelf. It's easier to move things accurately if perspective distortion is off. Press the X hotkey to enable symmetry for the Hair subtool. Press the W hotkey to switch to Move mode. This activates the Transpose handle.

9. There's a little known trick for moving subtools easily. While Move mode is active, hold the Alt key and drag on the hair; this allows you to position the Hair subtool without using the Transpose tool. This works for Scale mode as well but not for Rotate mode. Move the Hair subtool so that it fits over the head of the femaleHead and does not block her face (see Figure 4.32).

Figure 4.31

Rename the PolySphere as Hair.

ALWAYS NAME YOUR SUBTOOLS

There's a very good reason why you should always take the time to rename your subtools. When you open the tool library, the icon of each tool displays the currently selected subtool for that tool. If you had selected the Eyes subtool of the femaleHead model and then switched to the PolySphere, you would just see the Eyes in the tool library and not the female head. If you don't give your subtools unique names, you can start to get confused as the tool library becomes full of tools. The following graphic shows how bad this situation can get, and it can be frustrating to have to select each tool in order to find the one you want.

Figure 4.32

Move the Hair subtool to the back of the head.

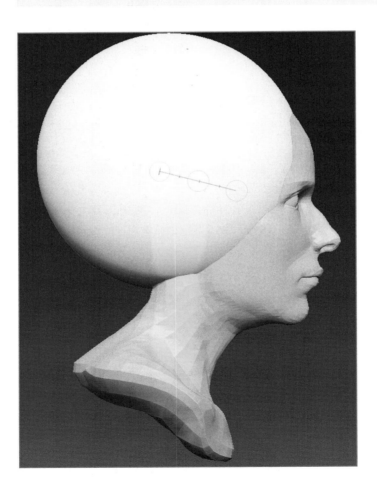

At this point you're set up to start sculpting some hair. This usually takes practice, but you can use many of the techniques you learned in previous sections. Using Dynamesh makes hair sculpting much easier and faster than in previous versions of ZBrush. Of course, you can create realistic strands of hair using FiberMesh, but there may be situations in which you want to sculpt hair from a single polygon mesh. For example, let's say you want to sculpt something that looks like a statue carved in stone. Creating realistic hair with FiberMesh is covered in Chapter 9; for this example we'll keep it simple and create some "statue-esque" hair using Dynamesh.

Before you start, though, you should save the project.

10. Click the Save button in the File palette to save the project as **femaleHead_02.ZPR**.

11. Make sure the Hair subtool is selected in the SubTool subpalette of the Tool palette. Set the Resolution slider below the Dynamesh button in the Geometry subpalette to **64**, and click the Dynamesh button to activate Dynamesh.

12. A warning box will appear asking you if you want to preserve the subdivision levels for the Hair subtool. Click the No button (see Figure 4.33).

13. Use the Move brush with a large draw size to start shaping the hair. Depending on the style you are looking for, you may want to deactivate Symmetry (press the X hotkey again to deactivate Symmetry).

Figure 4.34 shows some of the stages I went through during the hair development. Note that at the end the hair is low resolution and not very detailed. I used only the Move and DamStandard brushes to create the basic shape.

14. Once you have the basic shape established, save the project as **femaleHead_03.ZPR**.

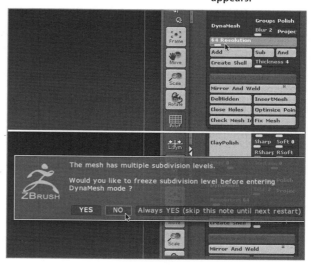

Figure 4.33

Set the Dynamesh Resolution to 64 (top image). Click the Dynamesh button and then choose No when the warning message appears.

FREEZING SUBDIVISIONS

When you activate Dynamesh for a surface that has multiple subdivisions, you get a warning asking you if you want to freeze subdivisions. It's not always necessary to freeze the subdivision levels, but in some cases you may want this option so that when you exit Dynamesh mode you still have multiple levels of subdivision. Be aware that whether you choose to freeze subdivision levels or not, the topology of your model will still be completely reorganized by Dynamesh.

Figure 4.34

The hair is sculpted in Dynamesh mode. The resolution is increased only when more detail is needed.

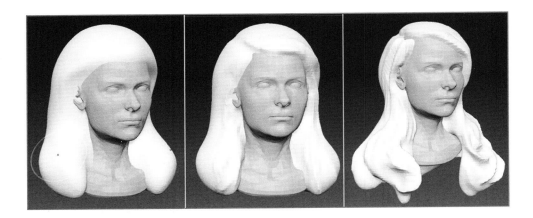

TIPS ON SCULPTING HAIR

- Have a reference close by (unless you're a beauty school graduate). Some artists who have spent most of their time reading sci-fi and horror novels may suddenly realize what they've been missing by not leafing through glossy glamour magazines! (It gets even worse when you start sculpting clothing, and you realize you don't know anything about fashion.) That's OK; the Internet can come to the rescue. Do an Internet search for hair styles and find a style that you like; then use it for reference.

- Use the Move tool to block out the basic shape. As long as Dynamesh is active, just Ctrl+drag on the canvas whenever the polygons appear stretched.

- Clay Tubes, Clay Build-up, DamStandard, and the Rake brush are all very helpful for defining hair.

- Avoid focusing too much on one part; instead, work the entire surface over.

- If things get too blobby, use the Trim Dynamic or hPolish brush to define the forms with flat planes.

- Don't worry about detail until you have the entire basic form blocked out.

- Toggle Persp on and off while you work so that you can see how perspective distortion affects the way the hair looks.

- The advantage of using a separate subtool for the hair is that if you don't like what you've done, you can add a new PolySphere and start over, and you can add more hairstyles as different subtools. Test them out by simply toggling the visibility of each hair subtool off and on.

- It's good to sculpt the hair at lower Dynamesh resolutions. You should only increase the resolution of Dynamesh when you feel you've done everything you can possibly do at the lower resolution. When you increase the resolution, do so by small increments. Go from 64 to 80, do as much work as you can, and then increase to 100 and then to 128 and so on. If you try to jump to a high resolution too early, you'll find it difficult to maintain the control you want over the design, and it will look lumpy and unappealing.

SAVING ZTOOLS VERSUS ZPROJECTS

You'll notice that in the previous exercise you loaded the PolySphere from the Tools section of Light Box instead of the Projects section. You can also save and load tools (aka ZTools) using the buttons at the top of the Tool palette. So how is this different from saving and loading projects?

Simply put, a *tool* is a model saved in the special ZTL file format. When you save a tool, you are saving only the tool that is presently loaded on the canvas in Edit mode. If the tool is made up of several subtools, then the subtools will also be saved.

When you save a *project*, you save the current tool as well as all the other tools in the tool library—materials, textures, and other elements.

Think of it this way: saving a project is like saving your entire sculpture studio exactly the way you left it. Imagine walking out of the studio and locking the door behind you. When you return, everything in the studio is just the way you left it.

When you save a tool, it's like putting a sculpture in a box and storing it. When you load that tool again, it's like taking the sculpture out of the box. Only what you put in the box is saved; nothing else is affected or saved when you save a tool.

I usually advise new students to save projects because it minimizes the risk of losing any work, and it's very similar to saving a scene in other 3D applications. Now that you are familiar with projects and tools, you may decide you want to save tools sometimes and projects other times. This is perfectly fine. There are some advantages of saving tools, including the fact that the file sizes of tools are usually smaller than those of projects, and there is less clutter in the tool library when you load a tool into ZBrush.

SubTool Master and Transpose Master Plug-Ins

ZBrush has a number of free plug-ins that extend the capabilities of the program. Most plug-ins are free and are preinstalled. The most common plug-ins and instructions on how to install new plug-ins are found in the bonus chapter, "Zscripts and Plug-Ins," which is included on the DVD that comes with this book.

The plug-ins (aka ZPlug-ins) are found in the ZPlug-in palette. If you don't see a particular plug-in listed, then you'll need to download it and install it. Plug-ins can be downloaded from Pixologic at this web address: www.pixologic.com/zbrush/downloadcenter/zplugins/.

SubTool Master adds a number of functions to help extend the capabilities of subtools. While many of these functions have been incorporated into the main interface in recent versions, there are still features that are very useful. In particular, the mirror function makes it easy to create a mirror copy of a subtool, which can either be added as a separate subtool or merged into the current subtool.

Transpose Master makes it possible to pose models that are made up of many subtools. It does this by making a clone of the current model. The clone is automatically set to the lowest SDiv level, and all the subtools are merged into a single object, allowing you to pose it easily with the Transpose handle. Once the model is posed, the plug-in allows you to automatically copy the pose back to the original model and all of its subtools. Transpose Master is demonstrated in Chapter 6, "Advanced ZSphere Techniques."

ZSpheres

ZSpheres are unique ZBrush modeling tools unlike anything you'll find in other 3D modeling programs. ZSpheres act as an armature for digital clay. Think of the wire skeleton a sculptor uses as the underlying structure for a sculpture. The wire armature is built and posed and then the sculptor adds clay to the armature to create the final figure. The armature acts as a support for the clay, but it can also be used to establish the initial pose.

ZSpheres are special spheres that can be connected into a network. The network of ZSpheres is then converted to a polygon mesh known as an adaptive skin. It is similar to a sculptor's armature except that instead of adding clay to the armature, you convert the ZSphere armature directly into a sculptable mesh.

The polygon mesh that results from the skinning process is placed as a copy in the Tool palette. The new mesh is just like any other 3D tool and can then be sculpted using the sculpting brushes.

You can form anything you want out of ZSpheres, but they are particularly useful for things such as figures, trees, and creatures. Because a copy is made, you're left with both a mesh and the original ZSphere armature, which can be reused as the basis for similar meshes in future projects. Let's take a look at how to use ZSpheres.

ZSphere Basics

In this section, you'll learn how to create and manipulate a basic ZSphere armature. Follow these steps to get started:

1. Save any projects you may have open and select the ZSphere 3D tool from the Tool palette. This is the red sphere that is colored in two different shades of red (see Figure 4.35). When you select the tool, it should appear on the canvas in Edit mode. If not, draw it on the canvas and switch to Edit mode (hotkey = T).

Figure 4.35

The ZSphere tool in the Tool palette inventory

2. Make sure the Draw and Edit buttons are on the top shelf. Move the brush over the surface of the ZSphere; you'll see a red circle connected to a line that starts at the center of the ZSphere (see the left image in Figure 4.36). The red circle will turn green as the brush appears over specific parts of the ZSphere.

3. Click and drag on the surface of the ZSphere. You'll see a new ZSphere grow out of the first as you drag (see the right image in Figure 4.36).

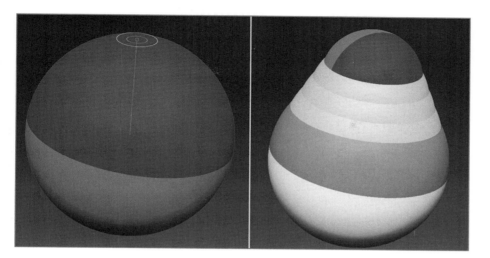

Figure 4.36

As you hold the brush tip over the ZSphere, a line appears from the center of the ZSphere (left image). To add another ZSphere to the first, click and drag on the surface while the Draw button is active on the top shelf (right image).

You can add a new ZSphere to any existing ZSphere while the Draw button on the top shelf is active. The cursor will turn green to indicate the best place to add a new ZSphere. The position of one ZSphere relative to another affects the topology of the final mesh, making it more or less easy to sculpt. ZBrush gives you hints, such as the green color of the cursor, to help you decide where to add new ZSpheres. In some cases you can bend the rules and place a ZSphere when the cursor is not green; it depends on what your final objective for the mesh is going to be. In general, when learning how to use ZSpheres, try to follow the hints suggested by the color changes.

4. Click the Move button on the top shelf (hotkey = W). Select the newly added ZSphere and move it away from the original ZSphere. You'll see a number of gray spheres appear between the original ZSphere and the newly added ZSphere. You'll also notice a triangle indicator that starts at the center of the first ZSphere and ends at the center of the second. This indicator resembles the way bones are drawn in other 3D applications.

You currently have a very simple ZSphere chain on the canvas. You've also established a simple hierarchy: The triangular icon indicates the relationship. The wide end of the triangle is at the center of the parent ZSphere, and the pointed end is at the center of the child ZSphere. The gray spheres in between are the connecting ZSpheres. These connecting ZSpheres act as a bridge. They can't be directly manipulated unless you convert them to standard ZSpheres.

5. Click the Draw button on the top shelf to switch to Draw mode (hotkey = Q). Click one of the connecting gray ZSpheres between the child and the parent. This will convert the connecting ZSphere to a standard ZSphere. You'll notice now there are two bones drawn between the three ZSpheres (see Figure 4.37).

Figure 4.37

Click a connecting ZSphere while in Draw mode to add a ZSphere between the two original ZSpheres. Drag on the ZSphere while in Move mode to change its position.

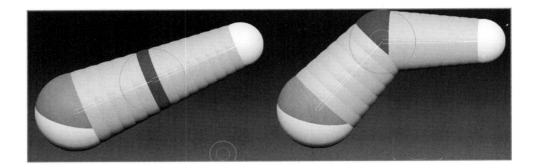

6. Click the Move button (hotkey = W) and try moving the ZSpheres around. If you drag on a ZSphere, it will move the ZSphere independently of the other two. If you drag on the connecting gray spheres, you'll move all of the child ZSpheres together. Hold the Alt key and drag on the last ZSphere while in Move mode. The other ZSpheres follow the movement.

The Rotate (hotkey = R) and Scale (hotkey = E) buttons work in a similar fashion. When you have the Rotate button activated, dragging on a ZSphere will cause it to pivot about its center, and dragging on the connecting sphere rotates all of the child ZSpheres. The Scale button allows you to scale individual ZSpheres by dragging on them or all of the child ZSpheres by dragging on the connecting ZSpheres.

7. Spend a few moments experimenting with adding, rotating, and scaling ZSpheres.

8. To delete a ZSphere, switch to Draw mode and Alt+click the sphere.

TIPS FOR WORKING WITH ZSPHERES

- In Draw mode, drag on a ZSphere and then hold the Shift key to add a second ZSphere that matches the size of the first.

- Lower your draw size to more precisely select and manipulate individual ZSpheres.

- ZSpheres can be added to existing tools as subtools, so you can use them to create additional props such as clothing or equipment for characters.

- ZSpheres work with symmetry; you can turn on radial symmetry to quickly create elaborate designs such as trees or cephalopods.

Skin ZSpheres

Skinning is the process of converting a ZSphere armature into a polygon mesh that can then be sculpted. ZBrush has two skinning methods: adaptive and unified. Usually a ZSphere armature uses adaptive skinning.

Adaptive Skinning

Adaptive skinning creates a polygon mesh based on the ZSphere armature. Think of wrapping the armature with a membrane made up of polygons. When you convert a ZSphere armature into an adaptive skin, the skin itself is stored as a copy in the Tool palette, and you can then continue to sculpt. While you are working with the ZSphere armature, you can preview the adaptive skin very easily, which can help you make decisions about the position of ZSpheres while you work, up until you are ready to convert the armature into an adaptive skin.

When starting a ZSphere model, you'll need to create a simple chain of at least three ZSpheres in order for the skinning process to work correctly. There is a simple workflow that ZBrush artists use when starting a typical ZSphere armature:

1. In ZBrush, select the ZSphere in the Tool palette library to start a new ZSphere armature. The ZSphere should appear on the canvas in Edit mode.

You're going to add two ZSpheres, one on each side of the original ZSphere, to start the ZSphere armature. You can use this trick to help precisely position the two child ZSpheres.

2. Press the X hotkey to activate Symmetry.

3. As you hold your brush over the ZSphere, you'll see two cursor icons. Position the icons so they meet at the center and both turn green (see Figure 4.38, upper-left image).

Figure 4.38

The basic approach to starting a ZSphere model involves creating a simple chain of three ZSpheres.

4. Create a new ZSphere by dragging from the center where the two brush tips meet (see Figure 4.38, upper-right image).

5. Drag on the canvas to rotate the view to the opposite side of the ZSphere (see the lower-left image in Figure 4.38). Repeat steps 3 and 4 to add a second ZSphere to the original. The simple three-ZSphere chain should look like the lower-right image in Figure 4.38.

6. Press the A hotkey. You'll see the ZSphere chain turn into a polygon mesh; this is actually a preview of the mesh.

7. To switch back to ZSphere mode, press A. Spend some time adding ZSpheres to these original three ZSpheres; move them around and press A to see the preview.

If you start with fewer than three ZSpheres, you'll end up with a hole at one end of the skin that will look strange and produce unpredictable results.

You can actually sculpt the preview mesh using the sculpting brushes while you work, but you should avoid doing this. If you sculpt the mesh while in Preview mode and then make a change to the armature by adding additional ZSpheres, your changes will be lost, and in some cases it can really mess up the model.

The best approach is to create your ZSphere armature, pose it, and preview often while you work. When you have a satisfactory ZSphere chain, you can then click the Make Adaptive Skin button in the Tool palette (this button appears only when you're working with ZSpheres; see Figure 4.39), and you'll find that the mesh is placed in the Tool palette library. The prefix *skin_* is added to the name of the mesh to distinguish it from the original ZSphere armature. Once you create the skin, you can append it to another tool as a subtool or draw it on the canvas and sculpt away.

Figure 4.39

The Make Adaptive Skin button converts the armature into a mesh that you can sculpt.

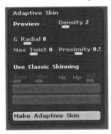

Creating a Body for the Dragon Using ZSpheres

In this section, you'll learn how to create a body for the dragon head model you sculpted in Chapter 3 using ZSpheres. Follow these steps to begin:

1. Click the Open button in the File palette to open the last version of your dragon head, or open the Dragon_Chapter4.ZPR project from the Chapter 4 folder on the DVD.

2. In the SubTool subpalette of the Tool palette, click the slot for the dragon's head. Currently, it is still named PolySphere. Click the Rename button below the stack and change the name to **DragonHead**.

3. Since the ZSphere is always available in the tool library, you don't need to load it as you did with the PolySphere earlier in the chapter. You can just append it to the dragon's head. Click the Append button in the SubTool subpalette of the Tool palette, and choose the ZSphere from the pop-up library (see Figure 4.40). It will be added to the subtool stack below the dragon's head.

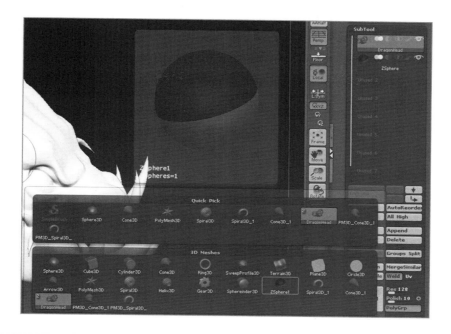

Figure 4.40

Append the ZSphere to the dragon head model.

CLASSIC ADAPTIVE SKINNING

The adaptive skinning process was upgraded with the release of ZSphere 3.5. The new adaptive skin created by ZSpheres more closely resembles the armature than the skin that was created using the original skinning method. However, there are advantages to using the old, original (aka classic), adaptive skinning method, and therefore ZBrush has an option for switching to classic skinning.

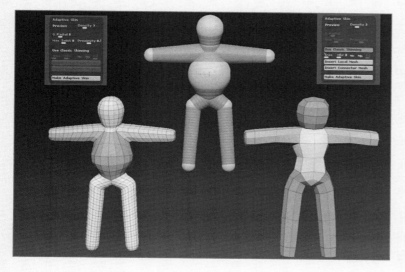

continues

continued

A number of options become available when you click the Use Classic Skinning button. These options can change the way the mesh is generated when you make the adaptive skin. You can see how these changes affect the mesh while the ZSpheres are in Preview mode.

When ZBrush creates an adaptive skin in Classic Skinning mode, it determines how many polygons each ZSphere will create. This is known as the mesh resolution. Some parts of the mesh are at a higher resolution than others: ZSpheres that have a number of child ZSpheres attached to them generate a higher resolution. The Ires slider determines how many child ZSpheres are needed before a parent ZSphere generates a high-resolution mesh.

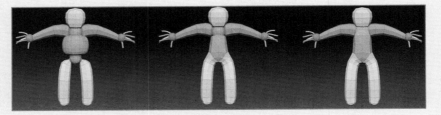

Raising the MC slider increases the amount of curvature in the membrane profile at intersections.

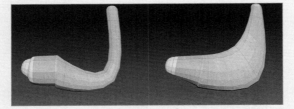

The Minimal Skin To Child (Mc) button reduces the resolution between a child ZSphere and its parent, which can create a kind of webbing between the ZSpheres. Minimal Skin To Parent (Mp) does the same thing but in reverse.

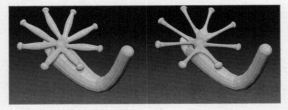

The Insert Local Mesh button lets you replace a selected ZSphere with a polymesh object. When you click this button, the tool inventory appears. If you select one of the polymesh objects in the inventory (non-polymesh objects are grayed out in the inventory), the selected ZSphere will be replaced by the mesh.

continued

The Insert Connector Mesh button also opens the tool inventory. The selected polymesh object replaces the connector ZSpheres between the selected ZSphere and its parent.

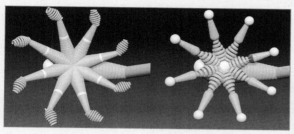

If you open the mannequin projects available in the Project section of ZBrush, you'll see a number of ZSphere mannequins that were created by replacing parts of a ZSphere armature with simple primitive shapes. These mannequins were created using the Insert Connection Mesh feature, which is active only when the Use Classic Skinning button is on.

Magnet ZSpheres can be used as a way to deform the skin when Use Classic Skinning is active. To create a magnet ZSphere, add a child ZSphere to the chain, pull it away from its parent, switch to Draw mode, and hold the Alt key while clicking the gray connecting ZSpheres. Press the A hotkey to see how the magnet ZSphere influences the adaptive skin.

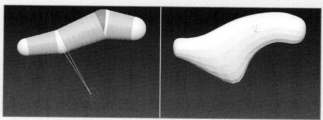

continues

continued

Negative ZSpheres create an edgeloop in the surface but only when using classic skinning. To create a negative ZSphere, use Draw mode to add a child ZSphere and then use Move mode to push it into the parent ZSphere. The ZSphere will become semitransparent, indicating that it has a negative ZSphere. Press the A hotkey to see the effect on the topology of the adaptive skin preview.

4. Lower your Draw size to **3** or **4**. Using a small Draw size will help you to place new ZSpheres more accurately as you build the armature.

5. Make sure the eyeball icons for both the DragonHead and the ZSphere are turned on in the SubTool subpalette stack. Otherwise, when you switch subtools, the head or the ZSphere may become hidden.

6. You probably can't see the ZSphere on the canvas because it's inside the DragonHead subtool. Select the ZSphere in the subtool stack so that its slot becomes highlighted. Click the Transp button on the right shelf. This button toggles on Transparency for all of the inactive subtools. Now, you can see the ZSphere in the center of the head (Figure 4.41, left).

7. Press the X hotkey to activate Symmetry for the ZSphere. Rotate the view so you can see the ZSphere from the front. Press the W hotkey to switch to Move mode and drag on the ZSphere; pull it toward the back of the dragon's head (Figure 4.41, center).

8. Press the Q hotkey to switch to Draw mode. Add a ZSphere to the front and back of the ZSphere by dragging on the original ZSphere. Rotate the view as you work as needed to do this (Figure 4.41, right).

9. Now you have the initial three-ZSphere arrangement discussed in the previous section. Next, you'll pull the ZSphere at the back of the head outward to form a neck. Press the W hotkey to switch to Move mode; drag on the ZSphere at the back of the head and pull it outward to form the neck. Pull it back quite a way; you'll add the body in between this ZSphere and the root ZSphere (Figure 4.42, top).

Figure 4.41

Turn on
Transparency so
that the ZSphere
is visible in the
dragon's head (left
image). Move the
ZSphere to the back
of the head (cen-
ter image). Add a
ZSphere to the front
and back of the
initial root ZSphere
(right image).

10. Switch to Draw mode (hotkey = Q), and click the gray connecting ZSpheres in three different places to add three ZSpheres, as shown in the second image from the top in Figure 4.42. You don't need to be terribly precise.

11. Switch to Scale mode (hotkey = E). Drag downward on each ZSphere to scale it up in size. You want to create a rough swelling in the middle, which will become the mass of the dragon's body (Figure 4.42, second from bottom).

12. Experiment with the position of each ZSphere, and think about how you would like the body to look (see Figure 4.42, bottom). Think about how much personality you can give to the body of your dragon using just this simple ZSphere armature.

13. When you have something that roughly looks like an interesting body, click the Save button in the File menu and save the project as **Dragon_Chapter4_Body.ZPR**.

In the next section you'll add legs and a tail.

ZSPHERE ERRORS

If it looks as though part of the ZSphere chain turns transparent while you are posing your armature or adding new ZSpheres, this is just ZBrush letting you know that the position of the ZSpheres may cause problems in the topology of the mesh that will be generated by the skinning process. The error is shown in the image. Try repositioning the ZSpheres until the display returns to normal.

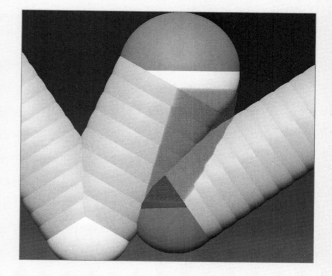

Figure 4.42

Pull the rear ZSphere back, and add three ZSpheres by clicking the connecting ZSpheres. Scale the new ZSpheres up, and use Move to position them to form the body.

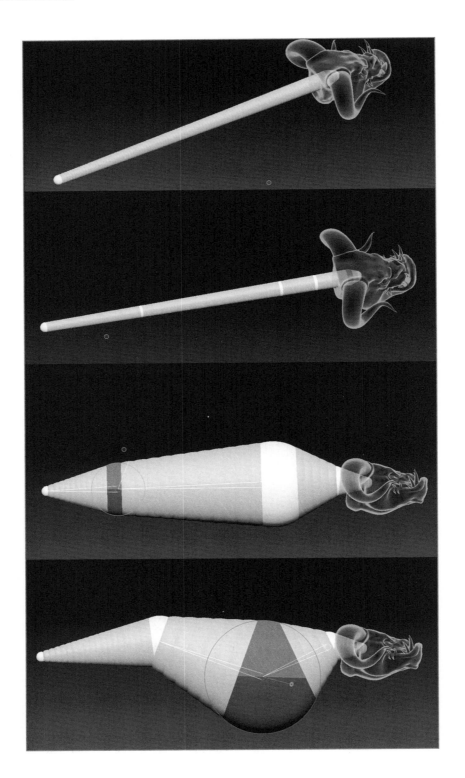

Adding ZSphere Legs and a Tail

In this section, you'll add legs, complete with feet and toes, and a tail. The emphasis will be on keeping things simple so that it's easier to sculpt the surface once it's converted to a mesh.

1. Continue with the project from last section; first, you'll add the front legs. Switch to Draw mode and hold the mouse over the large ZSphere of the body. The red dots may or may not turn green, indicating the best spot to create a new ZSphere, but that's OK. Click the side of the large ZSphere to add a new ZSphere. This will be mirrored on the other side; these two ZSpheres will be the shoulders (Figure 4.43, top left).

2. Press the A hotkey to see a preview of the mesh (see Figure 4.43, top right). If the surface is not twisted or if you don't see any obvious problems, then you should be OK. If there is a problem, you can press the A hotkey again to toggle back to ZSphere mode, move the offending ZSphere, and press the A key to preview the mesh to see if the problem has been fixed. It's usually a good idea to preview the mesh frequently as you work so that you can catch problems early when they are easier to fix.

3. Press the A hotkey again to switch out of Preview mode. Switch to Draw mode (hotkey = Q), and add another ZSphere to the shoulders. Switch to Move mode (hotkey = W), and drag this out to form the front legs (Figure 4.43, bottom left).

4. To add a knee, switch back to Draw mode and click the center of the leg; again, you don't need to be overly precise. Switch to Move mode and move the knee ZSphere to create an angle in the leg (bottom right in Figure 4.43).

5. Add another ZSphere at the end of the leg for the foot. Use Move and Scale modes to shape it as shown in Figure 4.44.

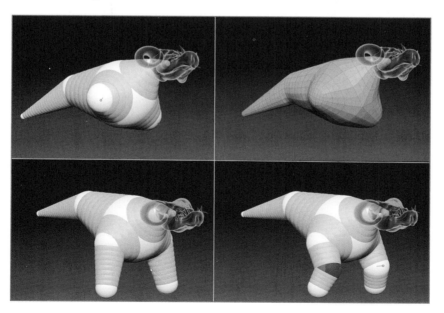

Figure 4.43

Add legs to the front of the Dragon (upper left). Press the A hotkey to check for errors in the mesh (upper right). Pull the legs downward to extend them (lower left). Insert knees in the model of the leg (lower right).

Figure 4.44

Add a ZSphere to the end of the front legs to create feet.

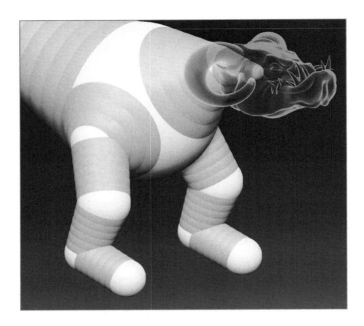

6. You can repeat steps 1 through 5 to create the back legs. Remember to preview often! In my version I added a second angle in the leg to create the typical dogleg-style anatomy (Figure 4.45, left).

7. The tail is pretty simple; just add a ZSphere to the ZSphere at the end of the body. Pull it out as far as you think it needs to go. To add a bend you can switch to Draw mode, click the gray connecting ZSphere, and add as many bends as needed (however, if you want to add large scales and other details later, you may want to keep the tail straight for now). To delete a ZSphere, hold the Alt key and click the ZSphere you want to remove while in Draw mode. Try to keep the body symmetrical along the x-axis; this will make it easier to sculpt later on (Figure 4.45, right).

Figure 4.45

Use ZSpheres to add back legs (left image) and a tail (right image).

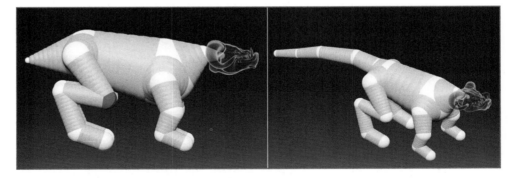

You can add toes using the same techniques; however, there's a trick you can use that will make toes easier. This trick also works well for human fingers.

8. Switch to Draw mode and click the foot ZSphere; drag out slowly to scale it up but keep the ZSphere fairly small. Think of this ZSphere as a knuckle (see Figure 4.46, top left).

9. Add a new ZSphere to the knuckle, but after you start dragging it, hold the Shift key. This will snap the ZSphere to the same size as the knuckle. Switch to Move mode and pull the finger ZSphere away from the knuckle (see Figure 4.46, top right).

This idea behind this technique for adding toes is that by first creating a knuckle ZSphere and then creating a finger ZSphere, you avoid the conical shape that would be created by simply adding the finger without the knuckle.

10. After you create the finger, you can switch to Draw mode and click the gray connecting ZSpheres to add more joints. Use Move mode to move the ZSpheres to create a bend in the finger (see Figure 4.46, bottom). Repeat these steps to add additional fingers. Try to keep some space between the fingers as you create them so that they're easier to sculpt later on.

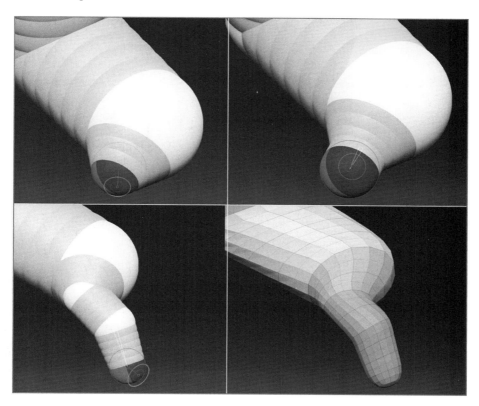

Figure 4.46

Add a knuckle to the foot (top left). Draw the toe and hold the Shift key as you draw to match the size of the knuckle; then pull this away from the foot (top right). Add a ZSphere in the finger to create a joint (bottom left). Press the A hotkey to preview the result (bottom right).

11. Repeat this process to create toes for the back legs.

12. Spend a few minutes using Move and Scale mode to adjust the ZSpheres of the armature. Take advantage of the simplicity of ZSpheres to experiment with different proportions and poses. Try to keep the pose symmetrical across the x-axis so that it's easier to sculpt later on (see Figure 4.47).

13. When you're happy with your dragon body, save the project. In the next section you'll convert the ZSphere armature to a mesh and merge it with the head.

Figure 4.47

Toes are added to the back feet, and the armature is adjusted to shape the dragon's body.

Skinning the ZSphere Dragon Body

The basic ZSphere body created in the previous section is your armature. To make the ZSpheres into a sculptable surface, you'll convert it to a mesh using adaptive skinning.

1. Continue with the project from the previous section. Make sure the ZSphere is the currently selected subtool in the subtool stack.

2. Scroll down to the Adaptive Skin subpalette of the Tool palette. (Note that this subpalette is visible only when you have a ZSphere selected. If you don't see it, chances are you have the wrong subtool selected in the subtool stack.)

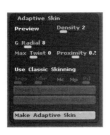

Figure 4.48

Click the Make Adaptive Skin button in the Adaptive Skin subpalette of the Tool palette.

3. Click the Make Adaptive Skin button (see Figure 4.48). You won't see any change in the model. When the skin is created, it is placed as a new tool in the tool library. The new tool has the prefix *skin_* attached to it. In this case it will be named skin_ZSphere1.

4. Click the Append button to add the skin_ZSphere1 tool to the subtool stack, as shown in Figure 4.49. Turn off the Transp button on the right shelf to deactivate Transparency.

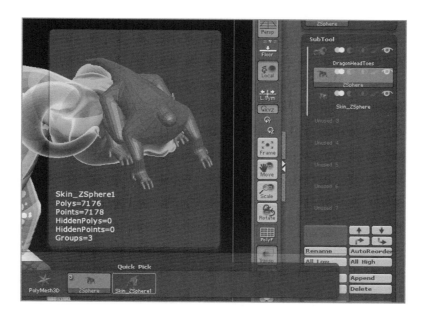

Figure 4.49

Append the skin to the dragon as a subtool.

Now the dragon model has three subtools: the dragon_head, the ZSphere, and the skin_ZSphere1 surface. You can neaten things up a little by renaming the skin_Zsphere1 subtool and deleting the original ZSphere tool. You don't have to delete the tool, and in some cases you may find that there's a good reason to keep it around. In this case, you can delete it to keep the subtool stack simple and uncluttered. Deleting a subtool is not undoable, meaning that if you change your mind after deleting it, it's too late to bring it back. For this reason I make it a habit to always save the project before deleting a subtool.

5. Click the Save As button in the File menu to save your project.

6. In the subtool stack, make sure that the ZSphere is selected (not the skin_ZSphere1 subtool). Click the Delete button in the SubTool subpalette of the Tool palette. You'll see a warning appear letting you know that this is not undoable. Click OK.

7. Select the skin_Zsphere1 tool in the subtool stack. Click the Rename button and rename the tool **DragonBody**.

8. Save the project again (sometimes I like to save the project with a new version number so that I can go back to the version that still has the ZSphere armature if I need to).

9. Select the DragonBody subtool in the subtool stack. Press the X hotkey to activate Symmetry. Spend a few minutes using the Move and Smooth brushes to sculpt the surface to make it look a bit more natural and less like a balloon animal.

10. Subdivide the model by pressing the Ctrl+D hotkey. This adds another level of subdivision to the body. Use the clayTubes, Standard, Move, Smooth, and DamStandard

brushes to shape the dragon body a bit more. Try to make the neck look as though it flows into the back of the head.

11. Add one more level of subdivision and continue sculpting (Figure 4.50). There is no need to go into detail such as scales just yet since the body will be merged with the head and dynameshed.

Figure 4.50

Subdivide and sculpt the body using the sculpting brushes.

ZSPHERE STRATEGIES

When creating a ZSphere armature, how many ZSpheres should you use? Should you pose the armature, or should you make sure the limbs are symmetrical along the x-axis? Should you use adaptive or classic skinning? The answers to these questions depend on the situation or your own personal style of working.

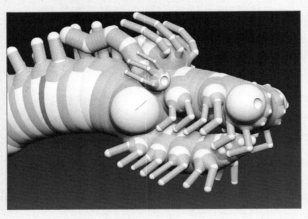

continued

Some artists prefer to keep things as simple as possible and add detail to the adaptive mesh after it's been converted or add detail using ZSketching techniques (described in the next section). Other artists like to add a lot of detail in the ZSphere armature before skinning.

The same is true when deciding whether or not to pose the ZSphere armature. For sculptors who work in clay, the pose is usually established at the very beginning when creating the wire armature. The following image shows how ZSpheres can be used to establish the pose before converting the ZSpheres into an adaptive mesh. However, clay sculptors don't have the benefit of automated symmetry that ZBrush sculptors enjoy. You may want to keep the ZSphere armature as symmetrical as possible so that when you create an adaptive skin, you can easily sculpt on both sides at the same time and then use the transpose tools or other methods to pose the mesh after conversion. This is a good approach for beginners.

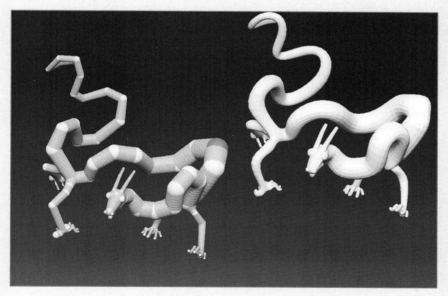

The choice to use classic adaptive skinning or to use the newer ZSpheres 2 adaptive skinning method (the default setting for ZBrush 4) will probably be made based on the situation. Use the A hotkey to toggle on and off the adaptive skin preview, and experiment with the settings to see what skinning method suits you the best. The following image compares the ZSphere 2 adaptive skinning (top) with classic adaptive skinning (bottom).

continues

continued

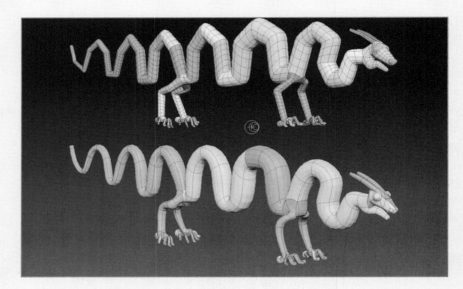

As you become more experienced with ZBrush, you'll develop your own strategies for modeling with ZSpheres. While you're first learning, it's probably a good idea to keep things simple. This will ensure that it will be easier to sculpt the meshes that you generate from your ZSphere armatures. That said, you should also take time to experiment and try making complex ZSphere armatures and posing them as well.

Merging the Head and Body

At this point you can merge the DragonHead and DragonBody subtools so that it will be easier to create a seamless transition between the head and the body. Merging subtools means that two subtools are collapsed into a single subtool. The geometry remains intact, but now the merged surfaces can be affected by the sculpting brushes as a single mesh.

It's important to understand that you don't have to merge subtools unless you want to; it's ultimately an artistic choice. I have created many ZBrush models over the years that consist of dozens of subtools, and that's perfectly fine. It is necessary to merge subtools if you want to create a single seamless surface using Dynamesh, which is why you'll merge the head and the body in this section.

1. Continue with the project from the previous section. Select the DragonBody subtool. In the Geometry subpalette make sure the SDiv slider is set to the highest subdivision level. Click the Delete Lower Subdiv button to remove all lower subdivision levels.

2. Select the DragonHead subtool. In the Geometry subpalette, turn off the Dynamesh button.

3. Merging subtools is *not* an undoable operation, so it's a good idea to save the project before merging subtools. Do this now using the Save As button in the File palette.

4. With the DragonHead subtool selected in the subtool stack, click the Merge Down button (see Figure 4.51). You'll get a warning again letting you know that this is not undoable. Click OK (see Figure 4.52). The subtools are now merged.

5. Click the Dynamesh button in the Geometry subpalette to "dynamesh" the merged head and body. Keep in mind that before you apply Dynamesh you can set the resolution using the Resolution slider below the Dynamesh button in the Geometry palette. Higher resolution will mean more detail from the original is transferred to the Dynamesh version. Lower resolutions may make it easier to sculpt primary forms into the mesh. The choice is yours. I recommend experimenting with different resolutions. If you don't like the result of a particular resolution setting after you use Dynamesh, you can press Ctrl+Z to undo and then try again using a different setting.

Figure 4.51

Click the Merge Down button to merge the head with the body.

6. Use the sculpting brushes to sculpt the surface a little more. Again, don't worry about details at this stage (Figure 4.53). I used my own variation of the InsertSphere brush to create the scaly armor on the back. This same technique was demonstrated in Chapter 3 for adding teeth to the dragon's mouth.

7. When you're happy with the result, save the project.

Figure 4.52

A warning message lets you know that merging is not undoable.

Figure 4.53

After the dragon is merged, it is dynameshed and sculpted

TIPS ON MERGING SUBTOOLS

- The Merge Down button merges the selected subtool with the subtool directly below it. If you need to merge two subtools that are not next to each other in the stack, use the arrow keys to move the subtools as needed.

- The Merge Similar button merges subtools that have the same polygon count and geometry. For example, if you have a separate subtool for each wheel on a car and the wheels are all duplicates of each other, you can use this button to automatically merge them all into a single subtool.

- The Merge Visible button creates a copy of the tool in the tool library in which all subtools that are currently visible are merged into a single tool. Note that when you use this button your current tool won't look any different; you have to keep in mind that the merged version has been placed in the tool library.

- When subtools are merged, the polygrouping is maintained so you can continue to isolate parts of the mesh for masking.

- You can use Group Split to split a surface into multiple subtools based on the polygrouping of the mesh. Make sure that before you use this feature, the polygroups have all been organized in a logical fashion so that you don't end up with a few hundred or so subtools.

- If you would like to merge two subtools while at the same time keeping their subdivision levels, make sure that both subtools have the same number of subdivisions and that both are set to their highest subdivision level before merging. This works most of the time, but always save your file before merging.

ZSketching with ZSpheres

ZSketching involves painting ZSpheres on top of an existing ZSphere armature or mesh object. It's an amazing process that feels just like adding strips of clay to a model. The ZSketch can then be skinned using unified skinning. The unified mesh creates a sculptable object made up of square and triangular polygons that evenly cover the surface. This is the same type of topology you get when using Dynamesh. This differs from an adaptive mesh introduced earlier in the chapter, which adapts the size and number of polygons based on the size of the ZSpheres (see Figure 4.54). Think of ZSketching as yet another tool in your arsenal that you can use to start a digital sculpture.

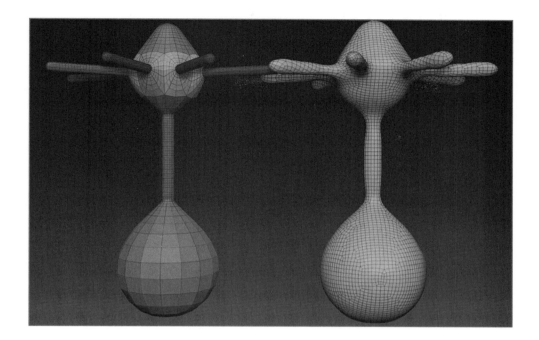

Figure 4.54

A ZSphere armature has been converted to an adaptive skin in the left image. The same armature has been converted to a unified skin in the right image.

Creating a ZSketch

In this example, you'll learn how to create another style of dragon head using ZSketching. ZSketching can be applied to an existing ZSphere armature, or you can simply start with a single ZSphere and then use the special ZSketch sculpting brush to create forms in empty space. Since this is the easiest way to ZSketch, you will use this method:

1. Start a new ZBrush session on a blank canvas.

2. In the Tool palette fly-out inventory, select the ZSphere. Draw it on the canvas and switch to Edit mode (hotkey = T).

3. Expand the Tool palette and find the ZSketch subpalette toward the bottom. This subpalette is available only when ZSphere is the current tool.

4. Click the EditSketch button (see Figure 4.55). You'll see the ZSphere turn to a single color.

Figure 4.55

The EditSketch button is enabled.

The sculpting brushes in the library switch to a subset of the sculpting brushes designed to work only when ZSketching (see Figure 4.56). These brushes can be divided into several groups:

Sketch Brushes Armature and Sketch 1: The Sketch brushes draw the ZSpheres on the original armature as well as on the canvas.

Figure 4.56

The ZSketch brushes

Figure 4.56

The ZSketch brushes

Smooth Brushes Smooth 1, Smooth 2, Smooth 3, and Smooth 4: The Smooth brushes smooth the position and size of the sketched ZSpheres. Each smoothing brush has a slightly different quality to the way it smoothes the surface. Just as with sculpting brushes, the smoothing brushes are mapped to the Shift key. If you choose one of these brushes, you'll see a reminder at the top of the screen letting you know that the chosen Smooth brush is only active when you are holding the Shift key while in Draw mode.

Bulge Brush This brush causes the ZSketch to swell—or shrink if you hold the Alt key.

Additional Brushes Flush, Float, Flush, Flush Dynamic, Flush Resize, and PushPull: The manipulation brushes help you fine-tune the position and size of the sketched ZSpheres. These brushes and other variations are found in the ZSketch section under Brushes in Light Box.

5. From the fly-out material library on the left shelf, select the SketchGummyShiny material. This is one of several materials designed to help you see your ZSketch as you create it.

6. Reduce your brush size and select the Sketch 1 brush. Press the X hotkey to activate Symmetry if it is not active already (you should see a red circle on the left and right side of the ZSphere if Symmetry is on).

7. Start drawing on the ZSphere. You'll see a series of spheres follow the stroke. Extend the stroke out into empty space.

8. Rotate the view of the ZSketch (see the top image in Figure 4.57).

The ZSpheres you add with the ZSketch brush are unlike the ZSpheres you used to make the dragon armature. These ZSpheres can only be added using the special ZSketch brushes when ZSketch mode is on. You need to have at least one ZSphere on the canvas, and the sketch has to start on a ZSphere, but after the initial stroke you can continue to add more ZSpheres and build up the model by drawing on existing strokes.

ONE UNDO TOO MANY

Sometimes you may find that if you press Ctrl+Z to undo the last ZSketch stroke, the ZSphere turns red, and it seems like the ZSketch brushes no longer work. What has happened? This is simply a result of going back too far in the undo queue. You've basically stepped out of ZSketch mode. To fix this, turn the Edit ZSketch button in the ZSketch sub-palette back on and continue working.

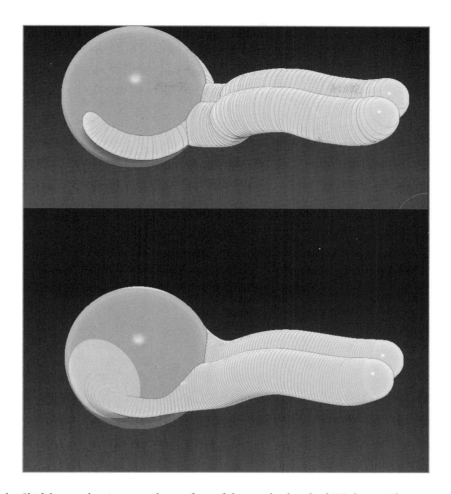

Figure 4.57

New ZSpheres are
sketched onto the
initial ZSphere
(top image). The
ZSpheres are
smoothed into the
surface when you
brush them with the
Smooth brush (bot-
tom image).

9. Hold the Shift key and paint over the surface of the newly sketched ZSpheres. This
   activates the Smooth 1 brush, which helps to straighten the position of the sketched
   ZSpheres. It also scales the ZSpheres at the ends to match the original ZSphere (see
   Figure 4.57, bottom).

The Smooth 2 brush will push the end ZSketched ZSpheres into the armature but it
will not change the radius of the ZSpheres.

The Smooth 3 brush will not change the radius of the ZSketched ZSpheres. It applies a
global smoothing to the sketch, which can help straighten the line of the ZSketch.

The Smooth 4 brush scales the end ZSpheres down and embeds them deeper onto the
other ZSpheres.

The typical method for adding ZSketched ZSpheres to an armature is to draw out a
single line using the ZSketch ZSpheres on the armature and then smooth the newly added
ZSpheres using whichever smoothing brushes you prefer. Do this each time you sketch on
the armature to ensure that the model is neat and easy to use. Think of it as adding strips

of clay to your model. Each time you add a strip, use a smoothing brush to push it into the rest of the models, just as if you used your thumbs to smooth out the strip of clay on a real model.

10. Hold the Alt key and draw on top of the ZSketch. Holding the Alt key deletes parts of the ZSketch, so use this to erase what you have drawn so far.

11. Click the Floor button on the right shelf to turn on the grid. Make sure Persp is off. Rotate the view so that you can see the ZSphere from the side.

12. Starting from the ZSphere, paint an S shape that moves up toward the right. This will be the neck for this version of the dragon's head (see Figure 4.58, left).

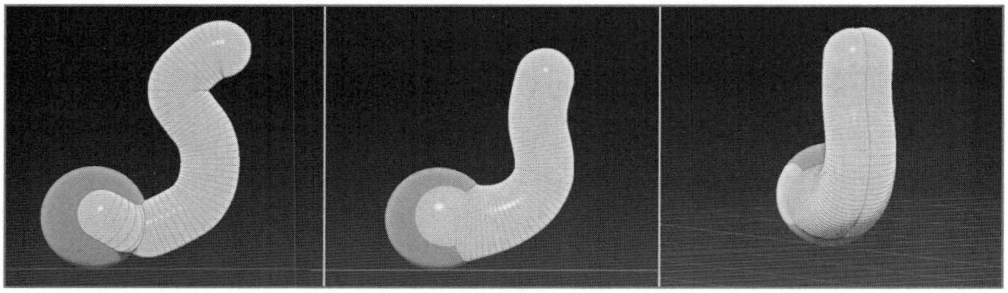

Figure 4.58

The dragon's neck is started by painting an S shape. The Smooth brush is used to refine the shape. In perspective view, you can see how two lines of ZSpheres overlap to form the neck.

13. After you draw out the neck, hold the Shift key and paint over the ZSketch to smooth their position and size (see Figure 4.58, center).

14. Rotate the view of the model. You'll see that since Symmetry is enabled, you have drawn two lines of ZSpheres. Using the Smooth brush has caused these lines to converge toward the end of the neck. That's okay. In fact, that's a big part of how ZSketching works. Overlapping lines of ZSpheres will become the basis for the model's form (see Figure 4.58, right).

15. Rotate back to a side view. Activate the Move button on the top shelf (hotkey = W). Drag on the ZSpheres to adjust the shape of the neck if you need to (see Figure 4.59, left).

Figure 4.59

Use Move and Scale modes to adjust the position and size of the ZSketch.

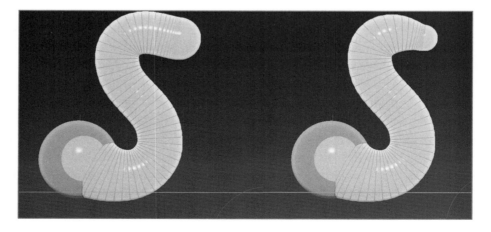

16. Switch to Scale mode (hotkey = E) and drag upward on the ZSpheres at the end of the neck to scale them down. This adds a taper to the neck (see Figure 4.59, right).

17. Switch back to Draw mode (hotkey = Q). Use the ZSketch 1, ZSketch 2, and ZSketch 3 brushes to form a triangular head at the end of the neck. Draw a few lines at a time and then hold the Shift key while painting over the ZSpheres to smooth the shape. Rotate the view and adjust your draw size as you work. Remember that you can erase ZSpheres by holding the Alt key, and you can move and scale ZSpheres by switching to Move or Scale mode. Figure 4.60 shows how I created the head for my dragon.

Figure 4.60

A basic head is created at the end of the neck using the ZSketch brushes.

When you're smoothing multiple lines of sketched ZSpheres, the smoothing brushes work on whichever sketched line of ZSpheres you touch with the smoothing brush first and then any lines sketched after that. For example, if you sketch three lines of ZSpheres on top of each other and then use the smoothing brush to straighten them, if you touch the third line first with the smoothing brush, only the third line will be smoothed. However, if you touch the second line first with the smoothing brush, both the second and third line will be smoothed. Touching the first line with the smoothing brush will smooth all three. This feature gives you precise control over how the smoothing is applied.

18. When you are happy with the look of the head and neck, click the Save As button in the File menu to save the project as **ZSketchDragon.ZPR**.

Absolute precision is not necessary when ZSketching. The process should feel natural and organic, which is why it's called ZSketching. The best approach is to add a few lines at a time, slowly and deliberately, and then hold the Shift key while brushing to smooth the forms of the model. Be mindful, but not obsessive, of how you paint the ZSpheres on the armature because their position and size can affect the look of the unified skin.

Previewing the Unified Skin

Just as when you created the ZSphere armature, you can preview the mesh that the ZSketch will create by pressing the A hotkey. Remember that you don't want to use the sculpting brushes on the ZSketch preview. Once you're finished with the ZSketching, you will convert the ZSketch into a skinned copy, which you can then sculpt into a more refined

Figure 4.61

The settings in the Unified Skin subpalette of the Tool palette

shape. A number of settings in the Unified Skin subpalette toward the bottom of the Tool palette will determine how the unified skin looks and behaves (see Figure 4.61).

1. Continue with the ZSketch you created in the previous section or use the ZSketchDragon_v01.ZPR project from the Chapter 4 folder on the DVD.

2. Press the A hotkey to preview the unified skin that will be created from the ZSketch (see the upper-left image in Figure 4.62).

Typically, ZSketch ZSpheres are converted into a unified mesh, as opposed to an adaptive mesh. As mentioned earlier in the chapter, a unified mesh is made up entirely of quadrilaterals that are all the same size. You can increase the number of polygons in the mesh and reduce their size by increasing the resolution of the preview.

3. Press the A hotkey again to switch back to the ZSketch. In the Unified Skin subpalette, set Resolution to **400** and create another preview. The result more closely resembles the ZSketch. The upper-right image in Figure 4.62 shows the preview when the resolution is set to 400.

Figure 4.62

The ZSketch dragon is previewed using various settings in the Unified Skin subpalette of the Tool palette.

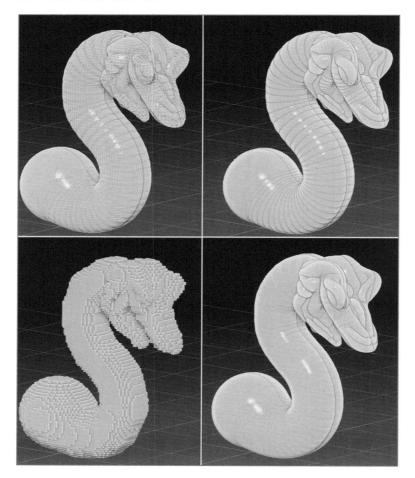

The ideal resolution value for your particular ZSketch will vary depending on the ZSketch; usually it takes some experimentation to find the value that's right for you. You try to get the lowest density mesh possible that still retains the level of detail that you want for the sculpt. Remember that eventually you'll be working over the converted mesh with the sculpting brushes, so you may not need to have a very high resolution to get the basic shape of the ZSketch.

TIPS ON CREATING UNIFIED MESHES

- SDiv subdivides the resulting mesh just as when you add subdivisions to a regular mesh object. The Preview button displays the mesh at the subdivision level specified by the SDiv slider.

- Smooth evens out the surface of the mesh. For an interesting look, try setting the resolution to 128 and the Smooth slider to 0. The mesh will look as though it is made of tiny cubes (see Figure 4.62, lower left).

- The Sdns slider will add ZSpheres in between every ZSphere that was sketched out. It will create a smoothing, in a way. For example, if you set it to 100, ZBrush will add 100 ZSpheres between the ZSpheres that were sketched out. The lower-right image in Figure 4.62 shows the unified mesh with a Resolution value of 400, Smooth value of 10, and Sdns value of 100.

- The Polish Surface slider is another way to smooth the surface. There are two Polish modes you can use to polish the surface. To choose a mode, click the tiny circle to the right of the Polish slider. The open circle ensures that the polished mesh will maintain the original volume of the ZSketch. The closed circle allows the skin to be stretched; the original volume is ignored, as shown in the following image. Experiment with different combinations of values for the Smooth and Polish sliders and see how they affect the mesh preview.

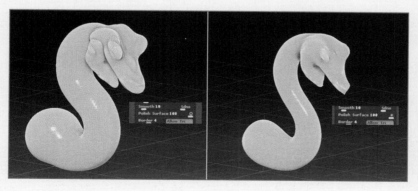

continues

continued

- The Border slider is active only when Polish is above 0. Each line of ZSpheres you sketch on a surface generates a new polygroup. The Border slider inserts loops of polygons along the borders of existing polygroups. The number of loops is determined by the value of the Border slider. The result is similar to when you apply the Group Loops button in the Geometry palette to a regular mesh object. The Smooth slider has to be more than 0 in order for ZBrush to generate the loops. The following image shows how loops are inserted in the mesh when the resolution has been set to 128.

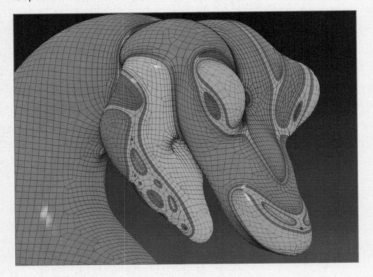

- The Allow Tri button lets ZBrush generate triangular polygons when needed. This can result in a smoother-looking mesh.

Adding Details

To create the face, use a small Draw Size value and scale up the view to zoom in on the head:

1. Switch out of Preview mode by pressing the A hotkey. Zoom into the head region. Use the Sketch 2 brush to add lips around the mouth and large nostrils (see Figure 4.63, top left).

2. Switch to Move mode (hotkey = W) to carefully reposition the lips and nostrils and eyebrows.

3. Switch back to Draw mode (hotkey = Q) and hold the Shift key. Paint over the ZSpheres to smooth the changes you have made (top right in Figure 4.63).

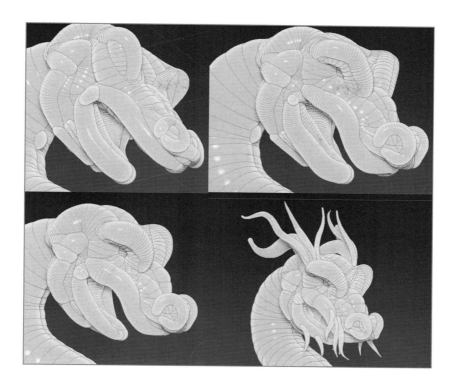

Figure 4.63

The face is formed using a variety of ZSketch brushes.

TIPS ON ZSKETCHING

Here are some tips to keep in mind while you create a ZSketch:

- To reposition the ZSpheres you paint on the surface, you can use the Push Pull brush or switch to Move mode (hotkey = W) and drag the ZSpheres to place them wherever you like, even away from the ZSphere armature.

- To erase ZSpheres, switch to Draw mode (hotkey = Q) and use any of the ZSketch brushes while holding the Alt key.

- The Armature brush lets you easily paint the ZSpheres in any direction on the canvas as long as you start the stroke on the armature or on part of the exiting sketch.

- The Float, Flush, and Fuse brushes are found in the ZSketch section of Light Box under Brush. The following image shows where to find the extra ZSketch brushes in Light Box.

continues

continued

- Float pushes the sketch out along the original stroke direction, and holding the Alt key while using Float pushes the ZSketch in toward the model.

- Flush pushes and scales the ZSpheres along the viewing axis toward the back of the canvas. Hold the Alt key to push the ZSpheres in toward the model along the viewing axis.

- Flush Dynamic positions the ZSketch along the same plane based on the stroke path.

- Flush Resize uses the viewing angle to flatten the ZSketch line as well as scale the ZSketched ZSpheres.

- Fuse blends the ZSpheres together.

- In the Tool directory of Light Box are several examples of ZSketches created by other artists, such as the ZSketch_Bug, ZSketch_Critter, and ZSketch_Facial Anatomy tools. It's a good idea to examine these sketches to pick up some useful techniques. The following image shows a facial muscle anatomy study created with ZSketching.

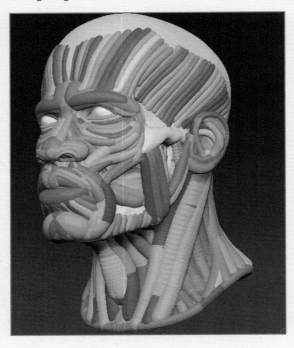

4. Choose the Bulge brush from the brush fly-out library and use it to resize parts of the face as needed. Hold the Alt key while brushing over the ZSpheres to shrink them (bottom left in Figure 4.63).

5. Choose the Armature brush and use small strokes to add short lines of ZSpheres. The Armature brush adds strips of ZSpheres parallel to the viewing angle, so you may want to rotate the view of the dragon to add the ZSpheres in specific spots.

6. Use these techniques to add and shape details such as teeth, flames, swirls of hair, and whiskers (see Figure 4.63, bottom right).

7. Use these techniques to add detail to the rest of the neck (see Figure 4.64).

8. Save the project as **ZSphereDragon_v02.ZPR**.

Binding and Posing the ZSketch

You can repose the ZSketch while you are working on it using a ZSphere armature. In this exercise you'll build a simple ZSphere skeleton for the ZSketch dragon and then use the skeleton to adjust the pose of the dragon.

1. In the ZSketch subpalette, deactivate the Edit Sketch button. The sketch will disappear; don't worry, it has not been deleted.

2. Click the ShowSketch button. The sketch reappears as a transparent mass over the original ZSphere (see Figure 4.65).

Figure 4.64

Details are added to the rest of the neck.

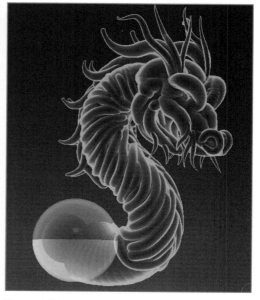

Figure 4.65

The ZSketch appears as a transparent mass over the original ZSphere.

3. Make sure the Draw button is activated on the top shelf. Hold the cursor over the ZSphere at the start of the neck. Symmetry should still be activated. Position the cursor so that the two red dots on the ZSphere come together to form a single green dot (upper-left image in Figure 4.66) and drag on the surface to add a ZSphere (Figure 4.66 upper right).

Figure 4.66

ZSpheres are added to the initial ZSphere to form a simple armature for the neck.

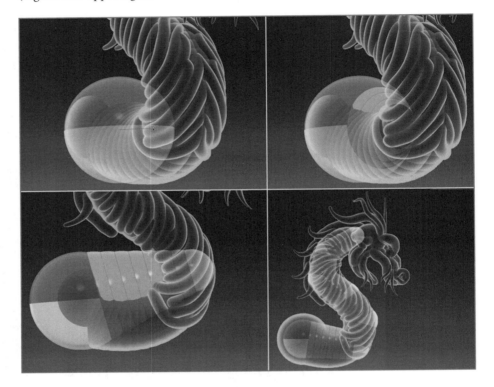

4. Switch to Move mode (hotkey = W) and pull this ZSphere outward (see Figure 4.66, lower left).

5. Add several more ZSpheres to this armature to match the curvature of the neck (see Figure 4.66, lower right).

6. Add more ZSpheres to the chain that fit inside the head and the jaw. Figure 4.67 shows the armature next to the ZSketch. I added extra branches for the horns.

Once you have created a basic ZSphere armature, you can bind the ZSketch to the armature and then move the ZSpheres around to adjust the pose of the ZSketch.

7. In the ZSketch subpalette of the Tool palette, click the Bind button.

8. Activate the Move button on the top shelf. Try moving the ZSpheres around and see how it affects the ZSketch (see Figure 4.68).

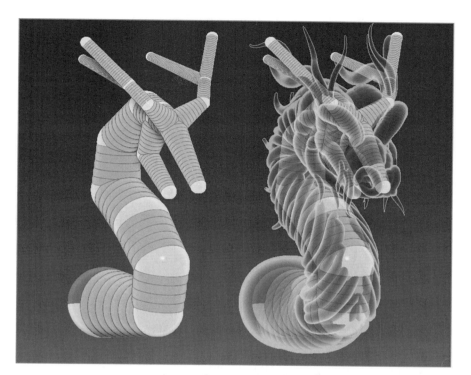

Figure 4.67
ZSpheres are added for the jaw and horns.

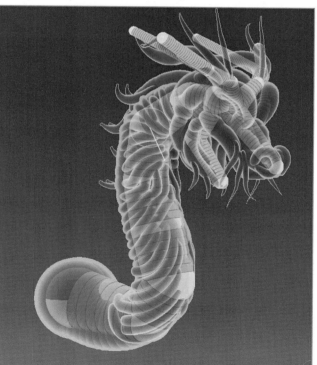

Figure 4.68
The ZSketch is posed by moving the underlying ZSpheres.

In all likelihood you'll need to spend some time cleaning up the model after posing. If you work slowly and methodically, you should be able to minimize the amount of touch-ups. The ZSketch is bound to the armature based on the distance between the ZSpheres and the ZSketch. You can turn off the Bind button, adjust the SoftBind slider, and even edit the position and scale of the ZSpheres in the armature and then click the Reset Binding button. Turn on Bind and continue posing.

9. When you have posed the dragon, turn off Bind Pose, and then turn on the Edit Sketch button and use the ZSketch brushes to clean up any problems. Remember that you can delete stray ZSpheres by pressing the Alt key while the Draw button is activated (see Figure 4.69).

Figure 4.69

After posing, edit the ZSketch to fix any problems.

Creating a Unified Mesh

The whole point of ZSketching is to allow for an intuitive way to sketch out a design in three dimensions. ZSketching is perfect for when you want to experiment with ideas and concepts. Once you have the initial ZSketch created, you can convert it into a unified mesh, which allows for easy sculpting. From there you can continue to develop your idea.

Just as with standard ZSpheres, creating a unified mesh means making a copy of the ZSketch that is made up of polygons instead of ZSpheres. Before creating this copy, you'll want to preview the unified mesh in order to fix any problems that may occur during the conversion process:

1. In the Unified Skin subpalette, set Resolution to **304**, which is a good resolution for this particular model. Of course, other models may require experimentation to determine the best resolution.

2. Experiment with the Polish Surface, Smooth, and Sdns settings. Try setting Smooth to **10**, Polish Surface to **5**, and Sdns to **50**.

3. Press the A hotkey to see the preview. Examine the surface from as many views as possible to see if there are any holes that need to be filled.

4. Press A to switch out of Preview mode. Make any last changes you need to fill holes by adding to the ZSketch or moving parts around (Figure 4.70). Adjust the unified skin settings as you see fit.

TIPS ON POSING

When using the techniques described in this section to pose and change the original armature, try to work slowly and deliberately. You can switch between posing the armature and editing the ZSketch as often as you like while you work. It's a very flexible workflow.

In some cases, you may find that the original armature is making it hard to add the details you'd like or parts of it are included in the mesh preview in an undesirable way. When this happens, try these steps to get the armature out of the way:

1. Turn off the Edit ZSketch button.

2. Turn on the Show ZSketch button so you can see the ZSketch as a transparent ghost over the armature.

3. Don't turn on the Bind button. Leave it off so that the changes you make don't affect the ZSketch.

4. Switch to Scale mode and reduce the size of the ZSpheres that are causing the problem.

5. Turn on Edit ZSketch and continue ZSketching.

5. Click the Make Unified Skin button in the Unified Skin subpalette of the Tool palette to create the unified mesh. The new mesh will appear in the tool inventory with the *skin_* prefix before the name.

6. Save the project as **ZSketchDragon_v03.ZPR**. This will save both the ZSketch version and the unified mesh in a single project file.

Sculpting the ZSketch

Once you have created the unified mesh, you can subdivide it just like any other 3D mesh and use your favorite sculpting brushes to shape it into a finished product. The unified mesh method of skinning creates a mesh in which all of the polygons are the same size and cover the mesh uniformly. This makes it easy to sculpt. However, if you want to use the geometry in an animation, you may need to retopologize the mesh so that it can easily be deformed in your animation software. Retopology is covered in Chapter 6, "Advanced ZSphere Techniques." The sculpted dragon is shown in Figure 4.71.

Save the final dragon as **ZSketchDragon_v04.ZPR**.

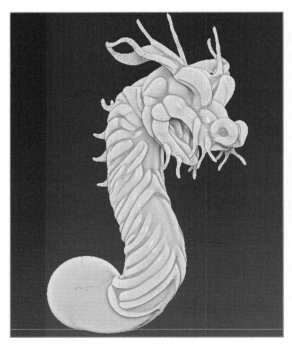

Figure 4.70

Inspect the preview for holes and the quality of the mesh.

Figure 4.71

The unified mesh is subdivided and edited using the sculpting brushes.

ZSKETCHING TECHNIQUES

There are additional techniques you can use that can make ZSketching even more powerful. For example, you can sketch ZSpheres on top of an existing mesh object. This is a great way to add details. To do this, follow these steps:

1. Append a ZSphere as a subtool to an existing mesh.

2. Select the ZSphere subtool in the SubTool subpalette of the Tool palette. Turn on the Edit ZSketch button in the ZSketch subpalette of the Tool palette.

3. You can turn on the Transp button on the right shelf if you'd like, but make sure that the Ghost button is off. Otherwise, you will not be able to draw on the mesh.

4. Use the ZSketch brushes in the sculpting brush library to paint ZSpheres on top of the mesh.

5. You can press the A hotkey to preview the unified mesh while you work.

6. When you are ready to convert the ZSketch to a mesh, click the Make Unified Skin button in the Unified Skin subpalette of the Tool palette.

7. The unified skin appears in the tool inventory. You'll need to append the skin to your original mesh if you want to incorporate it into your sculpt.

The following image shows how whiskers and flames can be drawn onto the surface of the Chinese dragon mesh using the ZSketch brushes.

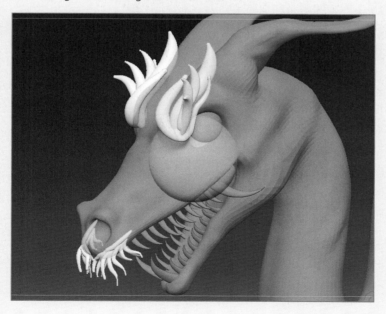

Summary

In this chapter you learned how to select parts of the mesh using the selection brushes. You learned how to organize the polygons of a surface into polygroups as well as techniques to use polygroups and masking together. You learned how to append subtools and work with the controls in the SubTool subpalette. You learned how to use the SliceBrush to cut apart a surface. ZSpheres were introduced as well as ZSketching techniques.

CHAPTER 5

ShadowBox and Clip Brushes

The digital sculpting tools you've encountered so far in this book lend themselves very well to the creation of organic surfaces. Subjects such as creatures, characters, clothing, and natural environments are easily achieved using sculpting brushes, ZSpheres, and ZSketching. ZBrush has long held the reputation of being the best way to create these kinds of organic objects.

ZBrush also has several tools that are designed to expand the power of digital sculpting to hard-surface objects as well. Things like vehicles, buildings, robots, and armor can now be created just as easily as organic surfaces.

This chapter introduces some tools that you can use to sculpt hard-surface objects including the ShadowBox tool, clip brushes, and curve brushes.

This chapter includes the following topics:

- **Creating meshes with ShadowBox**

- **Using radial symmetry in ShadowBox**

- **Using custom alphas in ShadowBox**

- **Refining surfaces using clip brushes and ClayPolish**

- **Using the InsertCube brush to cut into a surface**

ShadowBox

ShadowBox offers a completely different way to create meshes than anything you've seen in other 3D modeling packages. The technology is included as a special tool in ZBrush,

and you'll find that once you get the hang of the basic concept, it's easy to use and a lot of fun. In a nutshell, here's how ShadowBox works: A mesh is generated at the center of the ShadowBox tool based on the intersection of profiles that you draw on the three sides of the box (see Figure 5.1). You create the silhouettes on the sides of the box using the masking brushes, and as you edit the silhouettes the mesh at the center of the box instantly updates. Once you have the basic shape you want, you can turn ShadowBox off and you're left with a mesh that you can then refine using the sculpting brushes, Dynamesh, and other techniques. It's a very fast way to get an idea into three dimensions. Just as with the other ZBrush tools, the approach is artistic and intuitive, and there are only a few technical details that you need to worry about.

Figure 5.1

ShadowBox creates a mesh using silhouettes drawn on each side of a three-sided box.

Creating a ShadowBox

The easiest way to get started with ShadowBox is to open the ShadowBox128.ZPR project found in Light Box.

1. Start a new ZBrush session.

2. Open Light Box to the Projects section and open the DemoProjects folder.

3. Scroll to the left and find the ShadowBox128.ZPR icon (see Figure 5.2); double-click the icon to open the project. After a few seconds the project will open.

Figure 5.2

Open the ShadowBox128. ZPR project in the Projects/Demo Projects folder in Light Box.

The project consists of a cube that has three sides visible. This is a ShadowBox tool. You'll create your surfaces inside the box by drawing masks on the side. It's kind of weird but also very cool.

4. Rotate the view of the ShadowBox so that you can see the three sides, hold the Ctrl key to activate the MaskPen brush, and drag on one of the sides to paint a mask.

When you let go to complete the stroke, you'll see a flat blob appear at the center of the ShadowBox tool. The profile of the blob matches the shape of the mask painted on the side of the ShadowBox.

5. Turn on the Transp button on the right shelf. Make sure the Ghost button on the right shelf is activated, and rotate the view. Now you can see the mask on the side of the ShadowBox through the blob at the center (see Figure 5.3, left image).

Figure 5.3

Paint a mask on each side of the ShadowBox to create a mesh at the center.

6. Paint another mask on the other side of the ShadowBox (see Figure 5.3, middle image).

When you let go, the blob at the center updates. If you rotate the view, you'll see that from the sides, the profile of the blob matches each of the masks drawn on the sides of the ShadowBox. As you view the blob from a perspective view, you'll see that the shape of the blob is determined by the combination of the two masks.

7. Paint a third mask on the bottom of the ShadowBox. You can see that the blob is now generated based on the combination of the three masks (see Figure 5.3, right image).

8. In the SubTool subpalette, click the ShadowBox button in the Geometry subpalette of the Tool palette (see Figure 5.4). The box disappears, and you are left with the blob that was generated from the masks. At this point you have a mesh that you can subdivide and sculpt just like any other lump of digital clay (see Figure 5.5).

This is the basic workflow for creating a mesh using ShadowBox. However, you can get much greater control by taking advantage of the various options the mask brush has to offer. In the

Figure 5.4

Click the ShadowBox button in the Geometry subpalette of the Tool palette.

Figure 5.5

The resulting mesh created from painting masks in ShadowBox

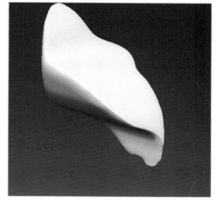

next sections, you'll learn how you can adjust the resolution of the mesh and how to use reference images within the ShadowBox tool.

The ShadowBox Tool

ShadowBox is a 3D tool similar to other 3D tools in that many of the options for controlling ShadowBox are found in the Tool palette, specifically in the Geometry subpalette of the Tool palette. You can also append the ShadowBox tool as a subtool to any existing 3D tool. This is a great way to add details to an object.

ShadowBox uses the unified skin method for generating the mesh created by the mask profiles. This means that the mesh is made up of quadrilateral polygons; this type of mesh is similar to the kind of mesh you create when you activate Dynamesh. So how do you set the number of polygons for the ShadowBox mesh? You do this using the Res slider in the SubTool subpalette of the Tool palette. The smoothness of the mesh can be adjusted using the Polish slider. However, you must set these sliders before you create the ShadowBox tool. Here are some tips on how to adjust the resolution of ShadowBox:

1. Continue with the tool created in the previous section. Click the ShadowBox button in the Geometry subpalette of the Tool palette.

The ShadowBox appears again, and the masks are regenerated on each side of the ShadowBox based on the profiles of the selected subtool.

2. On the right shelf, click the PolyF button to activate the wireframe display. Turn off the Transp button as well.

The wireframe appears on each of the sides of the ShadowBox (see Figure 5.6). This gives you an indication of the density of the mesh created by ShadowBox. Also, notice that the ShadowBox tool has been organized into color-coded polygroups so that each side is in its own polygroup.

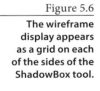

Figure 5.6

The wireframe display appears as a grid on each of the sides of the ShadowBox tool.

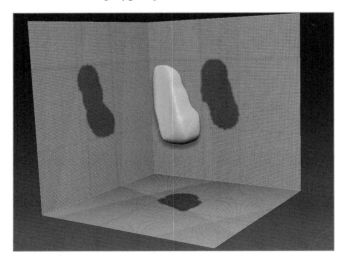

While the ShadowBox button is on, the Res slider is grayed out. In order to change the resolution of ShadowBox you need to leave ShadowBox by turning this button off, adjust the resolution, and turn ShadowBox back on.

3. Turn the ShadowBox button off, and you're left with a blobby little mesh but the Res slider is now available.

Take a look at the controls above the ShadowBox button in the Geometry subpalette of the Tool palette. The Res slider determines the resolution of the mesh, or in other words, the number of polygons that make up the surface of the mesh. The Polish slider determines how smooth the mesh is.

4. Set the Res slider to **244**, and click the ShadowBox button once to turn ShadowBox back on.

Notice that the squares that make up the wireframe display on the sides of the ShadowBox are larger and that the mesh at the center of the ShadowBox is at a lower resolution (see Figure 5.7, left image). At a setting of 24, each side of ShadowBox is made up of a grid that is 24 × 24 polygons.

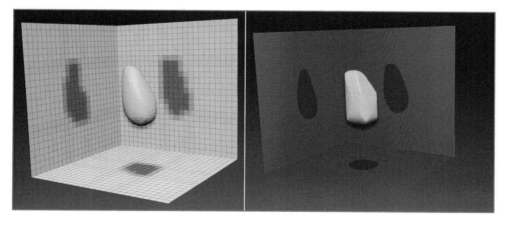

Figure 5.7

At a lower Res setting, the grid on the sides of the ShadowBox is larger and the resolution of the mesh is lower (left image). Higher-resolution settings for ShadowBox produce smoother masks and a denser mesh (right image).

5. Turn the ShadowBox button off, set the Res slider to **400**, and then turn ShadowBox on again.

This time the grid on each side of the ShadowBox is very dense, and the mesh at the center is at a much higher resolution. Notice that the edges of the masks on each side of the ShadowBox are smoother as well. The quality of the mask is directly related to the resolution of ShadowBox (see Figure 5.7, right image).

There are different approaches to how you use ShadowBox, and depending on how you want to use the mesh generated by ShadowBox, you may want to choose a medium or low resolution or a high resolution.

The purpose of ShadowBox is to allow you to quickly determine the shape of a surface, which you can then subdivide and sculpt with the sculpting brushes. If you plan to subdivide the mesh after you leave ShadowBox, then you may want to choose a low resolution so that you can take advantage of having a range of SDiv levels to work with. But if you plan to convert the mesh into a Dynamesh surface, then you can choose a higher ShadowBox resolution since Dynamesh is going to automatically retopologize the surface anyway. The workflow is very flexible, and how you choose to incorporate ShadowBox into your modeling process is up to you.

6. Turn ShadowBox off again, set the Res slider to **256**, and set the Polish slider to **0**. This time notice that the surface of the mesh is very "blocky" (see Figure 5.8).

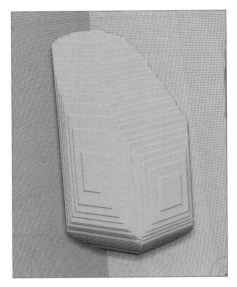

The Polish slider determines the smoothness of the mesh surface. Without smoothing, the surface will appear very blocky and rough. In some cases, you can use this aspect of ShadowBox as a creative advantage. Using a low or 0 Polish setting with a rectangular mask is a great way to create hard-edged surfaces. Later in this chapter you'll see how to use rectangular masks in ShadowBox.

7. Experiment with different Polish settings and see how they affect the appearance of the mesh.

You can save the ShadowBox tool for future use, and the settings you have established will be included whenever you load the tool into ZBrush.

Figure 5.8

Setting Polish to 0 creates a blocky-looking mesh.

8. Turn ShadowBox off, and set the Res slider to **256** and the Polish slider to **10**. This will establish the settings for the tool. Then turn ShadowBox back on.

9. Hold the Ctrl key and drag on the canvas to clear any masks that may be drawn on the sides of the ShadowBox. Clearing the masks will also clear any meshes that may be at the center of the ShadowBox.

10. Now click the Save As button in the Tool palette and save the tool as **ShadowBox256. ztl**. Save this in the ZBrush 4 R3/ZTools folder. The tool will appear in Light Box under Tools. Note that there is already a ShadowBox64.ZTL tool and a ShadowBox128.ZTL tool in Light Box. The numbers refer to the resolution of the ShadowBox.

POLISH VOLUME CONTROL

The Polish slider has two modes that can be set by clicking the circle on the right side of it. The open circle means that as the surface is polished, the volume of the mesh will be preserved. The closed circle means that the volume of the surface will not be preserved when it is polished. Experiment with these two modes when working with ShadowBox. You can create some interesting effects using one mode or the other. The difference is more noticeable on surfaces that have variations in thickness.

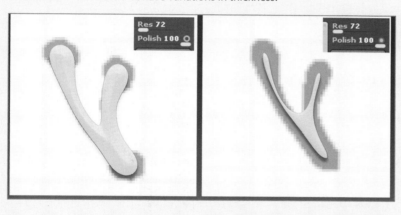

Using Reference Images in ShadowBox

Now that you have the basics of ShadowBox down, let's look at how you can use ShadowBox to create a sculptable mesh. The goal is to create the body for a hot rod (see Figure 5.9). It's tempting to jump right in and start roughing out the shape for the body inside ShadowBox, but it might be helpful to first create a guide within ShadowBox that can be used as a reference for the shape of the masks.

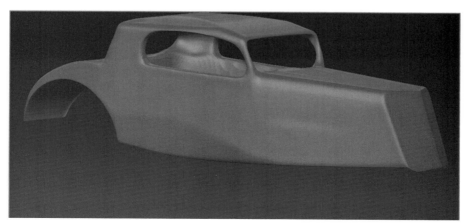

Figure 5.9

Image of the hot rod body

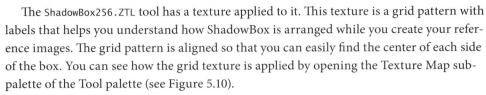

Figure 5.10

A grid texture is applied to the ShadowBox256.ZTL tool.

The ShadowBox256.ZTL tool has a texture applied to it. This texture is a grid pattern with labels that helps you understand how ShadowBox is arranged while you create your reference images. The grid pattern is aligned so that you can easily find the center of each side of the box. You can see how the grid texture is applied by opening the Texture Map subpalette of the Tool palette (see Figure 5.10).

Follow these steps to create a hot rod reference image for ShadowBox:

1. In the UV Map subpalette of the Tool palette, click the Morph UV button, as shown in Figure 5.11. This unfolds the ShadowBox tool so you can see how the texture corresponds to the sides of the ShadowBox tool.

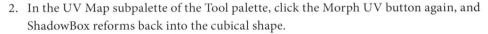

UV TEXTURE COORDINATES

UV texture coordinates (or UVs for short) are a set of coordinates used to tell 3D software how to map a 2D image onto the faces of a 3D object.

Figure 5.11

Click the MorphUV button in the UV Map subpalette of the Tool palette.

2. In the UV Map subpalette of the Tool palette, click the Morph UV button again, and ShadowBox reforms back into the cubical shape.

The texture that is applied to ShadowBox is an image file. This image is found in the ZBrush 4R3\ZTools folder. The name of the texture file is SBRef.PSD. This image file can be opened in your favorite digital painting program and used to place reference images. Just make sure you save the altered image file under a different name so that you don't overwrite the existing SBRef.PSD file.

3. You can exit ZBrush and open the SBRef.PSD image in your favorite painting program.

Figure 5.12 shows the reference image I created in Corel Painter. You can create a similar image using Photoshop or your favorite image-editing program. I created very simple silhouettes of the front, side, and top view of the hot rod body.

4. When you're happy with the reference image, save it as a BMP file to your local drive. Go back into ZBrush and make sure the ShadowBox256.ZTL tool is loaded on the canvas, and the Edit button on the top shelf is on.

5. Open the Texture palette and click the Import button. Find the saved reference image on your local drive and load it into ZBrush.

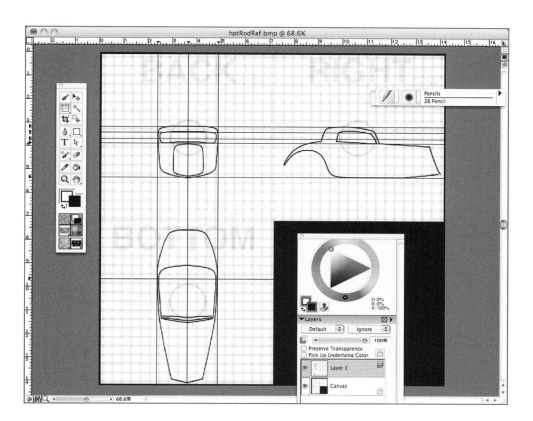

Figure 5.12

The reference image for the body of the hot rod is painted in Corel Painter.

6. To apply the reference image to the ShadowBox, open the Texture Map subpalette of the Tool palette, expand the texture fly-out library by clicking the large gray icon box, and select the texture as shown in the top of Figure 5.13. The Texture On button should activate automatically; if it does not, click it and you'll see the texture appear on the ShadowBox tool (bottom of Figure 5.13).

7. In the Tool palette, save the tool as **hotRodSB.ZTL**. The texture will be saved with the tool. Save the file in the Pixologic/ZTools folder so that it appears in Light Box.

Now you have a guide for creating the hot rod. You can use the reference I created if you'd like. Copy hotRodRef.BMP from the Chapter 5 folder on the DVD. The next step is to start roughing out the forms of the body by painting masks in ShadowBox.

Figure 5.13

Select the imported texture by clicking in the Texture subpalette of the Tool palette (top image). The reference image of the hot rod is applied to the ShadowBox tool (bottom image).

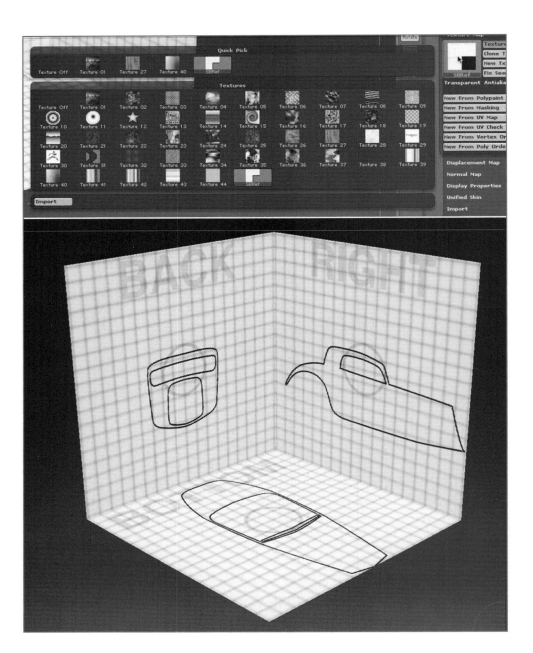

REFERENCE IMAGERY

Finding reference images for a project is not too hard as long as you have an Internet connection and some time to search the web. However, sometimes finding the exact image you need for a particular detail can be particularly difficult. This is why I always keep a camera on me; you never know what you might stumble across while wandering out in the wild. I accidentally came across these hot rods at a highway rest stop while on vacation in New Zealand. Who knew Kiwis loved cars so much! On a separate occasion I came across this bizarre engine design that powered a homemade hot rod that was parked in a convenience store lot on Sunset Boulevard in Los Angeles.

Create the Car Body in ShadowBox

Now you're ready to start working on the car body. When approaching a shape such as this one, think about how you might carve the body of the car out of a piece of wood.

You'll start by creating an overall block for the car and then whittling down each side using the Mask brushes:

1. Load the hotRodSB.ZTL tool into ZBrush, and make sure that it is on the canvas and that the Edit button on the top shelf is activated. This tool is available in the Chapter 5 folder of the DVD.

2. Make sure the Persp button on the right shelf is off. It will be easier to create masks in ShadowBox if Perspective mode is off.

3. Rotate the view of the ShadowBox tool so that you can see the plane labeled Back, and then click the Frame button on the right shelf (hotkey = F) to center the view. Turn on the Transp button on the right shelf so you'll be able to see the reference images through the mesh generated in ShadowBox. Make sure Ghost is on as well. The Ghost transparency style is easier to use in ShadowBox than the standard transparency style.

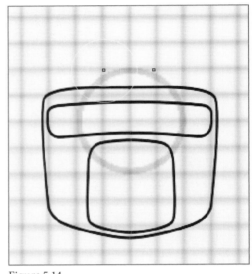

Figure 5.14

Activate Local Symmetry so that the brush tips are aligned symmetrically on either side of the center line of the reference.

4. Scale up the view of ShadowBox so that you can clearly see the reference image. Press X to activate Symmetry. Hold the brush over the ShadowBox tool. You should see two red dots indicating that Symmetry is activated along the x-axis (see Figure 5.14).

5. The two dots should meet at the center line in the middle of the back plane. If they do not, you'll need to press the LSym button on the right shelf to activate Local Symmetry.

6. Open the sculpting brush fly-out library on the left shelf. Press the M key and then the R key to select the MaskRect masking brush. A warning will appear reminding you that this brush is active only while you hold the Ctrl key (Figure 5.15). Click OK.

Figure 5.15

The MaskRect brush is automatically mapped to the Ctrl key.

7. Hold the Ctrl key and open the stroke type fly-out library on the left shelf. Click the Center button, as shown in Figure 5.16. Now whenever you draw a rectangular mask using this brush, the mask will be created from the center of the brush stroke.

Figure 5.16

Turn on Center in the options within the stroke type library.

8. Hold the brush over the ShadowBox tool. You want to place the brush stroke roughly at the center of the front view of the reference image.

9. Hold the Ctrl key and drag out from the center to create a rectangular mask that covers the front view (see Figure 5.17). Don't worry too much about being absolutely precise; you'll be reshaping the rectangle in the next section.

10. Let go of the brush and you'll see a gray transparent box appear. This is the ShadowBox mesh. The next step is to whittle the shape down a little to refine it.

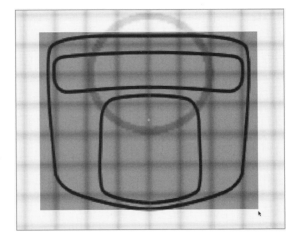

Figure 5.17

Hold the Ctrl key and drag from the center of the reference to create a rectangular mask that covers the reference image.

Using the MaskCurve Brush

To shape the front view, you can use the MaskCurve brush. The MaskCurve brush uses the Curve stroke type. This means that you use the brush to draw out a curve to define the mask. This can make your masking very precise.

To whittle down the rectangular mesh you created in the previous section, you'll actually be using the MaskCurve brush to erase parts of the mask drawn on the back of ShadowBox. This means that you'll hold the Alt key before releasing the masking brush.

Before you try it out, here's a little background on how the MaskCurve brush works. You'll draw the curve by holding the Ctrl key and dragging on the canvas. You'll see a dashed line appear as you drag. The curve starts at the point where you initially touch the canvas, and it will be a straight line as you draw it. One side of the curve is shaded with a gray gradient. This indicates which side of the curve will be masked. If you start the curve and then drag to the right, the shaded area appears on the top; if you start the curve and drag to the left, it appears on the bottom.

To make the line curved rather than straight, you add a point and then continue dragging. The point pins down a section of the curve, and then you can bend the line from there. To add a point to the curve, press the Alt key; to add a sharp corner, press the Alt key twice.

Once you release the mask by lifting the pen from the tablet (or releasing the mouse button if you're using a mouse), the area on the shaded side of the line becomes masked, and thus a mesh is created. The mask will extend all the way to the edge of the ShadowBox and so will the mesh. The following steps show how you use this technique to shape the front profile of the hot rod:

1. Open the sculpting brush fly-out library and switch the masking brush to the MaskCurve brush. This brush will now be mapped to the Ctrl key. Click the Skip Warning Until Next Restart button so you don't see the warning every time you switch masking brushes.

2. Let's take a little off the top. Hold the brush to the left of the reference image, near the top but outside of the area that has already been masked. Press the Ctrl key and drag out toward the right, as shown in the left image in Figure 5.18. Drag all the way past the center and outside of the original rectangular mask. The idea is that you'll be lopping off the corner of the rectangular mask.

3. Before you let go of the brush, press and hold the Alt key (it's OK to let go of the Ctrl key at this point). The dashed curve will turn white, indicating that you're in Erase mode.

4. Release the brush by lifting your pen from the tablet. The corners of the mask will disappear. Since Symmetry has been enabled, the corner on the other side will also disappear (see the right image in Figure 5.18).

Figure 5.18

Drag the MaskCurve brush out at an angle from left to right (left image). Release the stroke to cut off part of the top of the mask (right image).

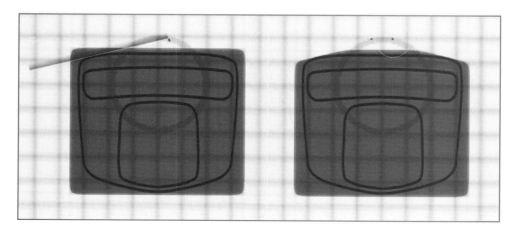

5. If instead you see two long masks shooting out at an angle, then you forgot to hold the Alt key or you let go before pressing the Alt key. This is an easy mistake to make. Just press Ctrl+Z to undo and try again.

6. To chop off any extra mask on the top, start the mask from the left side and drag toward the right. Hold the Alt key and then release to erase the little peak from the top of the mask (Figure 5.19).

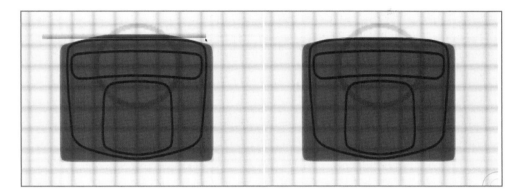

Figure 5.19
Use the MaskCurve brush to remove the very top of the mask.

Once you get the hang of refining the shape of the mask using straight lines, you can try using a curved line. To make a bend in the curve, press and release the Alt key while dragging out the curve. To make a sharper corner, press and release the Alt key twice.

7. Use Figure 5.20 as a guide for shaping the sides of the mask. Don't worry about detail at the moment; you just want to get a rough shape established. Sometimes it's easier to use series of mask curves rather than try to make a single mask curve that follows the reference perfectly.

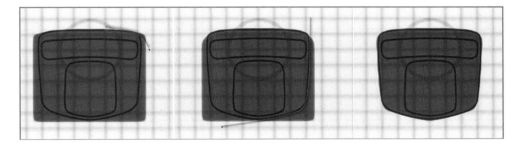

Figure 5.20
The MaskCurve brush is used to shape the mask so that it fits the shape shown in the reference image on ShadowBox.

8. When you're satisfied with how the front looks, rotate the view so you can see the result.

From the Perspective view, the mesh should look like a thick flat plane with angled corners, kind of like a piece of toast (see Figure 5.21). This is easier to see if you turn off the Transp button on the right shelf.

Figure 5.21

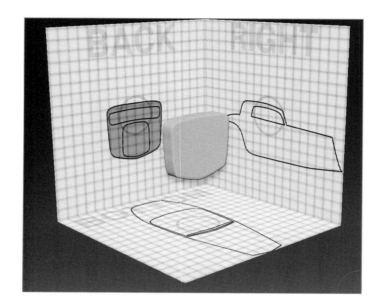

9. Rotate the view so that you can see the side view clearly (remember to hold the Shift key after you start rotating the view in order to snap to a side view), and then scale up the view so that you can clearly see the profile of the car. Turn the Transp button on the right shelf back on if it has been turned off.

10. Use the MaskRect masking brush to create a rectangle that covers the general shape of the profile. In this case, it may be easier to turn off the Center option in the Stroke palette and drag the mask out from the upper-left corner of the profile (see Figure 5.22).

Figure 5.22

Draw a rectangular mask around the overall shape of the car body profile.

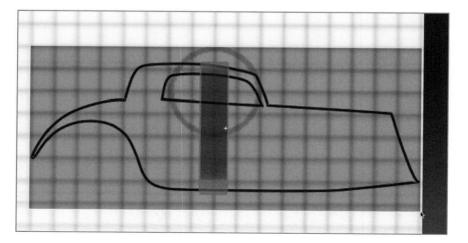

It doesn't matter how tall the mask is, only how long it is. The resulting mesh will use the mask you've already created on the back side to constrain the height and width of the mask you create on the right side.

11. Once you have created the rectangular mask, switch back to the MaskCurve brush. You'll use this brush again to whittle down the rectangular mask until it matches the profile of the car body.

12. Rotate the view a little so you can see what's going on. Ctrl+Shift+click the plane that displays the right profile of the car body to isolate its visibility.

13. Rotate the view again so that you can see the profile.

SHADOWBOX POLYGROUPING

Before you start slicing up the mask, I'd like to point out a tip that will save you some headaches while working in ShadowBox. Each side of the ShadowBox is grouped separately, as shown in the following image. This means that you can hide all of the planes of the ShadowBox except the one you are currently working on. This is helpful because a mask drawn on one side of the box can easily spill over to one of the other sides, which will cause strange behavior in the mesh created at the center. This is especially true when using the MaskCurve stroke type.

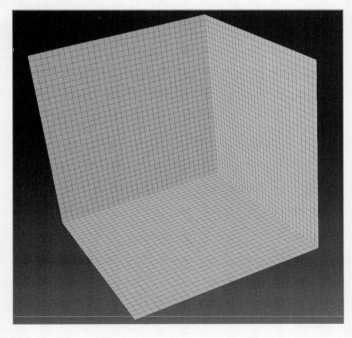

continues

continued

When you use the MaskCurve brush, the mask is generated on the shaded side of the curve, and the mask continues on to infinity out into space. So let's say you use the MaskCurve to erase part of the mask near the back of the car. When you release the mask and then look at the mesh in Perspective view, the top part has been chopped off, ruining all the work you did on the front. This is because the mask shoots out from the curve and erases not only part of the mask on the right side but also part of the mask on the back side.

The solution to this problem is simple. Since each plane is a polygroup, just Ctrl+Shift+click the plane you need to work on and the other planes will be hidden. If part of the ShadowBox is hidden, the masking brush won't affect it, so you won't lose parts of your model. You can see this in the following image where the back side of ShadowBox has been hidden. Now the MaskCurve brush can easily be used on the side view of the car.

Remember that you can Ctrl+Shift+click a polygroup to isolate its visibility, Ctrl+Shift+click it again to invert visibility, and Ctrl+Shift+click on a blank part of the canvas to unhide everything.

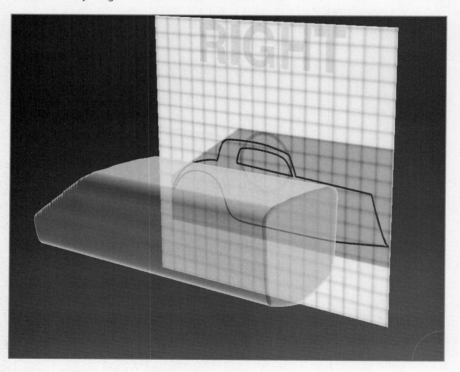

You'll continue to use the MaskCurve brush to work on the car, but now you'll add points to the stroke's curve so you can match the curves of the profile. You'll start at the back of the car, work your way around the top toward the front, and then work back toward the wheel well. This will take several strokes; it's not something you can do using a single curve.

To add a point to a curve, press and release the Alt key while dragging the curve out. Keep your curves as simple as possible.

14. Click near the back of the car and drag up toward the right along the curved edge of the rear of the car. Press and release the Alt key to add a point. Try to match the arc of the rear of the car. You should need to add only two points to match this curve in the reference image (see Figure 5.23, top).

15. When you reach the point where the rear trunk meets the back of the car's top (where the rear window is), tap the Alt key twice. This adds two points on top of each other, allowing for a sharp corner. Drag the curve up past the top of the car (see Figure 5.24, middle image).

16. Press and hold the Alt key and release the masking brush. The resulting mask should match the back of the car. It may take a couple of tries at first until you get used to creating masking curves.

17. Create another curve to form the rounded back of the top (see Figure 5.24, bottom image).

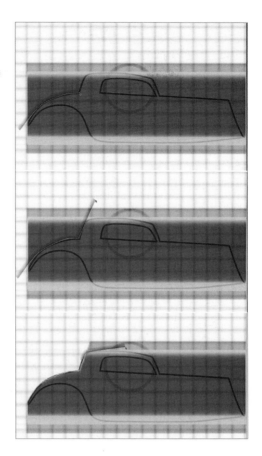

Figure 5.23

Draw the curve to match the shape of the trunk and the back of the car's top.

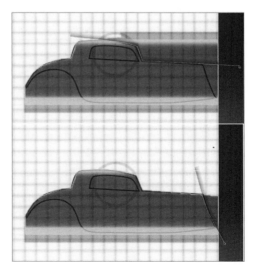

Figure 5.24

The profile of the top of the car is formed by using the MaskCurve brush to cut out parts of the mask.

Now you can create a curve that forms the roof, windshield, and hood (see Figure 5.24).

18. Finally, use a series of curves to refine the bottom. This time start each curve from the right and drag toward the left. The shaded side of the curve will face downward so that when you hold the Alt key and release the masking brush, the bottom parts of the mask will be erased. At this point, don't worry about creating the wheel well (see Figure 5.25).

19. This is a good place to save the project. Click the Save As button in the File menu to save the project as **HotRod_v01.ZPR**.

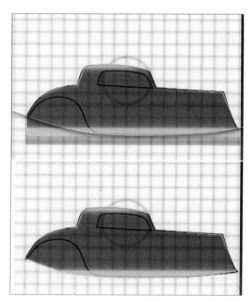

Figure 5.25

Use the MaskCurve brush to refine the bottom edge of the car.

Using the MaskCircle Brush

The MaskCircle brush simply creates the mask in the shape of an oval. This can be used to cut out the wheel well in the profile of the car. As with the MaskRect brush, you can activate the Center option so that the mask is created from the center of the stroke:

1. Continue with the project from the previous section.

2. Open the sculpting brush fly-out library and press M and then C to switch to the MaskCircle brush. Remember that this brush is active only while you hold the Ctrl key.

3. Hold the Ctrl key, open the stroke type fly-out library on the left shelf, and turn on the Center button.

4. Turn on the Square button as well. This means that the circle fits within a square area, so instead of being an oval it will be a perfect circle (see Figure 5.26).

5. Hold the Ctrl key and drag outward from the center of the circular area of the wheel well.

Figure 5.26

Turn on the Square and Center buttons in the stroke type fly-out library for the Mask Circle brush.

6. It's usually impossible to get the mask perfectly placed the first time you drag it out, but this is an easy problem to solve. Before you release the mask, hold the spacebar. You can then move the mask around until you find the best position. This technique also works with the other type of mask brushes, such as MaskRect and MaskCurve.

7. Once you have the mask positioned, hold the Alt key and release. This will cut a hole into the mask in the shape of a circle (see Figure 5.27).

8. Once you have used the MaskCircle brush to cut out the wheel well, switch back to the MaskCurve brush and use the curve to try to make the mask match the reference image a little better (see Figure 5.28).

9. Save the project as **HotRod_v02.ZPR.**

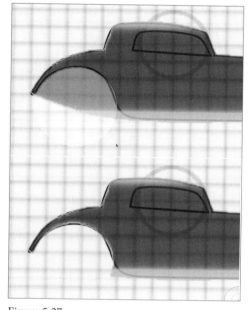

Figure 5.27

The MaskCircle brush is used to cut a circular hole for the wheel well.

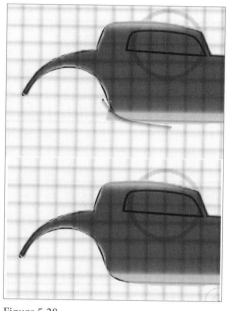

Figure 5.28

The extra parts of the mask are trimmed away using the MaskCurve brush so that the mask matches the profile.

Creating the Top View of the Hot Rod

If you rotate the view of the ShadowBox, the mesh at the center looks a little jagged or "chunky." That's okay. As you create the final mask for the top view, you'll see that the mesh becomes a bit smoother again. Here are the steps:

1. Continue with the project from the previous section or open the HotRod_v02.ZPR project you saved.

2. Rotate the view of the ShadowBox so that you can see the mesh. Hold Ctrl+Shift and click on a blank part of the canvas to unhide the rest of the box.

3. Hold Ctrl+Shift and click on the bottom plane of the ShadowBox tool to hide everything but the bottom.

4. Rotate the view so you can see the ShadowBox from the top. Press X to activate Symmetry.

5. Use the MaskRect brush to draw a rectangle around the top of the reference image. It's easy to forget to do this, and then when you start to refine the edges, it seems as though nothing is happening. Don't forget to first create a rectangular mask that covers the top view of the car, and then use the MaskCurve brush to shape the rectangular mask.

6. Use the MaskCurve brush to make the edges of the mask match the reference image. Use Figure 5.29 as a guide.

7. Save the file as **HotRod_v03.ZPR**.

Figure 5.29

Use the MaskCurve brush to trim the mask from the top view.

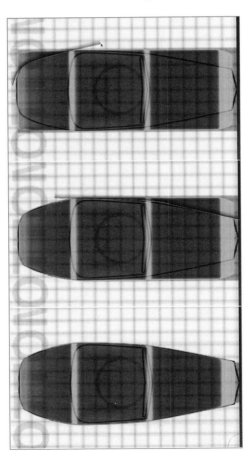

Using the MaskLasso Brush to Create Windows

To finish off the basic body of the hot rod, you can cut holes in the top for the windows. Using the MaskCurve brush won't work because you can't form a closed loop with the curve. Since the mask is created on one side of the curve, ZBrush won't understand how to create the mask when you try to make a loop. Instead, you can use the MaskLasso brush:

1. Continue with the project from the previous section or open HotRod_v03 .ZPR.

2. Hold the Ctrl key and select the Mask Lasso brush. Remember that the brush is active only when you hold the Ctrl key.

3. Rotate the view of the hot rod so that you can see the right side.

4. Hold the Ctrl key and use the lasso to draw a shape roughly matching the window. Hold the Alt key before releasing the brush so that the mask is in Erase mode; otherwise nothing will happen when you let go of the brush (see Figure 5.30).

Figure 5.30

Use the MaskLasso brush to create a window in the side view.

> **MASKLASSO OR MASKPEN?**
>
> The great thing about having so many masking options is that you can choose whichever mask brush fits your own modeling style. If you find that the MaskLasso brush is hard to use, try switching to MaskPen. Using MaskPen, you can hold the Alt key and simply erase the window area on the ShadowBox plane. It's really up to you which method you prefer.

5. Rotate the view of the ShadowBox so that you can see the back plane. Use the same technique to create the front windshield. Make sure Symmetry is active so that you only have to draw the mask on one side of the windshield (see Figure 5.31).

6. Click the Save As button in the File menu to save the project as HotRod_v04.ZPR.

Congratulations! You've created your first ShadowBox model. The next step is to use the clip brushes to refine the edges, but before you get to that you can use a few more tricks in ShadowBox to create hubcaps for the wheels.

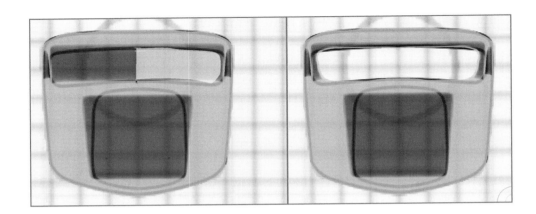

Using Radial Symmetry in ShadowBox

ShadowBox is a great way to explore shapes. Once you start to combine techniques, you can create some really interesting things. In this exercise, you'll look at some approaches for creating stylish hubcaps for the hot rod:

1. Start a fresh ZBrush session. Open Light Box to the Tool section and double-click the ShadowBox128.ZTL tool. Draw it on the canvas and switch to Edit mode.

2. To make nice, crisp designs in ShadowBox, you'll want to increase the resolution. In the Geometry subpalette of the Tool palette, turn the ShadowBox button off. This will make the Resolution slider available. Set the slider to **256**.

3. Click the ShadowBox button to turn it back on. After a few seconds it will appear. It will likely be filled with a cubical mesh. Ctrl+drag on a blank part of the screen to clear the mask from the sides of the ShadowBox. This will make the cubical volume disappear.

4. In the material fly-out library on the left shelf, select the skinShade4 material so you can easily see the grid texture on the tool.

5. Turn off the Persp button on the right shelf, and turn on Transp and Ghost.

6. Click the Frame button on the right shelf to center the view of ShadowBox (hotkey = F).

7. Turn on the L.Sym button on the right shelf so that Symmetry will be in line with the center of the back view of the ShadowBox.

8. Expand the sculpting brush fly-out library, and press M and then C to switch to the MaskCircle brush.

9. In the stroke type fly-out library, make sure the Square and Center buttons are on so that you can easily draw a perfect circle. (The Square button just makes sure that the mask is perfectly round, that is, it fits into a square.)

10. In the Transform palette, turn on Activate Symmetry if it's not on already. Turn on the >Z< button so that Symmetry is activated on the z-axis. Turn on the (R) button so that Radial Symmetry is active, and set RadialCount to **5** (see Figure 5.32).

Using Radial Symmetry, you can easily find the exact center of the back view of the ShadowBox.

Figure 5.32

Turn on Radial Symmetry on the z-axis and set RadialCount to 5.

11. Hover the brush over the ShadowBox. You'll see five red dots; these are the brush tips. Bring them toward the center until you see a single point. Hold the Ctrl key and drag outward to create a circular mask (the left image in Figure 5.33).

12. Let go of the brush to create the mask. The mesh at the center of the ShadowBox will be a circular disc (right image in Figure 5.33).

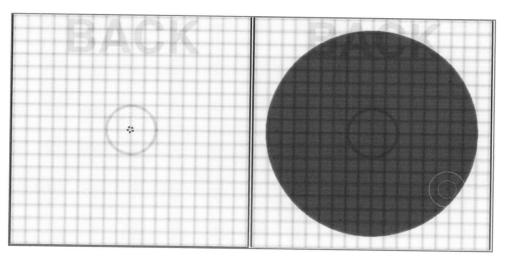

Figure 5.33

Use the five brush points to find the center of the back side of the ShadowBox. Create a circular mask from the center.

Now for the fun part. You can start to experiment with designs using Radial Symmetry. This can get a bit addictive.

13. Move the brush tip away from the center of the ShadowBox so that you see five red dots. Hold the Ctrl key and drag to create a circular mask. Make a small circle above the center. Hold the Alt key and release the brush to cut a circular hole into the mask (the left and center images in Figure 5.34). Five holes appear around the mask.

14. Create a second series of larger circles slightly offset from the first. The result is a nice "bat wing" design for the hubcap (the right image in Figure 5.34).

Figure 5.34

Figure 5.34

Circular masks are used to cut holes in the original mask. Using Radial Symmetry, you can easily create a pattern.

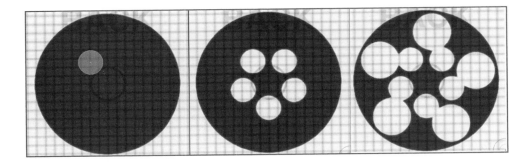

Experiment with different variations. You can try turning off the Square option in the stroke type fly-out library and use ovals. Try using the MaskRect brush. Add more or less detail if you want. Figure 5.35 shows a few variations using different masking techniques. Try making freeform shapes using the MaskLasso brush. Remember that you can hold the spacebar to reposition the mask before you release the masking brush.

Figure 5.35

Use a variety of mask brushes and Radial Symmetry to come up with alternate hubcap designs.

Using Alpha Textures within ShadowBox

You can apply alpha textures to the masking brush to create precise designs. These can be the alpha textures that come with ZBrush or even your own custom textures that you can create in paint programs such as Photoshop, Painter, and Illustrator. Follow these steps:

1. Continue with the hubcap design you created in the previous section. Make sure Radial Symmetry is still active along the z-axis.

2. Open the sculpting brush fly-out library and press M and then R to switch to the MaskRect brush. This is the best masking brush to use when you want to apply alpha textures to the ShadowBox. (Don't confuse this stroke type with the DragRect brush. You can use DragRect, but the alpha will be blurry and the resulting mesh will not be as well defined).

3. Open the alpha texture fly-out library on the right shelf and choose Alpha 09. This is a simple circle alpha (see Figure 5.36).

4. Hold the Ctrl key and drag out across the back of the ShadowBox, and then release the brush to create the mask (see Figure 5.37).

Figure 5.36

Select the MaskRect brush and choose Alpha 09.

Try variations to see what kind of designs you can create with this texture. You can also click the Import button in the Alpha palette to import your own alpha textures, as shown in Figure 5.38. The textures you import must be grayscale textures saved in TIFF, Photoshop, or BMP format.

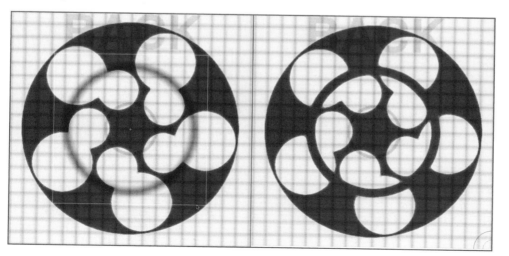

Figure 5.37

Using an alpha texture with the MaskRect brush allows you to add complexity to your hubcap design.

Figure 5.38

You can import custom alpha textures to create even more complex designs.

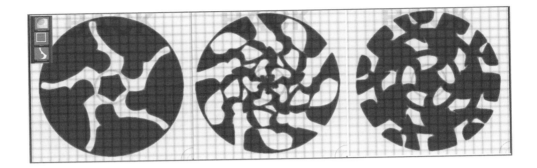

MatchMaker Brush

The purpose of the MatchMaker brush is to make one surface conform to another. For example, you can round the shape of the hubcap so that it's no longer a flat piece by using Match Maker to push the surface against a PolySphere. In this section you'll do just that. The technique is very easy to use and a lot of fun:

1. Open the HubCap_v01.ZTL tool from the Chapter 5 folder on the DVD. Draw the hubcap tool on the canvas and switch to Edit mode (hotkey = T).

2. The hubcap is currently still a ShadowBox object. Open the SubTool subpalette of the Tool palette and turn the ShadowBox button off. Now the hubcap is a mesh that you can sculpt with any of the sculpting brushes (see Figure 5.39).

You'll need a round surface to act as a template for the MatchMaker brush. A slightly flattened PolySphere should work just fine.

3. Open Light Box to the Tool section and double-click the PolySphere to load it into ZBrush. The canvas will automatically switch to the PolySphere in Edit mode. Don't worry if the hubcap disappears; it is still available in the Tool palette.

Figure 5.39

The hubcap is now a sculptable mesh.

4. Open the SubTool subpalette of the Tool palette and click the Append button. Choose the hubcap to append it to the PolySphere.

5. On the right shelf, click the Transp button and rotate the view. You should see the hubcap appear as a transparent object inside the PolySphere.

6. Chances are the hubcap and the PolySphere are not aligned very well (Figure 5.40). There is a quick way to fix this. Select the hubcap in the SubTool subpalette of the Tool palette. Expand the Deformation subpalette of the Tool palette, and click the Unify button at the top.

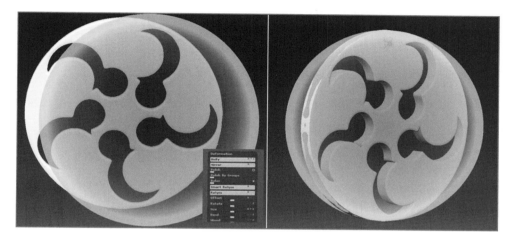

Figure 5.40

The hubcap is out of alignment with the PolySphere tool.

The MatchMaker brush pushes the selected subtool up against the other visible sub-tools to make the surfaces conform. For it to work properly, there should be no empty space behind the selected subtool, so the PolySphere needs to be scaled up a little so that the edges of the hubcap don't get distorted (see Figure 5.41).

7. In the SubTool subpalette of the Tool palette, select the PolySphere subtool. Expand the Deformations palette. Click the Size deformer slider so that the numeric value appears highlighted in red. Type the number **10** and press Enter. You'll see the PolySphere grow slightly so that now the hubcap easily fits inside.

8. Rotate the view of the PolySphere and hubcap so that you can see them from the side. In the Deformations subpalette, click the x and the y letters to the right of the Size slider to turn off these axes. Drag the Size slider all the way to the left; this will flatten the PolySphere a little (see Figure 5.42, left image).

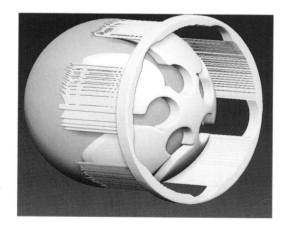

Figure 5.41

If there is empty space behind the subtool, the Match Maker brush will not function properly.

Figure 5.42

The PolySphere is flattened and moved to the left of the hubcap in the side view. From the front view the hub-cap is ready to be pressed against the PolySphere with the MatchMaker brush.

Figure 5.43

The MatchMaker brush is selected in the sculpting brush library.

9. In the Deformations subpalette of the Tool palette, turn off the x and y buttons for the Offset deformer. Drag the Offset slider to the right until the PolySphere appears to the left of the hubcap (see Figure 5.42, middle image).

10. Switch to the HubCap subtool and rotate the view so that you can see the hubcap straight on from the front (see right image in Figure 5.42). Turn off the Transp button on the right shelf.

11. Open the sculpting brush fly-out library. Press M and then M again to switch to the MatchMaker brush (see Figure 5.43).

12. On the top shelf, make sure the Zsub button is on. Set Z Intensity to **40**. At this strength you'll be able to deform the hubcap against the PolySphere while still having a fair amount of control.

13. Turn off Symmetry (hotkey = X). Position the brush at the center of the hubcap and then drag outward. You'll see the hubcap change, although it won't be clear what's happening until you've finished.

14. Once you've dragged all the way out past the edge of the hubcap, let go of the brush and rotate the view. You'll see that the hubcap now appears rounded, matching the surface of the PolySphere. The design on the hubcap has been preserved (see Figure 5.44).

Figure 5.44

The hubcap appears rounded after using the MatchMaker brush.

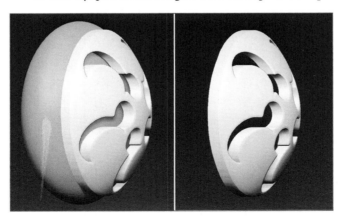

The MatchMaker brush is extremely useful and versatile. In the Tool section of Light Box, you'll find several example tools named MatchMaker1.ZTL, MatchMaker2.ZTL, and so on. These have been set up for you to experiment with.

15. In the SubTool subpalette of the Tool palette, select the PolySphere subtool. Click the Delete button at the bottom of the SubTool subpalette to remove the PolySphere. Click the Save As button in the Tool palette to save the tool as **HubCap_v02.ZTL**.

Clip Brushes

The ZBrush clip brushes are particularly well suited for hard-surface modeling, and, among their many possible applications, they do a good job of refining the edges of meshes created in ShadowBox.

Clip brushes use the same stroke types as the masking and selection brushes—namely the rectangular, circle, lasso, and curve stroke types. They are used to slice away parts of the surface, but it is important to understand that they don't actually delete geometry; rather, they squash the selected polygons so that they conform to the selected shape. Imagine taking a lump of clay and squashing it down on a flat surface; that's the basic idea behind how clip brushes work. Clip brushes work really well when combined with Dynamesh as a way to create hard-surface objects. After you flatten an edge with a clip brush, you can then "dynamesh" the surface, which will eliminate the "squished" polygons and rebuild the topology of the surface while retaining the hard edges.

In the following exercises, you'll get a taste for the kinds of things you can do with these brushes, but the creative possibilities stretch far beyond this simple introduction. Let's start by trying the brushes out on a PolySphere.

Clip Brush Basics

There are a few rules you have to be aware of when using the clip brushes. An understanding of these rules will help you make sense of how the brushes work. Clip brushes are automatically mapped to the Ctrl+Shift hotkey, just like the selection brushes. When you choose ClipCircle, ClipCircleCenter, ClipCurve, or ClipRect, you'll get a warning that lets you know that these brushes are activated by holding Ctrl+Shift together. Be aware that both the clip brushes and the selection brushes share the Ctrl+Shift hotkeys.

This example demonstrates the basics of using the clip brushes.

1. Start a fresh session of ZBrush, open Light Box to the Tool section, and double-click the PolySphere.ZTL tool. Make sure the tool is on the canvas and that Edit mode is enabled on the top shelf.

2. From the material fly-out library, choose the skinShade4 material.

3. On the right shelf, activate the PolyF button (hotkey = Shift+F) so that you can see the wireframe display on the polygons.

4. Open the sculpting brush fly-out library and press C and then R to choose the ClipRect brush. A warning appears reminding you that this brush is activated by holding Ctrl+Shift together (see Figure 5.45). Click the Skip This Note Until Next Restart button so that the next time you choose a Clip brush, you don't see the warning.

Figure 5.45

The ClipRect brush is assigned to the Ctrl+Shift hotkey combination.

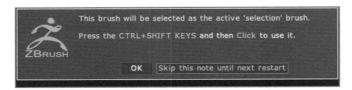

5. Make sure Symmetry is disabled.

6. Hold Ctrl+Shift and drag the rectangular shape over the top two-thirds of the PolySphere (see Figure 5.46, left image). When you release the brush, it appears as though the bottom has been chopped off (see Figure 5.46, middle image).

Figure 5.46

The ClipRect brush squashes all the polygons outside the rectangular selection so that they fit within the selection area.

7. Rotate the view and zoom in so that you can see the bottom. You can see that the polygons have not been deleted; they've just been flattened (see Figure 5.46, right image).

All the polygons outside the selected area are pushed up so that they fit within the rectangular selection.

8. Press Ctrl+Z to undo the last action. The PolySphere should return to its rounded state.

9. Now hold Ctrl+Shift and select just the upper third of the PolySphere (see Figure 5.47, left image).

The bottom two-thirds disappear, but notice that when you rotate the view, you can see what appears to be a flattened lip around the edge of the remaining section (see Figure 5.47, right image). This is because the lower two-thirds are pushed straight up to meet the outer edge of the selection rectangle, but they are not pushed inward toward the center. This creates a flattened rim. When using the clip brushes, keep this in mind.

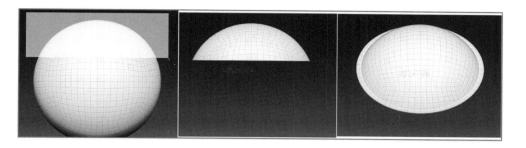

Figure 5.47

The top third is selected using the ClipRect brush, but this leaves a very thin lip around the edges of the selected area.

Holding the Alt key inverts the selection so that polygons within the selected area are pushed out of the selected area. Be careful when using this technique with the ClipRect brush because it usually creates very strange results (see Figure 5.48).

You can use the Square option in the stroke type fly-out library to make the selected area a perfect square and the Center option so that the selection starts at the center of the stroke rather than at the corner. To turn these on, hold Ctrl+Shift and open the stroke type fly-out library on the right shelf. Click the Square and Circle buttons.

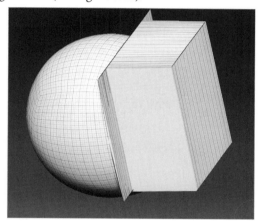

Figure 5.48

Holding the Alt key before releasing the ClipRect brush inverts the clipping action but can cause some odd results.

You can reposition the selection area before you release the brush. Just hold the spacebar and drag on the canvas. This allows you to precisely position the clipping area.

Using the ClipCircle Brush

The ClipCircle brush works just like the ClipRect brush except that the selection area is circular:

1. Press Ctrl+Z to undo any changes you've made to the PolySphere.

2. Open the sculpting brush fly-out library and choose the ClipCircle brush.

3. Hold Ctrl+Shift and drag an oval over the top two-thirds of the PolySphere. Release the brush.

Just as with the ClipRect brush, the area outside the selection is clipped away. When you rotate the view, you can see how the polygons outside the circular selection are pushed up to match the edges of the circle (see Figure 5.49).

Figure 5.49

The ClipCircle brush clips away everything outside of the circular selection area.

4. Press Ctrl+Z to undo the last action.

5. Press Ctrl+D twice to add two more subdivisions to the PolySphere.

6. Hold Ctrl+Shift and drag a small circular selection on top of the PolySphere. Hold the Alt key and release.

The result is strange but also kind of interesting. The polygons are pushed out of the selected area as much as possible, resulting in a flattened circular plane within the PolySphere. This can be used for interesting details (see Figure 5.50). This kind of detail is perfect for robotic or mechanical details. Notice that the wireframe on the PolySphere shows how this technique distorts the topology of the surface.

Figure 5.50

Hold the Alt key before releasing the ClipCircle brush on a small section of the PolySphere to create interesting details.

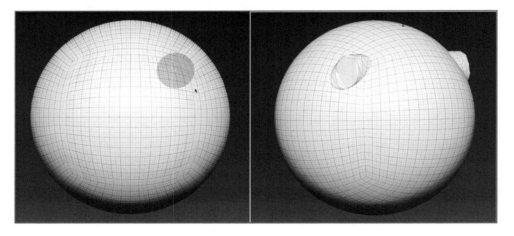

The ClipCircleCenter brush is just like the ClipCircle brush except that the Center and Square options in the stroke type fly-out library are already enabled.

7. Spend a few minutes experimenting with the ClipCircle and ClipRect brushes. They take a little practice to get used to. As you'll soon discover, they are great tools for creating crisp edges and details for hard-surface models.

CLIP BRUSH CENTER

At the center of the clip brush boundary, you'll see a little plus sign indicating the center of the selection area. When using the Clip Circle brushclip brush and the Alt key together to cut away part of a surface, you'll get better results if the plus sign remains outside the mesh.

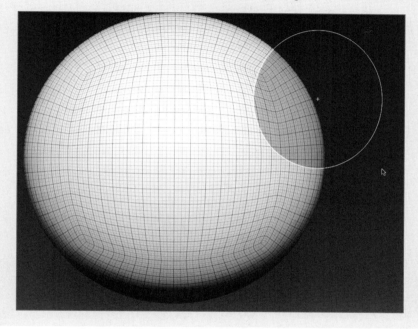

Creating a Tire Using Clip Brushes

Now let's get some practice using these techniques to create a tire for the hot rod. You'll use the ClipRect and ClipCircle brushes to shape a torus into a tire:

1. Start a fresh session of ZBrush.

2. In the Tool palette, open the tool fly-out library and select the Ring3D tool. Draw the tool on the canvas and switch to Edit mode.

   The Ring3D tool is a parametric 3D tool, meaning that it can't be edited using the sculpting brushes—including the clip brushes. You can convert it into a polymesh object, but first you can establish a few settings just to thicken it up a little.

3. At the bottom of the Tool palette, expand the Initialize subpalette.

4. Set SRadius to **60**. Set SDivide to **40** and LDivide to **80** (see Figure 5.51).

5. At the top of the Tool palette, click the Make PolyMesh 3D button. At this point the object has been converted into a sculptable mesh.

Figure 5.51

Set SRadius and the divisions in the Initialize palette.

6. In the material fly-out library, choose the Basic material.

7. Press **Ctrl+D** twice to add two levels of subdivision to the mesh.

8. Rotate the view of the tire so that you can see it from the side, as shown in the left image in Figure 5.52.

9. In the Transform palette, turn on the Activate Symmetry button. Turn the >Z< button on and the >X< button off so that symmetry is created along the z-axis.

10. Hold Ctrl+Shift and drag out a selection box starting from the right and moving to the left. The box should cover most of the torus, as shown in the middle image of Figure 5.52. Release the brush. The tire will be flattened on both sides because Symmetry has been activated, as shown in the right image of Figure 5.52.

Figure 5.52

The ClipRect brush is used to flatten the sides of the tire.

Next you'll use the ClipCircleCenter brush to flatten the area of the tire tread. However, it can be a little tricky to find the center of the tire since there's a big hole at the center. Using Radial Symmetry can help with this problem.

11. In the Transform palette, turn on Radial Symmetry and set Radial Count to **16**. Remember that to turn on Radial Symmetry you need to first activate Symmetry (hotkey = X) and then turn on the R button in the Transform palette.

12. Rotate the view of the tire so that you can see it from the front.

13. From the sculpting brush library, choose the ClipCircleCenter brush.

14. Hold Ctrl+Shift and drag out from the center of the tire. Drag just so the edge of the selection circle is about halfway between the flattened edge of the tire and the outer edge, as shown in the left image of Figure 5.53.

Figure 5.53
**The edges of the tire
are flattened using
the ClipCircleCenter
brush.**

15. Before you release the brush, hold the spacebar and move the selection circle. Try to center the selection with the tire as well as you can. Radial Symmetry will ensure that the clipping remains fairly circular.

16. Let go of the clipping brush to flatten the outer edge of the tire (see Figure 5.53, right image).

17. Repeat steps 14 and 15, but this time align the selection brush with the inner edge of the flattened side of the tire. Once it's aligned, drag back toward the center.

18. Hold the Alt key and release the brush. This will flatten out the inside edge of the tire. This is a little tricky and may take you a couple tries to get perfect (see Figure 5.54).

Figure 5.54
**The inside edge
of the tire is flat-
tened using the
ClipCircleCenter
brush.**

19. If you want to make the tire a little wider, expand the Deformations palette, turn off the x and y buttons to the right of the Size slider, and move the slider to the right.

20. Click the Save As button in the Tool palette to save the tool as **tire_v01.ZTL**.

Brush Radius and PolyGroup Clip Brush Options

You can activate two options that affect how the brushes clip the surface: Brush Radius and PolyGroup. The Brush Radius option constrains the size of the clipping based on the current radius of the brush. The PolyGroup option automatically divides the object into polygroups based on the clipped areas. These options are found in the Clip Brush Modifiers subpalette of the Brush palette. In this section you'll use these options to add a little detail to the hubcap.

1. Continue with the tire model you created in the last section or open the tire_v01.ZTL tool.

2. Open HubCap_v02.ZTL, which you created earlier in the chapter, using the Load Tool button in the Tool palette.

3. In the SubTool subpalette of the Tool palette, click the Append button. Choose the tire_v01.ZTL tool from the fly-out tool library to append it to the hubcap.

4. Turn on the Transp button on the right shelf. Expand the Deformation subpalette of the Tool palette.

5. Make sure the x, y, and z buttons are all active to the right of the Size slider. Move the slider to the left to scale down the hubcap so that it fits within the center of the tire (see Figure 5.55).

Figure 5.55

The hubcap is scaled down to fit within the tire.

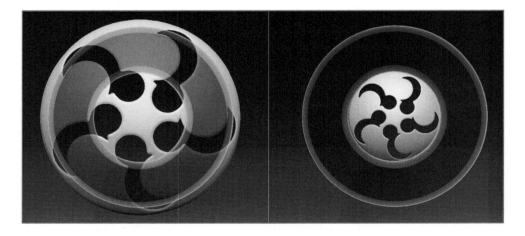

6. Rotate the view of the tire to the side. In the Deformations subpalette of the Tool palette, turn off the x button next to Offset and turn on the z button. Move the slider to the left to move the hubcap out a bit (see Figure 5.56).

7. Turn off the Transp button.

8. Hold Ctrl+Shift. In the sculpting brush fly-out library on the right shelf, select the ClipCircle brush. Turn on Radial Symmetry on the z-axis for the hubcap if it's not already on.

9. Set the Draw Size slider on the top shelf to **10**.

10. Rotate the view of the tire so that you can see the hubcap face on. Position the brush at the center of the hubcap.

11. Open the Brush palette and expand the Clip Brush Modifiers subpalette; turn on both the BRadius and the PolyGroup buttons, as shown in Figure 5.57.

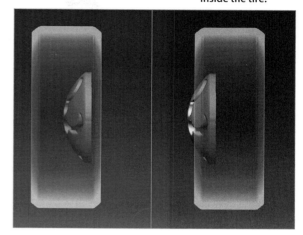

Figure 5.56

The hubcap is moved out from inside the tire.

12. Hold Ctrl+Shift and drag outward from the center, as shown in left image in Figure 5.58.

13. Hold the Alt key and release the brush. This creates a groove in the hubcap (see Figure 5.58, center and right images).

   Because the BRadius option is on, the size of the clip is restricted by the Draw Size setting on the top shelf. This is a great technique for creating hard-surface details such as grooves.

14. Turn on the PolyF button on the right shelf. You'll see that the face of the hubcap is now divided into polygroups based on the clipped area.

15. Save the tool as **wheel_v01.ZTL**. Save it to the ZBrush 4/ZTools folder so that it appears in the Tool section of Light Box.

Figure 5.57

Turn on the BRadius and PolyGroup button.

Figure 5.58

Create a circular selection with the clip brush. A groove is created in the hubcap because the BRadius option is on.

CLIP BRUSH OPTIONS HOTKEY

If you're using a clip brush you can access the BRadius and PolyGroup options by holding the spacebar. This means you're holding the Ctrl+Shift keys and the spacebar all at the same time. A little pop-up menu appears on the canvas that lets you turn these options on or off.

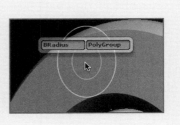

Using the ClipCurve Brush

The ClipCurve brush uses a curve stroke type and is similar to the MaskCurve brush except that instead of masking an area, it clips it so that all the polygons on the shaded side of the curve are squashed to match the shape of the curve. The ClipCurve brush is great for designing complex surfaces and also works well for refining the meshes you make with ShadowBox.

Let's take a look at how the ClipCurve brush works by trying it out on a PolySphere:

1. Start a fresh session of ZBrush, open Light Box to the Tool section, and double-click the PolySphere.ZTL tool. Make sure that the tool is on the canvas and that Edit mode is enabled on the top shelf.

2. From the material fly-out library, choose the skinShade4 material.

3. On the right shelf, activate the PolyF button so that you can see the wireframe display on the polygons.

4. Open the sculpting brush fly-out library and press C and then C again to choose the ClipCurve brush. If this is a new session of ZBrush, you'll see the familiar warning advising you that the brush is mapped to Ctrl+Shift.

5. Hold the Ctrl and Shift keys and start a curve above and to the right of the PolySphere. Drag out a straight line that goes down past the right corner of the center of the PolySphere. The shaded side of the curve should be on the right of the curve line.

6. Release the brush. You'll see that the side of the PolySphere is now flattened (see Figure 5.59). The clipping action goes all the way through the surface in a direction that is perpendicular to the canvas.

Figure 5.59

The surface is clipped on the right, the shaded side of the curve.

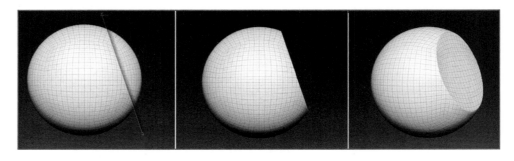

CURVE SNAPPING

You need to hold Ctrl+Shift only long enough to activate the brush and start the curve. Once the curve is started, you can let go of Ctrl+Shift. If you continue to hold the Shift key, the curve will snap to specific angle increments. This can be helpful in creating precise curves, but it can be confusing when you're just getting the hang of using the brush. If you notice that the curve is snapping from one angle to the next, let go of the Ctrl+Shift keys.

7. Press Ctrl+Z to undo and return the PolySphere to its unclipped state.

8. Now start a curve below and to the left of the center of the PolySphere; this time drag upward.

9. As you drag the curve up through the PolySphere, press the Alt key to add a point, and then change directions as you drag to make a curve. Add a few more points and then let go. The PolySphere is clipped so that it matches the curve (see Figure 5.60).

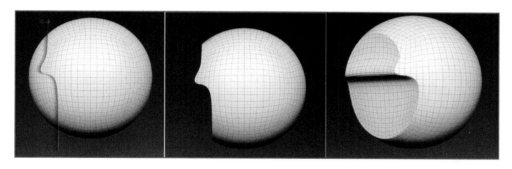

Figure 5.60
The clipped surface matches the contour of the curve.

There is a limit to the types of curves you can create. A curve that loops around will mangle the surface or create unpredictable results. Remember that all the polygons of the surface are squashed against the form of the curve in a straight line, so if the curve loops around, ZBrush will have a hard time clipping the surface (see Figure 5.61).

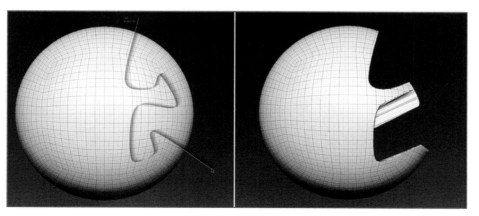

Figure 5.61
Complex curves cause unpredictable results when using the clip brush.

It's also important to pay attention to which side of the curve is shaded. If you drag the curve downward, the shaded side will be on the right; if you drag upward, the shaded side will be on the left. If you drag from right to left, the shaded side will be on top, and from right to left, the shaded side will be on the bottom. The shaded side is the clipping side. Holding the Alt key inverts the function of the brush so that the unshaded side becomes the clipping side. While you are first getting used to the way the brush works, avoid using the Alt key. Once you get the hang of it, you can start experimenting with using the Alt function.

If you need to reposition the curve, hold the spacebar and drag before releasing the brush. This is very helpful because it can be hard to draw the curve exactly where you want it on the first try. Typically you'll create a curve, then hold the spacebar and reposition the curve, and then let go. After a little practice this becomes somewhat second nature.

10. Press Ctrl+Z to undo and return the PolySphere to its unclipped state. Press X to activate Symmetry along the x-axis.

11. Rotate the view of the PolySphere so that you can see two red dots when you hold the brush over the surface.

12. Use the ClipCurve brush to create a curving line down the right side of the surface. Release the brush. The surface is clipped symmetrically on both sides (see Figure 5.62).

Figure 5.62

The surface is clipped symmetrically along the x-axis.

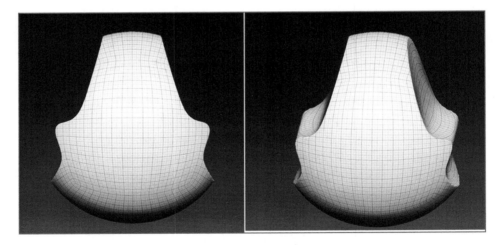

Using Symmetry with the clip brush, you can create some really interesting shapes, but be aware that if you draw a curve that crosses over the center while Symmetry is enabled, you'll get some strange results because the clipping action of one curve will overlap the area clipped by the symmetry (see Figure 5.63). Try using Radial Symmetry with the curve to create an interesting shape (see Figure 5.64).

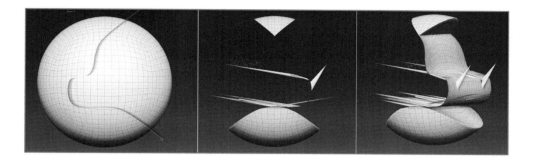

Figure 5.63

Curves that overlap the center point of the surface while Symmetry is enabled can cause unpredictable results.

Figure 5.64

Use Radial Symmetry to create interesting shapes.

There is no ClipLasso brush in the Brush palette, but you can use the Lasso stroke type with the clip brushes. To select this stroke type, select one of the clip brushes and then, while holding Ctrl+Shift, open the stroke type fly-out library and choose Lasso.

Refining the Car Body Using Clip Brushes

In this section, you'll get some hands-on experience using the ClipCurve brush to neaten up the edges of the hot rod car body created in ShadowBox. The general idea is to use the brush to refine the edges and prepare the model for detailing with the sculpting brushes. Here are the steps:

1. Click the Open button in the File menu to open the HotRod_v04.ZPR project you created earlier in this chapter.

2. At this point the body is still a ShadowBox tool. Expand the SubTool subpalette of the Tool palette and turn off the ShadowBox button to convert the mesh into a surface that can be sculpted.

3. Make sure the Persp button on the right shelf is off. The brushes work best when the tool is not in Perspective mode.

4. Rotate the view so that you can see the model from the side view. Open the sculpting brush fly-out library and press C and then C again to select the ClipCurve brush.

5. Scale up the view so that you are zoomed in to the car's roof. You'll use the curve to refine the back of the car's top.

6. Hold Ctrl+Shift and start a curve by clicking to the left of the car, as shown in the left image of Figure 5.65.

7. Let go of Ctrl+ Shift but drag the curve up to the right. Press the Alt key to add a bend in the curve. You want to create a curve that matches the shape of the top of the car. At the moment it's OK to draw the curve away from the car (see Figure 5.65, left image).

Figure 5.65

Draw the clip curve to match the contour of the surface, and then hold the spacebar to position the curve over the surface. Release to create the clip.

8. When you have a curve that you like, hold the spacebar and drag the entire car up so that it overlaps the edge of the surface slightly (see Figure 5.65, middle image). Release the brush to create the clip (see Figure 5.65, right image).

If you mess up, just press Ctrl+Z and try again. It usually takes a couple of tries. Even experienced users have to try a few times to get exactly the curve they want. The beauty of computer graphics is that you can undo the action, as opposed to sculpting in the real world where it is possible to permanently ruin your work!

9. Repeat these steps to refine the outside edges of the car's profile, as shown in Figure 5.66. Remember that to make a sharp angle, tap the Alt key twice.

10. For the wheel well, you can try using the ClipCurve brush or switch to the ClipCircleCenter brush. Position the circular selection but hold the Alt key before releasing to create the circular clip (see Figure 5.67).

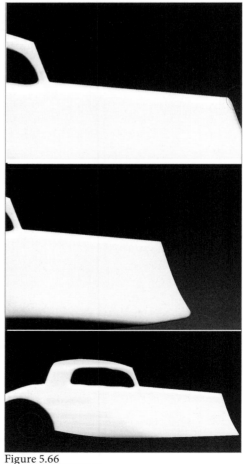

Figure 5.66

With the ClipCurve brush, clean up the edges of the car.

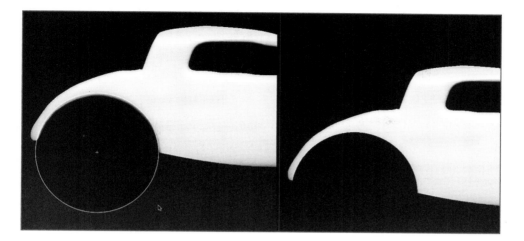

Figure 5.67

Use the ClipCurve brush to refine the wheel well.

11. You can use the same approach to refine the edges of the car from the top (see Figure 5.68). Press the X hotkey to activate Symmetry, and make sure the LSym button on the right shelf is on.

Figure 5.68

With the ClipCurve brush, clean up the edges of the car.

12. Click the Save As button in the File menu to save the project as **HotRod_v06.ZPR**.

Clipping at an Angle

For some parts of the car, you'll need to rotate your model to an odd angle in order to make a clean, straight cut. For example, in the reference drawings used in ShadowBox, the front of the car is pointed out like a wedge. In the side view, the front slopes down at an angle (see Figure 5.69).

Figure 5.69

From the top view (top image), the front of the car is angled to form a wedge. From the side view (bottom image), the front slopes at an angle.

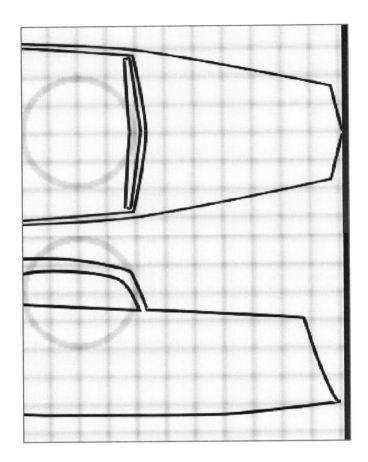

If you use the ClipCurve brush to cut the wedge from a straight-on, top view, you'll lose the sloping angle seen from the side. So in this case, to replicate that shape in 3D, you can simply rotate the view of the car to match the sloping angle of the front. It takes a little practice, but after a few tries you'll get the hang of it. Follow these steps:

1. Open your saved version of HotRod_v06.ZPR.

2. Rotate the view of the car while holding the Shift key, and snap the view so that you're looking at the car from the top (top image in Figure 5.70).

3. Carefully right-click drag on the canvas from right to left so that the front of the car rotates away from the camera. You want the slope of the front of the car to be perpendicular to the viewing angle (see Figure 5.70, bottom image).

4. Open the sculpting brush fly-out library and press C and then C again to choose the ClipCurve brush.

5. Make sure Symmetry is active across the x-axis, and click the LSym button on the right shelf to turn on Local Symmetry.

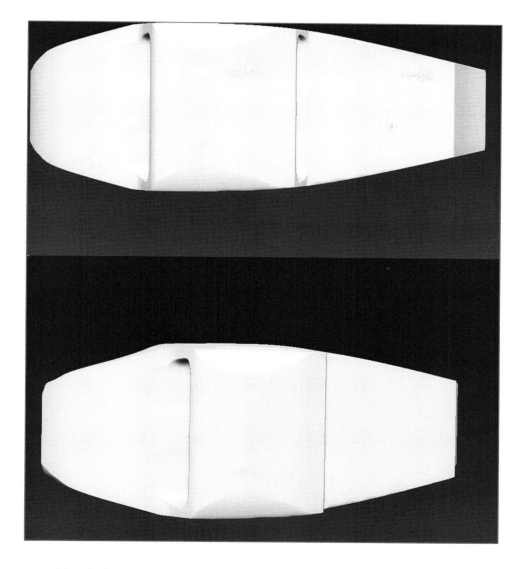

Figure 5.70
Rotate the view of the car so that you can see it from the top. Carefully rotate the view so that you're looking down along the slope of the car's front.

6. Hold Ctrl+Shift, and start dragging a curve down at an angle from left to right, as shown in Figure 5.71.

7. Release the brush, and then rotate the view and inspect the shape. If you didn't quite get it, press Ctrl+Z to undo and try again.

Once you get the hang of this, you can try creating a rounded curve for the edge of the trunk. This is a bit trickier because it requires making a curve line that clips the edge of the hood and goes from the front of the car up to the front plane of the windshield. Before you make the clip, you'll need to mask out the part of the car behind the windshield so it is not clipped as well.

Figure 5.71

Use the ClipCurve brush to clip the front of the car at an angle.

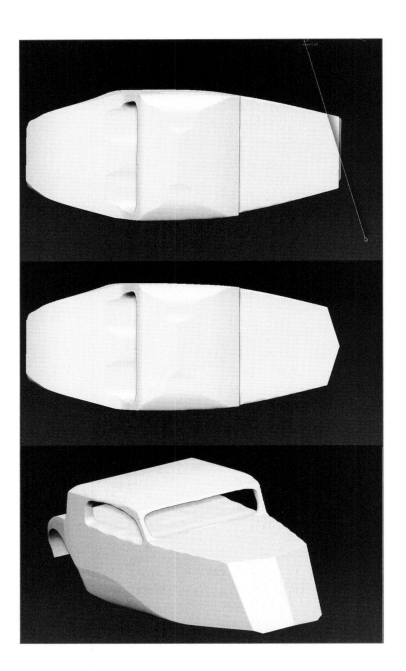

8. Rotate the car so that you can see it straight on from the side.

9. In the brush fly-out library, press M and then R to set the mask brush to MaskRect.

10. Hold the Ctrl key and drag a rectangular mask that covers the car from the windshield to the rear (see Figure 5.72).

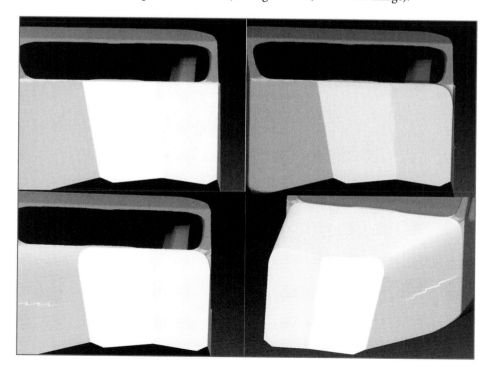

Figure 5.72

From the side view the car is masked from the windshield to the trunk.

11. Rotate the view so that you're looking at the car along the edge of the hood.

12. Hold Ctrl+Shift and draw a short curving line, as shown in Figure 5.73. In this example, I clicked the Alt key twice while drawing the curve to create the two points necessary to make a smooth curve.

13. Release the brush to make the clip.

14. Rotate the view and inspect the clip. Undo and try again if it wasn't quite right. This area will be cleaned up even further with the sculpting brushes, so it's okay if the clip leaves some small bumps on the trunk (see Figure 5.73, lower-left image).

Figure 5.73

The view of the car is rotated so that the car is viewed down the edge of the hood. A clip curve is used to create the rounded edge.

15. Use these techniques to add a rounded edge to the roof and the trunk. Remember to use masks to control which parts of the car are clipped.

16. Click the Save As button in the File menu and save the project as **HotRod_v07.ZPR**.

Refining the Windows Using Clip Brushes

The lasts parts of the car body that need some cleaning up are the window openings. This is a little tricky since you can't create a closed loop with the clip curve. Again, using masks will help a lot (see Figure 5.74):

Figure 5.74

The window edges are refined using masking and the clip brushes.

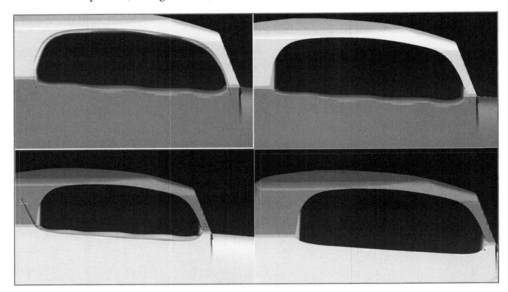

1. Open your saved version of the HotRod_v07.ZPR project.

2. Rotate the view of the car while holding the Shift key, and snap the view so that you're looking at the car from the side.

3. Use the MaskRect brush to mask everything below the top of the car.

4. Scale up the view so that you can see the window area up close.

5. Starting from the lower-right edge of the window, carefully draw out a curving line to match the shape of the upper part of the window opening.

6. Release the brush to make the clip.

7. Press Ctrl+I to invert the mask (or Ctrl+click on a blank part of the document). Draw the curve starting from the lower left and move toward the right to clip the bottom part of the window.

8. Use the same technique to clean up the edges of the opening for the front windshield. This time mask the bottom of the car as well as the back part of the car top so that the work you do on the front of the windshield does not affect the opening for the back window.

9. Enable Symmetry so you only have to draw a curve for one side of the windshield. Start from the lower right and draw a curve moving up and to the left around the top edge of the windshield. To eliminate kinks in the curve, press the Alt key to add points, even along the straight parts of the curve at the top (see Figure 5.75).

10. Save the project as **HotRod_v08.ZPR**.

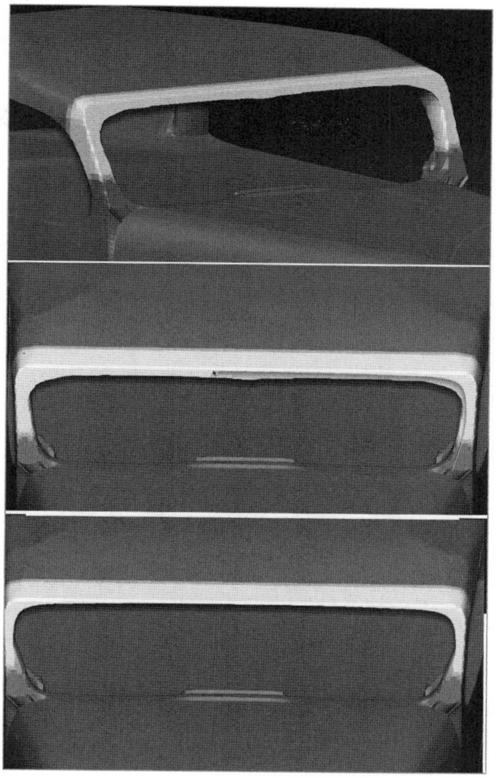

Figure 5.75

Use the ClipCurve brush to refine the opening for the windshield.

Dynamesh and ClayPolish

At this point the edges should appear more refined, but no doubt the geometry is starting to look mangled. To fix this you can use Dynamesh, which will replace the topology with a unified skin while retaining the shape of the surface. Dynamesh was first introduced in Chapter 3. Follow these steps to "dynamesh" the surface:

1. Open your saved version of the HotRod_v08.ZPR project.

2. Open the Tool palette, and expand the Geometry subpalette. Under the Dynamesh button set the Resolution to **304**. Based on the scale of this particular model I found that this resolution setting does a good job of retaining the overall contour of the body.

3. Click the Dynamesh button. After a couple seconds the body of the car will be retopologized. You can see the results of the new topology by turning on the PolyF button on the right shelf (Figure 5.76).

Figure 5.76

After you apply Dynamesh, the surface is retopologized.

Figure 5.77

Click the ClayPolish button to sharpen the edges of the surface.

4. Use the clip brushes to clean up any stray polygons, and click the Dynamesh button to retopologize again if needed. This removes any squished polygons created by using the clip brushes.

5. The edges may become "soft" or overly round after "dynameshing." To sharpen the edges click the ClayPolish button in the Geometry subpalette of the Tool palette (see Figure 5.77).

6. The ClayPolish button refines the corner of the mesh automatically. It also adds a mask that is not visible by default. After applying ClayPolish, hold Ctrl and drag on the canvas to remove the mask.

7. Save the project as **HotRod_v09.ZPR**.

You can turn the Polish option on in the Dynamesh settings. This automatically polishes the surface each time you apply Dynamesh.

Creating a Space for the Interior of the Car

The car model will look a little more convincing with space inside for the driver and passengers. To accomplish this, you can use Dynamesh and the InsertCube brush:

1. Open HotRod_v09.ZPR.

2. Make sure the LSym button is activated on the right shelf so that the symmetry is aligned with the center of the car. Leave Symmetry on so that it's easier to find the center of the car.

3. Select the InsertCube brush from the brush library.

4. Rotate the view so that you can see the car from the top.

5. Hold the Alt key and drag the cube. Make it large enough to cover the passenger area, and don't worry if it intersects with the roof. Use Symmetry on the stroke so that you can insert the cube at the center of the car (see the top image in Figure 5.78).

6. Let go of the brush. A mask will be applied to the car, but the inserted cube is unmasked.

7. Switch to the Transpose brush in Move mode (hotkey = W). Use Transpose to move and scale the cube so it fits under the roof but does not penetrate the bottom of the car (see Figure 5.78, middle image).

8. Once the cube is positioned, hold Ctrl and drag on a blank part of the canvas to clear the mask. Then Ctrl+drag on the canvas to dynamesh the surface (see Figure 5.78, bottom image).

Because you held the Alt key when you inserted the cube instead of combining the cube and the car, the cube is used to cut a hole in the surface when Dynamesh is activated.

9. Save the project as `HotRod_v10.ZPR`.

You now have the basic shape of the hot rod body, which is ready for sculpting and detailing.

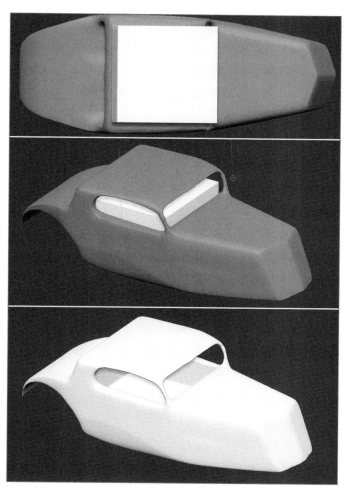

Figure 5.78

Hold the Alt key while drawing a cube using the InsertCube brush. When the surface is "dynameshed" a square space is cut into the surface.

USING DYNAMESH TO CREATE BOOLEAN OPERATIONS ON SURFACES

Boolean operations refer to common ways of using one surface to shape a second surface. Users of other 3D modeling programs frequently create surfaces through subtraction or intersection, for example, using a primitive cylinder to cut a round hole through a thick piece of geometry. Most 3D modelers complain that in many applications Boolean operations create a lot of topological problems and errors with the resulting surface. In ZBrush, Dynamesh creates very clean geometry, so by using the insert brushes (InsertCube, InsertSphere, and the like) in subtract mode (that is, while holding that key) you can create some very creative designs through Boolean operations that would create extremely messy topologies in other 3D modeling software.

Summary

In this chapter you learned how to use the ShadowBox tool to generate a mesh for a car body. You learned how to create a reference image and apply it to the ShadowBox texture. You learned how to use the masking brushes to create a shape and then the clip brushes to refine the edges. The ClayPolish button was introduced as a way to sharpen the edges. You learned that you could click the Insert Mesh button while holding the Alt key to cut away into the surface of the hot rod to create a passenger area. You also learned how to use Radial Symmetry to create intricate designs with ShadowBox as well as how to use the MatchMaker brush to create the rounded shape of the hubcap.

CHAPTER 6

Advanced ZSphere Techniques

The ZSphere was introduced in Chapter 4, where you saw how it can be used to create a basic armature for a dragon's body. In this chapter, you'll see how the ZSphere is actually an extremely versatile tool. In a sense, it's the Swiss army knife of ZBrush tools because it can be used not only to generate meshes but also as a tool for editing topology, deforming meshes, posing, and rigging characters.

This chapter demonstrates the many ways ZBrush can be used when sculpting a project. You'll also learn about the Curve brush and some of the ways it can be used to create mechanical pieces.

This chapter includes the following topics:

- **Retopologizing a character**
- **Transferring details using projection**
- **Deforming a mesh with ZSpheres**
- **Rigging with ZSpheres**
- **ZSphere mannequins**
- **Curve brushes**

Retopologizing a Character

So far in this book we've talked a lot about creating sculpting-friendly topologies using unified meshing. This was introduced in Chapter 3. A unified mesh is made up of uniformly sized polygons that are evenly distributed across the surface. This type of mesh is very easy to sculpt. However, sometimes you may need a mesh that is better suited for other purposes, such as animation in other 3D packages. Or, you may want to redistribute the polygons more efficiently across the surface. You may want a mesh where some areas, such as a character's face, have more polygons than other areas, such as the legs, where you can have fewer polygons. This is when retopology becomes a very useful technique.

Retopology is a process where a new mesh is created one polygon at a time using an existing mesh as a template. The details sculpted into the template mesh can then be projected onto the retopologized version. Then sculpting can continue using the retopologized version, or it can be exported and used in another 3D application for animation or other purposes.

ZSphere Retopology

Figure 6.1

The finished dragster-monster sculpt

Retopology in ZBrush is achieved through the use of ZSpheres. Essentially, you draw a cage of ZSpheres around the surface you want to retopologize. It's like connecting the dots in 3D. The ZSpheres are then converted into an adaptive skin, which is an entirely new, sculptable mesh that has the shape of your original object but with a different topology.

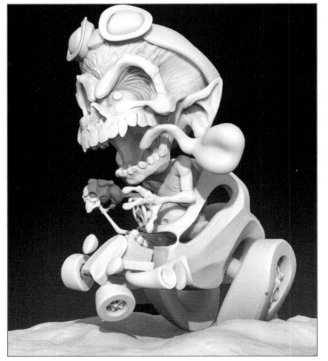

In this example, you'll see a fairly typical workflow for retopologizing a character mesh. This character has been designed as a cartoon-style demon reminiscent of the monster art/dragster style of artists such as Ed Roth, Bill Campbell, and "Dirty Donny." Figure 6.1 shows the finished sculpt. I like this style because it's fun, very loose, and completely different from what I usually do. Experimenting with a variety of styles is always good for an artist.

This demonstration shows some of the techniques I used in creating, sculpting, and retopologizing the character. Even though the style is cartoon, these techniques can be used on any mesh style from simplistic to fantastic to hyper-realistic.

The Basic Character Mesh

The character for this piece was started using basic ZSphere modeling techniques, as shown in the upper left of Figure 6.2. I converted the ZSpheres into an adaptive skin (Figure 6.2, upper right) and then used the sculpting brushes to work out the basic shape (Figure 6.2, lower left). Then I activated Dynamesh and refined the forms a little more (Figure 6.2, bottom right). These techniques are the same ones you used in Chapter 3 to sculpt the dragon and model the dragon's body.

You can retopologize any type of mesh; it doesn't matter if it's an adaptive skin created from ZSpheres, a Dynamesh object, a parametric primitive, or even a mesh created in a different program and imported as an OBJ file.

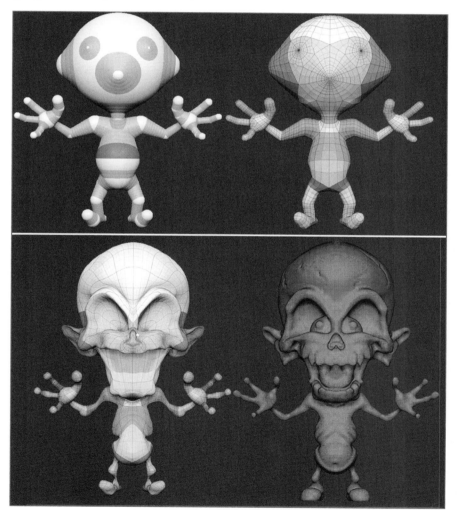

Figure 6.2

This basic character is created using ZSpheres and then refining the forms using the sculpting brushes and Dynamesh.

Personally, I prefer to retopologize a model when I feel like it's about 60 percent sculpted. Then I use retopology to create more polygons in the areas I think need more detail in the final mesh, usually around the eyes and mouth and other parts of the head. I like to use retopology as a way to introduce edgeflow into the model. *Edgeflow* means that the edges of the polygons flow along the contours of the surface. Think about the direction of wrinkles or folds in a person's flesh. The skin wrinkles and folds in the areas that deform the most, indicating the underlying anatomy of the surface. By establishing edgeflow into the topology, you'll find that characters deform more naturally when animated in other programs and, even if you don't intend to animate the character, sculpted details look more natural in the areas that stretch and compress.

Retopology with ZSpheres

The process of retopologizing a surface starts with adding a ZSphere to the mesh as a subtool. You can use your own model or the dynameshDemon.ZPR project found in the Chapter 6 folder of the DVD while you follow along.

1. Load the dynameshDemon.ZPR project into ZBrush.

2. Open the Tool palette and expand the SubTool subpalette. Click the Append button and append a ZSphere. It should appear in the stack below the demon model.

3. Select the ZSphere in the SubTool subpalette. Turn on Transp on the right shelf so that the demon is transparent. Press the X key to activate Symmetry along the x-axis.

4. Switch to Move (hotkey = W) and move the ZSphere up inside the head. You want to move it somewhere out of the way so you don't click on it while creating the new topology.

5. Turn Transp off on the right shelf.

6. Make sure the ZSphere is still the selected subtool. Scroll down in the Tool palette and expand the Topology subpalette.

7. Turn on the Edit Topology button (Figure 6.3).

8. Set the Draw Size on the top shelf to **1**. A low Draw Size makes it easier to precisely place the ZSpheres.

9. Zoom in on the head and click on it, as shown in Figure 6.4, upper left. This places the first ZSphere (the color of the head is set to gray so the ZSpheres are easier to see in the image). Click on the head again off to one side; you'll see a line connect the first ZSphere to the second, as shown in the upper right of Figure 6.4.

10. The idea here is that you want to draw a square on the head using the ZSpheres. Click again to add the third corner of the square, as shown in Figure 6.4, lower left. Click again to create a point for the fourth corner, and then click again on the first vertex to close the square. You have now made your first polygon.

Figure 6.3

Turn on Edit Topology in the Topology subpalette of the Tool palette.

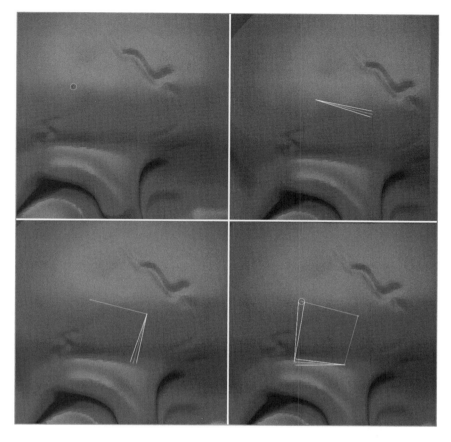

Figure 6.4

Start a polygon by clicking on the head to create the first corner. Click three more times, and then close the polygon by clicking on the first corner again.

11. Hold the Ctrl key and click on the head. This drops the ZSphere momentarily, allowing you to start a second polygon (another way to deselect the ZSphere is to click on a blank part of the canvas). Rotate the view of the head, and you'll see that a second square has been mirrored to the other side of the head (see Figure 6.5). Since Symmetry is on while you work on one side of the head, the second side is built automatically.

12. To start a second polygon that is attached to the first, hold the Ctrl key and click on one of the corners. This selects the ZSphere. Click again on the head, and you'll see a line attaching the corner to a new vertex (see Figure 6.6, upper left). Click twice more to add a third side, and then close the square.

The process of retopology really is like connecting the dots. You simply add vertices to the cage, building out the new topology one vertex at a time.

13. Add a third square that is connected to the second square. If you run into a situation where a ZSphere appears connected to the ZSphere at the center of the head (which is very easy to do by mistake), then press Ctrl+Z to undo and try again. Figure 6.6 shows how I added more squares to the ZSphere network.

Figure 6.5

Since Symmetry is turned on, the square is mirrored to the other side of the head.

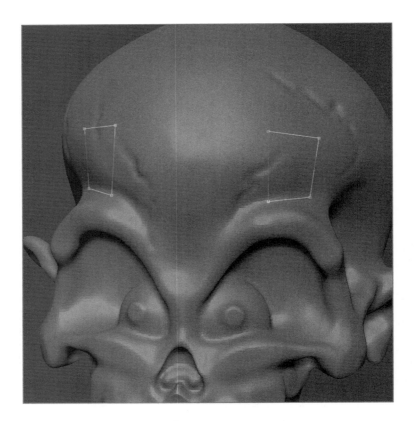

Figure 6.6

Ctrl+click on a vertex to select it, and then add a new line from the selected vertex. Continue to add more squares by connecting more lines to the existing ZSpheres.

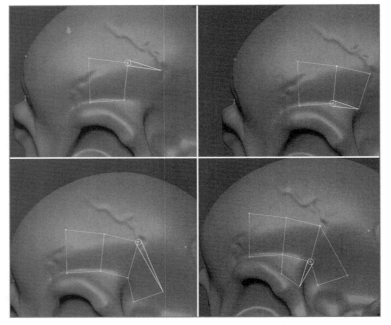

Generally, you want the edges of the squares to flow along the contours of the surface. It's good practice to stick to four-sided "quads" as much as possible. Avoid making polygons with more than four ZSpheres (known as n-sided polygons, or n-gons).

You can split a row of polygons by clicking on the center of one of the lines that connect the ZSpheres. You can then continue to extend this line by clicking on adjacent lines (see Figure 6.7). Notice that the cursor snaps to even divisions within the line so that you can easily split the line in half or into quarters.

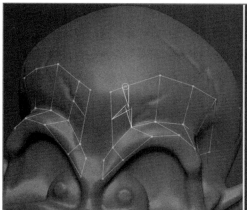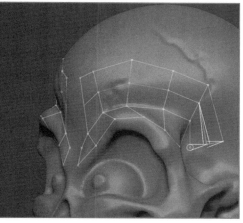

Figure 6.7

Split a row of polygon squares by clicking on the lines between ZSpheres.

If you must add a three-sided polygon (triangle, or "tris") try to do it in a place that is not terribly noticeable. By following these guidelines you'll ensure that the topology is clean and easy to sculpt or animate when it's finished (see Figure 6.8).

Figure 6.8

Try to use mostly four-sided polygons (quads). Place triangles in less noticeable areas.

Previewing the New Topology as You Work

As you add more quads to the network, you can preview the retopology by pressing the A hotkey. Follow these steps to preview:

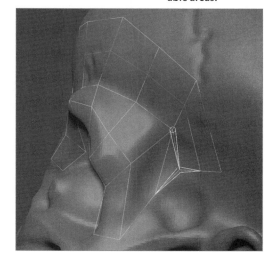

1. Continue to build up the surface of the head by adding new ZSpheres to the network.

2. Press the A hotkey, and the network is replaced by a small patch of polygons (see Figure 6.9, left image; Transparency is on in this image so that it's easier to see).

3. Turn on the PolyF button on the right shelf to see the wireframe on the preview. You can also click the Solo button to hide the other subtools (see Figure 6.9, right image).

4. Expand the Adaptive Skin subpalette of the Tool palette. If you want to see how the surface looks when subdivided, increase the Density slider.

5. Press the A hotkey again, and then continue working on building the network.

6. Remember to save often! Use the Save As button in the File menu to save the project as `demonRetopo.ZPR`.

Figure 6.9

Preview the retopology by pressing the A hotkey. The right image shows the topology with the PolyF and Solo buttons activated.

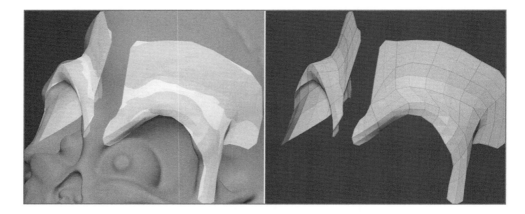

When you have completed the cage, save the project. Figure 6.10 shows the completed retopology cage.

Figure 6.10

The completed retopology cage for the demon character

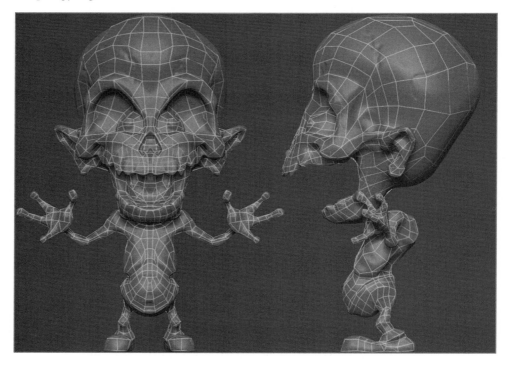

TIPS ON CREATING THE ZSPHERE NETWORK

Retopology with ZSpheres takes a little practice to get used to the process. But by the time you've retopologized an entire model, you should be pretty comfortable with the technique. Here are some tips that will help you when creating the network:

- You can move a ZSphere by switching to Move mode (hotkey = W) and dragging on the ZSphere. When you move a ZSphere, it will no longer snap to the surface.

- Hold the Alt key and click on a ZSphere (while in Draw mode) to delete it.

- If you make a connection that you don't want, press Ctrl+Z to undo, and click on a blank part of the canvas (or rotate the view slightly) to deselect the ZSpheres. Click on the model again to add a new ZSphere, and then click on a ZSphere in the network to make a connection.

- Preview the mesh frequently as you work. This is the only way to catch problems ahead of time!

- You can show or hide subtools while working as well as parts of the original model. The ZSpheres will snap to only visible parts of the model.

- You can hide parts of the network by holding Ctrl+Shift and dragging over the ZSpheres as well as hiding parts of the template mesh. This can be helpful if the visibility of the network makes it hard to see what's going on. The following image shows how hiding the head of the original geometry makes it easier to retopologize hard-to-reach parts such as the shoulder.

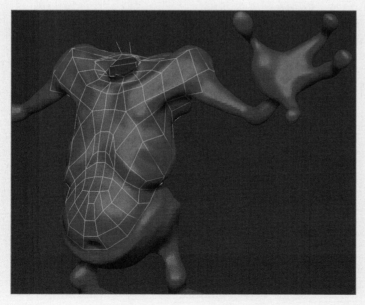

continues

continued

- Save often and save multiple iterations of the file so you have something to go back to if you mess up!

- If you find that the ZSpheres are behaving strangely, try turning Edit Topology off and then on again. Occasionally when you save and load a project that is midway through the retopology process, ZBrush gets a little confused; this trick usually fixes the problem.

- You can retopologize over multiple subtools at the same time, which will allow you to create a single surface that covers multiple parts. The ZSpheres will snap to any visible subtools.

- While Symmetry is enabled, you can easily retopologize both sides of the surface at the same time. However, creating a line of ZSpheres down the middle of the object can be a bit tricky. It's usually a good idea to create a pair of lines on either side of the center line, and then disable Symmetry and join the lines together, as shown in the following graphic.

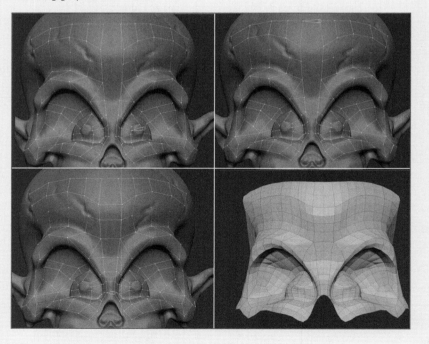

Converting the Retopology Cage to an Adaptive Mesh

Once you have completed the retopology of your model, you will need to convert it into an adaptive mesh. The process is the same for converting a ZSphere armature to a mesh.

1. Make sure the ZSphere retopology cage is selected in the SubTool subpalette.

2. Expand the Adaptive Skin subpalette and click the Make Adaptive Skin button (see Figure 6.11).

3. The adaptive skin is placed automatically in the tool library as a new tool. The tool name has the prefix Skin_ appended to it.

4. Click the Append button in the SubTool subpalette and choose the Skin_ZSphere tool as a subtool. You will end up with the original Dynamesh object, the ZSphere cage, and the Skin_ZSphere mesh as subtools of the same tool (see Figure 6.12).

5. Select the ZSphere subtool in the subtool stack and click the Delete button below the SubTool subpalette. A warning pops up letting you know that this is not undoable. Click OK to accept this change. You'll end up with the original Dynamesh version and the Skin_ZSphere subtool.

6. Select the Skin_ZSphere subtool in the subtool stack and click the Rename button. Type **DemonRetopo** in the Rename field.

7. Save the project under a new name.

I usually save a version of the project that has the retopology cage as a backup, so once I have deleted the ZSphere tool, I save the project with a different name. This way, if I decide I don't like something about the retopology later on, I can always go back a version and fix anything I don't like without having to completely redo the retopology.

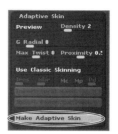

Figure 6.11
Click the Make Adaptive Skin button to convert the cage into an adaptive mesh.

Figure 6.12
Append the Skin_ZSphere tool.

Projection

After the surface has been completed, you can easily transfer the details from the original surface to the retopologized version by using projection.

Projecting a Retopologized Surface

ZBrush uses projection, which transfers detail from a source subtool (or subtools) to a target subtool. The topology of the source and the target can be completely different, but the surfaces themselves should be similar in shape for the best results. You can use projection for a variety of sculpting effects; the creative possibilities are endless. One of the more common uses of projection is to transfer details from a source subtool to a retopologized surface.

Figure 6.13

Click the ProjectAll button to project the details from the DynameshDemon subtool to the DemonRetopo subtool.

The following demonstrates how this can be done for the demon model:

1. Continue with the file from the previous section or open the demonRetopo_v03.ZPR project from the Chapter 6 folder on the DVD.

2. Select the DemonRetopo subtool. It should already have two levels of subdivision. Press Ctrl+D two times to create a total of four levels of subdivision.

3. Both the DynameshDemon and the DemonRetopo subtools should be visible.

4. In the SubTool subpalette of the Tool palette, select the DemonRetopo tool.

The original DynameshDemon will be the source for the projection and the DemonRetopo subtool will be the target. The projection process involves selecting the target subtool, making sure the source subtool (or subtools) is visible, and then clicking the ProjectAll button. The target will shrink to match the source. Usually there's a little bit of cleanup involved as well, and sometimes it takes a few tries to get it to work right. I find that I get the best results if I project on each SDiv level starting with the lowest level and then working my way up to the highest.

Figure 6.14

After projection, the DemonRetopo subtool matches the shape of the DynameshDemon subtool.

5. Set the SDiv slider to **1** and click the ProjectAll button in the SubTool subpalette of the Tool palette (see Figure 6.13). After a few seconds you'll see the DemonRetopo tool shrink to match the DynameshDemon subtool.

6. Move the SDiv slider up one level and click ProjectAll again. Repeat this process two more times for SDiv levels 3 and 4 (see Figure 6.14).

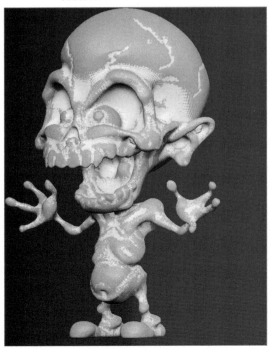

7. Once you have finished, you may need to do some cleanup, especially in thin parts such as the ears. Use the Smooth brush to clean up any stretched parts. (You may want to turn on the Double button in the Display Properties subpalette of the Tool palette so you can see both sides of the polygons. Otherwise, it may be hard to see the problem areas.)

Retopology can take a while to do, but the payoff is usually worth it. I prefer to retopologize my models before sculpting fine detail into the surface. This makes projection easier to deal with. Because I know I will be making changes to the model anyway, I'm not concerned if the projection is not 100 percent perfect. I usually retopologize a model whenever I know that the model will be sent to another program, such as Autodesk® Maya® or modo, for rendering and animation. Or sometimes I retopologize a model if I want to reorganize the mesh to support more detailed sculpting in specific areas such as the face.

ZBrush is not the only way to retopologize a surface, either. There are several solutions from third party software vendors which have more advanced retopology tools. Many of these are easier and faster than ZBrush retopology. I recommend trying Topogun (www .topogun.com) if you expect to be retopologizing surfaces on a daily basis.

After retopologizing the model, I'll spend some time sculpting details and making changes. I'll usually subdivide the model a few more times as well.

8. Once you're happy with the way the demon looks, you can delete the DynameshDemon subtool and save the project under a new name. Save it as **DemonRetopo_v04.ZPR**. Figure 6.15 shows the finished demon sculpt.

Figure 6.15

The sculpt of the demon is finished after retopology and projection.

ZPROJECT BRUSH

In the example shown in this section, projection is used to transfer details from a very simple mesh, so cleaning up problem areas is easily done using the Smooth brush. However, you may find yourself in a situation in which you want to project intricate details from one mesh to another. You can use the ZProject brush to clean up areas where ProjectAll did not produce a perfect result.

The ZProject brush is a sculpting brush that uses the same projection algorithm as ProjectAll, but the fact that it is a brush allows you to project in very specific areas. You can use this to fix parts of your mesh or explore creative ideas. There are a few rules you need to follow when using ZProject to ensure the best results.

continues

continued

Follow these steps when using ZProject:

1. Just as with ProjectAll, the ZProject brush uses a target mesh and one or more source meshes. Make sure the target mesh is selected and all source meshes are visible.

2. Make sure Symmetry is off. ZProject does not work well with Symmetry, and you can accidentally mess up one side of your model if Symmetry is enabled for the tool.

 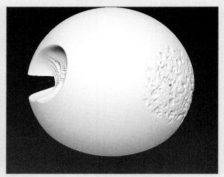

3. Rotate the model so that the surface is perpendicular to your view, and rotate frequently as you work. The brush will smear and squish parts of the surface that are brushed at an angle.

4. ZAdd should be active on the top shelf when using the ZProject brush. The brush brings the surface of the target subtool out to meet the surface of the source subtool. Hold the Alt key to push in the surface of the target subtool to meet the surface of the source mesh.

continued

5. Alternate between using ZProject and the Smooth tool on parts of the surface. Work over small parts, holding and releasing the Alt key to move the surface of the target mesh until you get the results you want.

6. It may help to have Transparency on while you work.

7. If the Rgb button is activated on the top shelf and Polypainting is on for both surfaces, the ZProject brush will transfer color information from one surface to the other. Polypainting is discussed in Chapter 8.

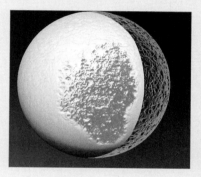

Deforming a Mesh with ZSpheres

Aside from generating sculptable meshes and retopologizing surfaces, ZSpheres can also be used as a deformer. You can create a network, bind it to a mesh, and then as you move the ZSpheres, the mesh can be bent, twisted, and distorted into any shape you like.

And what's more, you can use the Transpose Master plug-in as a way to use ZSpheres to deform multiple subtools at the same time. There are a few rules you need to follow to ensure that the deformation is smooth and controllable. In this section you'll see how ZSpheres can be used to deform a hot rod model.

Binding a Mesh with ZSpheres

Before jumping into the hot rod project, this exercise demonstrates the basics of how to bind a mesh to ZSpheres as well as some tips on how to make the process easier.

1. Open a new session of ZBrush.

2. Open Light Box to the Tool section, and double-click the Dog.ztl tool to load it into ZBrush (see Figure 6.16). Draw the dog on the canvas and switch to Edit mode (hotkey = T).

Figure 6.16

Load the Dog.ztl tool from Light Box.

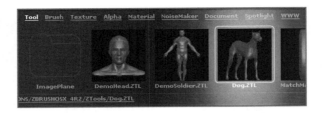

3. Switch to the SkinShade04 material in the Material library just so it's easier to see.

4. Open the tool library and select the ZSphere tool. The dog on the canvas is replaced by the ZSphere. That's OK. It just means that you have switched to the ZSphere; the dog is still safe and sound in the tool library.

5. Scroll down in the Tool palette to the Rigging subpalette. Click the Select Mesh button. This opens up the tool library. Select Dog_1 from the tool library (see Figure 6.17).

6. The dog appears transparently over the ZSphere. You can use the dog as a guide for building the ZSphere rig (see Figure 6.18, left).

Figure 6.17

Select Dog_1 from the pop-up tool library when you click the Select Mesh button.

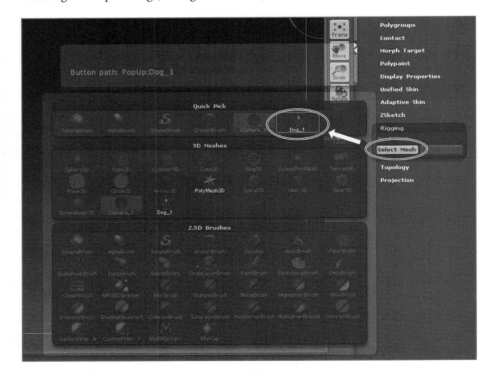

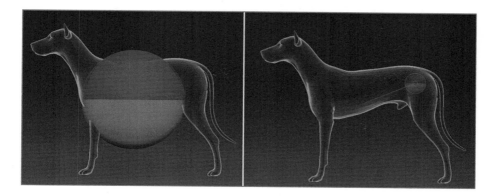

Figure 6.18

The dog appears over the ZSphere (left). Move the ZSphere to the pelvis of the dog (right).

Notice that in the SubTool subpalette, there is still just the ZSphere subtool. The dog is in Rigging mode, meaning that it is not a separate subtool; it is combined with the ZSphere while you prepare the rig. The idea here is to build a simple skeleton out of ZSpheres to use to pose the dog.

7. Press the X key to turn on Symmetry across the x-axis.

8. Switch to Scale mode (hotkey = E) and scale down the ZSphere. Use Move (hotkey = W) to position the ZSphere at the pelvis of the dog (see Figure 6.18, right image).

9. Switch to Draw mode (hotkey = Q) and build out a very simple ZSphere armature like the one shown in Figure 6.19.

Figure 6.19

Create a simple armature for the dog.

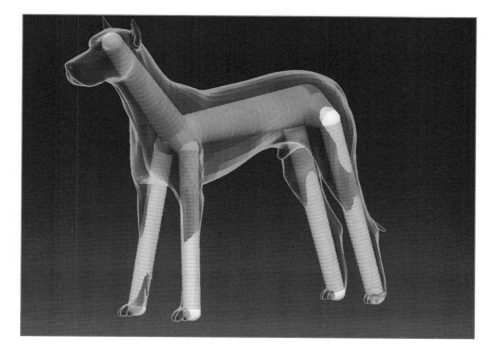

Figure 6.20

Click the Bind Mesh button in the Rigging subpalette.

10. Once the armature is complete, click the Bind Mesh button in the Rigging subpalette (see Figure 6.20).

11. Switch to Rotate, and try moving some of the ZSpheres. The dog stretches as you move the ZSpheres (see upper right in figure 6.21).

ZSpheres act similar to joints in other 3D applications, such as Maya. However, the system is designed for very simple manipulation, so it is not as sophisticated as an animation rigging system. ZSpheres are bound to the mesh based on proximity alone, so size does not affect how the ZSpheres influence the mesh. This means that sometimes a ZSphere will affect part of the mesh that you don't want affected. To fix this you need to add some ZSpheres strategically to influence the mesh to be the way you want. This takes practice and some experimentation, depending on the mesh you are trying to rig.

12. Click the Bind Mesh button in the Rigging subpalette. The dog snaps back to its original shape. Press Ctrl+Z a few times to make the ZSphere rig go back to its original position.

Figure 6.21

The mesh is deformed as the ZSpheres are rotated (upper-left image). The ZSphere armature can be edited (upper-right image), and when the mesh is bound again, the deformation is more precise (lower left). The lower right shows the adaptive mesh.

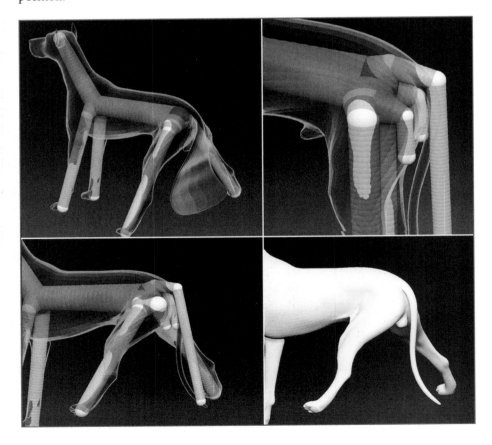

13. Switch to Draw mode and add a few ZSpheres, as shown in Figure 6.21, upper-left image.

14. Click the Bind Mesh button again and try moving the ZSpheres. You can see how the added ZSpheres help control the deformation of the mesh (see Figure 6.21, lower left).

15. In the Adaptive Skin palette, click the Make Adaptive skin. This places a copy of the deformed dog mesh in the tool library just like when you convert a ZSphere armature into an adaptive skin. The lower right of Figure 6.21 shows the deformed mesh.

When you use this technique to deform a mesh, you'll find that it works best on a model that is not very dense. The deformations are much cleaner and the response is much faster. If you try to deform a mesh made up of a lot of polygons, such as a model in Dynamesh mode, you'll get a lot of unsightly ripples in the surface that will need to be cleaned up (see Figure 6.22). This is another reason why you may choose to retopologize models you've created using ShadowBox or Dynamesh even if you don't intend to export the model for animation.

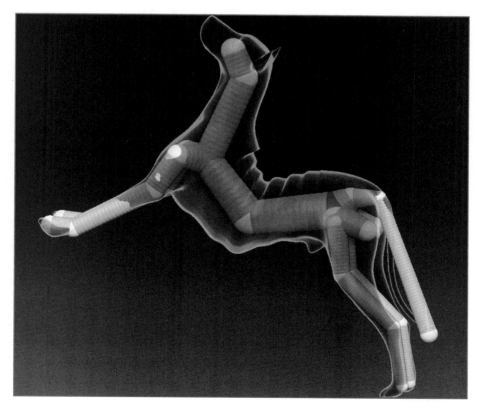

Figure 6.22

Using ZSphere rigging on dense meshes can cause ripples in the surface when the ZSpheres are rotated.

Deforming Multiple Subtools with Transpose Master

The technique of deforming a mesh with a ZSphere skeleton can also be used to deform a model made up of multiple subtools. This is achieved through the use of the Transpose Master plug-in. When the ZSphere Rig option is activated in Transpose Master, ZBrush will automatically set up a copy of the tool that is set up to be bound to the ZSpheres. Once the deformation is complete, the changes are automatically transferred back to the original and all of its subtools. The example shows how this technique is used to add cartoonish deformations to the hot rod model.

The model was created by retopologizing the ShadowBox car mesh created in Chapter 5. The mesh was then sculpted and the tires and engines were modeled and added as subtools. All of the subtools have multiple levels of subdivision (see Figure 6.23).

Figure 6.23

The hot rod is created by retopologizing and sculpting the ShadowBox hot rod created in Chapter 5.

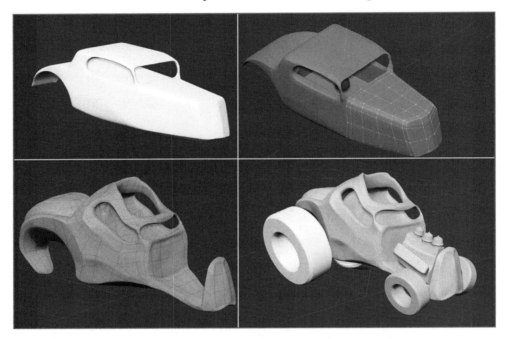

Figure 6.24

Turn on the ZSphere Rig button in the Transpose Master options.

1. Open the hotrod.ZPR project from the Chapter 6 folder on the DVD.

2. The model has subtools for the body, tires, and engine parts. Each part has multiple levels of subdivision. To deform all of these as a single object you'll use Transpose Master. Open the ZPlug-in palette and expand the Transpose Master subpalette.

3. To create the ZSphere rig you must turn on the ZSphere Rig button before activating the plug-in (see Figure 6.24).

4. Click the TposeMesh button in the Transpose Master plug-in.

The plug-in now automatically goes through each subtool in the SubTool subpalette and sets it to the lowest SDiv level. Then all the subtools are cloned and merged. This merged, cloned version is placed into the tool library. Then ZBrush automatically selects the ZSphere tool and attaches the merged version of the hot rod. When the plug-in is finished, you have a low-resolution version of the hot rod all set up and ready for rigging (see Figure 6.25).

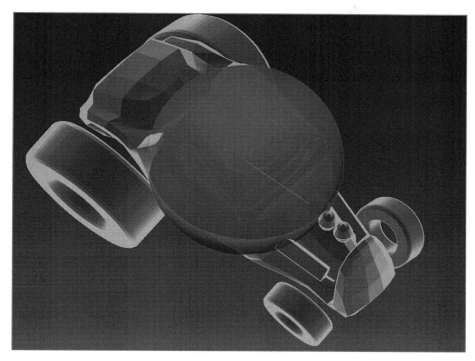

Figure 6.25

The hot rod model is readied for rigging.

5. Turn on Symmetry (hotkey = X). Create a very simple ZSphere armature similar to what you created for the dog in the previous section. Create ZSpheres that branch out and meet the center of the wheels (see Figure 6.26).

6. It's always a good idea to save the Transpose project so that you can make changes or reuse the rig later on. In the Transpose Master plug-in, click the Save TM Prj button. Save the project as **HotRod rig**.

7. Once you think you have a good enough rig, scroll down in the Tool palette and click the Bind Mesh button in the Rigging subpalette.

8. Use Rotate and Move to manipulate the rig. If you mess up or feel like you need to add or remove ZSpheres from the rig, deactivate the Bind Mesh button, edit the rig, and then reactivate Bind Mesh and continue. It usually takes a few tries before you get a rig you like.

Figure 6.26

The rig is created by adding ZSpheres to the initial ZSphere root.

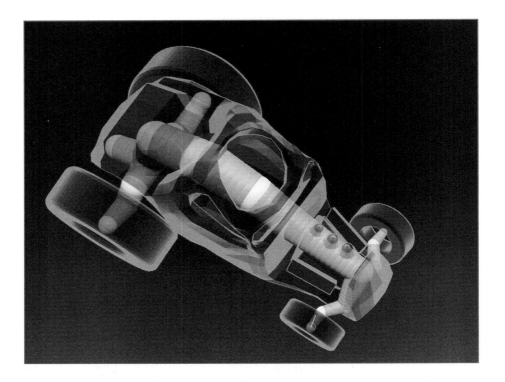

If you edit the rig significantly, then remember to save the project using the Save TM Prj button in the Transpose Master plug-in!

This technique works really well with cartoony subjects since you can try out new ideas with a good rig that you would not think of otherwise. Figure 6.27 shows a few variations. You can always deactivate Symmetry and see how that affects the deformations you created.

9. When you are satisfied with the deformation, open the Transpose Master plug-in interface and click the TPose To SubT button.

ZBrush will automatically transform the deformations from the copy back to each subtool of the original. The SDiv levels of the original subtools are preserved as well, so you can continue sculpting when it's done.

Note that the ZSphere rig is deleted in the process of transferring the deformation back to the original. This is why it's very important to save the transpose project whenever you create a rig you like. That way you can reload it later if you need to change the pose, or you can use it to develop multiple poses for the same character.

ZBrush has become popular as an illustration tool for graphic novels. The ability to use the same rig to come up with many different poses for a character is an indispensible tool for ZBrush graphic novel artists!

10. Click the Save As button in the File menu to save the project as **hotrod_v02.ZPR.**

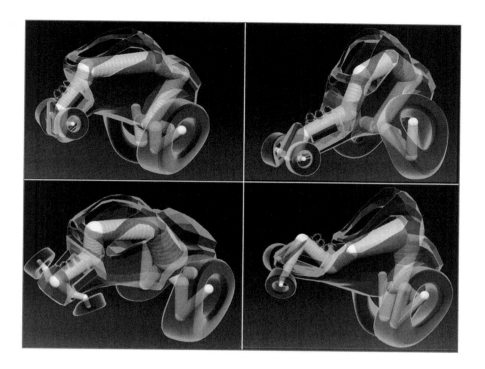

Figure 6.27
Variations are created by moving, rotating, and scaling the ZSphere rig.

Posing Characters with ZSpheres and Transpose Master

You can use the same techniques you used to deform the car to pose characters, and this is where Transpose Master really shines (see Figure 6.28). There are a few things to keep in mind when rigging and posing characters using ZSpheres.

Figure 6.28

A character is rigged and posed using ZSpheres and Transpose Master.

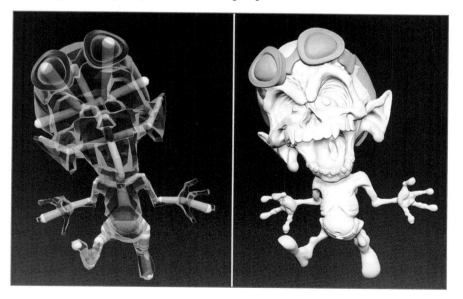

To create better deformations of joints like elbows and knees, place an extra ZSphere before and after the joint ZSphere. In Figure 6.29 you can see how extra ZSpheres were placed on either side of the elbow ZSphere as well as after the shoulder and before the wrist. Try not to go crazy though; too many ZSpheres will make it hard to pose.

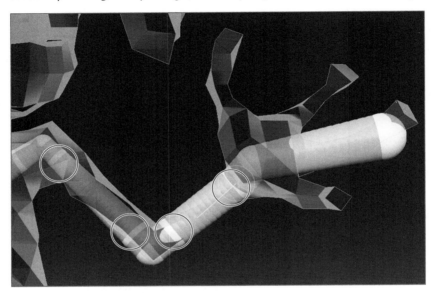

When posing the figure it's easiest to use Rotate mode and drag on the gray connecting ZSpheres above the joint you want to rotate. To twist a joint, drag directly on the ZSphere.

Move mode allows you to stretch the joints. If you hold the Ctrl key while dragging on the connection ZSpheres, the joint will not stretch; instead, the behavior is similar to Rotate mode.

You can lock a ZSphere by masking it. Simply hold Ctrl and drag a mask over the ZSpheres you want to lock.

Mannequins

The ZSphere mannequin projects that come with ZBrush are a starting place for exploring character poses. Using the mannequins, you can develop poses and multicharacter compositions very quickly and easily without the need to create new ZSphere armatures or to sculpt new models. The mannequins are all set up and ready to pose. What's more, using Dynamesh you can use the mannequins as a starting point for creating your own unique sculpts.

In the following sections, we'll take a look at how to create poses with the mannequins, how to create multicharacter scenes, and also how to model the body of a penguin character by remeshing a mannequin.

Posing a Mannequin

A mannequin is simply a premade ZSphere armature. Some of the ZSpheres in the armature have been replaced with simple mesh objects, and the result is something that looks like a mannequin. Several example mannequin projects ship with ZBrush. Let's open one and look at how it works. Mannequins are useful for creating quick character armatures or for exploring poses as a way to "previsualize" a composition.

Figure 6.30

Load the Mannequin.ZPR project from the Project folder in Light Box.

1. Start a fresh ZBrush session. Open Light Box to the `Projects/Mannequins` folder.

2. Find the `Mannequin.ZPR` project, and double-click it to load it on the canvas (see Figure 6.30).

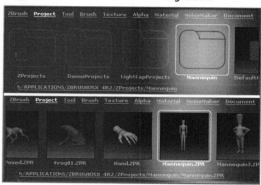

The mannequin looks like a gray figure on the canvas. There are several ways you can pose the limbs of the mannequin.

3. Press the X hotkey to activate Symmetry on the x-axis.

4. Click the Move button on the top shelf (hotkey = W).

5. Select the long tube that represents the forearms of the character and drag upward. This action rotates the lower arm (see Figure 6.31, left).

6. Select the upper arm and try moving it upward as well (Figure 6.31, right).

You get the same effect by holding the Ctrl key and dragging on the ZSpheres themselves. If you drag on the ZSphere without holding the Ctrl key, the position of the ZSphere is changed relative to its position in the armature. You can use this technique to reposition the joints of the mannequin (see Figure 6.32).

Figure 6.31

Drag on the forearms to move the arms upward.

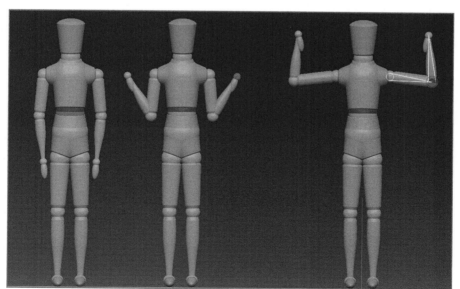

Figure 6.32

Drag on the ZSphere to change the position of a joint.

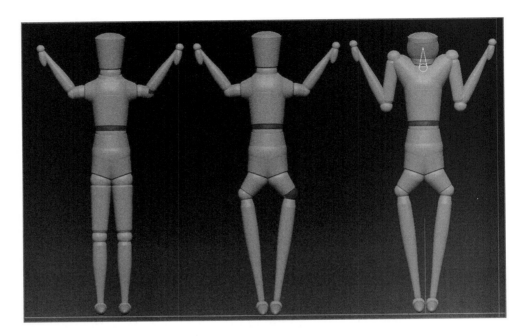

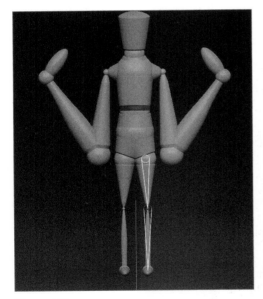

Figure 6.33

Scale mode allows you to change the size of parts of the mannequin.

You can use the Scale mode (hot key = E) to resize parts of the armature. To scale a joint, click and drag on a ZSphere. If you click and drag on the connecting cylinder, you will increase the size of it and all the child ZSpheres and cylinders. Use Alt+drag on the connecting cylinders to make them appear fatter or skinnier (Figure 6.33).

Rotate mode allows you to rotate the ZSpheres by dragging on them. In most cases, it is easier and more intuitive to pose the limbs using Move mode than using Rotate mode.

To move the entire mannequin, switch to Move mode, hold the Ctrl key, and drag on the root ZSphere.

Creating a Multicharacter Scene

In this example, you'll learn how you can easily create a scene using multiple characters.

1. Open Light Box and switch to the Project/Mannequins section. Double-click the Mannequin3.ZPR project to load it on the canvas. This project has a single mannequin in a simple pose (Figure 6.34).

2. In the Tool palette, expand the SubTool subpalette. You'll see that the mannequin is a single subtool at the top of the palette.

3. Toward the bottom of the SubTool subpalette, click the Duplicate button to make a copy of the mannequin. The copy is appended as a new subtool (see Figure 6.35).

Figure 6.34

Select the Mannequin3.ZPR project from Light Box.

4. Use the Rename button to name one mannequin **Man1** and the other **Man2**.

The easiest way to rotate an entire mannequin is to use the Rotate slider in the Deformations palette while the mannequin is at the origin.

5. In the SubTool subpalette, select the Man2 subtool.

6. In the Deformation subpalette, click the Z button on the Rotate slider to turn the z-axis Rotation off. Click the Y button to turn on Rotation on the y-axis (see Figure 6.36).

7. Drag the Rotate slider all the way to the right to rotate the Man2 subtool.

8. Expand the Deformation subpalette, and click the X button on the Offset slider to turn off the x-axis. Click the Z button on the Offset slider to turn on the z-axis.

9. Drag the Offset slider all the way to the left. Repeat this a second time to move Man2 in front of Man1 (see Figure 6.37).

Figure 6.35

Use the Duplicate button to copy the mannequin.

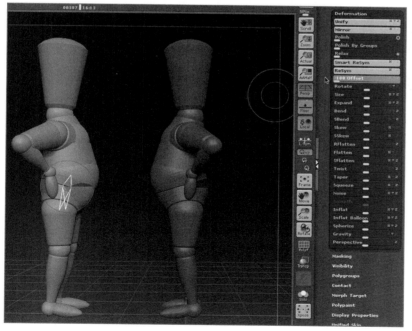

Figure 6.37

Drag the Offset slider to move one mannequin in front of another.

Figure 6.36

Turn off the Z button on the Rotate slider, and turn on Y.

Once the two mannequins are no longer overlapping, you can move them around by holding the Ctrl key and dragging on the root ZSphere.

10. Switch to Move mode and experiment with poses for the two characters using the techniques described in the section "Posing a Mannequin," earlier in this chapter (see Figure 6.38). For best results, reduce your Draw Size so that you can easily move one part of the mannequin at a time.

Figure 6.38

The second manne- quin is posed using Move and Scale modes.

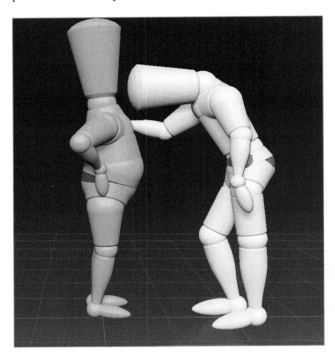

SWITCH BETWEEN MANNEQUINS

You can quickly switch from one character to the other by holding the Alt key and clicking the mannequin.

Editing a Mannequin

In this section, you'll learn how you can edit the mannequin to create different types of creatures and characters. These techniques will be applied to creating a penguin model.

1. Just as in the previous section, open Light Box and switch to the Project/Mannequins section. Double-click the Mannequin3.ZPR project to load it on the canvas. This project has a single mannequin in a simple pose.

2. Switch to Rotate mode (hotkey = R) and rotate the upper arms to move the arms away from the body (left image in Figure 6.39).

3. To turn the arms into flippers you can delete the ZSpheres at the elbow. Switch to Draw mode and hold the Alt key. Click on the elbow ZSphere to delete it (center image in Figure 6.39).

4. Use the same technique to remove the hands.

5. Switch to Move mode and pull the flippers out toward the back (right image in Figure 6.39).

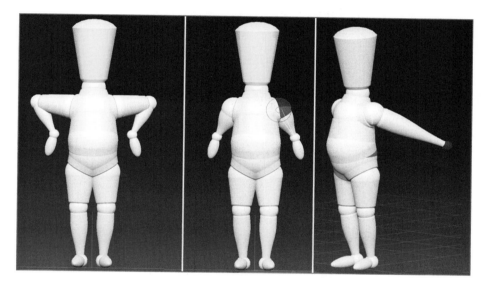

Figure 6.39

The arms are edited to look like flippers.

6. Use the same technique to delete the knees (see upper-left image in Figure 6.40).

7. Switch to Move mode (hotkey = W), and move the upper part of the body down to form the belly.

8. Switch to Draw mode (hotkey = Q), and add a tail to the rear (upper-right image in Figure 6.40).

9. Turn the head into a beak by rotating it forward (lower-left image in Figure 6.40).

10. Switch to Scale mode and scale the head up and the end of the beak down (lower-right image in Figure 6.40).

11. Using Move, Scale, and Draw, enlarge the belly of the penguin, position the legs, and add eyes to the head (see Figure 6.41).

12. Save the project as **penguinMannequin.ZPR**.

Figure 6.40

The mannequin is edited to resemble a penguin.

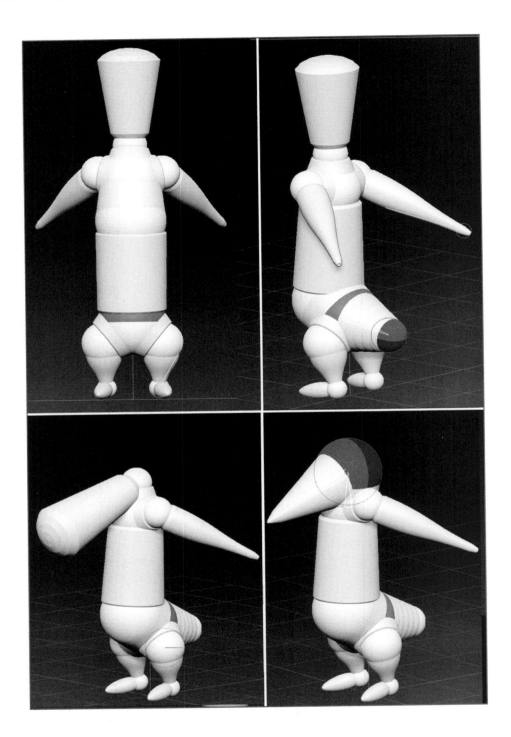

Figure 6.41

Scale the belly and add eyes to the head.

Converting the Mannequin into a Mesh

The next step is to convert the penguin into a mesh, which can then be sculpted. Dynamesh makes this extremely easy.

1. Continue with the project from the last section.

2. Press the A hotkey; this gives you a preview of the mesh. However, if you turn on the PolyF button on the right shelf, the wireframe shows that the mesh is made up of separate parts (left image in Figure 6.42).

3. Click the MakePolyMesh 3D button on the top of the Tool palette. This makes a sculptable copy of the mesh from the ZSphere preview. The new copy can be found in the tool library and should be labeled **PM3D_ZSphere**.

4. In the Geometry subpalette of the Tool palette set the Resolution slider to **40**. The scale of the original ZSphere model is fairly large, so by lowering the resolution you'll make a low-res mesh of the penguin that is easier to sculpt. You can use a higher-resolution setting if you want the Dynamesh version to more closely resemble the mannequin.

5. Click the Dynamesh button. The result is a continuous mesh based on the penguin mannequin ready for you to sculpt (see the right image in Figure 6.42).

6. Use the sculpting brushes and the Dynamesh controls to sculpt a penguin character like the one shown in Figure 6.43.

7. Save the penguinMannequin.ZPR project. Because the Dynamesh version is based on a copy of the mannequin, both the Dynamesh version and the original penguin mannequin are saved as tools in the project.

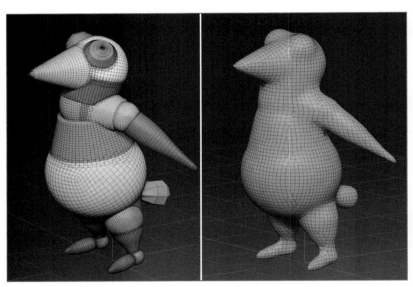

Figure 6.42

The preview shows that the mesh is made up of separate parts (left image). Convert the mesh to a Dynamesh object to make a continuous sculptable mesh (right image).

Figure 6.43

The mesh is sculpted into a penguin character.

Curve Brushes

Curve brushes are a subset of the sculpting brushes that allow you to draw a stroke using a curve in 3D space and then manipulate the stroke by pulling and pushing on the segments of the curve. You can use the curve either to insert new geometry into a 3D tool or to manipulate the placement of a stroke after it has been drawn. This increases the flexibility and the precision of the strokes you make in ZBrush.

This section demonstrates how you can use these brushes to add details to a model.

Curve Mode

The Curve brushes are really the same brushes you have been using but with one important difference. These brushes use a special mode called Curve mode, which is activated using the settings in the Transform palette.

Before getting into using this feature in a project, a little background concerning how this mode works would be a good place to start. Let's try out Curve mode on the Standard brush using a simple surface.

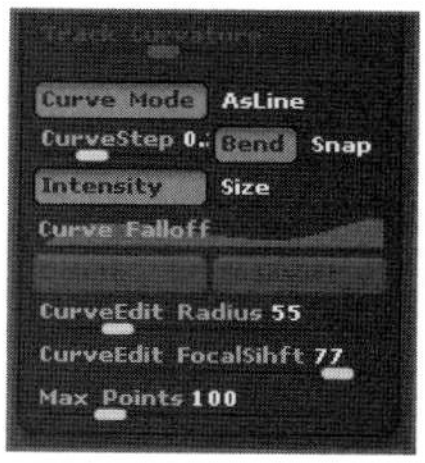

1. Start a new session of ZBrush, open Light Box, and load the DefaultSphere.ZPR project from the Projects section. Set the color in the color picker to white so that it's easier to see what's going on.

2. Press the X hotkey to turn Symmetry off, so that Symmetry does not obscure the results of the brush.

3. The Standard brush should be loaded in the Brush palette. Place the Stroke palette in the tray so that you can access the controls.

4. Turn on the Curve Mode button (see Figure 6.44), and then draw across the surface of the sphere; you'll see a line appear as you draw.

5. After you draw the line, hold the brush tip over the line; the circles of the brush icon turn light blue. Drag on the curve, and you'll see the surface bulge out along the curve (see Figure 6.45).

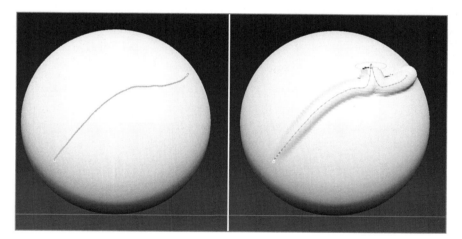

As you continue to drag, the curve around it extends the deformation of the surface. If you draw on another part of the sphere, the deformations are baked into the surface and a new curve is drawn. If you change the Draw Size while the curve is still active, the next time you adjust the curve, the size of the deformation will update automatically.

6. Undo your changes so that the sphere returns to its original state.

7. In the stroke library, select the DragDot stroke type (see Figure 6.46). Draw a new curve on the surface with the Standard brush and try moving the curve around. This time the deformation moves with the curve (see Figure 6.47). This is a great way to edit the stroke after it has been drawn.

Figure 6.44

Turn on Curve mode in the Stroke palette.

Figure 6.45

Draw a curve across the surface (left image), and then drag the curve to create a bulge (right image).

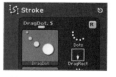

Figure 6.46

Switch to the DragDot stroke type.

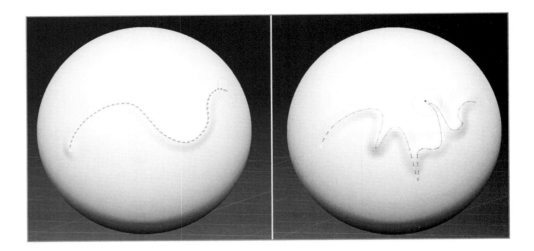

The options in the Stroke palette let you change the behavior of Curve mode for the current stroke:

As Line This option makes the curve a straight line.

Curve Step This determines the amount of space between each point in the line. A low setting makes a very smooth, continuous line. A high setting places more space between each point. If you wanted to create a line of bolts along the surface, then you would increase the size of Curve Step.

Bend This allows you to change the shape of the curve after it has been drawn. This is usually on by default. If you turn this option off, then you can drag the entire curve across the surface.

Snap This option forces the curve to follow the contours of the surface you're drawing on. This can be really helpful for generating zippers and continuous rivets, bolts, and even scars.

Intensity When this is on, the intensity of the stroke is varied along the length of the curve.

Size When this is on, the size of the stroke is varied along the length of the curve.

Curve Falloff This edit curve modulates the amount of pinching along the line when the Bend button is active and the size of the stroke from the start to the end when the Size button is active.

Curve Edit Radius This adjusts the size of the light blue circles representing the brush tip when you are adjusting the curve itself. A large Curve Edit Radius setting means that after you draw the curve you can grab and drag more points along the curve. A small Curve Edit Radius setting means that you can move around fewer points.

Curve Edit Focal Shift This adjusts the falloff of the curve edit area. If you want a smooth bend in the curve as you drag it around, set this to a low or negative number. If you want to pull out sharp corners in the curve, set this to a high value.

Max Points This sets an overall limit on the number of points in the curve.

Curve mode gives you the power to make some really interesting types of brush strokes. If you look in the Brush palette, you'll see a number of presets that have Curve mode already applied. These include CurveEditable, CurveStandard, and CurvePinch.

You can turn Curve mode on for almost any type of brush preset. Try activating Curve mode for brushes such as Dam_Standard, ClayBuildup, and Move, and see how this affects the types of marks you can make. See what happens when you use Curve mode together with Radial Symmetry (see Figure 6.48).

In Chapter 8 you'll see how powerful this option is when used to paint colors on the surface of your model.

Figure 6.48

Stroke mode is enabled for the Move brush, and Radial Symmetry is applied.

CurveTube Brush

Things get truly interesting when you apply Curve mode to the insert mesh type of brush. A number of brush presets combine the power of these options to make it possible to draw out long extruded tubes, create lathed surfaces, and insert rows of bolts and other details. This example shows how these techniques are used to add details to the model of the demon's cartoon hot rod.

The first thing we'll do is add some ridiculous-looking exhaust pipes that start from the engine and flare out at the ends. To do this you'll use the CurveTube brush with a few modifications.

1. Load the MonsterCarPosed.ZPR project from the Chapter 6 folder on the DVD.

To use any of the curve brushes that insert geometry, you need to have a mesh that has no subtools or a mesh in Dynamesh mode. At the moment all the subtools of this model have subdivisions, and it would be nice to keep them the way they are. So as a workaround, you can append a simple primitive and place it inside the model out of sight. Then you can use the brushes to add the exhaust pipe geometry to the unseen primitive.

2. Scroll to the bottom of the subtool stack and click the Append button. Append the Sphere3D tool to the model.

3. Turn on Transp on the right shelf so that the other subtools become transparent.

4. Press the E hotkey to switch to Scale mode. Use the Transpose handle to scale the sphere down; switch to Move (hotkey = W) mode and move the sphere inside the engine block. Make sure that it's small and is not visible when Transp is turned off (see Figure 6.49).

Figure 6.49

Append the Sphere3D tool (left image). Use Transpose to scale it down and move it inside the engine block.

5. From the Brush palette select the CurveTube brush (Figure 6.50).

6. Set the Draw Size to **30**; this will make the radius of the tube small enough to work with. Draw a curve starting from the engine block out into space (see Figure 6.51).

Figure 6.50

Select the CurveTube brush.

7. In the Stroke palette, increase the CurveEdit Radius to **100**. This will make it easier to shape the curve as you work since you'll be able to grab more points on the curve.

8. Try shaping the curve by dragging on it. Try not to draw a new stroke. If you mess up, you can press Ctrl+Z to undo to go back a step (or steps if needed!).

9. You want to shape the extruded tube so that it looks like a pipe coming off of the engine block and curving out toward the back of the car. The curve may be tough to work with if there are too many points. In the Stroke palette set Max Points to **10**. This means there are fewer points so it's easier to shape the curve. Think of the max points as kinks in a pipe that allow you to easily bend the pipe at certain intervals.

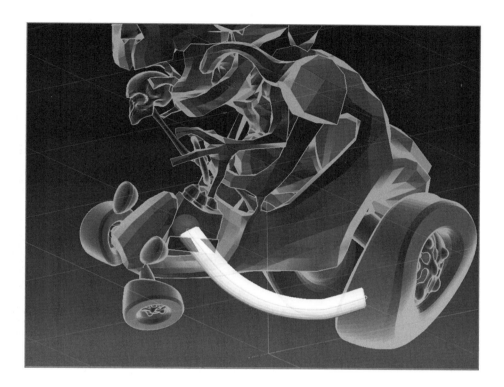

Figure 6.51
Draw a tube from the engine block out into space.

Every time you adjust the Draw Size or the settings in the Stroke palette, the stroke will update the next time you touch the curve. This adds a lot of flexibility to the process because you can change a setting, edit the curve, change another setting, edit the curve again, and continue the process until you have exactly what you want.

10. Try to shape the curve so that the extruded tube looks something like the left image in Figure 6.52.

11. To add a flare, expand the Curve Falloff graph in the Stroke palette, and edit the curve as shown in Figure 6.53. Then turn on the Size button.

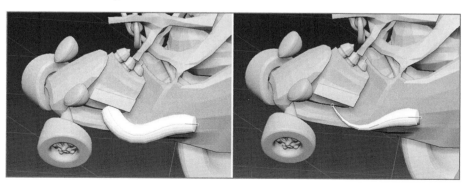

Figure 6.52
Shape the extruded tube using the curve (left image).

Figure 6.53

Edit the Curve Falloff graph.

Figure 6.54

The exhaust pipe is shaped and placed so that it is coming out of the engine.

12. Touch the end of the curve that controls the extruded tube. The tube will become flared at the end but probably very small and thin as well (see Figure 6.52, right).

13. Increase the Draw Size on the top shelf and touch the end of the curve again. Now it becomes thicker.

The Curve Falloff graph applies the shape of the graph to whichever point you touch on the curve, so if you touch the start of the curve, then the flare is reversed; if you touch the middle of the curve, then a bulge appears around the center. This odd behavior is actually a neat feature, but it takes getting used to as you shape the curve. If you get frustrated while you're shaping the curve, simply turn the Size button off in the Stroke palette, adjust the Draw Size, shape the curve, and then turn the Size button back on again in the Stroke palette. Touch the end of the curve and the flare returns.

14. Spend a few minutes adjusting the look of the exhaust pipe by editing the curve, the settings in the Stroke palette, and the Draw Size slider on the top shelf. It's important to understand how all of these elements work together so that you can get control over the CurveTube brush. Figure 6.54 shows what I came up with.

15. To add another exhaust pipe you can use a cool trick: simply press the 5 hotkey. This will mask the original exhaust pipe and make a copy; you can then move the curve over to place a second exhaust pipe next to the first. I did this twice to create a series of exhaust pipes, as shown in Figure 6.55.

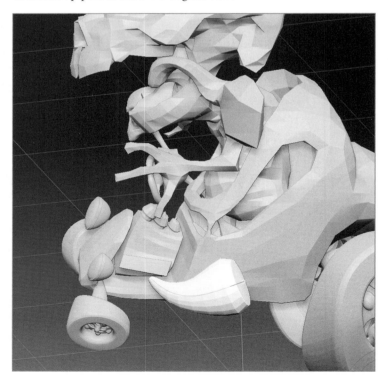

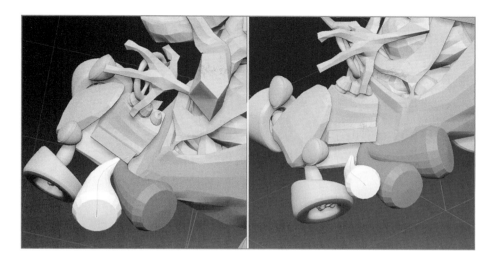

Figure 6.55
Create copies of the pipes by pressing the 5 hotkey.

16. Keep in mind that these exhaust pipes will be sculpted once you have finished placing them, so don't stress out too much if they are not perfect!

17. Save the project when you are happy with the way the pipes look.

Creating Wings with the CurveSurface Brush

The CurveSurface brush is another curve brush that allows you to create geometry by drawing out a curve. It differs from the CurveTube brush in that it lofts a surface across multiple curves, making it perfect for making things such as wings. In the demonstration you'll create some bat wings for the demon character.

1. Open ZBrush and use the File menu to load the demonWings .ZPR project from the Chapter 6 folder on the DVD.

2. Just like the CurveTube brush, the CurveSurface brush must be used on a surface that has no subdivision levels, so again you can append a sphere and hide the sphere within the body of the demon. Append the Sphere3D tool and use Transpose to place it in the back of the demon, as shown in Figure 6.56.

3. Rotate the view of the demon so that you can see the back. Select the CurveSurface brush from the brush library (see Figure 6.57).

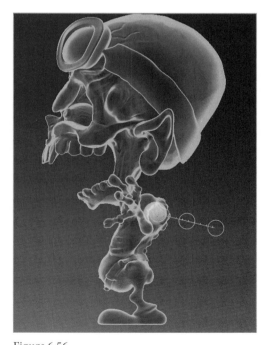

Figure 6.56

Append a sphere, and then scale and move it to the back of the demon using Transpose.

Figure 6.57

Select the CurveSurface brush.

4. Make sure Symmetry is activated (hotkey = X). Draw a curve from the sphere in the back up in an arc to represent the top of a bat wing (as shown in Figure 6.58, upper left).

5. You're going to draw a second curve, but before you do this you'll want to lower the CurveEdit Radius in the Stroke palette so that you have an easier time drawing; otherwise, you will accidentally grab the first curve. Lower the CurveEdit Radius in the Stroke palette to **10**.

6. Draw a second curve below the first, as shown in Figure 6.58, upper right.

7. When you let go, the space between the two curves is filled with a surface.

8. Draw a third curve as shown in Figure 6.58, bottom left. This will be the bottom edge of the curve.

9. When you let go, the space between the second and third curves is filled in, as shown in Figure 6.58, bottom right.

10. As long as the curves are active you can edit them. In the Stroke palette, make sure the Bend button is active. Move the curves around to shape the wings. You can rotate the view of the demon and shape the wings in three dimensions to give them more of a curve (see Figure 6.59).

11. As you shape the wings, you can lower the Draw Size to reduce the thickness of the wings. Lower the Max Points settings in the Stroke palette if you find that there are too many points to work with.

12. When you have a wing shape you like, click the Delete button in the Stroke palette (Figure 6.60). This removes the edit curves and commits the surfaces.

Figure 6.58

As each new curve is drawn, the space between is filled in with a lofted surface.

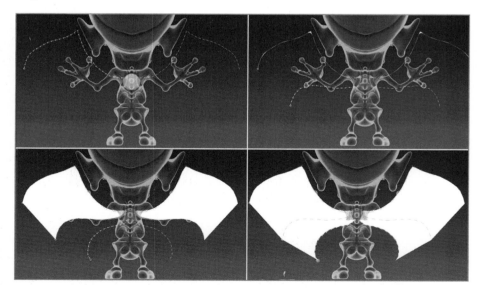

Figure 6.59

Shape the wings by rotating the view and dragging on the curves.

Figure 6.60

Click the Delete button in the Stroke palette to remove the active curves.

13. Ctrl+drag on the canvas to clear any masks, and then activate the Dynamesh button in the Geometry palette. The wings are retopologized to a more sculpting-friendly mesh. You can now edit them using the sculpting brushes. Figure 6.61 shows the demon character with the wings attached.

Figure 6.61

The demon character with the wings attached

Summary

In this chapter you learned some more advanced ZSphere techniques. You learned how to retopologize a character using ZSpheres and how to deform a mesh and rig a character using Transpose Master and ZSpheres. You also learned about mannequins and how they can be converted into a sculptable mesh.

In addition, you learned how to use Curve mode for brushes and how to create and edit geometry using the CurveTube and CurveSurface brushes.

CHAPTER 7

Advanced Brush Techniques

The secret to creating fantastic models in ZBrush lies in the power to customize the sculpting brushes. Up to this point, the exercises in this book have primarily focused on different ways to generate general forms, and the sculpting techniques have been fairly basic. In this chapter, you'll switch into high gear as you learn how to detail your models using the sculpting brushes.

Once you understand how the various controls can be used to customize the brush presets, you'll see that you can design a brush that can do just about anything you want. In this chapter, you'll learn how to design your own brushes to achieve specific results. Each section shows an example of how to use the custom brushes on one of your models.

This chapter includes the following topics:

- **Brush base types**
- **LazyMouse**
- **Alpha textures**
- **Curve brushes**
- **Planar brushes**
- **Depth masking**
- **NoiseMaker**
- **The Picker palette**

Brush Customization

You really don't have to create custom brushes in ZBrush. The existing brush presets found in the brush fly-out library are powerful enough to allow you to sculpt an astonishing amount of detail into your models, from wrinkles in skin to smooth hard-surface models and even dragon scales. So why should you take the time to learn how to customize the sculpting brushes? By learning how the brush controls work, you'll be able to get more out of the existing brush presets. Sometimes just the slightest change to the settings in the Brush palette can make all the difference. Plus, creating your own brushes is a lot of fun. This is probably why there are so many presets available in the brush library—the developers at Pixologic can't seem to stop creating and adding new brushes. If you look in the Brush section of Spotlight, you'll find a large number of folders containing hundreds of variations on brush types. ZBrush users often share their own special variations online through community websites, such as www.zbrushcentral.com.

Creating a custom brush involves adjusting a number of settings throughout the ZBrush interface. The Alpha, Brush, Picker, and Stroke palettes all contain controls that affect how the brushes manipulate the surface of your model. In fact, it would be possible to write a whole book devoted to how these controls work. Rather than overwhelm you with detailed descriptions of each and every button and slider, this section will give you an introduction to how these settings can be combined. As you go forward in your career as a digital sculptor, you'll be able to build on the knowledge gained in this chapter.

We'll start with the fundamentals of how the brushes actually work. The brush presets that you see in the brush fly-out library are all variations created from a number of base brush types. Each brush base uses its own specific algorithm to determine how the surface of the model will be altered. You can find out the base type used by the various presets by holding your cursor over the brush in the fly-out library. The brush base is listed at the bottom of the info pop-up (Figure 7.1).

As you apply the brush tip to the surface, ZBrush samples the polygons within the area defined by the Draw Size setting. Sampling is like a short conversation that takes place between the brush tip and the surface. This sampling action helps ZBrush to determine the properties of the surface, such as the direction of the normals, the number of polygons within the area defined by the brush, which polygons are masked, and so on. The polygons of the surface are then altered by the brush depending on the algorithm used by the brush base and, if you're using a digital tablet, the amount of pressure applied to the tablet.

The following list contains a brief, simplified description of how each brush base affects the surface as you sculpt:

Standard This brush type moves the polygons of the surface outward based on an average of the normal direction (Figure 7.2). Holding the Alt key causes the surface to be pushed inward.

Figure 7.1

The brush base type is displayed at the bottom of the brush info pop-up.

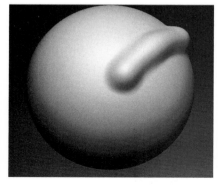

Figure 7.2

The Standard brush base displaces the surface based on an average of the surface normals sampled by the brush.

Move This brush type allows you to push and pull the polygons of the surface around depending on how you move the brush (see Figure 7.3). Holding the Alt key moves the surface along the normal face.

Blur This is the base type used by all the smooth bushes. The positions of the points of the surface are averaged, which causes the details to be smoothed away (Figure 7.4). Holding the Alt key reverses this action, causing details to become more prominent.

Polish This brush base flattens details on the surface, which can reduce the amount of detail in the surface, kind of like the Blur base type. It does this by averaging the normals so that they lie along the same plane, but at the same time the brush continually evaluates and updates the normal direction. Brushes that use this base type work well when sculpting hard edges and flat areas. They are also useful for eliminating lumps in the surface (see Figure 7.5). Holding the Alt key reverses the direction of the polishing action, so, for example, the mPolish brush (medium polish) pushes the surface inward, and holding the Alt key pulls the surface outward.

Clay This brush base affects recessed areas in the model before affecting the protruding parts of the surface (Figure 7.6). This results in a very organic type of deformation that is reminiscent of pressing clay into an actual model. The Clay brush base is used by a lot of the brush presets. Holding the Alt key reverses the direction of the deformation. Be careful when using this brush base on thin parts of the model; the opposite side of the model can become distorted.

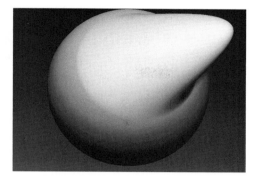

Figure 7.3

The Move brush base lets you pull and push the polygons of the surface.

Figure 7.4

The Blur brush base is used by the smooth brushes. They let you smooth the surface to remove detail.

Figure 7.5

The Polish brush base smoothes the surface and allows you to sculpt hard edges.

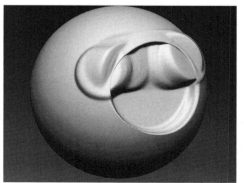

Figure 7.6

The Clay brush base fills in recessed areas of the surface faster than raised parts of the surface.

Figure 7.7

The Hide/Show brush base lets you select the polygons of a surface and hide them.

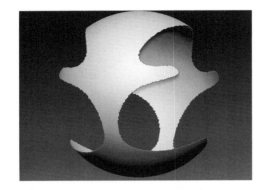

Figure 7.7

The Hide/Show brush base lets you select the polygons of a surface and hide them.

Figure 7.8

The Mask brush base is used to mask the polygons of the surface.

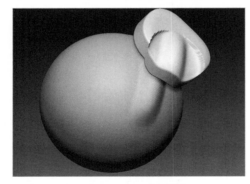

Figure 7.9

The Project brush base moves the polygons of the active subtool so that they match the polygons of visible, inactive subtools.

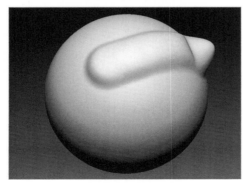

Figure 7.10

The Elastic brush is similar to the Standard brush except that the points of the surface are relaxed as the stroke is drawn.

Hide/Show This brush base type is used by the selection brushes when hiding or showing the polygons of the surface (see Figure 7.7). The selection brushes are explained in detail in Chapter 4, "Polymesh Editing."

Mask This brush base is used by the various masking brushes to apply masks to the surface (see Figure 7.8). Masks are covered in detail in Chapter 3, "Basic Digital Sculpting."

Project This brush base moves the surface of the model to match the surface of visible subtools close to the surface (see Figure 7.9). The ZProject and MatchMaker brushes both use this base. Projection is discussed in more detail in Chapter 6, "Advanced ZSphere Techniques."

Elastic This brush base is similar to the Standard brush (see Figure 7.10). However, the position of each point is relaxed immediately after the brush deforms the surface. Holding the Alt key reverses the direction of the deformation.

ZBrush
Color Image Gallery

On the following pages you will find a gallery of color renderings of some of the example projects used in this book's exercises. In addition, there are images created by ZBrush users. Some of these images were created by my students at the Gnomon School of Visual Effects in Hollywood, and some have been created by my friends and mentors.

"Subterranean" by Jared Krichevsky. Jared is a graduate of the Gnomon School of Visual Effects and currently works as an artist at the Aaron Sims Company in Hollywood (http://jaredkrichevsky .blogspot.com/).

"International Traveler" by Scott Spencer. Scott is a fellow instructor at the Gnomon School of Visual Effects. Currently he is an artist at the Weta Workshop in New Zealand. This image is the result of a tutorial found in his new book *ZBrush Creature Design: Creating Dynamic Concept Imagery for Film and Games* (Sybex, 2012).

LEFT: "Bust of Alfred Hitchcock" by Padhia Avocado (http://www.avocado3d.com/). **RIGHT:** "Blue-Eyed Devil" by Jamin Joseph Lackie (http://artofjamin.blogspot.com/). **BOTTOM:** Dragon design from an animation by Sabra Haskell (http://www.sabrafx.com/). Padhia, Jamin, and Sabra were students in my Introduction to ZBrush class at the Gnomon School of Visual Effects.

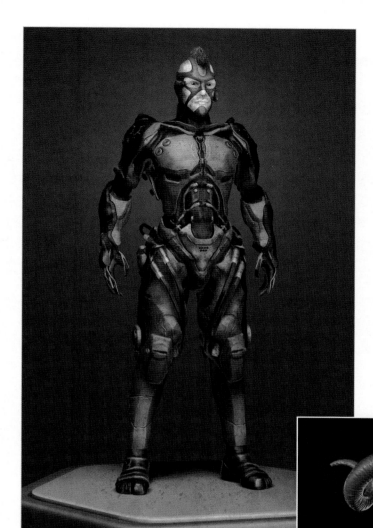

LEFT: "Quantum Armor Prototype VII" by Ara Kermanikian (www.kermaco.com). Ara is a freelance concept artist working in Hollywood. He is also the author of *Introducing Mudbox* (Sybex, 2010).

RIGHT: Concept sketch by John Mahoney. John teaches ZBrush at CalArts and has taught a number of classes at the Gnomon School of Visual Effects as well. (http://mahoneyart.carbonmade.com/)

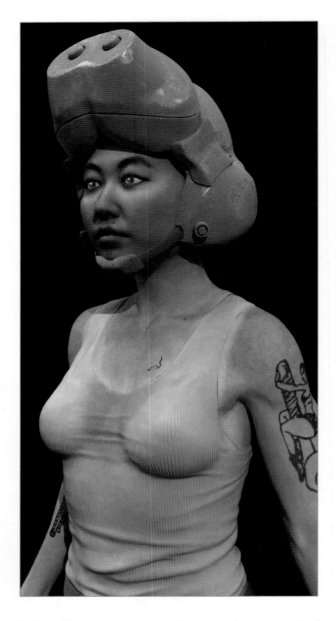

"Mousy" by Mark Dedecker. Mark is a character artist for video games and a fellow instructor at the Gnomon School of Visual Effects (http://monkeymuscle.blogspot.com/).

TOP LEFT: The demon character from Chapter 9, rendered using a custom MatCap material created using the LightCap editor. **TOP RIGHT:** Materials are blended on the surface of the character's face using the Material Mixer and polypainting technique demonstrated in Chapter 9.

BOTTOM LEFT: A model is integrated into a panoramic image of an art gallery using the BPR rendering techniques demonstrated in Chapter 9. **BOTTOM RIGHT:** The finished polypainted dragon's head from Chapter 8.

The completed demon character rendered using BPR and custom materials. Although ZBrush is often used to create realistic characters, this image was designed to demonstrate how easily ZBrush can be adapted and exploited to create any style image, including cartoons.

SingleLayer This brush base moves the surface outward while retaining existing details (see Figure 7.11). Holding the Alt key reverses the direction of the deformation.

SnakeHook This brush base allows you to pull the surface outward in thin wiggly strands (see Figure 7.12). This brush works really well when used on a surface in Dynamesh mode. This is because the SnakeHook can cause polygons to become stretched. However, the stretching is easily eliminated when Dynamesh is activated. This technique is introduced in Chapter 3.

Displace This brush base is similar to the Standard brush in that the surface is pushed out based on the normal direction of the sampled area; however, the specific sampling algorithm is slightly different, causing the deformation to move directly outward from the surface (see Figure 7.13) or inward when holding the Alt key. Try comparing the results of using this brush with the results of using the Standard brush.

Pinch This brush base pulls the points of the surface together (see Figure 7.14). It's great for refining details such as wrinkles and for realistic folds in clothing. Normally, the brush pinches the points up away from the surface. Holding the Alt key causes the pinched areas to be pushed down into the surface.

Figure 7.11
The SingleLayer brush displaces the polygons of a surface by an equal amount while retaining existing details.

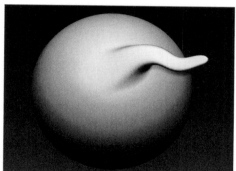

Figure 7.12
The SnakeHook brush base lets you pull snakelike strands out of the surface.

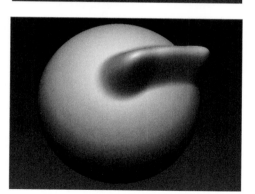

Figure 7.13
The Displace brush base moves the surface directly outward based on the direction of the sampled surface normals.

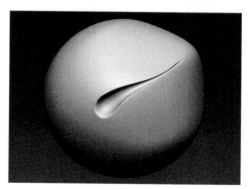

Figure 7.14
The Pinch brush base pulls the points of the surface together.

Figure 7.15
The Trim brush base
is used by the clip
brushes to flatten
the polygons of the
surface to a plane.

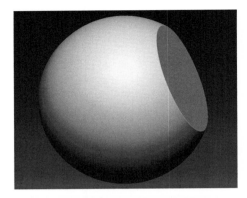

Figure 7.15
The Trim brush base
is used by the clip
brushes to flatten
the polygons of the
surface to a plane.

Trim This brush base pushes the points of the surface to create a flat plane (see Figure 7.15). It is used by the Clip brushes, which were explored in Chapter 5, "ShadowBox and Clip Brushes." It is ideal for sculpting hard surface details and mechanical objects.

Pump This brush base pushes each point outward based on its individual normal direction, so the result is kind of a bulging action (see Figure 7.16). Holding the Alt key reverses the direction of the deformation.

Figure 7.16
The Pump brush
base moves the
points of the surface
outward based on
the individual nor-
mal direction of the
sampled polygons.

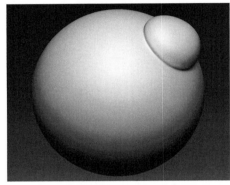

InsertMeshDot This brush base lets you insert a mesh into an existing surface (see Figure 7.17). The InsertSphere, InsertHead, and InsertEar brushes are examples of this brush type. You can edit the brush so that it can be used to insert a custom mesh of your own creation. This technique was covered in Chapter 3. Keep in mind that this brush can only be used on a mesh that has no levels of subdivision.

Figure 7.17
The InsertMeshDot
brush base lets you
insert a mesh into
an existing surface.

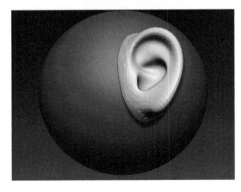

Make a note of the brush base listed in the icon for each of the brushes as you experiment with the presets. Understanding how each base type works will help you decide which brush to use for specific situations.

Designing a Brush

In the exercises in the following sections, you'll create a custom detailing brush and then see how the brush can be used to refine the details of your models. Creating the brush is very easy, and you'll see how adjusting a few settings can change the character of a sculpting brush. This brush will also be useful for creating organic details such as wrinkles.

You'll use the Standard brush as a starting point and begin the design of the brush by applying the LazyMouse feature to the Standard brush.

LazyMouse

LazyMouse stabilizes your brush stroke, allowing you to sculpt straight lines into the surface. This gives you more control over details you create. It seems odd that the feature is called LazyMouse. Technically, it should be LazyBrush, since most people do not sculpt with the mouse, but that's just my opinion.

Figure 7.18

A red line connects the tip of the brush to the stroke on the surface. The length of the line indicates the amount of delay created by the LazyMouse feature.

The LazyMouse feature works by creating a delay between the end of the brush and the actual change made to the surface of the geometry. This delay minimizes the effect of small movements made while sculpting, making it easier to create straight lines as you sculpt. The feature uses a red line to indicate the amount of delay applied to the brush (see Figure 7.18). To adjust the amount of delay as well as other LazyMouse properties, use the controls in the Stroke palette. For many brushes, such as the Standard brush, LazyMouse is already turned on by default. You can turn LazyMouse on or off using the LazyMouse button in the Stroke palette.

When I design a brush, I like to test it using a simple primitive surface, such as a sphere or cube, to easily see what effect the brush settings have on the surface. There are a number of projects in Light Box that work perfectly for brush testing. You'll use some of these in the next few exercises.

1. Open Light Box to the Projects section and double-click the defaultSphere.ZPR project. This project contains a simple PolySphere on a grid. The PolySphere has three levels of subdivision already.

2. Press Ctrl+D twice to add two levels of subdivision. If you like, set the color in the color picker to white so that you can easily see the brush strokes on the surface.

3. Open the brush fly-out library and select the Standard brush. This will be the starting point for your custom detailing brush.

4. Set Draw Size to **20** and Z Intensity to **50** to make a nice, strong stroke that is easily visible on the surface. Make sure there is no alpha selected for the brush in the alpha library. (If there is, open the alpha library and select Alpha Off to remove any alpha textures from the brush.)

5. Draw a stroke on the surface of the PolySphere. Move the brush back and forth in small motions as you drag on the surface. This gives you an idea of how the brush works using the default settings.

6. The LazyMouse controls are found in the Stroke palette. To make it easy to access these controls, open the Stroke palette and move it to the right tray.

By default, the Standard brush has the LazyMouse feature activated already, but LazyRadius is set to 1, so the effect of LazyMouse is not very noticeable. To see how LazyMouse works, increase the LazyRadius value.

7. Set LazyRadius to **80**. Drag across the surface of the PolySphere and move the brush back and forth again. Compare this stroke with the one you made in step 5 (see Figure 7.19).

Figure 7.19

Increasing the LazyRadius value stabilizes the stroke as you draw on the PolySphere.

The stroke is more stable, so there is less variation in the mark created on the PolySphere. By increasing the LazyRadius setting, you increase the amount of delay, and this is indicated by the length of the red line that connects the tip of the brush with the beginning of the mark made on the surface. To make it easier to create straight lines, set LazyRadius to **100**.

CREATE A VERTICAL LINE

You can make the brush stroke move straight up or down by holding the Shift key after you start dragging the brush across the surface. Then pull the brush up or down, and the stroke will snap to a vertical line. This also works when creating horizontal lines or lines moving at a 45-degree angle. It takes a couple of tries to get the hang of this.

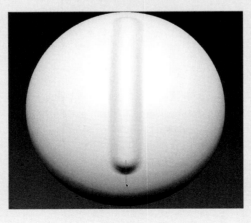

There are several other settings associated with LazyMouse:

LazyStep Increasing the value of this slider increases the space between the marks made by the brush. At the maximum value of 2, you'll see individual dots placed on the surface (see Figure 7.20). This can be really use-ful when creating the effect of bolts or stitches on the surface. Try setting this to the maximum value of 2 while using the Spray stroke type for an interesting effect.

Relative When this button is on, the Draw Size setting influences the space between steps as well. Use this as a way to modify the LazyStep setting.

LazySmooth This adjusts the overall strength of the LazyMouse settings. Use this as a way to modify or fine-tune the LazyRadius setting.

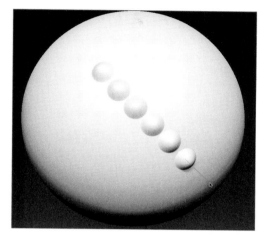

Figure 7.20

Increasing the LazyStep setting increases the space between each step in the stroke.

8. Experiment for a while with different settings for the sliders in the LazyMouse sub-palette of the Stroke palette. Once you get the hang of it, use the following settings:

> LazyMouse = On
> Relative = Off
> LazyStep = **0.1**
> LazySmooth = **10**
> LazyRadius = **20**

Saving Your Custom Brush Preset

You're not finished creating your custom brush yet, but it's a good idea to save the brush now so that you can use it and modify it in future ZBrush sessions.

1. Make sure the Standard brush is the currently selected brush in the sculpting brush fly-out library. Make sure all the settings you created in the previous section are still applied.

2. In the Brush palette, click the Save As button. This will open your computer's file browser window.

3. Use the file browser to navigate to the `Program Files\Pixologic\ZBrush 4R3\ZBrushes` folder (in Mac OS, navigate to the `Applications/ZBrushOSX 4R3/ZBrushes` folder).

Keep in mind that the ZBrush version number may be different on your computer depending on which version of ZBrush you are using. In this folder you'll see a number of subfolders. Each of these folders corresponds to the folders you see in the Brush section of Light Box. I usually save my own custom presets in the Misc folder. Inside each of the subfolders there are a lot of files with the .ZBP filename extension. This is the file format ZBrush uses for brush presets.

4. Save the brush file in this directory using the name detailBrush.ZBP (see Figure 7.21).

5. Once the file is saved, open the Brush section of Light Box. The brushes are listed alphabetically. Scroll the folders to the left, and click the Misc folder. Inside you should see the detailBrush.ZBP file.

6. To load the brush, just double-click the icon. Currently the icon looks the same as the Standard brush icon. Later in the chapter you'll learn how to create your own custom brush icon.

Figure 7.21

Save the brush as detailBrush.ZBP within the ZBrushes folder.

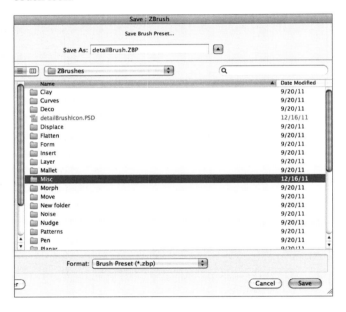

Using the Brush Modifier Slider

The Brush Modifier slider is one of the many controls found in the Brush palette. When you change the settings in the Brush palette, the changes affect all the currently selected brushes in the brush fly-out library. The settings found in the Smooth Brush Modifiers subpalette of the Brush palette, however, affect only the Smooth brush.

The Brush Modifier slider adds a pinch effect when applied to brushes that use the Standard base type. Positive values increase the pinch effect; negative values create more of a bulging effect. By adding this pinch effect to the custom brush created in the previous section, you'll have a brush that works very well for creating wrinkles and precise details on a surface.

Figure 7.22

The Brush Modifier slider is set to 70 in the Modifiers subpalette of the Brush palette.

1. Make sure you have the defaultSphere.ZPR project loaded in ZBrush. If you've made a lot of changes to the PolySphere while testing the brushes, you can either undo the changes or use the Revert button in the File palette to send the surface back to its initial, unsculpted state.

2. Select the detailBrush you created in the previous section.

3. Set Draw Size to a medium Draw Size, such as **20**. Drag across the surface of the PolySphere so that you can see how the brush behaves with its current settings.

4. In the Modifiers subpalette of the Tool palette, set Brush Modifier to **70** (shown toward the bottom of Figure 7.22).

5. Drag across the surface of the PolySphere. Notice that a pinch effect has been added to the marks made by the detailBrush (see Figure 7.23). This will help add to the precision of marks made by the brush.

6. Use the Save button in the Brush palette to save the brush as detailBrush.ZBP. Overwrite the previous version of the brush that you saved in the ZBrushes folder.

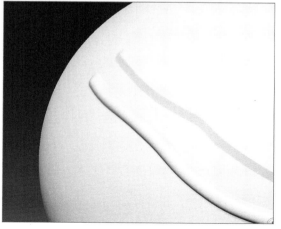

Figure 7.23

Increasing the Brush Modifier slider adds a slight pinch to the Standard brush.

Tablet Pressure Settings

The Tablet Pressure settings found in the Brush palette allow you to fine-tune how the amount of pressure applied to the digital tablet affects various settings in the Brush palette. You can use this feature to further customize your brush and create some very interesting brush properties. An edit curve is used to manipulate each Tablet Pressure setting.

In this section, you'll adjust the edit curves so that the pinching effect of the detailBrush is stronger when more pressure is applied to the tablet. In addition, the Z Intensity will be stronger when pressure is increased and the Draw Size will be larger when less pressure is applied.

1. Open Light Box to the Projects section and double-click the brushTest.ZPR project.

2. Select the detailBrush you created in the previous section.

Figure 7.24

The Tablet Pressure subpalette of the Brush palette

3. Set Draw Size to a medium size such as **20**. Drag across the surface of the PolySphere so that you can see how the brush behaves with its current settings.

4. Place the Brush palette in the right tray so that you can easily access the controls.

5. Expand the Tablet Pressure subpalette so that you can see the controls (see Figure 7.24). Click the BrushMod box toward the bottom to expand the edit curve (see the left image in Figure 7.25).

This curve modifies the intensity of the Brush Modifier setting that you adjusted in the previous section. Currently, the edit curve interface is filled with a light shaded color because the curve itself is set to 100 percent all the way across the top of the graph.

6. Hold the mouse pointer over the edit curve box; you'll see two orange dots appear in the upper left and upper right. Drag the orange dot in the upper left all the way down to the bottom of the graph (see Figure 7.25, right).

The graph now looks like a diagonal line moving from the lower left to the upper right. This particular edit curve is tied to brush pressure in such a way that the horizontal axis of the graph corresponds to brush pressure and the vertical axis corresponds to the

Figure 7.25

Expand the edit curve labeled BrushMod to fine-tune the intensity of the Brush Modifier setting. Drag the dot on the left down to the bottom of the graph to create a diagonal line that slopes upward from left to right.

strength of the effect.

By creating a diagonal line from the lower-left corner to the upper right, you are adjusting the intensity you set earlier using the Brush Modifier slider so that when the pressure is at 0, the intensity of the Brush Modifier is also 0. As you press harder on the digital tablet, the intensity of the Brush Modifier increases so that the pinching effect becomes more pronounced. At full pressure, the maximum value of 70 (which is the value I had you set in step 4 of the previous section) is achieved.

7. Try dragging the brush across the surface of the PolySphere. Vary the pressure as you drag across the surface.

8. The effect is fairly subtle. To make it a bit more obvious, click the center of the line in the BrushMod edit curve window and drag down and toward the right. Add a fourth dot near the upper-right corner of the graph. See if you can make the curve match the one shown in Figure 7.26.

9. Try drawing on the surface again and vary the pressure. Now it should be more obvious that by increasing the pressure on the digital tablet, you get more of a pinching effect (see Figure 7.27).

10. Expand the Size edit curve in the Tablet Pressure subpalette of the Tool palette. Edit the curve so it looks like the left image in Figure 7.28.

11. Expand the Z Intensity edit curve in the Tablet Pressure subpalette of the Tool palette and edit the curve so it looks like the right image in Figure 7.28.

12. To make it more obvious how these changes affect the stroke, on the top shelf, set Draw Size to **60** and Z Intensity to **80.**

13. Drag on the surface of the PolySphere again and vary the pressure as you draw. Now the marks made by the brush become more narrow, pinched, and more intense as you press on the surface (see Figure 7.29).

14. Use the Save button in the Brush palette to save the brush as detailBrush.ZBP. Overwrite the previous version of the brush that you saved in the ZBrushes folder.

Figure 7.26

Two points are added to the graph in the BrushMod edit curve window. The points are moved to shape the curve.

Figure 7.27

Varying the pressure on the tablet causes the strength of the pinching effect to change as the stroke is drawn on the surface.

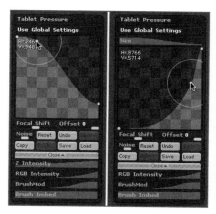

Figure 7.28

The left image shows the altered edit curve for Size, and the right image shows the altered edit curve for Z Intensity.

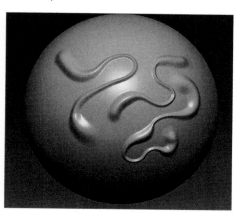

Figure 7.29

Marks made by the brushes vary in width, Z Intensity, and the amount of pinching based on pressure changes made while drawing the stroke.

Congratulations. You've created your first custom brush and it was really pretty easy. This is just the beginning, though. There are endless combinations of settings that can be applied to brushes, and you'll find that you can design a brush to do almost anything once you get some more experience working with the settings.

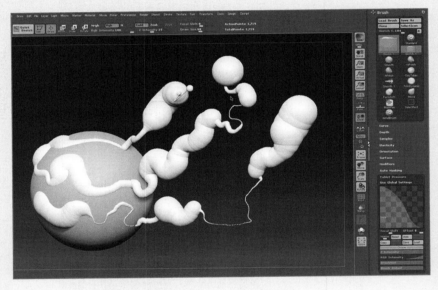

APPLY PRESSURE SETTING TO ZSKETCH BRUSHES

Try editing the Size edit curve for one of the ZSketch brushes and see how it affects the shapes you create when using the ZSketch feature. You'll have to turn off the Use Global Settings button in the Tablet Pressure subpalette of the Brush palette in order to access the edit curves for the ZSketch brushes. For more on ZSketching, consult Chapter 4.

Creating a Custom Brush Icon

It's very easy to create your own custom icon in ZBrush. The icon display can give you a good idea of what a brush does while you're searching through the library of available brushes. This exercise shows you how to create a custom icon for the detailBrush created in the previous section.

Figure 7.30

Set the Width and Height sliders in the Document palette to 512.

1. Open the Document palette. Turn off the Pro button next to the Width and Height sliders. This disables the Preserve Proportion option.

2. Set both the Width and Height sliders to **512** (see Figure 7.30).

3. Click the Resize button. This will resize the canvas and drop any tools that may be in Edit mode to the canvas in the process.

4. Press Ctrl+N to clear the canvas.

5. Set the Range slider to **0** to eliminate the gradient in the canvas background.

6. Click the square labeled Back, and drag down to the black color swatch underneath the color picker. This will set the background color to black.

7. Open the Tool section of Light Box and select a fresh PolySphere. Draw it on the canvas and switch to Edit mode (hotkey = T).

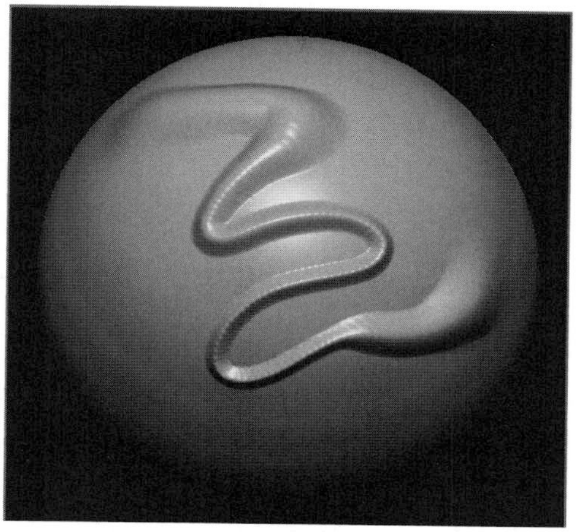

Figure 7.31

Draw a design on the PolySphere using the detailBrush.

8. Click the Frame button on the right shelf to frame the view of the PolySphere (hotkey = F).

9. From the materials fly-out library, choose the BasicMaterial2 material.

10. Press Ctrl+D twice to subdivide the PolySphere two times.

11. Make sure the detailBrush is loaded into ZBrush and is the currently selected brush from the brush fly-out library.

12. Draw a simple design on the PolySphere, something that gives a good indication of the type of mark made by the brush (see Figure 7.31).

13. Click the AAhalf button on the right shelf to shrink the canvas by 50 percent. This will make the anti-aliasing on the edges of the icon appear smooth.

14. In the Document palette, click the Export button to export the image to the document. The file browser window will appear.

15. Use the file browser to navigate to the Pixologic folder. Create a new folder here called **myIcons**.

16. Export the icon as **detailBrushIcon.psd**.

17. In the Brush palette, click the SelectIcon button. Use the file browser to find and select the detailBrushIcon.psd file. You'll see that the icon now appears in the Brush palette (see Figure 7.32).

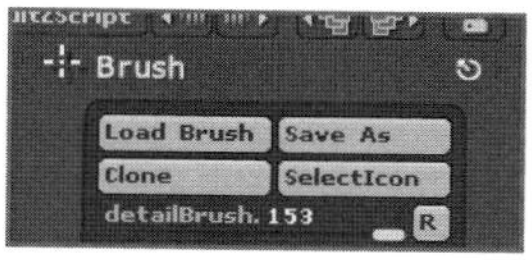

Figure 7.32

Use the SelectIcon button to select the image as the brush icon.

18. Use the Save button in the Brush palette to save the brush as detailBrush.ZBP. Overwrite the previous version of the brush that you saved in the ZBrushes folder.

You'll see the icon appear whenever the brush is loaded into ZBrush as well as in the Brush section of Light Box (in the Misc folder). You can use any image you like as an icon, but the image can't be in color and should be square for best results.

Using the detailBrush

The detailBrush can be used for creating wrinkles and folds of skin on your dragon. Test it out on one of the dragon heads you created in Chapters 3 and 4. I find that this brush works well when refining details such as the edges of the eyelids and lips. I alternate between the detailBrush, the Smooth brush, and the hPolish brush to create wrinkles around the eyes like the ones on the dragon head shown in Figure 7.33.

Figure 7.33

The detailBrush is used with the Smooth and hPolish brushes to create the wrinkles and details of the dragon's eyelids.

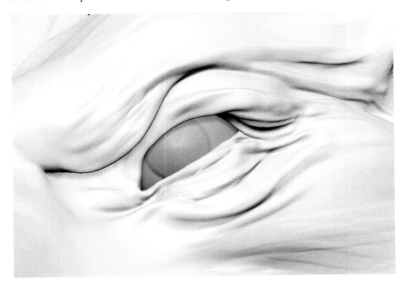

Alpha Textures

In Chapter 2 you were briefly introduced to alpha textures and how they can be used. You have probably noticed that some of the sculpting brushes, such as ClayBuildup and Rake, already have special alpha textures applied. In the following sections you'll dive into alphas and get a taste for the many ways in which alpha textures can be used and manipulated.

An alpha texture (frequently referred to in ZBrush as just an alpha) is a grayscale texture, meaning that it has no color values other than black, white, and gray. Try not to confuse alphas with alpha channels, which are used in compositing programs such as Photoshop.

In ZBrush, alphas are most often used to alter the way a sculpting brush affects the surface of a model. The alpha acts as a mask for the tip of the sculpting brush. White areas in the texture allow the brush to affect the surface, dark areas mask the effect of the brush, and gray values in between moderate the strength of the brush (see Figure 7.34).

An alpha can be an image created in another program such as Photoshop, or it can be created directly in ZBrush. Let's start by seeing some ways in which an alpha can be created.

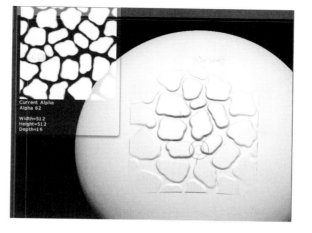

Figure 7.34

Alpha textures are used to modify sculpting brushes. Dark colors in the alpha mask the effect of the brush on the surface.

Creating an Alpha in Photoshop

The easiest way to create an alpha is to simply import an image into the Alpha palette. To see how, you'll do a little simple editing to a photograph in Photoshop. The image is a photograph I took of some snake scales, which is certainly something that could be adapted for use on a dragon model.

If you don't have Photoshop, you can use a similar image-editing program or skip ahead to the next section.

1. Open Photoshop or a similar editing program.

2. Open the snakeScales.PSD file from the Chapter 7 folder on the DVD.

3. The image currently has color information. One way to remove this is to set the mode to Grayscale. Choose Image → Mode → Grayscale (see Figure 7.35).

4. Photoshop may display a warning that the image needs to be flattened. Click OK to accept this.

5. The image could use a little more contrast. Choose Image → Adjustments → Levels to open the histogram. Move the white marker below the histogram (the histogram is depicted as a graph labeled Output Levels) to the left and the black marker to the right. Move the central gray marker a little to the left. Match Figure 7.36.

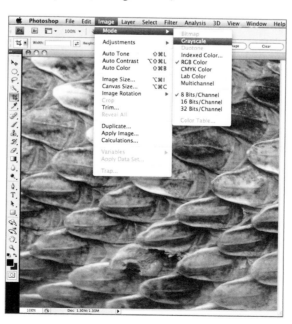

Figure 7.35

The snakeScales image is converted to grayscale, which removes color information.

Figure 7.36

Figure 7.36

The levels are adjusted to add more contrast to the snakeScales image.

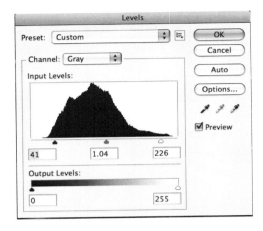

You can use whatever means you prefer to adjust the contrast. If you like using curves or the Brightness/Contrast controls instead of levels, go ahead and do that.

6. Click OK to accept the change.

7. Choose File → Save As and save the image as `scalesAlpha.psd`. Save the image in the ZAlphas folder (in the ZBrush 4R3 folder) so that the alpha appears in the Alpha section of Light Box.

Figure 7.37

The scalesAlpha.psd file is found in the Alpha section of Light Box.

Alternatively, you can save the file in the ZBrush 4R3\ ZStartup\Alphas folder if you want the alpha to load into the fly-out alpha library on the left shelf whenever you start ZBrush. However, you'll need to restart ZBrush if it's currently open to see the file.

8. Open Light Box to the Alpha section and scroll to the right to find the `scalesAlpha.psd` file (see Figure 7.37).

9. To load the alpha from Light Box into the alpha library, hold the Shift key and double-click the icon in Light Box.

10. Load the `defaultSphere.ZPR` project into ZBrush. Subdivide the PolySphere by pressing Ctrl+D twice. Dividing the PolySphere will give it enough polygons so that you can see the effect of the alpha clearly on the surface.

11. Choose the Standard brush and set the stroke type to DragRect.

12. In the alpha fly-out library, select the scalesAlpha.

13. Drag across the surface of the PolySphere. You'll see the impression of the scalesAlpha image appear on the surface of the PolySphere (see Figure 7.38).

This exercise demonstrates how a photograph can be used as an alpha, but I'd like to point out a few limitations related to this particular technique.

The image used in the example has light and dark spots that, in the photograph, appear as colors on the scales and the shadows cast by the scales. This looks natural in an image, but when the image is applied as an alpha, ZBrush interprets these light and dark values as lumps on the surface created by the brush, so it can look less like snake scales and more like just a bumpy surface. In my experience, using a photograph as an alpha to create a specific effect can be a little tricky for these reasons.

Simple alphas with clear shapes and less detail tend to work better than highly detailed images. In addition, if the image is low resolution or if the image suffers from heavy compression, artifacts can appear on the surface as lumps even if the surface itself is very dense. If you're set on using an image as an alpha texture, you'll want to spend some time editing the image to

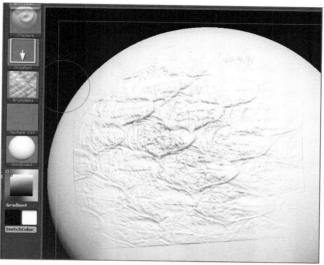

reduce noise and unnecessary detail. Also notice that the brush stroke has a hard edge created by the edges of the photograph. You'll learn how to eliminate this problem in the section titled "Editing an Alpha" later in this chapter.

If you want to load an image from another directory on your hard drive, you can use the Load button at the bottom of the alpha fly-out library, which will open your computer's file browser. If you load a color image, ZBrush will automatically convert it to a grayscale image, removing all of the color information for you. You can also convert a texture in the texture fly-out library on the left shelf into an alpha. Simply select the texture and then click the Make Alpha button at the bottom of the texture fly-out library. Working with textures is covered in more detail in Chapter 8.

Creating an Alpha in ZBrush

You can generate an alpha texture directly in ZBrush by capturing the image that has been drawn on the canvas. ZBrush will not only convert the image to a grayscale texture; it will also use the inherent depth information to shade the alpha in varying degrees of brightness, depending on what is closest to the front of the camera and what is farthest away.

In this exercise you'll create a seamless tiling alpha texture that can be used as a dragon scale brush.

1. Start a new ZBrush session. Open the Document palette and turn off the Pro button.

2. Set the Width slider to **400** and the Height slider to **600.** Click the Resize button. The canvas now appears as a narrow rectangle.

You're going to use a PolySphere to shape a basic dragon scale, which will be used to create a dragon scale pattern.

3. Open Light Box to the Tool section. Double-click the PolySphere.ZTL tool. Draw the PolySphere on the canvas and switch to Edit mode (hotkey = T). If you load a project file such as defaultSphere, the project will alter the document size you created in step 2. This is a case where it's better to load a tool file (.ZTL) rather than a project (.ZPR).

4. Open the Deformation subpalette of the Tool palette. To the right of the Size slider, turn off the Y and Z buttons so that the Size deformer applies only to the x-axis.

5. Move the slider gradually to the left. You'll see the PolySphere become flat; essentially you want to create a rounded disc (see Figure 7.39).

Figure 7.39

Use the Size deformer to flatten the PolySphere.

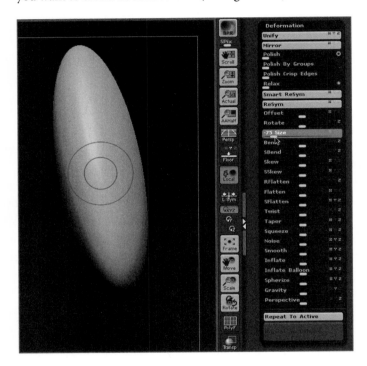

6. Rotate the view of the PolySphere so that you can see it from the flat side (not the edge).

7. Press the X hotkey to activate Symmetry. In the Transform palette under Activate Symmetry, turn off the >X< button and turn on the >Z< button so that Symmetry is now calculated across the z-axis.

8. Open the sculpting brush fly-out library and select the Move Elastic brush. Use the brush to shape the PolySphere into a rounded triangle, as shown in Figure 7.40.

9. Rotate the view of the PolySphere so that you can see it from the edge. Use the Move Elastic brush to shape the PolySphere so that it is bent. The pointed end should be

bent toward the left of the canvas, as shown in Figure 7.41. This will make it easier to overlap the dragon scales.

10. Rotate the view of the PolySphere so that you can see it from the flat side again. Center and scale the view of the PolySphere as shown in Figure 7.42.

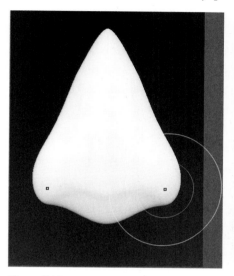

Figure 7.40

Shape the PolySphere into a rounded triangle using the Move Elastic brush.

Figure 7.41

From the side view, use the Move Elastic brush to bend the tip of the PolySphere toward the left side of the canvas.

Figure 7.42

Center the view of the PolySphere.

Here's where things get interesting. To make a seamlessly tiling alpha of dragon scales, you'll use a special feature of ZBrush that allows you to wrap the view of an object across the edges of the canvas. To do this, you have to switch out of Edit mode.

1. Turn off the Edit button on the top shelf to switch out of Edit mode (hotkey = T).

2. Make sure the Draw button is still on. On your keyboard, press and hold the tilde key. This is the squiggly line (~) that is usually just below the Esc key on most keyboards.

3. Drag downward on a blank part of the canvas while holding the tilde key. The PolySphere moves down, but notice that the image wraps around to the top of the canvas so that the bottom of the PolySphere is seen at the top of the canvas.

4. Stop dragging at the point where about half of the PolySphere is seen at the top and half at the bottom of the canvas (see left image in Figure 7.43).

5. Let go of the tilde key and drag on the center of the canvas where it is blank to create a new copy of the deformed PolySphere.

6. Press the T hotkey to activate Edit mode. Rotate the view of the PolySphere and adjust the scale so that the new PolySphere is at the center overlapping the other PolySphere, as shown in the right image in Figure 7.43.

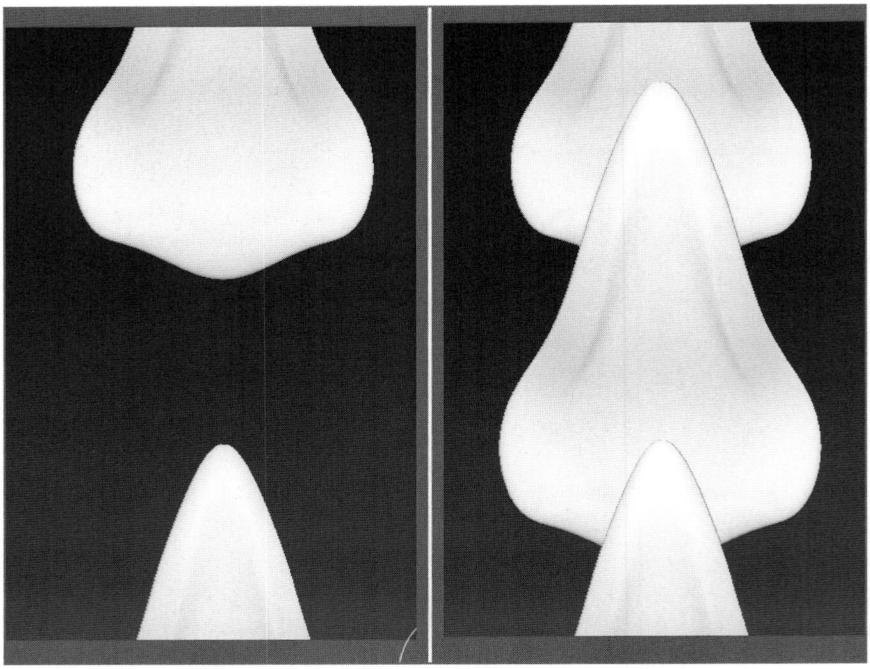

Figure 7.43

Drag downward on the canvas while holding the tilde key to wrap the image of the PolySphere (left). Create a new instance of the PolySphere and position the view so that it overlaps the original image (right).

7. Open the alpha fly-out library on the left shelf and click the GrabDoc button (see Figure 7.44). This takes a snapshot of the canvas. The new alpha appears as the currently selected alpha.

8. Hold the cursor over the newly created alpha to see a preview (see Figure 7.45).

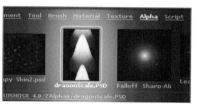

Figure 7.44

The GrabDoc button is at the bottom of the alpha fly-out library.

Figure 7.45

The GrabDoc button creates an alpha based on the image on the canvas.

You can see how the alpha is shaded so that the parts of the image that are closer to the front of the canvas are lighter in value than those that are farther away. This is because when you grab the document, the alpha grabs the depth information from the canvas as well as the overall shape of what is drawn on the canvas.

9. In the Alpha palette, click the Export button and save the alpha as **dragonScale.psd**. Save the alpha to the ZBrush 4 R3\ZAlphas folder. The alpha will appear in Light Box under the Alpha heading (see Figure 7.46).

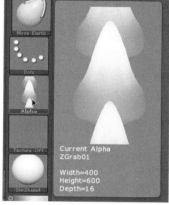

Alpha Roll

Now you can use the dragonScale.psd file as an alpha texture to create a new dragon scale brush that tiles perfectly. To ensure that the tiling is even, you'll use the Roll feature in the Stroke palette. You can see how creating custom brushes often requires using controls that are in a number of different ZBrush palettes. Just as in the previous example, you can test the brush on a PolySphere.

Figure 7.46

The new dragon-Scale.psd alpha appears in the Alpha section of Light Box.

1. Load the defaultSphere.ZPR project from Light Box, and subdivide the mesh a couple of times as you did before.

2. Select the Clay brush in the sculpting brush fly-out library on the right shelf.

3. In the Stroke palette, turn on LazyMouse and set LazyRadius to **10**.

4. Open the alpha fly-out library on the left shelf and select the dragonScale.psd that you created in the previous section.

5. Drag across the PolySphere.

Initially the marks made by the brush don't look very much like scales; this is because the alpha pattern is not spaced correctly, so it looks like a bunch of triangles (see the left image in Figure 7.48).

6. In the Stroke palette, click the Roll button (see Figure 7.47). Drag across the PolySphere again (see the right image in Figure 7.48).

Figure 7.47

The Roll feature is activated in the Stroke palette.

Now you have something that looks more like the scales of a dragon. As you change direction in the stroke, the pattern bends around the curves as well. The Roll Distance slider adjusts the spacing between each stamp created by the alpha. With most tiling textures, the default value of 1 works very well, but you can experiment with different values for Roll Distance to see what kind of effect it has on the marks made by the brush.

7. Use the Save As button in the Brush palette and save the brush as **dragonScales.ZBP**. Save the brush in one of the subfolders of the ZBrushes folder so that it appears in Light Box. If you'd like to create a custom icon, follow the instructions in the section titled "Creating a Custom Brush Icon" earlier in this chapter.

Your custom alpha will be saved with the brush preset so you won't need to load it separately into the Alpha palette when you use this brush in future sessions of ZBrush. It will automatically appear in the alpha library when you load the brush from Light Box.

Figure 7.48

The dragonScale alpha is applied to the Clay brush, which is used to edit the PolySphere (left image). When Roll is activated, the dragonScale.psd alpha tiles seamlessly as it is used to edit the PolySphere (right image).

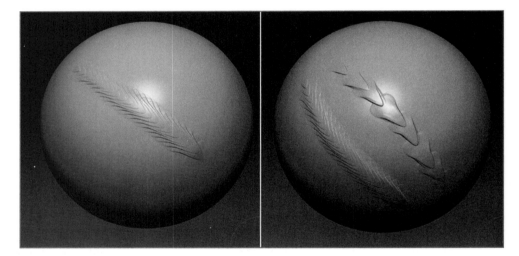

SCALE BRUSH PRESETS

Take a moment to look through the brush presets in the sculpting brush fly-out library as well as the presets available in the Scales folder inside the Brush section of Light Box. You'll notice that there are a fair number of brush presets devoted to creating scale effects.

Editing an Alpha

In this section, you'll take a look at how the settings in the Alpha palette can be used to change the behavior of an existing alpha. You'll use one of the basic alphas that is already loaded into the alpha fly-out library, but these settings can be applied to alphas that you create as well.

1. Load the `defaultSphere.ZPR` project from the Projects section of Light Box. Subdivide the sphere a couple of times as you did before.

2. In the brush fly-out library, select the Standard brush.

3. Set the stroke type to DragRect.

4. Open the alpha fly-out library and choose Alpha 62. Figure 7.49 shows the Standard brush with the DragRect stroke type and Alpha 62 applied.

5. Place the Alpha palette in the tray so that you can easily access the control.

6. Drag on the surface of the PolySphere. You'll see the pattern appear on the surface of the PolySphere.

The hard edge of the square alpha is clearly visible in the mark made on the PolySphere (see the left image in Figure 7.50). To eliminate this, you can use the Radial Fade feature.

7. In the Alpha palette, set the Rf slider to **10** and draw on a blank part of the surface of the PolySphere again. Now the hard edge is eliminated (see the right image in Figure 7.50).

8. You can add some noise to the alpha to increase detail. The noise is applied to the lighter parts of the alpha. Set the Noise slider to **50** and NScale to **24**. Drag across a blank part of the surface of the PolySphere to see how noise affects the stroke (see the left image in Figure 7.51).

9. You can adjust the repetition of the tiling across the vertical and horizontal axes independently using the H Tiles and V Tiles sliders. Try setting H Tiles to **3**. Test the brush again (see the right image in Figure 7.51).

Figure 7.49

Select the Standard brush, set the stroke type to DragRect, and choose Alpha 62 from the alpha library.

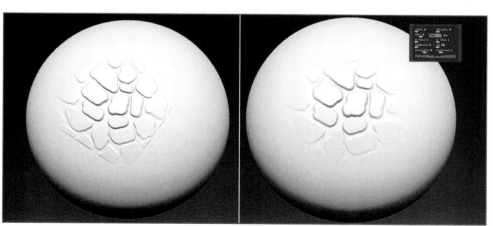

Figure 7.50

The hard edge of the alpha border is visible in the pattern created on the PolySphere (left image). The Radial Fade slider in the Alpha palette eliminates the hard edge (right image).

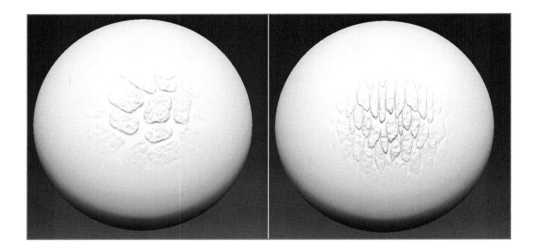

10. Expand the AlphaAdjust edit curve below the Intensity slider. Try adding some points to the curve, and notice how the alpha behaves. The curve controls the intensity of the black and white values. If you reverse the curve so that it slopes from the upper left down to the lower right, the alpha is inverted.

11. Try editing the curve so that it looks like Figure 7.52, and drag on a blank part of the PolySphere.

12. The changes you make in the Alpha palette are applied to whichever alpha the current sculpting brush uses. Switch to Alpha 56 and see the effect you get when the settings are applied to this alpha.

Figure 7.52

Adjust the edit curve for the alpha.

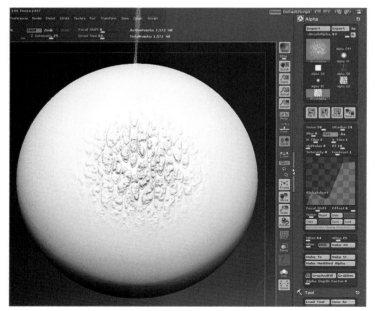

13. Switch back to Alpha 62. Click the Make Modified Alpha button. This creates a new alpha texture in the alpha fly-out library based on the current settings in the Alpha palette. This is another way you can generate new alpha textures within ZBrush.

Now that you have created a new alpha, you can save the brush, but before you do you'll need to set the alpha options back to their original state. Otherwise, these settings are applied to the newly created alpha texture, which doubles the effects applied to the alpha.

1. Set the following options:

 H Tiles = **1**

 Noise = **0**

 Rf = **0**

2. Under the AlphaAdjust curve, click the Reset button to restore the curve to its natural state.

3. In the Brush palette, click the Save button and save the brush as `noisySpots.ZBP` in the `ZBrushes/Misc` folder.

You can experiment with the other options in the Alpha palette. Here's a brief description of what each setting does:

Blur softens the alpha as well as any noise or other effects applied to it.

Max maximizes the range of the alpha so that the lightest values become 100 percent white and the darkest values become 100 percent black.

Aa adds anti-aliasing to the alpha, which can be helpful when using imported images that are not high quality.

MidValue adjusts how the alpha affects the depth of the alpha displacement. When this is at 0, lighter values in the alpha push the surface outward, and as you increase the setting, the amount of displacement caused by the lighter values is lowered. At a value of 100, the brush no longer pushes the surface outward. Instead, the impression made by the alpha is pushed into the surface.

Intensity increases the overall intensity of the alpha. The AlphaAdjust curve also affects the intensity of the alpha but allows you greater control over the adjustment than the Intensity slider.

Contrast increases the overall contrast of the alpha.

CREATE FROM NOISEMAKER

The Create From NoiseMaker option in the Create subpalette of the Alpha palette is a new feature in ZBrush 4R3. This lets you create a new alpha from a fractal noise pattern generated by the NoiseMaker plug-in. To learn more about how the plug-in works, read the section titled "Noise" later in this chapter.

Tilt

The Tilt settings cause marks made by a brush to slant slightly. This option is a great way to create overlapping scales and works best when an alpha is applied to the brush.

1. Load the defaultSphere.ZPR project from the Projects section of Light Box. Subdivide the sphere a couple of times as you did before.

2. From the sculpting brush library, choose the Elastic brush.

3. Open the alpha fly-out library and select Alpha 50, which is a simple, blurry, white dot.

4. In the Stroke palette, turn on LazyMouse and set LazyStep to **0.4** and LazyRadius to **5**.

5. Set Z Intensity to **80**.

6. Drag across the PolySphere; the stroke looks like a bumpy line (see Figure 7.53, left image).

7. Open the Brush palette and expand the Modifiers subpalette. Set Tilt Brush to **70**.

8. Drag across the surface. You can see that now the bumps in the stroke are tilted, creating a scale effect (see the right image in Figure 7.53).

9. Use the Save button in the Brush palette to save the brush as **scalesLine.ZBP** in the ZBrushes/Misc folder.

Figure 7.53

The Tilt Brush setting in the Brush palette tilts the marks made by the alpha in the direction of the stroke (right image).

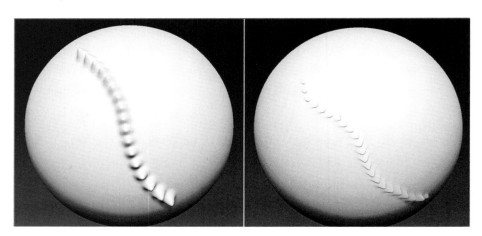

RESET BRUSHES

After you have played with brush settings for a while, you may lose track of all the changes you've made. If you want to return the brushes to their initial states, just click the Reset All Brushes button at the bottom of the Brush palette (this button is also found in the brush library). Make sure that you've saved any custom brushes that you want to keep before clicking this button!

Spin Alphas

The Spin Alpha feature causes the alpha to rotate with each step as you create a stroke across the surface. It's used by the deco brushes and is perfect when you want a brush that generates elaborate designs.

1. Load the `defaultSphere.ZPR` project from the Projects section of Light Box. Subdivide the sphere a couple of times as you did before.

2. Select the Layer brush from the brush fly-out library.

3. In the Stroke palette, turn on LazyMouse. Set LazyStep to **0.1** and LazyRadius to **20**.

4. In the Alpha palette, click the Load button and load the `centipede.PSD` alpha texture from the `chapter7\alphas` folder on the DVD. This is a simple alpha I created by grabbing an image from the ZBrush canvas (see Figure 7.54).

5. Open the Brush palette and expand the Tablet Pressure subpalette. Click the Size edit curve, and edit the curve so it resembles Figure 7.55.

6. Press the X hotkey to activate Symmetry. Set Z Intensity to **35** and drag across the surface of the PolySphere (see the top image in Figure 7.56).

It looks pretty interesting, but now you'll add spin to the alpha and see how easy it is to create elaborate designs.

7. Expand the Brush palette. In the Orientation subpalette, set SpinRate to **1** and drag across a blank part of the surface of the PolySphere (see the middle image in Figure 7.56).

The SpinRate setting determines how much the alpha spins around during each step of the stroke. Already it should be apparent how this setting changes the nature of the brush. The other Spin settings won't do anything unless SpinRate is set to a nonzero value. Positive values cause the alpha to spin clockwise, and negative values cause the alpha to spin counterclockwise.

8. Set the SpinCenter slider to **1.2**. Drag across a blank part of the PolySphere (see the bottom image in Figure 7.56).

Figure 7.54

The centipede.PSD alpha was created by grabbing the depth information of simple objects drawn on the canvas.

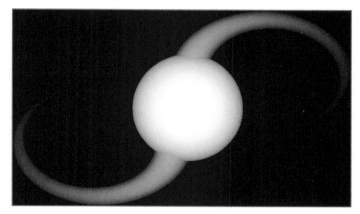

Figure 7.55

Adjust the shape of the Size edit curve in the Tablet Pressure subpalette of the Brush palette.

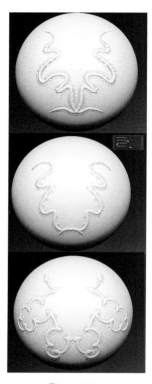

Figure 7.56

The SpinCenter setting adds an offset to the center of the alpha spin, which makes creating elaborate designs very easy.

SpinCenter adds an offset to the center of the alpha. This creates a looping action to the stroke. The higher you set the slider, the greater the offset, so the loops become larger. Negative values cause the loops to go in the opposite direction.

The SpinAngle slider sets the starting angle for the spinning action.

9. Experiment with different settings applied to the three sliders in the Orientation subpalette. Also, try combining this effect with different settings for H Tiles and V Tiles in the Alpha palette.

10. Save the brush as `centipede.ZBP` in the `Brushes\Misc` folder.

THE LAYER BRUSH

The Layer brush works well for creating decorative designs on a surface because it pushes the surface out in a single layer. When you store a morph target for the model, the Layer brush always pushes the surface out the same amount even when strokes overlap each other.

Figure 7.57 shows some ways in which the alpha texture brush techniques described in this section can be used to create details and designs on the surface of some dragon models.

Figure 7.57

Details and designs are added to the surfaces of some dragon models using the techniques described in this section.

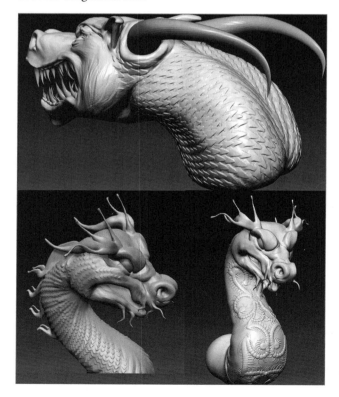

BRUSH TWIST

The settings in the Twist subpalette of the Brush palette have a similar effect on the brush except instead of rotating the alpha, the Twist options rotate the end of the brush that twists the surface in a spiral motion. The Twist Rate setting determines how many turns occur per brush step. The Centrifugal option determines how much of the surface is pulled, and the Radius option determines the falloff of the twisting effect. Try using these options on the SnakeHook brush when sculpting a Dynamesh surface. Use a Twist Rate setting of **0.05** and a Centrifugal setting of **0.1**. Lower the Z Intensity to around **40**. You should be able to create some very interesting shapes when you use the brush to pull out parts of a surface. The image at right shows how this brush can be used creatively on a Dynamesh surface.

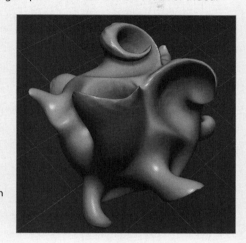

Brush Effects

A number of settings in the Brush palette can add special effects to your custom brushes. In some cases, using these features in combination with alpha textures can add really interesting behaviors to your brush, allowing you to create details on your surfaces that would be difficult to achieve otherwise. In the following sections, you'll continue to add to your library of customized sculpting brushes by implementing some of these features.

Trails

You can think of the Trails feature as adding a kind of echo effect to your brush stroke. The Trails slider is found in the Brush Modifiers subpalette of the Tool palette. There is a Trails slider that, when set to a value above 1, adds another iteration of the stroke that "trails" behind the initial stroke. As long as you continue to apply the stroke to the surface, the trails continue to repeat until you release the stroke. A number of additional settings below the Trails slider fine-tune how the trail effect is applied to the stroke.

In this exercise, you'll design a brush that uses the Trails feature. This brush can be used to create a kind of calligraphy stroke.

1. Load the defaultSphere.ZPR project from the Projects section of Light Box. Subdivide the sphere a couple of times as you did before.

2. From the sculpting brush fly-out library, choose the Clay brush.

3. Set the Z Intensity to **60** and Draw Size to **15**, and turn on the Zsub button so that the brush cuts into the surface.

4. From the alpha fly-out library, select Alpha 60.

5. In the Stroke palette, turn on LazyMouse and set LazyRadius to **5**. Turn on the Roll button.

6. Create a few test strokes on the surface of the PolySphere (see Figure 7.58).

7. Place the Brush palette in the tray so that you can access the controls.

Figure 7.58

Test strokes are created on a blank part of the PolySphere.

8. In the Modifiers subpalette of the Tool palette, set the Trails feature to **85**.

9. In the Tablet Pressure section, turn off the Use Global Settings button. Expand the Size edit curve and adjust the curve so that it resembles Figure 7.59.

10. Create a few more test strokes on a blank part of the PolySphere surface (left image in Figure 7.60). As you make the stroke, observe the area behind the stroke. You can see that as the stroke continues, the earlier parts push deeper into the surface. This is because of the echo effect created by the Trails feature.

11. Set GPosition and GOrientation to **1**. These settings adjust the global position of the trailing strokes as well as the orientation. The effect on the stroke is fairly dramatic.

12. Create a few more strokes. At this point, the Trails feature should appear more obvious (right image in Figure 7.60).

13. Save the brush as **Calligraphy.ZBP** in the ZBrushes/Misc folder.

Figure 7.59

The Trails slider in the Modifiers subpalette of the Brush palette is set to 85 and the edit curve for Size in the Tablet Pressure subpalette is modified.

Figure 7.60

The Trails feature echoes the brush stroke as you draw on the surface (left image). Set GPosition and GOrientation to 1 for a dramatic effect.

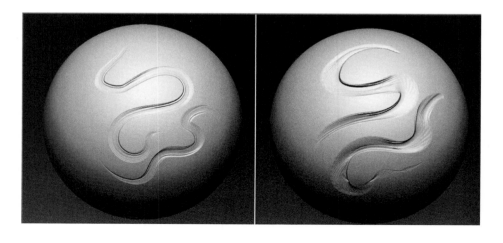

Elasticity

In Chapter 3 you used the Move Elastic brush to create the basic shape of the dragon head. The Move Elastic brush is a variation of the basic Move brush with additional Elasticity settings activated. The purpose of the Elasticity settings is to reduce stretching in the surface when it is pulled by the Move brush. As you use the Move Elastic brush, you can see the surface update while you work. In addition, pulling out and then pushing back in with the brush creates a tapering in the altered part of the surface.

The Elasticity settings can give other brushes some interesting behaviors as well. It works best when using the Move brushes, but let's see what happens when it is applied to the Nudge brush.

Because of the fact that ZBrush needs to reevaluate the surface as you work, it's best to use the Elasticity settings on low polygon surfaces.

1. Load the defaultSphere.ZPR project from the Projects section of Light Box. Subdivide the sphere a couple of times as you did before.

2. In the Tool palette, expand the Geometry subpalette and set SDiv to **3**.

3. Open the sculpting brush fly-out library and choose the Nudge brush.

4. Set Z Intensity to **60** and Draw Size to **45**. Set Focal Shift to **-100**.

5. Place the Brush palette in the tray and expand the Elasticity subpalette. This is where you will find the various Elasticity settings.

Elasticity Strength determines how much effort ZBrush will use to recalculate the topology of the surface with each brush stroke. In the case of the Nudge brush, you'll get more noticeable results using a lower value. If you crank the value all the way up, ZBrush will try to preserve the shape of the surface so much that it will appear as if the brush does nothing at all.

Figure 7.61

The Elasticity settings in the Brush palette

6. Set Elasticity Strength to **10** (see Figure 7.61).

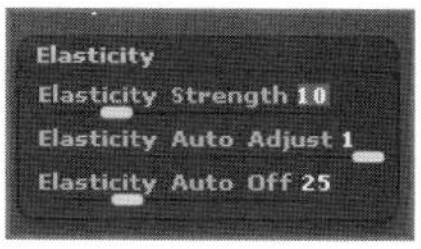

The Elasticity Auto Adjust setting controls the amount of tapering that occurs when you change directions while brushing on the surface. When applied to the Nudge brush, it creates more of a ripple effect as you move the brush back and forth.

7. Set Elasticity Auto Adjust to **1**.

Elasticity Auto Off sets a polygon limit for the elasticity effect. If the surface has more polygons than the slider value, then the elasticity effect is automatically disabled. This prevents ZBrush from slowing down too much or crashing when trying to reevaluate the surface. The value set by the slider is multiplied by 1,000, so the default setting of 25 means 25,000. A PolySphere at SDiv 3 is 24,578 polygons, just under the default limit.

You can raise this limit and use the Elasticity settings on a dense mesh, but do so with caution.

8. Try shaping the PolySphere with the Nudge brush. This brush should work well when developing facial expressions for characters because of the way that it pushes the surface around (see Figure 7.62).

9. Save the brush as **nudgeElastic.ZBP** in the ZBrushes\Misc folder.

Figure 7.62

The surface of the PolySphere is pushed around using the Nudge brush with an Elasticity Strength setting of 10.

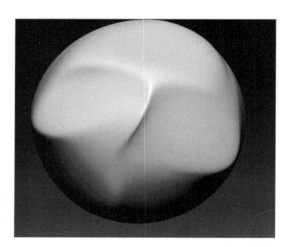

Noise

The Noise option adds a fractal-based noise effect to the marks created by a brush. You can use the NoiseMaker plug-in to custom design the look of the noise that is applied to the brush.

Using the Noise effect on a brush is a great way to sculpt rocky surfaces or create the look of damage for armor or mechanical objects. In this exercise, you'll create your own custom noise brush based on the Inflate brush so that you get a better understanding of how the feature works.

1. Load the defaultSphere.ZPR project from the Projects section of Light Box. Subdivide the sphere a couple of times as you did before.

2. From the sculpting brush fly-out library, choose the Inflate brush.

3. Place the Brush palette in the tray so that you can access the controls.

4. Expand the Surface subpalette of the Brush palette.

5. Click the Noise button; this opens up the NoiseMaker plug-in. This is a special interface you can use to design custom noise effects.

7. In NoiseMaker set the Scale slider to **40** so that the noise is easier to see, and set the Strength to **0.002**.

8. Expand the edit curve below the noise sliders. Experiment with different shapes for the curve, and test the brush while you make changes. Try matching the curves in the left side of Figure 7.63.

9. Use the Inflate brush to sculpt the surface of the PolySphere. The noise effect is applied to the surface as you sculpt.

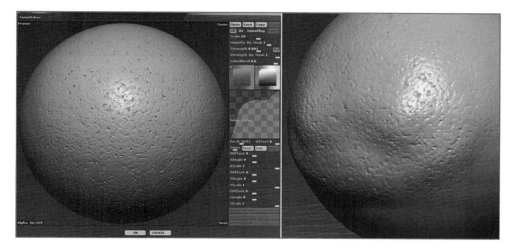

Figure 7.63

Change the shape of the Noise edit curve to create different looks for the noise patterns created in the stroke.

The Scale slider controls the size of the noise distortion. A low value creates tiny bumps, which is good for fine detail. A large value creates very large details, which works well for rocky surfaces.

The Strength slider controls how much noise is added to strokes created by the brush. This is also affected by the Z Intensity of the stroke. By using a Strength value of 1 on a brush with a lower Z Intensity, you'll get more of the noise effect with less of a change to the shape of the surface. Set the Strength slider to a negative value to invert the noise. This will cause strokes to create craters instead of bumps.

The Noise edit curve allows you to change the pattern of the noise itself. You can create a wide variety of different noise textures by experimenting with different shapes for the curve.

10. Save the brush as **noisyInflate.ZBP** in the myBrushes/Misc folder.

The NoiseMaker feature can be applied creatively to different brush types for interesting effects. Try adding noise to the Move brush; then hold the Alt key while dragging on the surface.

This same plug-in can be used to create alphas using the Create From NoiseMaker button in the Alpha palette. You'll find more examples of how to use NoiseMaker in Chapter 10, "Surface Noise, Layers, and the ZBrush Timeline."

Hard Surface Detail Brushes

The developers at Pixologic first introduced the Planar and Trim brushes in ZBrush version 3.5 as a way to make sculpting hard surface details easier. If you've tried using these brushes, you may have found that their behavior is a bit mysterious. In the following sections, hard surface modeling with these brushes will be demystified, and you'll learn how you can create your own variations of these brushes as well as use them to model mechanical surfaces.

Planar Brushes

The planar brushes are used to sculpt flat surfaces onto an object. When applied to a surface, they press all of the points within the area defined by the brush tip into a flat plane. This is very similar to the way in which the clip brushes described in Chapter 5 work.

Each planar brush has been created through different combinations of settings applied to brushes that use the Clay or Polish base. Many of these settings will be described in detail throughout this chapter. Before we get into how these settings are applied, let's just see how the brushes can be used on a surface. We'll start by creating a good test surface.

1. Load the defaultCUBE.ZPR project from the Projects section of Light Box. This project has a cube as a starting primitive that will work perfectly for demonstrating the planar brushes.

2. Set the color in the color picker to white so that it's easier to see the strokes you'll make with the brushes on the cube surface. Press Ctrl+D twice to add two levels of subdivision to the surface (see Figure 7.64).

3. From the brush fly-out library, choose the Planar brush. Use the brush to sculpt on one of the flat ends of the cube.

Nothing happens when you use the Planar brush. What is going on? The Planar brush is used to extend the sampled area into a flat plane. If you use the brush on a flat surface, you won't see any change.

4. Increase the Draw Size to **200**. Hold the brush over one of the rounded edges. Notice the angle of the brush icon as you hold it over the rounded corner.

Figure 7.64
After the cube is subdivided, the edges become rounded.

This gives you a visual indication of the angle of the plane that will be created when you use the brush on the corner (top image in Figure 7.65).

5. Drag along the corner with the Planar brush. Now a flat, beveled edge appears based on the angle of the brush icon (bottom image in 7.65).

This is a great brush to use when you need to flatten an edge or smooth out bumps on a surface.

Brush Depth

When you stroke along the surface of a mesh with the sculpting brush, the concentric circles give you an indication of the size, the falloff, and the angle of the stroke. However, the circles that represent the tip of the brush tell only part of the story. ZBrush actually understands that the tip of the brush is a spherical volume. The concentric circles you see as you sculpt on the surface are a cross section of that volume. And any part of the surface within the volume will be affected by the brush. Figure 7.66 illustrates this concept.

By altering the position of this spherical volume relative to the surface of the mesh, you can change the depth of the marks made by the brush. To do this, you adjust the Imbed setting in the Depth subpalette of the Brush palette.

The Depth subpalette has a picture that represents a cross section of the brush tip viewed from the side. The circle represents the spherical volume of the brush tip, while the horizontal line represents the surface of a sculptable mesh. The black dot represents the center of the brush tip (see Figure 7.67).

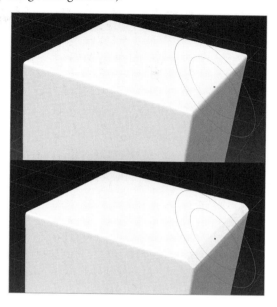

Figure 7.65

The angle of the circle as you hold it over the surface indicates the planar cut that will be created by the brush (top image). As you drag on the surface, a planar cut is made along the edge of the cube.

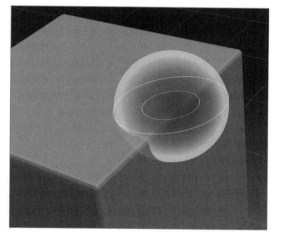

Figure 7.66

The concentric circles that represent the tip of the sculpting brush are a cross section of an invisible spherical volume.

Figure 7.67

The Depth subpalette contains an interactive diagram that represents the depth of the brush tip.

You can change the position of the brush tip's center by dragging it up or down within the diagram. You can achieve the same thing by moving the Imbed slider back and forth.

Let's take a look at how changing the Imbed setting affects the way the brush reacts with the surface.

1. Load the defaultCUBE.ZPR project from the Projects section of Light Box. Set the color picker to white and Press Ctrl+D twice to add two levels of subdivision to the surface.

2. From the sculpting brush library, select the Planar brush. Set Draw Size to **100**.

3. Place the Brush palette in the tray and expand the Depth subpalette.

4. Drag on one of the flat sides of the cube with the brush. Nothing happens.

Take a look in the Depth subpalette. The black dot at the center of the circle is in line with the horizontal line representing the mesh surface. At the moment, the brush has no depth, so the surface is unaffected.

5. Drag the black dot in the diagram down a little, or set the Imbed slider to **20**, and drag the brush across the surface (see Figure 7.68).

6. Try moving the black dot in the Depth subpalette above the line, or set the Imbed slider to **-20**. Drag on the surface of the cube.

This time nothing happens. Why is this? Take a look at the top shelf. The Planar brush has Zsub on by default.

7. Turn on the Zadd button and set Imbed to **20**. Now as you drag on the surface, the brush pulls the surface up to a flat plane (see Figure 7.69).

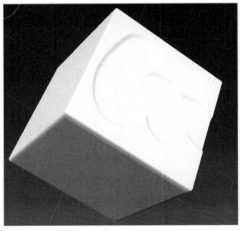

Figure 7.68

Setting the Imbed slider to 20 causes the Planar brush to cut into the surface of the cube.

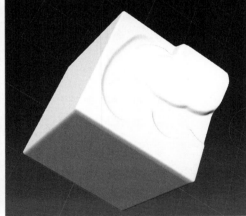

Figure 7.69

When the draw mode is set to Zadd and Imbed is set to 20, the Planar brush lifts the surface up.

The Zadd and the Zsub buttons work together with the Imbed feature. This can trip you up a little if you're not paying attention. Make a note of whether the brush is in Zadd or Zsub mode when you are adjusting the Imbed option. Notice that as you switch between the Zadd and Zsub buttons, the black dot at the center of the diagram flips positions across the central line. Remember that you can also hold the Alt key to switch between Zadd and Zsub.

8. Set Imbed to **-40** and draw on one of the rounded corners of the cube. The corner is not affected, but the area behind the corner is pulled up to a flat plane (see Figure 7.70).

This behavior illustrates that, because the center of the tip is imbedded below the surface, the deformation of the surface occurs below the point of contact.

9. Play with the Imbed feature using the Planar brush for a while, and experiment with different combinations of Imbed settings and Zadd or Zsub. After a while, it should start to make more sense.

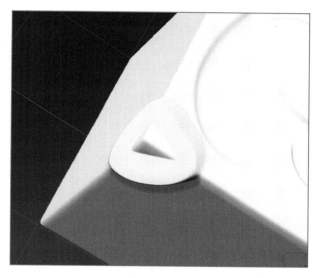

Figure 7.70

When Imbed is set to -40, the brush affects the area below the surface. This is most easily demonstrated by brushing on the corner of the cube.

DEPTH AND Z INTENSITY

Up to now you have probably been thinking that the depth of the stroke is controlled by the Z Intensity slider. Actually, Z Intensity controls how quickly you achieve the depth set by the Imbed setting in the Depth palette. Think of Z Intensity as the accelerator pedal on a car. Increasing the value is like applying more pressure to the accelerator pedal. The Imbed setting represents your destination. The more pressure you apply to the accelerator pedal of a car, the faster you go and the sooner you reach your destination. So the higher the Z Intensity, the sooner the brush meets its maximum depth.

Depth Masking

Depth masking lets you change the spherical shape of the brush tip itself, which creates some very interesting brush effects. When you activate the Depth Mask button in the Depth subpalette of the Brush palette, a black dot appears at the top and the bottom of the brush diagram. By dragging these dots toward the center of the circle, you're actually masking out part of the volume of the brush tip. This exercise demonstrates how this works.

1. Load the defaultCube.ZPR project from the Projects section of Light Box. Set the color picker to white and press Ctrl+D twice to add two levels of subdivision to the surface.

2. Choose the Standard brush from the sculpting brush fly-out library.

3. Make sure the Brush palette has been docked in a tray so that you can easily access the controls.

4. Set Draw Size to **60** and Z Intensity to **75**, and draw some strokes on the surface of the cube.

5. In the Depth subpalette of the Draw palette, click Depth Mask. Drag the black dot at the top of the circle down; you can also adjust the OuterDepth slider to achieve the same result.

6. Create some new strokes on the surface.

The strokes have a much flatter quality because the outer depth of the brush tip is masked (see Figure 7.71).

Figure 7.71

Mask the outer depth of the Standard brush to create a flatter stroke.

BACKTRACK

BackTrack is a special set of modifiers that become available when LazyMouse is activated for a brush. The BackTrack settings are most often used with the planar brushes as a way to help create hard surface details. These settings are also available for other types of brushes and can be used for creating interesting effects.

The BackTrack options are found in the Stroke palette and become available when the LazyMouse button is enabled. Once LazyMouse is activated, you can turn on the BackTrack button, which applies this feature to the current sculpting brush.

BackTrack has four modes: Plane, Line, Spline, and Path. The following exercises demonstrate how each of these different BackTrack modes works.

Plane—The Planar brush uses the Plane mode of BackTrack to create the virtual cut plane. This means that the stroke cuts along a plane established by the initial angle of the brush.

Line—This mode lets you set the angle of the cut plane interactively. You create a start point and an end point by clicking on the surface and then move the stroke back up toward the starting point, hence the name *BackTrack*. A red line appears as you drag. At each end of the line is a perpendicular green line indicating the starting and stopping points. By dragging this line out, you are setting the angle of the cutting plane interactively.

Spline—This mode is designed to make it easier to create a rounded bevel. It is similar to Line mode in that you draw a line between two points and then backtrack toward the start of the point. But rather than cut along a flat plane defined by the two points, Spline creates a rounded bevel by interpolating a curve between the two points.

Using the Spline option is made easier by enabling SnapToTrack, which restricts the stroke to the initial line of the stroke. The PlanarSpline brush uses both Spline mode and SnapToTrack. The way in which the curve is cut into the surface can be adjusted by increasing the value of Track Curvature. Higher values create a shallower curve.

Path—This mode restricts the stroke of the brush to the initial path that you draw on the surface. This can add precision to the details you create in a surface. Just as with Line and Spline modes, you first draw out the initial path and then move back and forth to create the cut. Unlike Line and Spline, the initial path you create does not have to be a straight line; it can be a curve.

The SnapToTrack option can be used with Line and Spline mode as well. This is a great way to create a perfectly straight line.

The Picker Palette

Even though the brush tip is a spherical volume, the actual deformation in the surface created by the brush is not. In many cases, the angle of the brush tip can make a big difference in how the brush deforms the surface. The Picker palette contains the controls for how ZBrush determines the angle of the brush.

This exercise shows you how to work with the orientation controls in the Picker palette.

1. Load the defaultCube.ZPR project from the Projects section of Light Box. Set the color picker to white and press Ctrl+D twice to add two levels of subdivision to the surface.

2. Press the X hotkey to turn off Symmetry.

3. From the sculpting brush fly-out library, select the Planar brush.

4. Open the Depth subpalette of the Brush palette and set the Imbed slider to **20**.

5. Place the Picker palette in the tray so you can access the controls easily.

The controls that affect the angle of the sculpting brush are the Once Ori and Cont Ori buttons and the area to the left of these buttons (see Figure 7.72).

Figure 7.72

The orientation settings in the Picker palette

Once Ori stands for Once Orientation, meaning that the orientation of the brush is set based on the normal direction of the surface at the point where the brush first makes contact with the surface. The brush is kept at this angle for the rest of the stroke.

Cont Ori stands for Continuous Orientation, meaning that the angle of the brush is continuously updated during the brush stroke based on the sampled normal direction of the surface.

The area to the left of these buttons contains the image of a three-dimensional arrow that becomes active when you click it. By default, the arrow is pointed directly at you so it looks like a colored circle. Once you click in this area, you can drag within the defined box to rotate the view of the arrow. The direction of the arrow indicates the angle of the brush stroke for every stroke made with the brush.

Let's see a demonstration of how this works.

6. Drag on the surface of the cube with the PlanarCut brush. You can see how the angle of the planar cut of the stroke is set based on the first point of contact with the surface (left image in Figure 7.73). This is what allows you to easily make a flat surface using the brush.

7. In the Picker palette, click the Cont Ori button.

8. Drag on the surface again. Now as you continue to draw on the surface, the angle of the planar cut made by the brush changes constantly to match the angle of the surface (right image in Figure 7.73).

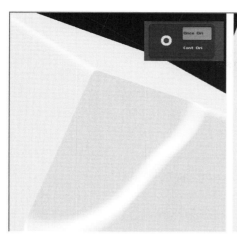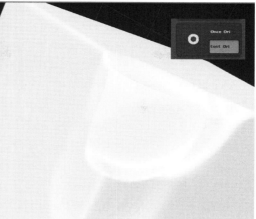

Figure 7.73

Once Ori sets the angle of the stroke based on the first point of contact on the surface. Cont Ori continuously updates the angle of the stroke while dragging on the surface.

9. Click below the arrow icon in the Picker palette to the left of the Once Ori and Cont Ori buttons to activate selected orientation. Drag in this area to rotate the arrow. The direction of the arrow indicates the angle of the brush.

10. Draw on the surface and make a note of the angle of the planar cut of the stroke. Compare the angle to the orientation of the 3D arrow in the Picker palette (see Figure 7.74).

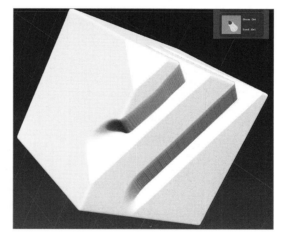

Figure 7.74

Use the three-dimensional arrow icon to establish a specific orientation for the brush.

To set the arrow icon so that it faces the screen, click the Once Ori button and then click back in the area surrounding the arrow. When the arrow is pointed directly at the screen, all strokes made by the brush are parallel with the screen.

Curve Stroke Type

The Curve option in the Stroke palette lets you draw out a curve that can be edited after you draw it on the surface. This option is extremely powerful and opens up endless possibilities for some amazing effects. In Chapter 6, "Advanced ZSphere Techniques," this option was used to help create wings for the dragon model.

This section introduces the basics of how to apply this option to change the behavior of a brush.

1. Open Light Box to the Projects section and open the DefaultSphere.ZPR project. As you did earlier in the chapter, press Ctrl+D twice to add two levels of subdivision, and set the color picker to a white color. Press X to deactivate Symmetry.

2. Just for fun you'll use the Inflate brush for testing, but these techniques can be applied to any brush preset. Select the Inflate brush from the brush library.

3. Place the Stroke palette in the tray so you can access the controls.

4. Set the Z Intensity to **40**. This will make it easier to see how the brush strokes are applied to the surface.

Figure 7.75

Turn on Curve mode in the Stroke palette.

5. In the Stroke palette, turn on the Curve Mode button (see Figure 7.75), and draw a line across the surface of the PolySphere. You'll see a dashed line appear and the brush cursor turn light blue (see Figure 7.76, left). This dashed line is created with each stroke when Curve mode is activated.

6. Hold the brush over the curve and then drag on part of the curve. As you drag on the curve, you'll see that the stroke is dragged along the surface (see Figure 7.76, right). As long as you don't start another stroke, you can continue to edit the shape of the curve and its effect on the surface as long as the curve is live. If you start drawing on another part of the surface, a new curve is created.

Figure 7.76

When Curve mode is on, a dashed line appears as you draw on the surface (left image). As you drag the curve, the surface is deformed along the length of the curve (right image).

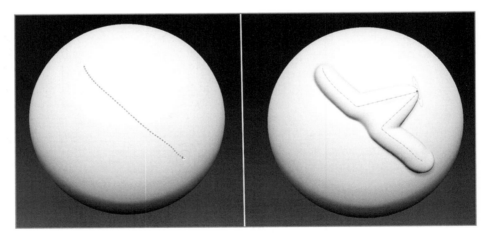

But if you're like me, you might be a little indecisive. Wouldn't it be nice to be able to use the curve feature to precisely position the stroke on the surface? This is really easy to do.

7. In the left shelf, open the stroke library and choose the DragDot stroke type.

8. Press Ctrl+Z (Undo) until the sphere returns to its initial state, and then draw a new curve along the surface.

9. While the curve is live, try moving the shape of the curve. You can edit the shape of the curve to your heart's content and the surface will update (see Figure 7.77). The changes to the surface are committed only when you draw a new stroke on a different part of the surface or switch to a different brush. You can even rotate the view and then continue to edit the curve.

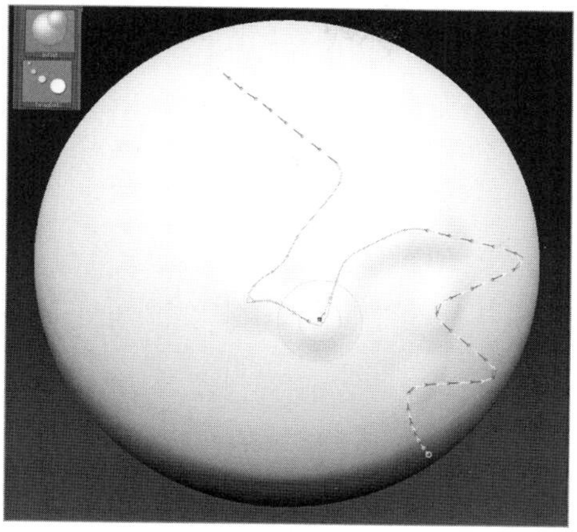

Figure 7.77

Choose the DragDot stroke type so that the stroke can be edited after the curve is drawn.

If you mess up, you can return to Curve editing mode by pressing Ctrl+Z to undo.

Now let's try something interesting. Let's say you want to precisely position a number of dots on the surface. These could be bolts or buttons or some similar type of detail.

Try this:

1. Press Ctrl+Z (Undo) until the sphere returns to its initial state.

2. Open the alpha library and choose Alpha 14. This is the circular alpha with a hard edge.

3. In the Stroke palette under the Curve options, set Max Points to **8**. By lowering this setting, you're decreasing the number of edit points on the curve, which means instead of a solid line of deformation, the stroke will appear as eight discrete dots along the length of the curve.

4. Lower the Draw Size to about **45**. This ensures that the dots of the stroke do not overlap.

5. Draw a curve along the surface, and edit the shape of the curve. Notice that the curve is now made up of a series of straight lines. This is because you lowered the Max Points setting. You can edit the stroke to place the line of dots exactly where you want them (see Figure 7.78). Note that sometimes there are display artifacts on the canvas that may look as though the stroke is leaving stray marks. To fix this just rotate the view a little while you work, and you can see how the stroke is actually affecting the surface.

Figure 7.78

Add an alpha to the stroke and lower the Max Points slider to create a movable line of dots on the surface.

6. Use the Save As button in the Brush palette to save the brush as **boltsBrush.ZBP** in the Brushes/Misc folder.

Here's a short description of the other settings in the Curve Mode subpalette of the Stroke palette. Note that we'll revisit this topic in Chapter 8, where you'll learn how these settings can help you paint a surface.

As Line—This option makes the curve drawn on the surface a straight line.

Curve Step—This establishes the spacing between each step on the curve. A lower value means a smoother, more continuous line.

Bend—This option is what allows you to edit the curve after it has been drawn. If you deactivate this button, then when you draw a curve and then drag on it, the entire curve follows like a rake in the sand.

Snap—This option causes the curve to snap to the surface as you draw it.

Intensity—When this option is enabled, the Z Intensity of the stroke is varied along the length of the curve. Disable this if you want all parts of the curve to have an equal amount of deformation on the surface.

Size—When this option is enabled, the size of the stroke is varied along the length of the curve. Disable this if you want all parts of the curve to have an equal size on the surface.

Curve Falloff—This is an Edit Curve interface that can be used to modulate the variation in size along the length of the curve.

Delete—This deletes the current curve from memory so that a new, fresh curve can be drawn on the surface. It's similar to starting a new curve on another part of the surface. Using the Delete button can be useful when you're drawing curves on the surface that are very close together.

Snapshot—This is an extremely useful option that creates a copy of the curve on the surface after the initial stroke has been applied. So, for example, if you want to create a series of matching lines on the surface, you can draw out a curve, deform it, click this button (hotkey = 5), and then move the curve; you can repeat as necessary to create a series of matching lines on the surface (see Figure 7.79). This works best when Size, Intensity, and Bend are disabled.

Figure 7.79

Use the Snapshot button to leave copies of the curve on the surface as you draw.

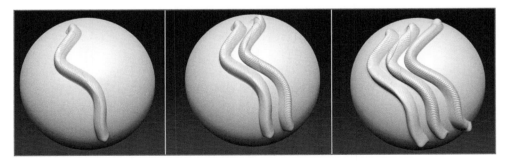

Curve Edit Radius—This slider adjusts the radius of the blue circle used to edit the curve on the surface while it is live. If you want to create sharp corners in the curve as you edit it, lower this setting. A higher value means that you will move a larger portion of the curve as you edit it.

Curve Edit Focal Shift—This setting adjusts the falloff of the blue circles used to edit the curve while it is still live.

Max Points—As mentioned before, this controls the number of points along the curve. A high setting means a smooth continuous curve; a low setting means that the curve will have fewer points and this become more like a series of connected straight lines. Each point along the curve makes a mark on the surface.

The possibilities for creative exploitation of this feature are almost limitless. Check out the many curve brushes in the brush library such as CurveEditable, CurveLathe, CurveLineTube, CurveStandard, and CurveTriFill. See what happens when Curve mode is enabled for one of the insert brush types.

Combining Settings

At this point you should start to see how much power you have over the behavior of the sculpting brushes. By combining various combinations of settings, you can create a brush that will do almost anything. Even if you're happy with the existing brush presets available in the sculpting brush library as well as in the Brush section of Light Box, understanding how the brush settings work will help you understand how best to use each brush.

Experiment with different combinations of settings in the Alpha, Brush, Stroke, and Picker palettes. Apply these settings to different brush base types and see what happens. Here are a few ideas you may want to try:

- Adjust the Size edit curve in the Tablet Pressure subpalette of the Tool palette for one of the ZSketch brushes. ZSketching is covered in Chapter 4.

- Apply an alpha texture to the Planar brush. Increase the SpinCenter and SpinRate sliders in the Orientation subpalette of the Brush palette. Then set the BackTrack mode in the Stroke palette to Line.

- Turn on the Noise button in the Surface subpalette of the Brush palette to the Nudge brush.

- Apply the Path mode in the BackTrack settings of the Stroke palette to the Blob brush, and use the Color Spray stroke type for this brush.

- Turn on Curve mode for the InsertCube brush, and activate the Size option in the Curve mode subpalette of the Stroke palette.

These are just a few ideas to get you started.

There are many more advanced settings that you can continue to explore while you grow as a ZBrush artist. In the Brush palette, you'll find the Samples subpalette, which contains a number of settings that determine how the tip of the brush gathers information from the surface and applies it to the behavior of the brush. To find out more about what each of these settings does, place the mouse cursor over the setting while holding the Ctrl key.

Examples of each of the custom brushes created in this chapter can be found in the Chapter 7 folder on the DVD.

CHAPTER 8

Polypainting and SpotLight

Polypainting is the process of applying color values directly to the polygons of a mesh using the sculpting brushes. It's like painting a real 3D object: You can blend and mix colors on the model's surface to create the look of realistic skin, details on hard surfaces, even decals and logos. You can use many of the advanced brush features to design your own special polypainting brush presets that suit your own style of working.

SpotLight is an advanced image-editing program built into the ZBrush interface that allows you to edit images and then project the colors of those images onto the surface of the model. SpotLight's unique interface makes this process very easy and fast, so you don't need to leave ZBrush to edit your image files in another program.

This chapter introduces polypainting techniques and gives you a tour of SpotLight with practical examples. We will cover the following topics:

- **Painting colors on a surface**
- **Using cavity and occlusion masking**
- **Editing images in SpotLight**
- **Saving SpotLight files**
- **Projecting colors from SpotLight images onto a surface**
- **Painting colors with curves**

Polypainting

The technical aspects of polypainting sound complex at first, but in reality they are quite simple. Using polypainting, you apply RGB values (red, green, and blue) to each vertex of a model. The color values are blended across the face of the polygons that share those vertices, creating what appears to be very smooth and detailed coloring. Figure 8.1 illustrates this point.

Polypainting is performed using many of the sculpting brushes you've been using throughout this book. Polypainting looks better on a surface with a lot of polygons, so polypaint your 3D tools when they are set to their highest subdivision.

To polypaint a 3D tool, it must be on the canvas, in Edit mode, and with the Colorize button in the Tool palette activated. The sculpting brushes you use to paint the surface should have Rgb mode activated. You can actually have Rgb mode and Zadd on together, which means the brush can be used to paint and sculpt at the same time, but most artists prefer to polypaint their models after they have been sculpted.

The exercises in the following section demonstrate a typical workflow for polypainting a 3D tool.

Figure 8.1

Color values are applied to each vertex and then blended across the polygon face.

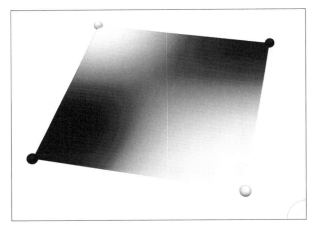

Polypainting Basics

Let's look at the general concepts behind polypainting. In this exercise, you'll see how to polypaint on a basic PolySphere and how the resolution of the mesh affects the quality of the brush strokes painted on the surface:

1. Open a new ZBrush session.

2. Open LightBox to the Tool section and double-click the `PolySphere.ZTL` tool.

3. Draw it on the canvas and switch to Edit mode.

4. Press Ctrl+D three times to subdivide the model three times. The PolySphere already has three levels of subdivision, so this gives the PolySphere a total of six subdivision levels. At SDiv 6, the surface has 1.572 million polygons.

5. Open the materials fly-out library and select the SkinShade4 material (see Figure 8.2). This material is completely white, so the appearance of color values applied to the surface will accurately reflect their color values.

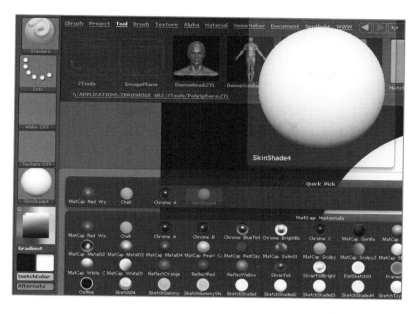

Figure 8.2

Select the SkinShade4 material.

Some materials, such as the MatCap Red Wax material, have a color component to them. If you paint color on surfaces that use a colored material, the colors you paint on the surface will combine with the color of the material and look "off." Materials are discussed in Chapter 9, "FiberMesh, Materials, and Rendering."

6. Use the Save As button in the File palette to save the project as **PolyPaintTest.ZPR**. Save the project in the ZBrush4 R3 \ZProjects folder in which the project appears in LightBox. In Windows, this folder is found in Program Files\Pixologic. On a Mac, the folder is found in the Applications folder.

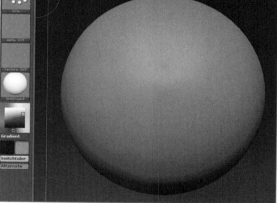

Figure 8.3

Use the color picker to select a blue color. This causes the entire PolySphere to turn blue.

Now let's take a look at how to activate polypainting. This is a simple but important step, and understanding it will explain some mysteries about ZBrush.

7. On the left shelf, drag the mouse pointer within the color picker and select the blue color (see Figure 8.3). The PolySphere turns blue when you do this. As you continue to select colors in the color picker, the color on the surface changes.

8. Open the Tool palette and scroll down until you see the Polypaint subpalette. Expand this subpalette and click the Colorize button (see Figure 8.4). When you do this, the PolySphere turns white.

Figure 8.4

Turn on Colorize in the Polypaint subpalette of the Tool palette.

9. Make sure the Standard brush is the currently selected brush stroke. On the top shelf, turn off the Zadd button and turn on the Rgb button. Make sure Rgb Intensity is set to **100** (see Figure 8.5).

Figure 8.5

On the top shelf, turn on Rgb and set Rgb Intensity to 100. Turn off Zadd.

10. Drag on the surface of the model. The brush leaves a blue stroke (see Figure 8.6).

11. In the color picker, select a red color and drag on the PolySphere again. Now the brush leaves a red stroke.

Figure 8.6

Drag on the surface to create a blue-colored stroke.

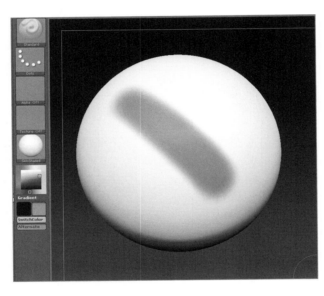

So what just happened here? When the Colorize button is off, the color of the surface changes each time you pick a new color using the color picker. Once you turn on the Colorize button, you have activated polypainting for the surface. Now the surface turns white and you can use the sculpting brushes to apply the current color picker value to the surface of the model. If you turn Colorize off, the strokes you painted disappear and the model goes back to a solid color. Turn Colorize back on and the colored lines reappear.

The color values of the strokes you paint on the surface are stored within each vertex, so they won't be erased if you turn off the Colorize button; you just won't be able to see the strokes until you turn Colorize back on. When you save your model to a disk as a Ztool (ZTL) or as a Zproject (ZPR), the polypaint information is saved as well.

Masked areas of the surface will be protected from colors painted on the surface.

12. Continue on to the next section using the same PolySphere.

ACTIVATING POLYPAINT

The Colorize button in the Polypaint subpalette of the Tool palette enables polypainting on the surface. Constantly going back to this button to turn on polypainting can get tiring. There are two other ways to enable polypainting:

1. Turn on the paintbrush icon for the subtool you want to polypaint in the SubTool subpalette of the Tool palette. This is shown in the image that follows.

2. Brush on the surface of the model with any sculpting brush that has the Rgb button activated. This will enable polypainting even if the Rgb Intensity slider is set to 0. You may have to rotate the view of the surface to get the display to update properly after brushing on the surface.

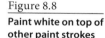

Secondary Color

So what happens if you do want to erase the colored strokes on the surface? Below the color picker are two color swatches. These swatches are a way to store a backup secondary color so you can erase strokes or just have a second color stored in memory for use when you need it (see Figure 8.7).

To erase the strokes you've painted on the surface, you can set the secondary color to white and then paint over the strokes. Here's how this works:

1. Below the Color palette, click the swatch on the left to activate the secondary color selection.

2. Choose a white color by moving the picker to the upper-left corner of the center square within the color picker. The swatch on the left becomes white.

3. Click the SwitchColor button below the swatches (hotkey = V). The colors in the two swatches are swapped, so now the main color is white and the secondary color is whatever the main color was.

4. Paint over the red and blue strokes you painted in the previous section.

   The white color of the brush is painted on top of the colored strokes, essentially erasing them from the surface (see Figure 8.8).

5. Press the V hotkey to switch the colors back so the secondary color is white again. This time paint red strokes on the surface, and when you want to erase, hold the Alt key.

Figure 8.7

The color swatches below the color picker store a main color and a secondary color.

Figure 8.8

Paint white on top of other paint strokes to erase them.

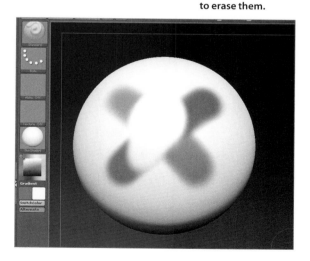

The Alt key temporarily switches the primary and secondary colors so that you don't have to constantly switch. The option for this behavior is activated whenever the Alternate button below the color swatch is on. If you don't want the Alt key to switch colors while you are painting, just turn the Alternate button off.

Now let's try something a little more interesting.

6. Click the Gradient button below the color picker.

7. Select a red color for the secondary color.

8. Paint some strokes on the surface.

   When the Gradient button is on, the main and secondary colors are blended together. When you paint on the surface, the main color is at the center of the brush stroke and the secondary color is at the edges. This produces something like a watercolor effect (see Figure 8.9).

9. Set the secondary color to yellow and paint a few more strokes; the red and yellow are blended together. Hold the Alt key while you paint to see what happens when the colors are switched.

10. Click the SwitchColor button again to swap the main and secondary colors. Paint some more strokes.

11. From the alpha fly-out library, select Alpha 34. Paint some brush strokes.

    When an alpha is applied to the brush stroke, the Gradient feature can be used to create some interesting color effects (see Figure 8.10).

12. Continue on to the next section using the same PolySphere.

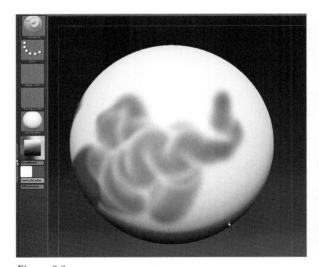

Figure 8.9

Activate Gradient to blend the main and secondary colors with each brush stroke.

Figure 8.10

Apply an alpha texture to the brush and turn on Gradient to get some interesting effects in the brush stroke.

Color Blending

You can blend colors together by adjusting the Rgb Intensity slider on the top shelf.

1. In the color picker, select a dark blue color for the main color.

2. Turn off the Gradient button below the color picker. Choose Alpha Off from the alpha fly-out library on the left shelf to turn the alpha off.

3. Set the Rgb Intensity slider to **15**. Paint some strokes on the surface.

   The blue color of the stroke is faded. At 15, it is 15 percent of the intensity selected in the color picker (see Figure 8.11). This is similar to reducing the opacity of a paintbrush when using a paint program such as Photoshop.

4. Paint repeated strokes over the same area to build up the color.

   As you paint repeatedly over the same strokes, the color of each new stroke is blended with the stroke below it.

5. Choose a red color and paint on top of the blue strokes.

   When you paint red over blue, the colors are mixed together, resulting in a purple color.

   If you're using a digital tablet, you'll notice that the color intensity is pressure sensitive, so the harder you press, the more intense the color becomes. You can build up color slowly by repeatedly brushing lightly over an area of the surface. You can also change the way in which pressure affects color intensity by editing the RGB Intensity edit curve in the Tablet Pressure subpalette of the Brush palette (see Figure 8.12). Expand the RGB Intensity edit curve in the Tablet Pressure subpalette to access the curve. Editing tablet pressure settings is covered in detail in Chapter 7, "Advanced Brush Techniques." These settings may be different depending on which brush preset you choose from the sculpting brush fly-out library.

6. Continue to the next section using the same PolySphere.

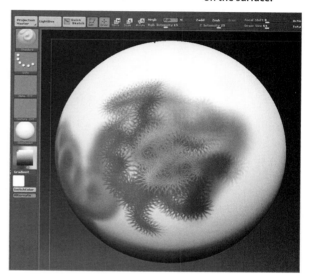

Figure 8.11

Lower the Rgb Intensity slider on the top shelf to reduce the intensity of the color painted on the surface.

Figure 8.12

Click the RGB Intensity button in the Tablet Pressure subpalette of the Brush palette to adjust how the pen pressure affects the intensity of the color.

CUSTOM POLYPAINTING BRUSHES

Many of the brush settings discussed in Chapter 7 can be adjusted to affect how a sculpting brush applies color to a surface. Tablet Pressure settings, Orientation, LazyMouse, BackTrack, and other features can be customized to create a wide range of polypainting effects. You can quickly create your own library of special polypainting brushes by customizing the brush settings and then saving the presets. Save them to the ZBrushes/Misc folder within the ZBrush 4R2 folder so that they appear in LightBox. It's a good idea to give the brushes all the same prefix so that you can easily find them using the search feature in LightBox.

Blurring Strokes

The Smooth brush can be used to blur the edges of a colored stroke painted on the model surface.

1. From the alpha fly-out library on the left shelf, select Alpha 28. This is a simple white square.

2. Choose a red color and paint some strokes on the surface of the PolySphere.

3. Hold the Shift key and turn off the Zadd button on the top shelf. Make sure Rgb is on and Rgb Intensity is set to **100**. By making these adjustments while holding the Shift key, you're setting the properties of the Smooth brush.

4. Hold the Shift key and paint over the strokes on the surface of the PolySphere. This blurs the edges of the strokes (see Figure 8.13).

You can adjust the intensity of the Smooth brush's blurring effect by lowering the Rgb Intensity slider while holding the Shift key.

Figure 8.13

Use the Smooth brush to blur the strokes painted on the surface.

Filling an Object with Color

At this point your PolySphere probably looks like a mess. How do you clear the entire surface? You can do this by filling the entire object with a single color.

1. Set the color picker to white if it's not already.

2. Set Rgb Intensity to **100**.

3. Open the Color palette and click the FillObject button (see Figure 8.14). The entire PolySphere turns white.

    This button is like a paint bucket that covers the whole object with the color currently selected in the color picker. You can use the FillObject button as a way to tint the surface as well.

4. Select a bright red color in the color picker.

5. Paint some strokes on the surface of the PolySphere.

6. Set Rgb Intensity to **10**.

7. Select a dark blue color in the color picker.

8. Open the Color palette and click the FillObject button.

    The PolySphere is tinted slightly blue. This is because the Rgb Intensity setting determines the intensity of the color applied to the surface when you use the FillObject button. Each time you click the button, the object is filled at an intensity of 10, so you can click it repeatedly to gradually increase the amount of blue applied to the surface (see Figure 8.15).

Masked areas of the surface will be protected from the colors applied to the surface when the FillObject button is used. The FillLayer button will clear the canvas and fill it with the current color.

Figure 8.14

The FillObject button fills the entire surface with the current color.

Figure 8.15

When Rgb Intensity is set to a low value, each time you press the FillObject button, the surface is tinted with the current color.

Using Brush Texture

You can apply a 2D texture to the surface of a model using the sculpting brushes. The texture will override the color set in the color picker so that with each brush stroke, the colors in the texture are applied to the surface. Here is a quick demonstration:

1. Clear the PolySphere using the FillObject button, or load the `PolyPaintTest.ZPR` project you created earlier in this chapter.

2. Make sure the Standard brush is the current sculpting brush preset. On the top shelf, Zadd should be off and Rgb Intensity should be set to **100**.

3. From the texture fly-out library on the left shelf, choose Texture 12. This is the orange and yellow star (see Figure 8.16).

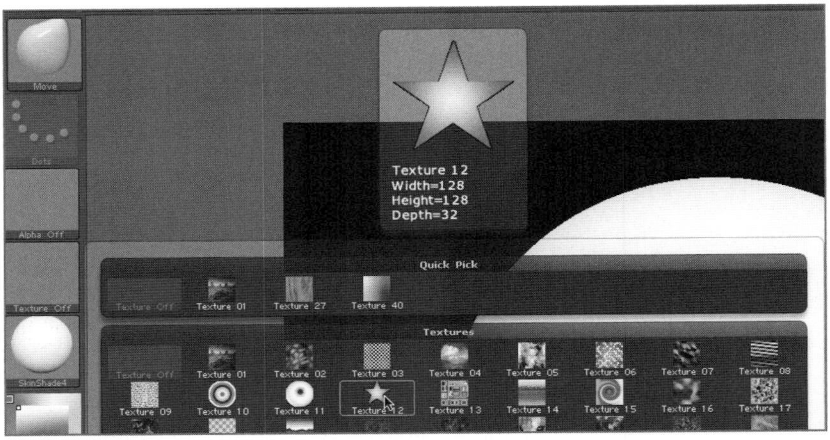

Figure 8.16

Choose the star texture from the texture fly-out library.

4. Open the stroke type fly-out library on the left shelf and select the DragRect stroke type.

5. Drag on the surface of the PolySphere. The star appears on the surface.

6. Release the brush and drag again. Each time you drag on the surface, a new star appears on top of the previous stroke (see Figure 8.17).

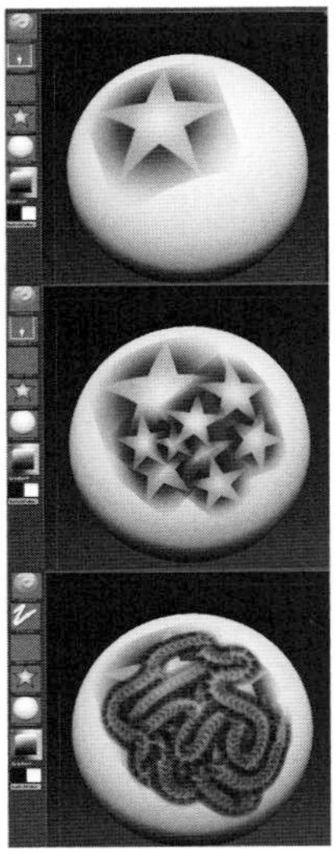

7. Experiment with painting on the surface using other stroke types such as Spray, FreeHand, and DragDot.

8. Lower the Rgb Intensity slider on the top shelf to decrease the opacity of the texture.

Figure 8.17

The star texture appears on the surface of the PolySphere when it is applied to the Standard brush. Use the FreeHand stroke type to create patterns with the texture.

FILL WITH TEXTURE

If you click the FillObject button in the Color palette while a texture is selected in the texture fly-out library, the texture will be applied to the unmasked portions of the 3D tool.

Polypainting and Subdivisions

As you learned earlier in this chapter, the quality of the strokes painted on the surface is directly related to the number of vertices in the mesh. The more vertices you have, the smoother the edges will appear in the strokes painted on the surface. This is why it is often best to polypaint your models at the highest possible subdivision level.

This exercise demonstrates this principle:

1. Load the `PolyPaintTest.ZPR` project you created earlier in this chapter.

2. Open the Geometry subpalette of the Tool palette and set the SDiv slider to **1**. You can also press Shift+D repeatedly until the model is at its lowest subdivision level.

3. Select a red color from the color picker and paint a stroke on the surface.

   The edges of the stroke are very blocky because at SDiv level 1, there aren't very many vertices in the surface.

4. Open the Geometry subpalette of the Tool palette and set the SDiv slider to **6**. You can also press D repeatedly until the model is at its highest subdivision level.

Notice that even though the surface is increasing in subdivisions, the edges of the brush stroke look very blocky (see Figure 8.18). This is why you'll get the best results if you paint a surface at the highest subdivision level.

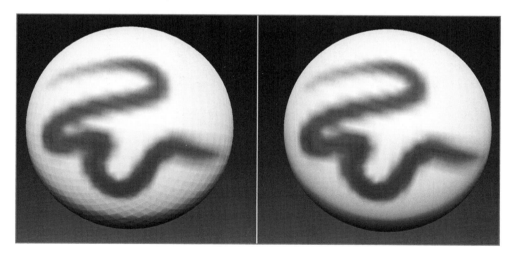

Figure 8.18

Paint strokes applied to a surface at a low subdivision level will appear blocky even when the surface is set to a high subdivision level.

Polypainting Techniques

Now that you have a basic understanding of how polypainting works, let's take a look at some techniques for painting a model. There are as many approaches to polypainting as there are ZBrush artists, so there's no one way to do it. Generally speaking, I like to use techniques that are similar to those used by effects artists who paint actual models. I use brushes that emulate the behavior of air brushes. I like to apply several coats of color at a low Rgb intensity. The following sections demonstrate some of the techniques I prefer to use. As you become more comfortable painting your models, no doubt you will develop your own approach.

I have recorded a color movie based on this demonstration. The movie file is named polyPaintDragon.mov and is found in the Movies folder on the book's DVD.

TIPS ON POLYPAINTING

- Here are just a few helpful tips you can use when polypainting an object:

- If you use the Spray stroke type to paint colors on the surface, the value (or brightness) of each dot in the stroke will be varied randomly. You can increase the amount of randomness by setting the Color slider in the Stroke palette to **1**. To turn this feature off, set this slider to **0**. You can also find this slider in the stroke type fly-out library. This is shown in the image at right.

- The Color Spray stroke type varies the hue of each dot in the stroke randomly (see the image below). Again, to change the behavior of this feature, adjust the Color slider in the Stroke palette.

- To select a color from the surface, hold the mouse pointer over the color you want to pick and press the C hotkey. You can also do this by dragging from the color picker to the color you want to select. The selected color value will not include the colors of preview shadows or the color of the material.

- If you want to select the color exactly as it appears on the canvas (that is, the color of the surface, shadows, and material), hold the Alt key and drag from the color picker to the color you want to select.

- You can convert the colors painted on the surface into a mask using the Mask By Intensity, Mask By Hue, or Mask By Saturation button in the Masking subpalette of the Tool palette. Each button creates a mask from the colors in a slightly different way (that is, based on the intensity, hue, or saturation of the colors painted on the surface).

- You can convert the colors painted on the surface into polygroups by clicking the From PolyGroup button in the PolyGroups subpalette of the Tool palette.

- The FillObject button will fill only the visible or unmasked parts of the surface on the model. Hide or mask parts of the object you don't want colored.

- Colorize can be activated per subtool. The SubTool Master ZPlug-in (discussed in Chapter 4, "Polymesh Editing") has a button for filling all the visible subtools at once with a color.

- Colorize is automatically activated for a surface when you paint on it with a brush that has Rgb activated on the top shelf. This is true even if Rgb Intensity is set to 0.

- You can use layers to create and blend different polypaint layers together on the same surface. This technique is discussed in Chapter 10, "Surface Noise, Layers, and the ZBrush Timeline."

Figure 8.19

The dragon head model that will be used in this section can be found in the Chapter 8 folder on the DVD.

Creating a Base Coat

You can start painting a model at any point during the sculpting process; however, many artists prefer to paint the surface after they have done most of their sculpting and detailing.

In this example, you'll start with a dragon head I created. The file is called polyPaintDragon_v01.ZPR and can be found in the Chapter 8 folder on the DVD (see Figure 8.19). Of course, you're also welcome to use this approach on your own model.

As mentioned earlier in the chapter, you'll get the best results if you paint the model at the highest possible subdivision level. The model I'm using has five subdivision levels. At SDiv 5, the model uses 3.2 million polygons. Normally I would subdivide the model one more time for a total of six levels of

subdivision. The model would be around 12 million polygons at SDiv 6; however, I want to make sure the example model can be easily used by readers using laptops or less-powerful machines.

1. Use the Open button in the File palette to load the `PolyPaintDragon_v01.ZPR` project from the `Chapter 8` folder on the DVD.

2. Open the Geometry subpalette of the Tool palette, and make sure the model is set to the highest subdivision level; this should be SDiv 5.

3. Make sure the SkinShade4 material is selected in the materials fly-out library.

I've decided that this dragon will be mostly reddish in color. So I'll start by experimenting with a color for the base coat.

4. Drag the cursor in the outer square of the color picker to the upper-left corner to select a red hue. Drag the cursor to the center square toward the middle to select a color that is not too dark or saturated (see Figure 8.20).

5. The color on the model should update as you move within the color selector. If the color is not updating, open the Polypaint subpalette of the Tool palette and make sure the Colorize button is off.

Figure 8.20
Use the color picker to choose a reddish color.

6. Once you have selected a suitable color for the base coat, make sure Rgb Intensity is set to **100**, open the Color palette, and click the FillObject button.

The dragon won't look any different when you fill it with the color, but the color has now been applied to the entire surface. Note that Colorize is automatically activated when you fill the object, so the model is all ready for polypainting. This is also indicated by the paintbrush icon, which is activated for the dragon's head in the SubTool subpalette of the Tool palette. The Colorize but-

Figure 8.21

When you fill an object with color, the Colorize button is automatically turned on, as is the paintbrush icon in the SubTool subpalette of the Tool palette.

ton in the Polypaint subpalette and the paintbrush icon in the SubTool subpalette share the same function: they both activate polypainting for the model (see Figure 8.21).

7. Choose a white color in the color picker. Note that the teeth, eyes, and other subtools on the head all turn white while the head remains red (see Figure 8.22). This is because Colorize has not been activated for these subtools, just the head. If you turn off the Colorize button, the head will turn white again. Turn it back on and the head returns to red.

8. Use the Save As button in the File menu to save the project as **PolyPaintDragon_v02.ZPR**.

Creating Color Zones

Now that you have a solid color chosen for the base coat, you can start painting color zones on the head. Color zones are areas of color painted on different areas of the head. By dividing the head into areas of color, you can suggest something about the anatomy beneath the skin or scales of your character or creature. Areas of the head that have more blood vessels may have more red and purple hues. Areas close to bone may have more yellow or white. This is true of humans as well as many other types of animals. Of course, when you're painting a fantasy creature, you have much more liberty in terms of the colors that you use or the placement of color zones. When you divide the head into regions of colors, your model will look less like it has been simply covered with a coat of paint.

Color zones are often painted using very vibrant colors. It's okay to go a little over the top. Keep in mind that these color zones will be covered up with successive coats of color later on in the painting process, so even though they look exaggerated when you first paint them, they will be much more subtle in the final version.

1. Let's start by painting deep red and purple around the area of the eyes. In the color picker, select a deep, dark purple.

2. Click the SwitchColor button below the color picker so that purple becomes the secondary color.

3. Use the color picker to choose a deep, dark red. This will become the main color.

Figure 8.23

Click on each color swatch so that a shadow appears at the top of both swatches. Turn on the Gradient button.

4. Click on both color swatches so that you can see a slight shadow at the top of the swatch. This indicates that both the main and secondary colors are active. Click the Gradient button to activate the Gradient feature (see Figure 8.23).

5. Choose the Standard brush in the sculpting brush fly-out library. Make sure the Zadd button is off on the top shelf. The Rgb button should be on. Set Rgb Intensity to **10**.

6. Set the stroke type to Spray. In the stroke type library, set the Color slider to **0.1**. This reduces the randomization of the color values used by the Spray stroke type.

7. In the alpha fly-out library, choose Alpha 58. This has a series of scribbled vertical lines (see Figure 8.24).

8. Use the Save button in the Brush palette to save the brush as **pPaint_spray.ZBP**. Save the brush to the ZBrush 4R3\ZBrushes\Misc folder so that you can easily find it in the Brush section of LightBox later on (see Figure 8.25).

9. Make sure that Symmetry is active across the x-axis in the Transform palette.

10. Set the Draw Size to **25**. Zoom in on the area of the eye and start painting strokes in this area. You don't have to be particularly neat about it; in fact, the more varied your stroke, the better it will look in the end.

11. On the right shelf, click the Solo button to hide the eyes and other subtools. Paint inside the eye socket (see Figure 8.26).

12. As you paint, make sure to vary the colors applied to the surface. You can do this by switching the main and secondary colors (hotkey = V). You can also sample the colors you've painted on the surface by holding the C key while holding the mouse pointer over the surface. This is a great way to blend colors across the surface.

13. Add additional color zones. Paint bluish colors along the lips; paint deep reds around the nostrils; paint pale pinks, yellows, and reds on the larger scales, horns, and bony parts. Paint dark reds in the larger folds of flesh.

Figure 8.24

Choose Alpha 58 in the alpha fly-out library.

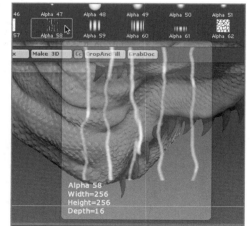

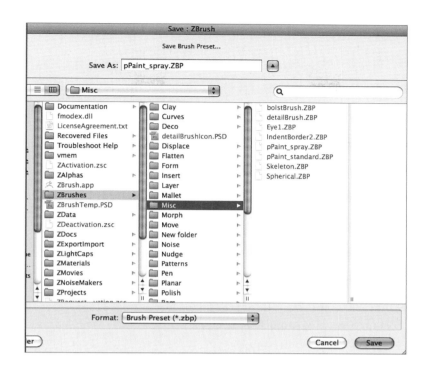

Figure 8.25

Save the brush preset so that you can use it for future ZBrush sessions.

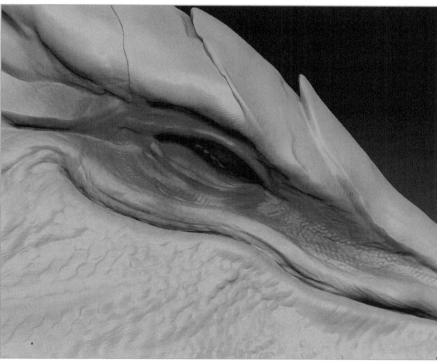

Figure 8.26

Paint purple and red in the eye socket and around the area of the eye.

Neatness does not count. Go ahead and be very loose with your strokes. The end result should look almost like a clown. Experiment with using different alphas and other settings while you work. Figure 8.27 shows the model using the Flat Color material after the color zones have been painted. To see the image in color, watch the `PolyPaintDragon.mov` movie in the `Movies` folder of the DVD.

14. While working, you should occasionally select the Flat Color material from the material fly-out library so that you can see exactly how the colors are applied to the surface without the influence of lights or shadows.

15. Use the Save As button in the File menu to save the project as **PolypaintDragon_v03.ZPR**.

Painting a Mottling Pass

Once you have the colors of the head segregated into zones, you'll need to break up the color using what's known as a *mottling* pass. This technique is taken directly from artists who have been painting masks and maquettes in the movie industry for years. It was introduced to me by Scott Spencer, and even though it may seem like an odd approach at first, it always seems to look great in the final process. Check out Scott's book *ZBrush Creature Design: Creating Dynamic Concept Imagery for Film and Games* (Sybex, 2012).

To create a mottling pass, you'll paint white squiggly lines all over the surface. These lines break up the color zones, making the face look less clownlike. In the end, it will also look as though the skin and scales are made up of layers of organic material.

1. Continue with the dragon model from the previous section.

2. Select the Standard brush from the sculpting brush library. Set the stroke type to DragRect.

3. From the alpha fly-out library, select Alpha 22 (see Figure 8.28). This is a series of squiggly lines.

Figure 8.27

Color zones have been painted on the surface of the model.

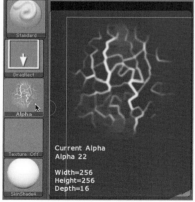

Figure 8.28

Choose Alpha 22 from the alpha fly-out library.

4. In the color picker, set the main color to white.

5. Set Rgb Intensity to **20**. Make sure the Rgb button on the top shelf is on and the Zadd button is off. Turn off the Gradient button below the color picker.

6. Use the Save button in the Brush palette to save the brush as `PolyPaintMottle.ZBP`.

7. Drag on the surface to add the stroke. The pattern will appear larger if you continue to drag before releasing. Rotate the pattern by dragging left or right before releasing (see Figure 8.29, top image).

8. Drag repeatedly over the surface to create a pattern with overlapping strokes (see Figure 8.29, bottom image).

9. Continue to cover the entire surface of the head. Create smaller strokes near the lips and eyes, larger strokes over the scales.

   You don't need to completely obscure the colors of the underlying layers; just use the mottling pass to break up the color zones. Once the surface is covered, you'll paint a light reddish color over the surface to tie the colors together. You may want to turn off Symmetry when creating the pattern along the center of the model. Figure 8.30 shows the result using the Flat Color material.

10. Select the Standard brush from the sculpting brush library. Set the stroke type to Color Spray.

Figure 8.29

Create overlapping patterns using the PolyPaintMottle brush to break up the colors of the model.

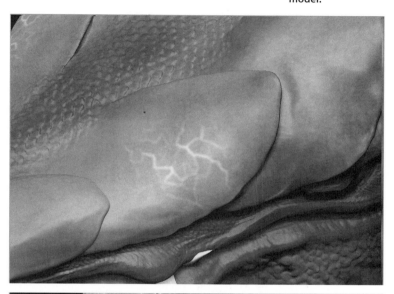

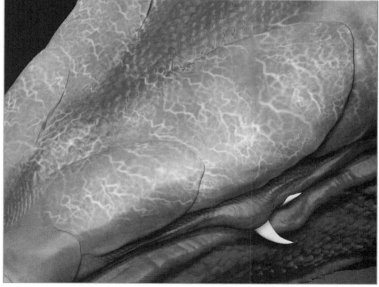

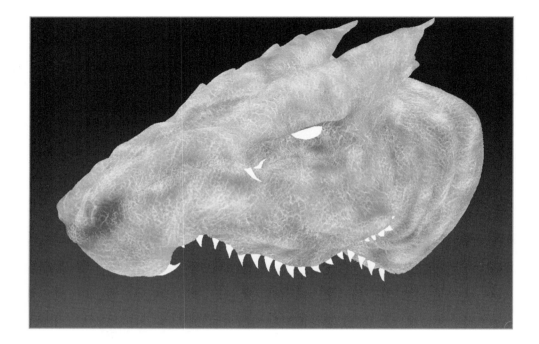

11. Turn off the Zadd button and turn on Rgb. Set Rgb Intensity to **5**.

12. Choose a light red color from the color picker.

13. From the alpha library, choose Alpha 23 (see Figure 8.31).

14. Use the Save button in the Brush palette to save the brush as `PolyPaintDust.ZBP`.

15. Set Draw Size to **30**. Use the brush to paint lightly over the surface (see Figure 8.32). Again, you don't want to completely obscure the colors of the previous passes. The light red color is meant to make the color zones and the mottling pass seem more cohesive.

16. Continue with this file in the next section.

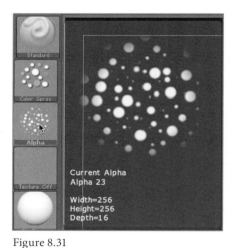

Figure 8.31

Choose Alpha 23 from the alpha fly-out library.

Figure 8.32

Paint over the surface with a light red color.

Painting Subsurface Details

Blood vessels and scar tissue are good examples of subsurface details. They appear just below the skin, which gives the impression that the surface is made up of overlapping layers of organic material. This particular dragon is covered in a lot of different-size scales, so it's unlikely that you would see as many subsurface details as you would on other models, such as an old man. Even so, many faint blood vessels can be added to the bases of the larger scales. Blood vessels close to the surface of a creature expose the blood to air, which helps to keep him cool. In addition, you can imagine that the dragon may have scars from ancient battles. The tissue near the old scars may appear dark just below the skin.

In this section, you'll add these details to the dragon:

1. To paint veins on the surface, you can use the detailBrush you created in Chapter 7. If you have not created this brush, you can use the Load button in the Brush palette to load the preset from the Chapter 7 folder on the DVD.

2. On the top shelf, set Z Intensity to **5** and Rgb Intensity to **20**. Set Draw Size to **10**.

3. Select a dark blue-purple color from the color picker. Turn off the Activate Symmetry button in the Transform palette.

4. Open the Stroke palette and turn LazyMouse off.

5. Use the Save button in the Brush palette to save the brush as `PolyPaintVein.ZBP`.

This brush is designed to use tablet pressure. As you paint on the surface, vary the pressure. Increase the pressure to make the stroke appear thin or dark and raise the surface.

6. Use the brush to create squiggly lines near the bases of the larger scales and in the areas near the eyes and other parts of the head where you might imagine blood vessels would be visible.

7. Choose the PolyPaintSpray brush to paint dark reds, blues, and purples. Create dark splotches on the surface. Figure 8.33 shows the model with the Flat Color material applied.

8. Use the Save As button in the File menu to save the project as `PolyPaintDragon_v04.ZPR`. Continue with this project in the next section.

Figure 8.33

Veins and dark splotches are painted on the surface.

POLYPAINTING AND SYMMETRY

You may want to try turning Symmetry off while painting a model. You can achieve more realistic coloring if the colors have an asymmetrical quality.

Using Cavity Masking

You can increase the detail on the surface and make the scales more apparent by using cavity masking. When you create a cavity mask, the recessed areas of the surface are protected from changes. You can invert the mask and fill the recessed areas with a darker color. This will make the spaces between the scales and other areas appear darker.

1. Open the Masking subpalette of the Tool palette.

2. Below the Mask By Cavity button, set the Intensity slider to **50** (see Figure 8.34). This slider determines the intensity of the cavity mask. You need to set this value before creating the mask.

Figure 8.34

Set Intensity to 50 in the Masking subpalette of the Tool palette.

3. Click the Mask By Cavity button. After a few seconds you'll see a mask appear on the surface. The mask appears in the recessed areas of the surface (top image in Figure 8.35).

4. Press Ctrl+I to invert the mask. You can also Ctrl+click on a blank part of the canvas to invert the mask (bottom image in Figure 8.35).

5. Use the color picker to choose a dark red color. On the top shelf, set Rgb Intensity to **5**.

6. In the Masking subpalette of the Tool palette, turn off the ViewMask button. This will make it easier to see how the color is applied.

7. In the Color palette, click the FillObject button. The dark red color will be applied to the recesses of the surface. No doubt it may be hard to see much of a difference since the Rgb Intensity setting is very low. Click the button repeatedly, and you'll start to see the dark red color between the scales. Figure 8.36 shows how the color looks when the Flat Color material is applied to the model.

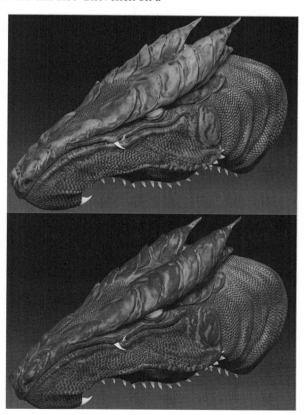

Figure 8.35

Cavity masking creates a mask in the dark recesses of the surface (top image). The mask is inverted (bottom image).

Figure 8.36

The unmasked parts of the dragon are filled with a dark red color.

8. Once you're satisfied with the color, Ctrl+drag on a blank part of the canvas to remove the mask.

9. Use the Save button in the File palette to save the project as **PolyPaintDragon_v05.ZPR**.

TIPS ON USING CAVITY MASKS

Cavity masking is a very powerful feature that can be applied to a wide variety of sculpting and polypainting techniques. Here are some tips on using the cavity mask controls in the Masking subpalette of the Tool palette:

- The Blur slider to the right of the Mask By Cavity button applies blurring to the cavity mask when it is generated. This can help reduce jagged edges in the mask.

- You can blur the cavity mask after you create it by Ctrl+clicking on the mask.

- To fine-tune the way the cavity mask is applied, expand the Cavity Profile edit curve in the Masking subpalette of the Tool palette.

- Cavity masking can be applied to the brush rather than the surface. Use the CavityMask options in the Auto Masking subpalette of the Brush palette. When you apply cavity masking to a brush, the mask is updated with each stroke.

Using Ambient Occlusion Masking

Ambient occlusion is a type of shadowing that occurs when light rays are unable to reach the cracks and crevices of a surface. This kind of shadowing is most apparent on overcast days or in a room that is illuminated with diffused light. ZBrush can create a special type of mask in the recessed areas of a surface that simulates this type of shadowing. The mask is much softer and broader than masks created using cavity masking.

In this exercise, you'll create an ambient occlusion mask, invert the mask, and then paint dark colors into the unmasked areas. This will create darker areas in the folds of flesh and in the cracks between the larger scales. Ambient occlusion masks tend to be fairly faint and hard to see. You can turn off polypainting and use the Flat Color material to make the mask easier to see.

1. Continue with the project from the previous section.

2. Use the color picker to set the main color to white.

3. From the materials fly-out library, select the Flat color material.

4. In the Polypaint subpalette of the Tool palette, turn off Colorize. The dragon will appear solid white. Don't worry; you haven't lost any of the colors painted on the surface.

5. Expand the Masking subpalette of the Tool palette. Under the Mask Ambient Occlusion button, set Occlusion Intensity to **1.3**.

6. Set the AO Scan distance to **0.35**. This sets the maximum distance ZBrush will use when creating the mask. Higher values mean that more of the surface will be masked, but they will also take longer to calculate (see Figure 8.37).

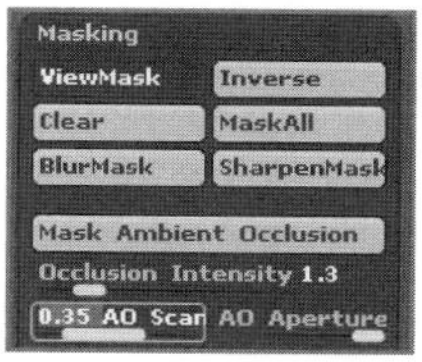

Figure 8.37

Adjust the settings for ambient occlusion masking before creating the mask.

7. Leave AO Aperture at the default setting of 90. Lowering this value will diminish the size of the ambient occlusion mask.

8. Calculating an ambient occlusion mask on a complex surface that has a lot of polygons can take a long time. It's usually a good idea to save your work before creating the mask. Use the Save As button in the File palette to save the project as `PolyPaintDragon_v06.ZPR`.

9. Click the Mask Ambient Occlusion button. This change takes a few minutes to occur. The countdown will appear at the top of the ZBrush interface along with a progress bar (Figure 8.38). This is a good time to take a break!

Once the mask has been calculated, the dragon should look something like Figure 8.39.

Figure 8.38

The progress bar at the top of the interface indicates the time it will take to calculate the ambient occlusion mask.

Figure 8.39

The ambient occlusion mask has been applied to the dragon head.

10. Press Ctrl+I or Ctrl+click on a blank part of the canvas to invert the mask.

11. In the Masking palette, turn off the View Mask button.

12. In the Polypaint subpalette of the Tool palette, turn on the Colorize button. The colors will appear on the surface.

13. Set Rgb Intensity to **14**. Use the color picker to choose a dark purple color. In the Color palette, click the FillObject button to fill in the unmasked areas. Click the button repeatedly until you're satisfied with the strength of the dark color applied to the surface (see Figure 8.40).

14. Hold the Ctrl key and drag on a blank part of the canvas to clear the mask.

15. Save the file as **PolyPaintDragon_v07.ZPR**.

Figure 8.40

Fill the unmasked areas with a purple color.

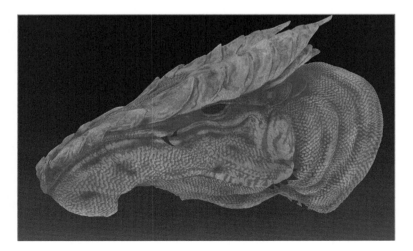

Painting Surface Details

The colors for the dragon are meant to serve as a foundation. For the final pass, you'll paint the surface details. By building a foundation of color through successive passes, you'll ensure that the final model looks interesting, has variation, and seems believable.

The details on the surface can be as elaborate as you like. I recommend doing an image search for snake and lizard scales. Take a look at what kinds of patterns appear on the scales of venomous snakes. How do they differ from nonvenomous snakes? Look at dinosaurs and birds for inspiration as well. Also check out the work of other fantasy artists, such as John Howe and Frank Frazetta. *Dracopedia* by William O'Connor (Impact Books, 2009) is a book I find particularly entertaining and inspiring.

I've included several photographs from my own reference library. These are images I took of various snakes and lizards at the Desert Museum in Arizona. These images are found in the Chapter 8 folder of the DVD. Note the color variations on each individual scale as well as the repeating patterns in the overall surfaces of the animals.

Generally speaking, the techniques for creating surface detail are not that different from the techniques used to paint the underlying layers. In my version of the dragon, I painted the large scales on the top of the head using the Standard brush with an Rgb Intensity of 25. I painted dark red strokes to create simple designs on the scales based on the color of the

Figure 8.41

Images of snake and lizard scales can be used as reference.

scales in the upper-left image in Figure 8.41. I applied Alpha 08 from the alpha fly-out library to the brush and varied the colors as I painted the strokes. Figure 8.42 shows the result. The Flat Color material is applied to the surface to make the strokes more apparent.

For the smaller scales of the neck, I used the upper-right image in Figure 8.41 as inspiration. I lightly painted individual scales, alternating light and dark colors to create a pattern (see Figure 8.43).

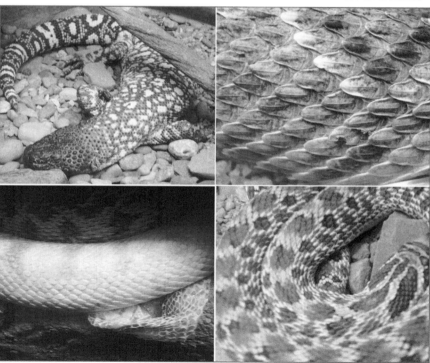

Figure 8.42

Dark red and brown brush strokes are added to the large scales on the head.

Figure 8.43

A pattern is created on the smaller scales of the neck by alternating light and dark colors on the scales.

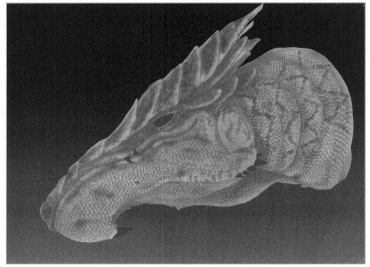

For the lips, I painted dark colors using repeating thin lines. I painted light, reddish colors on the inside edges of the eyelids as well. You can continue to work over the surface, adding color details where needed. It's never finished until you feel that it's finished. The important thing to keep in mind is that if you take the time to build up layers of colors for the undercoat, the details you paint on the surface will look much more organic and interesting.

When you feel that you have done enough, save the file as `PolyPaintDragon_v08.zpr`. Figure 8.44 shows the final version. A high quality version of this image can be found in the color insert section of this book.

Figure 8.44

The final version of the dragon

USE COLOR TO CREATE A STORY

The colors you paint on the surface can create a sense of story for your dragon. Does your dragon have elaborate markings? Battle scars? Do the colors indicate danger? Attract mates? Do dragons have tattoos? Do the markings indicate rank? Age? Class? Number of slain knights or burned villages? You can have a lot of fun thinking up the history behind the colors of your dragon.

Image Editing with SpotLight

SpotLight is designed to give artists the ability to manipulate images within the ZBrush interface. This eliminates the need to leave the ZBrush environment to edit images in a second software package such as Photoshop. Using SpotLight, you can color correct, transform, smudge, smear, and layer digital images and then project the result directly on your model.

In the following sections, you'll learn the basics of using SpotLight, starting with a tour of the interface.

Opening and Closing SpotLight

SpotLight is used for editing textures, so to launch SpotLight, you'll need to select a texture either from the texture library on the left shelf or from the Texture section of LightBox. A texture is simply an image file that's loaded into ZBrush. ZBrush accepts the most common image formats, such as Photoshop (PSD), Pict (PCT), bitmap (BMP), Tif (TIF or TIFF), Jpeg (JPG or JPEG), and Gif (GIF).

The following sections show you two ways to launch SpotLight.

Launching SpotLight from the Texture Palette

This exercise demonstrates how to add an image to SpotLight from the Texture palette.

1. Start a fresh session of ZBrush.

2. Place the Texture palette in a tray so you can access the settings easily.

3. Click a texture such as Texture 01 (see Figure 8.45).

Figure 8.45

Choose Texture 01 from the Texture palette.

4. In the Texture palette, click the Add To SpotLight (plus/minus) button in the Texture palette (see Figure 8.46). These buttons are grayed out if there is no texture selected.

The texture now appears on the canvas in full size. You'll also see a ring of small icons. This ring is the control interface for SpotLight. Note that the texture on the canvas appears slightly transparent (see Figure 8.47).

To remove the texture from SpotLight, just select it in the Texture palette and click the plus/minus button again.

5. To close SpotLight, press Shift+Z.

Figure 8.46

Click the Add To SpotLight button in the Texture palette.

Figure 8.47

The texture appears on the canvas when it has been added to SpotLight. The SpotLight interface appears as a ring of icons on top of the image.

As long as images have been added to SpotLight you can turn it on and off again using the Shift+Z hotkey combination. The images you have added to SpotLight will remain as part of SpotLight unless you remove them or close and restart ZBrush. The Shift+Z hotkey combination turns off SpotLight so that you can work on models or other artwork in ZBrush. ZBrush remembers which images have been loaded and their current status. Press Shift+Z again to turn on SpotLight at any time.

When you press Z without the Shift key modifier, the SpotLight interface (the ring of icons) is hidden. Press it again to display the interface. There are essentially two modes to SpotLight: Edit mode and Projection mode. You know you are in Edit mode when you see the interface dial (the ring of icons). In this mode, you can edit the SpotLight images. In Projection mode, the dial interface is hidden and the images you see on the canvas can be projected onto your models. In the following sections, you'll learn how to work in these two modes. Like many things in ZBrush, it takes a little practice to get used to it.

Launching SpotLight from LightBox

LightBox is described in detail in Chapter 2. Recall that the icons in SpotLight are a preview of files saved to your local drive within the subfolders of the ZBrush 4R3 directory. Adding a texture from LightBox to SpotLight is very easy:

1. Click the LightBox button on the top shelf to open LightBox (hotkey = ,).
2. Click the Texture heading in LightBox.
3. Click one of the textures to select it. A white border will appear around the texture indicating that it is selected (see Figure 8.48).

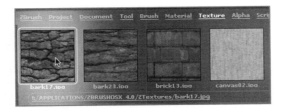

Figure 8.48

Select a texture from the Texture section of LightBox.

4. Double-click the texture. In some cases you may need to double-click the image twice. If SpotLight is already open, the picture is automatically added to SpotLight. If SpotLight is not open, then the texture is loaded into the texture library. Select the image in the library and then click the Add To Spotlight button as you did in the previous section.

Figure 8.49

When a new texture is added to SpotLight, the other image appears scaled down at the bottom of the interface.

Note that any images you may have added to SpotLight will be scaled down and positioned at the bottom of the interface. (See Figure 8.49. The smaller image may be hidden by the LightBox interface. Close LightBox so that you can see the smaller image.)

The last image you add to SpotLight always appears enlarged at the top of the interface, and previously added images appear at the bottom, scaled down. You'll learn how to resize and reposition images later in this section. At this point, you're simply building up a layout of active images. Imagine that you're pulling images out of a box and placing them on a table. That's basically what's going on when you add images to SpotLight. You can add new images at any time while working in SpotLight.

Note that you can load multiple copies of the same image into SpotLight if you want to.

Typically you'll use several images within a single SpotLight session. For example, let's say you're working on dragon scales. You may end up with a number of images that have been added to SpotLight from various locations such as your hard drive, the Internet, and so on. You can save the SpotLight session as a file that can be loaded the next time you start ZBrush. This saves you the trouble of having to add the images all over again the next time you start ZBrush.

You can create separate SpotLight files for use in different ZBrush sessions. So you might have a SpotLight file dedicated to images of snake scales, another one dedicated to vehicle decals, and another one dedicated to eyeballs, and so on. A SpotLight file uses a special format that contains the image files and their status.

This exercise demonstrates how to save and load a SpotLight session:

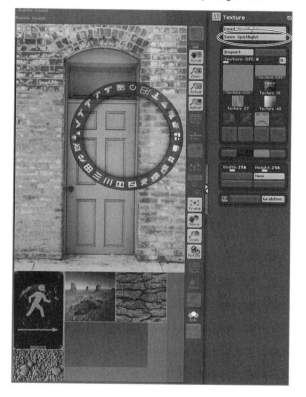

Figure 8.50

Use the Save SpotLight button in the Texture palette to save the SpotLight file.

1. Make sure you have three to five images loaded into SpotLight and that the images are visible on the canvas.

2. Open the Texture palette and click the Save SpotLight button (see Figure 8.50). This will open your computer's file browser.

3. Save the file as `SpotLighTest.zs1`. You'll use this file for practice in the next few exercises.

4. To load a SpotLight file, use the Load SpotLight button in the Texture palette. You can have only one SpotLight file open at a time.

If you have been working in SpotLight, save your work before loading a different SpotLight file.

Transforming Images

Now that you understand how to start SpotLight, let's take a look at how you can do some actual work. The ring of icons that appears when you launch SpotLight functions as a menu and a manipulator at the same time. I think of it as a dial. This exercise demonstrates how to move images around using the manipulator.

1. Continue with the SpotLight file from the previous section or use the Load SpotLight button in the Texture palette to load the `SpotLightTest.ZSL` file from the Chapter 8 folder on the DVD.

2. Click and drag on the largest image on the canvas.

   The SpotLight menu pops over to the center of your brush cursor, and the largest image moves as you drag on the canvas. This is how you move an individual image. Note that a red border appears around the image, indicating that it is selected.

3. Click and drag on one of the smaller images.

Each time you want to move an image around, just click and drag on it (see Figure 8.51).

Figure 8.51

Drag on an image to move it.

4. Click and drag on a blank part of the canvas. Now all the images move together. This is a handy way to move everything aside if you need to make space on the canvas.

5. Double-click one of the smaller images.

This rearranges all of the images so that the small image now becomes enlarged and the other images are scaled down and aligned at the bottom of the screen.

6. Click and drag in the center of SpotLight (within the small circle). This allows you to move the SpotLight interface without affecting the image.

7. Click the largest image again to place the interface on top of it. Click and drag the circular arrow icon at the top of SpotLight (see Figure 8.52).

This rotates the image. Drag this icon right or left to rotate the image clockwise or counterclockwise, respectively. The SpotLight interface acts like a dial. Each of the menu icons around the ring of the interface is a switch. Select an icon such as the circular arrow at the top of the ring. Drag on the menu icon left or right to rotate the dial and activate the selected function.

The pivot point for the center of the rotation is indicated by the circle at the center of the SpotLight interface. To change the pivot point, just click somewhere else in the image.

If you want the pivot point of rotation to be outside the image, select the image by clicking it (the red border will indicate that the image is selected). Then drag the center of the SpotLight interface, reposition the interface outside the image, and then drag the rotate icon.

If you want to rotate all of the images in SpotLight at once, click outside the image to deselect it (the red border will disappear), drag the center of the dial to reposition the SpotLight interface, and then drag the rotation icon at the top of the interface.

Figure 8.52

Drag the circular arrow in the SpotLight interface to rotate the selected image.

8. Click one of the smaller images to select it. Click and drag the box icon to the right of the rotate icon. This scales the image. Drag to the right to scale the image up; drag to the left to scale it down (see Figure 8.53). The name of the icon's function appears at the center of the SpotLight dial so when you drag on the scale icon you'll see the word "Scale" appear at the center of the dial.

Figure 8.53

Drag the rectangular icon to scale the selected image.

The scale function is similar to the rotate function in that the scale pivot is based on the circle at the center of the interface. Just as with the rotate function, you can scale the selected image or deselect the image and scale all the images at the same time.

SpotLight Functions

Each icon on the SpotLight interface indicates a different function. The icons are grouped together based on their purpose. Some SpotLight functions are used to transform the images, like rotate and scale, demonstrated in the previous section. Some of the functions are used to edit the image. Some of the functions affect how the image is projected onto a surface. This section gives a brief description of each function, going clockwise around the interface starting at the top. Many of these functions will be explored in more detail in the exercises of this chapter.

 Rotate As demonstrated in the previous section, drag this icon left or right to rotate the selected image or all of the images together. The center of LightBox is the pivot point for rotation.

 Scale As demonstrated in the previous section, drag this icon left or right to scale the selected image or all of the images together. The center of LightBox is the pivot point for the scaling.

 Pin This icon keeps the image at the center of the brush tip when you project the image onto a surface. Projection is discussed in the next section. Click this icon to toggle pinning on or off. When you see a white bar above the icon, this means that SpotLight is pinned. If pinning is off, the image will be projected onto the surface based on its current position on the canvas. When pinning is on, the area of the image at the center of the SpotLight image is pinned to the sculpting brush.

 SpotLight Radius Drag left or right on this icon to set the SpotLight radius. This feature is used when projecting the image onto a surface. It allows you to see a small, transparent, circular preview of the image while you project it on the surface.

 Opacity This is used to dim the interface while you are projecting the SpotLight images onto a surface. It does not affect the opacity of the projected image, however. Drag left or right to control the opacity of the SpotLight images. Drag left to reduce opacity; drag right to increase opacity. A low opacity makes it easier to see the surface while projecting images onto your model. A medium level of opacity is helpful when you are using SpotLight as a sculpture reference.

 Fade This controls the opacity of the image as it is projected onto the surface. You can vary the opacity of overlapping images to blend them together in SpotLight and then project the result onto a surface.

 Tile Proportional Click this icon to arrange the images in SpotLight on the left side of the canvas. The images are scaled down to fit on the screen, but their relative sizes are maintained. The image that is the largest size will be the largest on the screen, and then the next largest size image will be the second biggest on screen, and so on down to the smallest image.

Tile Selected Click this icon to arrange the images on the left side of the canvas. The selected image is shown at full size, and unselected images are scaled down and placed below the selected image.

Tile Unified Click this button to arrange the images on the left side of the canvas. The images are all scaled to the same size.

Front Click this image to move the selected image to the front. The unselected images are placed behind. This becomes more apparent when the selected image is overlapping another image.

Back Click this icon to move the selected image to the back. The unselected images are placed in front. This becomes more apparent when the selected image is overlapping another image.

Delete This function removes the selected image from SpotLight.

Flip H This function flips the image horizontally.

Flip V This function flips the image vertically.

Tile H This tiles the images horizontally. To use this function, select an image by clicking it and drag the icon clockwise. As you drag, the image is repeated horizontally. If no images are selected, then this function is applied to all the images in LightBox. If you hold down the Shift key when dragging this icon, it will tile the texture horizontally and vertically and respect the aspect ratio.

Tile V This works just like tile H but the images are tiled vertically instead of horizontally.

Grid This applies a grid or a checkerboard pattern to the image. Drag the icon counterclockwise to add a grid. As you drag to the right, the squares of the grid are enlarged. Drag clockwise to add a checkerboard pattern. As you drag to the left, the squares of the checkerboard are enlarged. When you release the icon, the grid is applied to the image. If you drag the icon again, a new grid is applied to the image in addition to any existing grid. This function works only when an image is selected.

Restore This function restores the image to its original state. To use this, select the image and drag the restore icon clockwise. As you drag, the changes made to the image will fade away. If you keep dragging, eventually the image will be completely restored.

Some of the SpotLight functions, such as restore, can be applied to the whole image or just parts of the image. If you click the icon and drag it counterclockwise, the restore function is applied to the whole image. If you click the icon and then drag on the image,

the restoration occurs only where you paint on the image. The Draw Size, Focal Shift, and Z Intensity sliders will determine the size, falloff, and intensity of the restoration effect.

 Nudge This function is used to smear the image. To use this feature, click the nudge icon to activate it and then paint on the image. As you paint, the image will be smeared. The Draw Size and Z Intensity sliders on the top shelf control the size and the strength of the smearing. If you click the nudge icon and drag left or right, the strength of the nudged areas is reduced. If you drag the icon far enough, the nudged strokes will disappear altogether.

 Clone This function copies part of an image to other parts of the same image or other images that have been loaded into SpotLight. To use this function follow these steps:

1. Place the center of the SpotLight interface over the area that you want to clone. This is the clone source.

2. Click the clone icon to activate it.

3. Drag on another part of the image or another image loaded within SpotLight. The area at the center of the SpotLight interface will be copied to wherever you paint. If there is an image selected, when you click another image, the image will be selected instead of being cloned.

4. Use the Draw Size and Z Intensity sliders to determine the size and opacity of the cloned image.

5. To reposition the clone source, drag on the edge of the circle at the center of the SpotLight interface.

The cloned stroke will not be applied to blank parts of the canvas. It appears only on images loaded into SpotLight. The clone feature is very useful but can be tricky. Watch the SpotLightClone.mov movie in the Movies folder on the DVD to see a demo that better explains this feature.

 Smudge This is similar to nudge. If you select this icon and drag left or right, the selected image is blurred. Click this icon and drag on the image to create smudged strokes. The Draw Size and Z Intensity sliders on the top shelf control the size of the smudge and the intensity.

 Contrast Click this icon and drag clockwise to increase the contrast of the image; drag counterclockwise to reduce contrast. As the dark colors in the image reach 100 percent black, they will appear transparent. Click this icon and drag on the image to paint areas of high contrast. The Draw Size and Z Intensity sliders control the size of the stroke and the intensity of the contrast. Hold the Alt key to paint areas of low or negative contrast.

 Saturation The feature works very much like contrast. Drag the icon clockwise to increase the saturation of the color; drag counterclockwise to remove saturation. Click the icon and drag in the image to paint saturation into the image. Hold the Alt key and paint to remove areas of saturation. The Draw Size and Z Intensity sliders control the size of the stroke and the intensity of the saturation.

 Hue Click the hue icon and drag clockwise or counterclockwise to adjust the hue of the image.

 Intensity This feature works very much like contrast and saturation. Drag the icon clockwise to increase the intensity of the color, and drag counterclockwise to remove intensity. If you keep dragging counterclockwise, eventually all the colors in the image become 100 percent black and the image becomes transparent. Click the icon and drag in the image to paint color intensity into the image. Hold the Alt key and paint to remove areas of intensity. The Draw Size and Z Intensity sliders control the size of the stroke and the color intensity.

 Paint Click and drag clockwise on this icon to fill the image using the main color in the color picker. Drag counterclockwise to fill the image with the secondary color in the color picker. Click and drag in the image to paint colored strokes on the image. The colors are determined by the main color in the color picker. Hold the Alt key and drag in the image to paint with the secondary color. The Draw Size and Z Intensity sliders control the size of the stroke and the opacity of the color. Hold the Ctrl key to smart-fill selected color. Remember, black is seen as transparent. This will allow you to mask out parts of the textures. Watch the SpotLightPaint.mov video in the Movies folder of the DVD to see how this can be useful.

This concludes a brief tour of the SpotLight functions. To make sense of all this, you'll need to practice. In the next few sections you'll get some practical experience using SpotLight to perform a number of tasks.

SpotLight Projection

SpotLight's power lies in its ability to project the images you edit in SpotLight directly onto the surface of a digital sculpture. This means it's very easy to incorporate photographic elements as well as digital painting and custom textures into the colors you paint on your models.

In the following sections, we'll take a look at the basics of projecting images onto a surface using SpotLight.

Projecting an Image

Imagine shining a spotlight onto a surface, but rather than seeing just a bright light on the surface, you see an image instead. That's kind of the idea behind SpotLight. The sculpting brush is kind of like a spotlight, and you use it to project images onto the surface. The process is very simple but very powerful. This exercise demonstrates a typical workflow for using SpotLight to project colors onto a surface.

1. Open a new session of ZBrush.

2. Use the Open button in the File menu to open the `PolyPaintTest.ZPR` project created earlier in this chapter.

3. Use the Load SpotLight button in the Texture palette to load the `SpotLightTest.ZSL` file created in the previous section.

4. When the SpotLight file loads, you'll see the images on the canvas in front of the PolySphere. The SpotLight interface may be hidden. Press the Z hotkey to show the SpotLight interface.

   When the SpotLight interface is visible, then you know that you are in Edit mode. This means you won't affect the PolySphere behind the images when you drag on the canvas.

5. Select the largest image and drag it away from the others toward the center of the canvas.

6. Select each smaller image and move them out of the way so you have some space to work.

7. Click the largest image. Use the scale icon on the SpotLight interface to increase the scale of the largest image. To do this, click the scale icon and drag the SpotLight dial clockwise until the image covers the PolySphere behind it.

8. Drag on the largest image to position it in front of the PolySphere (see Figure 8.54).

9. Click the opacity icon on the SpotLight dial. Drag counterclockwise until the image is almost completely invisible and you can clearly see the PolySphere (left image in Figure 8.55).

Figure 8.54

Arrange the SpotLight images so that the largest image is in front of the PolySphere. Scale the image up so that it covers the PolySphere.

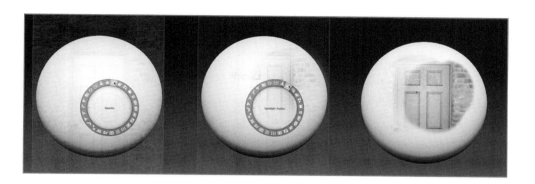

Figure 8.55

Reduce the opacity of SpotLight (left image), increase the SpotLight radius (center image), press the Z hotkey to enter Projection mode, and drag on the surface (right image).

10. Click the SpotLight Radius icon, and drag the dial clockwise to increase the size of the SpotLight radius. You'll see part of the image appear as you drag within a faded circle. The circle increases in size when you drag clockwise (center image in Figure 8.55).

The SpotLight radius function does not affect the brush size. The radius feature creates a preview of the SpotLight image so you can see which parts of the image will be projected as you work. Increasing the radius lets you see more of the projected colors, but it does not affect how the colors will be projected onto the surface.

11. Press the Z hotkey. This hides the SpotLight interface and puts SpotLight into Projection mode.

12. Hold the tip of the brush over the PolySphere. You can see a preview of the projection at the center of the brush tip. This is the SpotLight style projection.

13. On the top shelf, turn off Add and make sure Rgb is on. Set Rgb Intensity to **80**.

14. Click and drag on the surface. The image is projected onto the PolySphere (right image in Figure 8.55).

15. Rotate the PolySphere and paint some more. You can cover the whole surface by rotating and positioning the PolySphere within the projected area (see Figure 8.56).

Continue with this project in the next section.

Figure 8.56

Rotate the view of the PolySphere and continue to paint on it to cover the surface with the projected image.

Pinning the Projection to the Brush

When SpotLight is in Projection mode, the images remain fixed exactly as they have been arranged. SpotLight projects straight through the image onto the surface. If you want to use the location of the brush to place the image, you can use the pin function.

Figure 8.57

Click the pin icon on the SpotLight dial to turn on the pin function.

1. Press the Z hotkey to reenter SpotLight Edit mode.

2. Click the pin icon, which resembles a thumbtack, in the upper right of the SpotLight dial. A white bar appears above the icon, indicating that the pin function has been enabled (see Figure 8.57).

3. Press the Z hotkey again to hide the SpotLight dial and return to Projection mode.

4. Drag on the surface of the model. Lift the brush and drag on another part of the surface.

   Each time you release the brush and paint on another part of the surface, the projected image is placed at the point where the brush makes contact with the surface. The center of the projection source is based on the center of the SpotLight dial relative to the position of the image in SpotLight (see Figure 8.58).

Continue with this project in the next section.

Figure 8.58

The projected image is pinned to the brush, so each time you touch the surface, the image is projected based on brush placement.

Blending Images Together Using Fade

Using the fade function, you can control the opacity of the image as it is projected onto the surface. You can use this feature to blend two or more images in SpotLight and then project the result.

1. Press the Z hotkey to reenter SpotLight Edit mode.

2. Drag the opacity icon clockwise until you can see the images clearly.

3. Click and drag on one of the smaller images, and drag it over so that it overlaps the larger image. The smaller image may not be visible when it overlaps the larger image; this is because it is behind the larger image.

4. Select the large image by clicking it, and click the back icon on the SpotLight dial. The smaller image should appear now that the largest image has been sent all the way to the back (see Figure 8.59).

5. Click the smaller image to select it. The red border of the image indicates that is selected.

6. Drag the scale icon clockwise to enlarge the smaller image. The two images should be overlapping, and the PolySphere should be behind both.

7. On the dial, drag the fade icon counterclockwise to decrease the opacity of the selected image (Figure 8.60). Set the fade of the selected image to about 50 percent of its original opacity.

8. Drag the center of the SpotLight dial so that it is above an area where the two images are overlapping.

9. Press the Z hotkey to leave the Edit mode and enter Projection mode.

10. Drag on the surface of the PolySphere. The resulting projection is the combination of the two overlapping images blended together (see Figure 8.61).

Figure 8.59

Click the back icon to send the selected image behind the other images.

Figure 8.60

Reduce the opacity of the overlapping image by dragging the fade icon counterclockwise.

Figure 8.61

The blended images are projected onto the PolySphere.

Sculpting with SpotLight

SpotLight not only projects the colors of the images onto the surface; it can also be used to sculpt the surface based on the values of the projected images. To enable this ability, you simply need to turn on Zadd on the top shelf while in Projection mode. Any of the sculpting brushes can be used to create a wide variety of texturing effects. The projected image acts as a stencil for the sculpting brush. The darker values of the image mask the effect of the brush.

This exercise shows how to enable this feature:

1. Start a fresh session of ZBrush.

2. Open LightBox to the Projects section.

3. Double-click the `DefaultCube.ZPR` project. This will load it into ZBrush.

4. Turn off the Persp button on the right shelf. Rotate the view of the cube so that you can see it from the side.

5. Open the SubTool subpalette of the Tool palette. Click the paintbrush icon for the PolyCube_1 subtool to activate Colorize mode.

6. Press Ctrl+D three times to subdivide the model. The model should be 1.572 million polygons at the highest subdivision level.

7. Open LightBox to the Texture section. Scroll to the left by dragging on the images until you find the blue grate texture. It is labeled `IMG_4760.jpg` (see Figure 8.62).

8. Double-click this image to load it into SpotLight (you may need to double-click it twice).

9. Drag the scale icon on the SpotLight dial counterclockwise to reduce the size of the image.

10. Drag the opacity icon on the SpotLight dial counterclockwise to reduce the opacity of SpotLight so that you can easily see the cube.

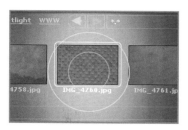

Figure 8.62

Select the blue grate image from the Texture section of LightBox.

11. Drag the SpotLight radius icon on the SpotLight dial clockwise to increase the radius of SpotLight (see Figure 8.63).

Figure 8.63

Increase the SpotLight radius.

12. Press the Z hotkey to leave Edit mode.

13. Open the sculpting brush fly-out library and select the Layer brush.

14. On the top shelf, turn on the Zadd and Rgb buttons. Set Z Intensity to **50** and Rgb Intensity to **10**.

15. Set Draw Size to **100**.

16. Drag on the surface of the cube.
You'll see the colors of the grate image appear on the surface, and you'll also see the details of the image sculpted into the geometry of the cube (see Figure 8.64).

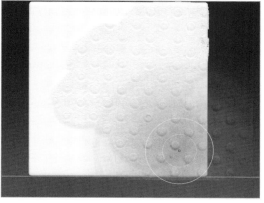

Figure 8.64

The sculpting brush sculpts the details of the image into the surface of the cube.

Try this technique with other sculpting brushes. Try TrimDynamic, ClayBuildup, or Blob. Note that you can use all of your sculpting tricks in combination with SpotLight. This means you can use alphas on the sculpting brushes, masks, stroke types, and so on. It's amazing how many interesting effects you can achieve using SpotLight as a sculpting tool.

IMAGE RESOLUTION AND SPOTLIGHT

You'll get better results in your SpotLight projection techniques if you use high-resolution images. Any image artifacts in the projected textures will affect the quality of the surface. So even if your model has been subdivided to millions and millions of polygons, if you project through a low-resolution or highly compressed image, the result will look blocky and pixelated.

Symmetrical Projection

Use Symmetry when projecting SpotLight onto a surface in order to paint both sides of an object at the same time. For example, this technique can be used to paint two sides of a face using the same image.

This exercise demonstrates how this works.

1. Start a new session of ZBrush.

2. Open LightBox to the Project/DemoProjects section and double-click the DemoDog.zpr project to load it into the current session.

3. Set the main color to white using the color picker. Make sure Symmetry is active for the dog across the x-axis (hotkey = X).

4. Open the Texture palette. Click the Import button. Use your computer's file browser to load the houndDog.jpg image from the Chapter 8 folder on the DVD.

5. If SpotLight is open, the image is automatically added when you import, as shown in Figure 8.65; if not, click the Add To Spotlight button to load it from the Texture palette into SpotLight.

6. Use the SpotLight dial to scale the image down a little and move it toward the center of the screen.

7. Press the Z hotkey to exit Edit mode.

8. Scale the view of the dog model so that it matches the size of the head in the image. Rotate the view of the dog to match the angle of the head as well. It will be impossible to get a perfect match, but that is okay; just try to get it close.

9. Press the Z hotkey to switch back to the SpotLight Edit mode.

Figure 8.65

Add the houndDog image to SpotLight.

10. Scale and rotate the image using the SpotLight dial to see if you can make the image line up with the model a little better.

11. Click the nudge icon so that a bar appears above the icon. Drag on the image to push the pixels of the image. Use nudge to make the image match the model of the dog. Use the Draw Size and Z Intensity sliders on the top shelf to adjust the radius of the brush and the strength of the nudge effect (see Figure 8.66).

12. Drag counterclockwise on the opacity icon to reduce the opacity of the image. Remember, this does not affect the opacity of the projection, just the opacity of the image. This makes it easier to see what's going on when you start to project the image onto the model.

Figure 8.66

Rotate and scale the view of the dog model to match the SpotLight image (left image). Rotate the SpotLight image to match the view of the model (center image). Use nudge to push parts of the image to match the model.

13. Press the Z hotkey to switch out of the SpotLight Edit mode.

14. Press Ctrl+D three times to subdivide the model.

15. Make sure Zadd is off and Rgb is on. Set Rgb Intensity to **80**.

16. Paint on the face of the dog to project the image.

17. Press Shift+Z to hide SpotLight. Rotate the view of the dog. The image has been projected onto both sides (see Figure 8.67).

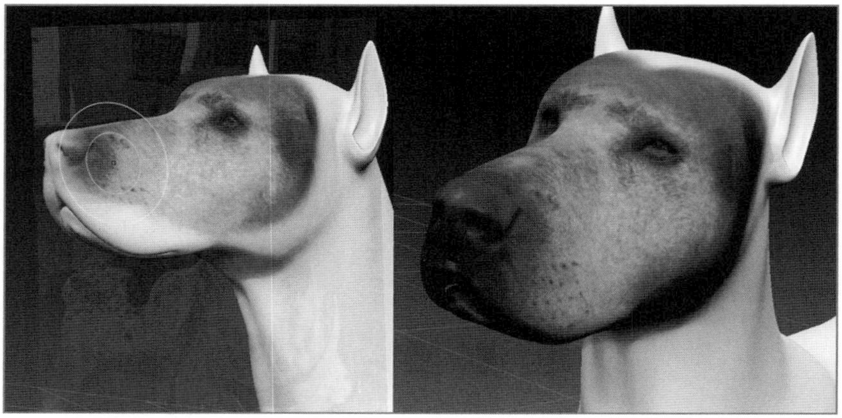

Figure 8.67

The image of the dog is projected onto the dog model. With Symmetry enabled, the image is projected onto both sides of the model.

Using symmetrical projection and the SpotLight nudge feature, it's not hard to texture an entire face very quickly. If you have a series of images from different views, then you can easily blend the projections together to create a convincing texture. The amazing thing is that you don't have to struggle with making sure everything lines up perfectly. You can easily edit each image in SpotLight to match the view of your model.

Sculpting References in SpotLight

SpotLight can be used as a convenient way to load reference images into ZBrush. This can eliminate the need to switch to an image-editing program or a web browser while sculpting, allowing you to stay comfortably within the ZBrush environment.

My original vision for the hot rod body created in Chapter 5 was to create a sculpture of a cartoon car in the monster art style of Ed Roth. I created a quick sketch of what I thought the end result should be. In this exercise, you'll see how the sketch can be used as a reference for sculpting the body.

1. Start a new session of ZBrush.

2. Use the Open button in the File palette to open the HotRodModel.ZPR project from the Chapter 8 folder on the DVD.

    This model was created by combining the hot rod body and wheel tools created in Chapter 5 (see Figure 8.68).

Figure 8.68

The hot rod model is made up of tools created in Chapter 5.

3. Open the Texture palette and click the Import button. Load the hotRodRef.psd file from the Chapter 8 folder on the DVD.

4. Open the Texture palette and click the Add To SpotLight button. The image appears on the canvas in SpotLight (see Figure 8.69).

5. Drag counterclockwise on the scale icon to scale the image down. Move it off to the side so that you can see the model.

6. If you have a large number of images on the canvas in SpotLight, take a few minutes to arrange them so that you can see the model on the canvas.

7. Drag counterclockwise on the SpotLight radius icon all the way to make sure it is set to **0**.

8. Press the Z hotkey to switch out of SpotLight Edit mode.

9. Open the Brush palette and expand the Samples subpalette. Turn off the SpotLight Projection button (see Figure 8.70).

Figure 8.69

Import the image and click the Add To SpotLight icon in the Texture palette.

This last step is the most important. If you don't turn off SpotLight projection, the sculpting brushes will not work unless they are used to project colors and details on the surface. If the images disappear when you press the Z hotkey, it means you need to set the SpotLight radius to **0**. Doing this keeps the images visible when SpotLight Edit mode is off (see Figure 8.71).

Figure 8.70

Turn off the SpotLight Projection button in the Samples subpalette of the Brush palette.

Figure 8.71

Model the car with the reference images in the background.

Now you are free to model the surface. Press Z whenever you want to toggle back into SpotLight and rearrange the images. Press Shift+Z when you want to hide SpotLight completely.

Check out the engineRefImages.ZSL SpotLight file in the Chapter 8 folder of the DVD. I created this SpotLight from photographs I took of a hot rod parked on my street.

Painting with Curves

The Curve mode you first encountered in Chapter 6 can be applied to brushes used for polypainting. You can use this option to develop some interesting brush effects as well as to increase the precision of your strokes.

Using Curve Mode with Polypaint

If you are not familiar with how Curve mode works, review Chapter 6, which demonstrates how curves work. In this exercise, you'll see how Curve mode is applied to a brush and used to paint designs on a face.

1. Load the femaleHead.ZPR project from the Chapter 8 folder on the DVD.

2. In the SubTool subpalette select the femaleHead subtool and turn on the paintbrush icon to activate polypainting.

3. Select the Standard brush from the brush library.

4. On the top shelf make sure Zadd is off and Rgb is on. Set Rgb Intensity to **50**.

5. Choose a red color in the color picker. Lower the Draw Size to around **20** and set the Focal Shift to **-60**. This ensures that the strokes are more precise.

6. In the Stroke palette, activate Curve mode.

7. Make sure Symmetry is activated (hot key = X), and then draw a curve starting from the outside corner of the upper lip toward the center, as shown in Figure 8.72. Follow the upper ridge of the lip. Since Symmetry is activated, you only need to draw the curve to the middle of the upper lip (Figure 8.72, top image).

8. Drag the curve downward; you'll see the lip fill in with color (Figure 8.72, middle image). Try this on the lower lip. Kind of neat, but let's try something a bit more exotic.

9. In the Stroke palette, turn off Bend. When you drag on the curve after you draw it on the surface, the entire curve will move so the curve itself acts as a brush tip.

Figure 8.72

Use Curve mode to paint the lips red.

10. In the Stroke palette, turn on Snap. As you drag the curve, the paint stroke snaps to the surface so that the stroke follows the contour of the face. If this is not on, the stroke will disappear as you move the curve along the face.

11. Set the main color to purple. Draw a curve just below the eyebrow and then drag the curve down. This fills in the area above the eye with purple; it looks like clown makeup, but you get the idea (see Figure 8.73). Drag the curve up and down to fill in the color more.

Figure 8.73

The curve is used to color in the area above the eyes.

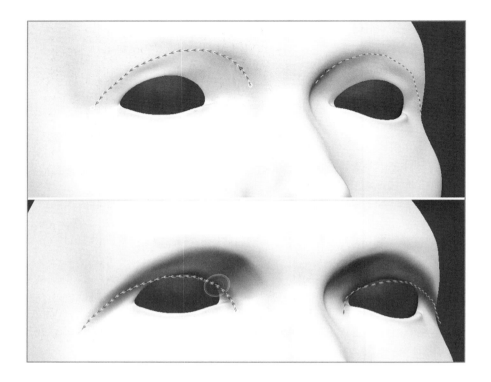

Creating a Design

Now for something interesting—let's say you want to add a row of stars on the face as a garish tattoo, and you want to control the position of the stars. Try these settings for the brush:

1. Continue with the scene from the previous section. Set the primary color to blue.

2. Set the Rgb Intensity to **100**. In the Alpha palette select Alpha 10; this is the star alpha.

3. In the Stroke palette, turn on Bend so that you can bend the curve after drawing it. Turn on Snap so the curve follows the contour of the face, and turn on Size And Intensity so the size and intensity are varied along the curve's length.

4. Set Max Points to **8**. This is important. If the Max Points setting is high when painting, it can slow down and even crash ZBrush. This also makes it easier to control how the stars are placed.

5. Set the Stroke type to DragDot. This allows you to position the stars as you adjust the curve.

6. Draw a curve down the side of the cheek. Once the curve is drawn, drag one of the ends of the curve. A row of stars follows wherever you drag the curve (Figure 8.74).

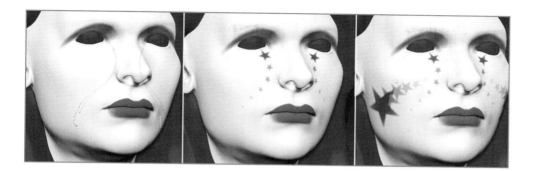

Figure 8.74

Use the DragDot stroke type to position a design precisely on the face.

You can continue to manipulate the curve until the stars are positioned on the face exactly where you want them. If you want the stars to be the same size and intensity, turn off the Size And Intensity button in the Stroke palette.

The poor girl looks like a 1970s glam rock star, but hopefully this exercise has shown you how you can use Curve mode to create interesting designs when painting a model.

Painting colors on a model is very useful for creating textures to use in other 3D programs such as Autodesk® Maya®. For tutorials on converting polypainting into a texture that can be exported, consult Bonus Content Chapter 1 on the DVD that comes with this book.

Summary

In this chapter you learned how to paint colors on a model using polypainting. You learned how to create the look of believable dragon skin by building up layers of color. You learned how cavity and occlusion masking can be used to add visual interest to your designs. SpotLight was introduced as a tool for projecting images onto a model. You learned how to use Curve mode to control how strokes are painted onto a model.

CHAPTER 9

FiberMesh, Materials, and Rendering

Once you have created a model in ZBrush, you will want to show it off to the world. Whether sharing your work online, presenting a model for approval from a director, or building up your portfolio, you'll want to make your models look as good as they possibly can. To help you accomplish this, ZBrush offers several features that achieve spectacular images. FiberMesh can be used to create hair, plants, and other special effects. The new lighting system can be used to integrate models realistically into an image. To bring it all together, ZBrush offers a variety of materials and rendering options that create both stylized and realistic images without using an additional program.

This chapter gives an overview of how to create hair with FiberMesh and several examples of how to use the lighting and materials in ZBrush renders.

This chapter includes the following topics:

- FiberMesh
- Rendering basics
- Standard lighting
- Advanced lighting with LightCap
- Material basics
- Standard materials
- MatCap materials
- Applying materials
- BPR rendering techniques
- BPR render filters

FiberMesh

FiberMesh is the newest addition to the ZBrush toolset. ZBrush artists no longer must use other graphics programs, such as Photoshop, Autodesk® Maya®, or Autodesk® 3ds Max®, to add hair to characters, leaves to trees, or fur to beasts. FiberMesh generates fibers for these models and then sculpts the fibers into shape using a special set of sculpting brushes. The process involves two basic steps: creating a preview of the fibers and then accepting the settings that convert the fibers into strands, which then can be shaped, combed, and sculpted using the special hair brushes. In this example, you'll work with the preview settings.

FiberMesh Preview Settings

The FiberMesh preview settings are located in a subpalette of the Tool palette and are available only when the current tool is a polygon mesh. If the current tool is a ZSphere or a Parametric 3D primitive, the Preview button in the FiberMesh subpalette will not be functional. Let's use the preview settings to create a Mohawk hairstyle for the demon character introduced in Chapter 6.

1. Load the demon.ZPR project from the Chapter 7 files on the DVD.

2. Before turning on the FiberMesh preview, paint a mask on the surface where you will place the hair; otherwise the fibers will cover the entire mesh. To create a Mohawk, hold the Ctrl key and use the MaskPen brush to paint a strip on the demon's head from the top to the base of the skull, as shown in Figure 9.1.

3. In the Tool palette, expand the FiberMesh subpalette and activate the Preview button. After a few seconds a small strip of hair appears on the demon's head.

Figure 9.1

Paint a mask on top of the head where you want to place the fibers.

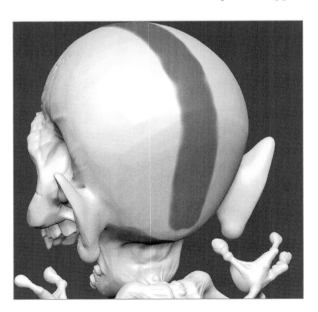

There are a lot of sliders in the FiberMesh subpalette: those in the upper portion affect the preview and hence the overall qualities of the fibers; those at the bottom control the fibers after they have been converted into a mesh. Figure 9.2 shows how the subpalette is divided. Each slider in the Preview portion controls the strength of the attribute. The small sliders on the right of the palette offer the ability to add a degree of randomness to each attribute. Let's look at how this works.

4. The Mohawk is looking a little short. To make it longer set the Length slider to **400**.

5. The black hairs are a little tough to see. Click the Base color swatch toward the bottom of the FiberMesh subpalette, and select a bright purple from the color picker.

6. The hair has Gravity automatically applied. To make the Mohawk stick up, set Gravity to **0**. This makes the hair stick straight out from the head like a classic punk rock hairstyle (see Figure 9.3).

7. Try the following settings to shape the Mohawk:

   MaxFibers: **100**

   LeV: **0** (This is the slider to the right of the Length slider. This controls the variation in length; by setting this to 0 you get an even length for the hair.)

   ByMask: **5** (This modulates the length of the hairs based on the masked part of the surface.)

   ByArea: **0.3** (This modulates the length of the hair based on the size and density of the polygons. A low setting keeps the hair even but also prevents the hair from going through the character's face.)

   Coverage: **90** (This setting increases the density of the fibers.)

   ScaleRoot: **1** (This sets the size of the fibers at the root.)

   ScaleTip: **0.5** (This sets the size of the fibers at the tip.)

   Tip color: Bright blue

   BColorize, TColorize: **1** (This adds saturation to the colors applied at the base and the tips.)

Figure 9.2

Turn on the Preview button in the FiberMesh subpalette in the Tool palette.

— Preview setting:

— Mesh settings

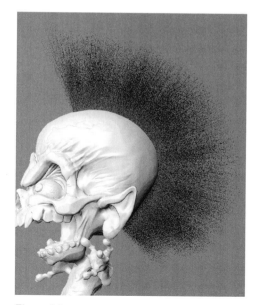

Figure 9.3

Set Gravity to 0 in the FiberMesh subpalette to make the hair stick straight out. The demon is a punk rocker now.

HAIR GRAVITY EFFECTS

The direction of the gravity is dependent on the viewing angle of the model. You can use this gravity to style hair. If you rotate the view of the model and increase the Gravity slider, the hair is pulled toward the bottom of the screen, or to the top of the screen if Gravity is set to a negative number. You can use Gravity to make hair appear windblown. The following image shows how Gravity pulls hair to the bottom of the screen when viewed at an odd angle; when the model is rotated to face the camera, you can see how it affects the hair.

8. To create a hairstyle you like, experiment with the modifier sliders to the right of each attribute to add more or less variation to each attribute.

9. Save the project as **demonHair.ZPR**. It's always a good idea to save once you have a hairstyle you like. Figure 9.4 shows the results of these settings.

Creating the Hair Mesh

Once you have a hairstyle you like, you can accept the changes, which converts the hair into a subtool.

1. Continue with the project from the previous section.

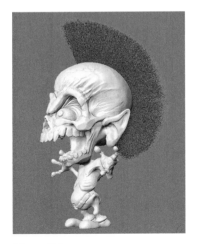

Figure 9.4

The results of the settings create a classic 1980s punk rock Mohawk.

2. Click the Accept button at the top of the FiberMesh subpalette. This converts the preview into a new subtool. A message appears asking if you want to activate Fast Preview mode (see Figure 9.5).

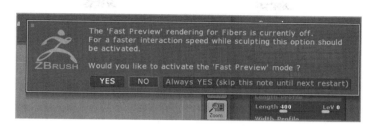

3. Fast Preview increases the performance when sculpting the hair. For this example click the No button since the Mohawk does not need to be styled. In the next section you'll learn more about sculpting and styling hair with the hair brushes.

4. The hair is now a new subtool (see Figure 9.6). If you decide you don't like it, delete the subtool. The hair settings you created are saved with the Demon subtool, so you can activate the Preview button and continue creating variations on your style. In fact, you can continue to create as many hair subtools as you'd like. ZBrush can easily become your virtual hair salon.

Figure 9.6

The hair is added as a new subtool.

Styling FiberMesh

Styling hair created with FiberMesh is easy, thanks to the powerful sculpting brushes that can be directly applied to the fibers. In this example you'll use the brushes to create a hairstyle for a female character. For this character you'll create long hair and style it so it looks somewhat realistic. The trick to styling long FiberMesh models is to start with short hair and then use the brushes to lengthen the hair as you work. This approach is much easier than shaping long fibers, which can be frustrating. It's also important to use masking strategically as you work.

1. Open the `femaleHeadHair.ZPR` project from the `Chapter 9` folder on the DVD.

2. Make sure that the Head subtool is selected in the SubTool subpalette and that it is set to SDiv level 4 in the Geometry subpalette.

3. Hold the Ctrl key and use the MaskPen brush to paint a mask on the scalp. Once the scalp is covered, lower the Draw Size and hold Ctrl and Alt together to erase a line in the mask to create a part line on the character's right side (see Figure 9.7).

Figure 9.7

Paint a mask on the woman's head, and then erase a line in the mask to create a part line.

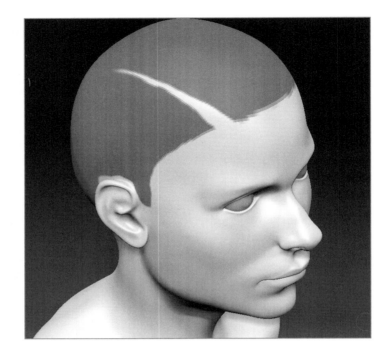

4. In the FiberMesh subpalette of the Tool palette adjust the sliders to create the following settings (any slider that is not mentioned can be left at the default value):

> MaxFibers: **100**
>
> ByMask: **5**
>
> ByArea: **0.5**
>
> Length: **90**
>
> LeV (Length Variation): **0**
>
> Coverage: **200**
>
> CoV (Coverage Variation): **0**
>
> Gravity: **0.8**
>
> Base: light brown
>
> Tip: light yellow

The result should look like a very short hair style with a part on the character's right side, as shown in Figure 9.8.

5. Click the Accept button at the top of the FiberMesh subpalette. ZBrush will ask you if you want to activate Fast Preview. Click Yes. This will improve performance while sculpting the hair.

6. In the SubTool subpalette, select the newly created Fibers subtool. The subtool looks slightly thinner than the original settings; this is because Fast Preview has been enabled.

7. Expand the sculpting brush library and choose the GroomHairShort brush (open the library and press G and then I to select the brush quickly). This brush is a variation of the Nudge brush that has been modified to sculpt short hair easily.

8. Drag the brush across the hair. Try styling the hair to move away from the part naturally. As you work, rotate the hair frequently to sculpt the hair from all possible views. Think of how a hairstylist moves around the customer and rotates the styling chair as he works. Figure 9.9 shows the steps I used while styling the short hair.

9. Hold the Shift key so the Smooth brush is activated. While continuing to hold the Shift key, expand the Brush palette and find the FiberMesh subpalette. Set the Preserve Length slider to **100**, as shown in Figure 9.10. This setting ensures that the length of the hairs is not affected by the Smooth brush.

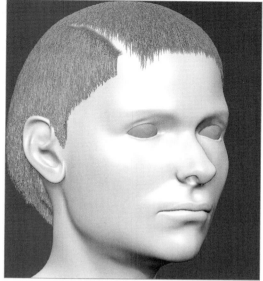

Figure 9.8

The settings create a short hairstyle on the female's head.

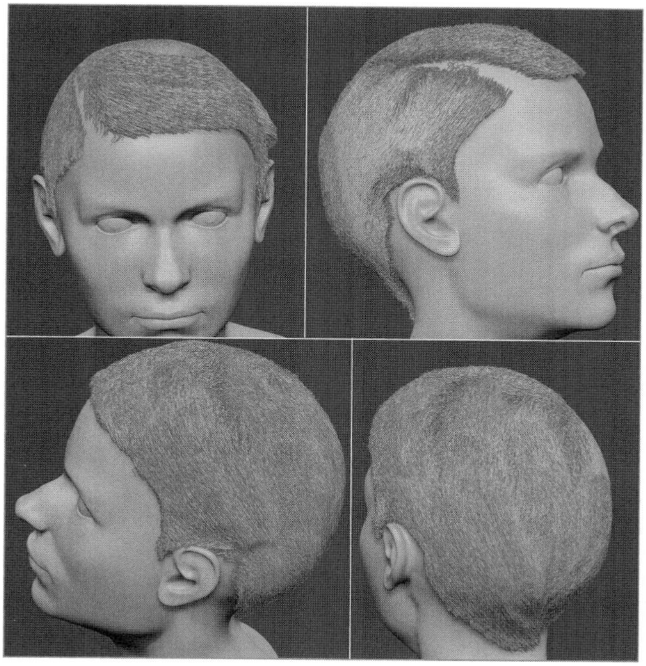

Figure 9.10

Set the Preserve Length slider in the Brush palette for the Smooth brush.

Figure 9.9

The short hair is styled using the GroomHairShort brush.

10. Now as you sculpt the hair, hold the Shift key to smooth the strokes. Use the GroomHairShort brush and then alternate with the Smooth brush to create neatly styled short hair. I find it useful to use a large brush size while working on hair.

11. Once you have something you like, save the project. Save frequently while sculpting hair so you can fall back on a version you like if the style takes a turn for the worse.

Lengthening the Hair

Now to add length you'll switch to another brush, which allows you to pull out the hair. We'll start by lengthening the hair on the back of the head (at the risk of creating a mullet hairstyle!). To make this easier you can isolate this area with a mask.

1. Hold the Ctrl key and choose the MaskLassoBrush from the Brush palette. Use the MaskLassoBrush to mask the hair on the back of the head from the side view. Then hold Ctrl and tap on a blank part of the canvas to invert the mask (see Figure 9.11).

2. Open the sculpting brush library and choose the GroomLengthen brush. Work slowly and deliberately, pulling the hair out and downward. Rotate the head as you work to see it from all sides. I find it's easier to do this when I use a large brush size and zoom out so that I can grab large areas of hair.

Figure 9.11

Mask all of the hair except for the back of the head.

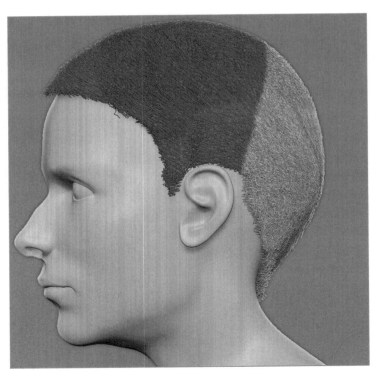

3. Once the hair is about shoulder length, switch to the GroomHairLong brush and use the brush to comb the hair. Alternate using this brush and the Smooth brush (see Figure 9.12).

4. Hold the Ctrl key and tap on a blank part of the canvas to invert the mask. Hold the Ctrl key and select the MaskLasso brush from the sculpting brush library. Hold Ctrl and use the MaskLasso brush to create a mask over the hair on the character's right side. Leave just the hair on the character's right side and the back unmasked.

5. Use the GroomLengthen brush to pull this hair out. And just as you did with the hair on the back, use the GroomHairLong and Smooth brushes to neaten the hair once it is pulled out (see Figure 9.13).

6. You may run into a situation where the hair starts to frizz out as you comb over the areas near the mask. If this happens, clear the mask and then redraw it so the hair on the right side and the back are unmasked. It also helps to click the Solo button so the head is hidden. This allows you to sculpt the hair from the inside.

7. You don't need to make the hair perfect at this point. You're just trying to get it nice and long; it will look strange for a while as you work. Ctrl+click on a blank part of the canvas to invert the mask, and repeat these steps to pull out the hair on the character's left side.

8. Once you have the hair pulled out to a fairly uniform length, clear the mask and then start styling. The best way to do this is to experiment with the grooming brushes and see how they react with the hair. Save your work before you start styling so you have a fallback version.

Figure 9.14 (left) shows the hair after it has been lengthened. The image on the right shows the finished hairstyle. I used the GroomColorize brushes to change the hair color to brown.

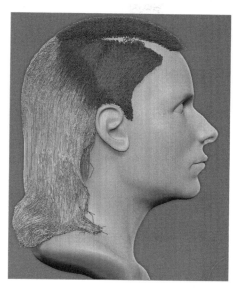

Figure 9.12

Lengthen the hair on the back of the head; then use the Smooth and GroomHairLong brushes to keep it fairly neat.

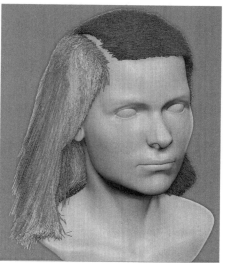

Figure 9.13

Pull the hair out on the side to match the length on the back of the head.

Figure 9.14

The hair is length-ened and then styled and colored using a variety of special grooming brushes.

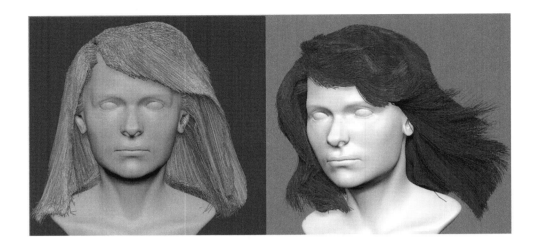

TIPS ON GROOMING HAIR

- If the ends of the hair are uneven in length, hold the Shift key and lower the Preserve Length setting in the FiberMesh subpalette of the Brush palette. The Smooth brush averages the length of the hair within the area of the brush tip and smooths the ends of the hair to make them less frayed.

- Always have a reference nearby! You can use fashion magazines, image searches on the Internet, shampoo commercials, or whatever else you can find. Styling hair without a reference is asking for trouble!

- Store a Morph Target by clicking the StoreMT button in the Morph Target subpalette of the Tool palette. Then as you work you can use the Morph brush to comb hair back to the stored state if it gets out of control. Chapter 10 discusses using Morph Targets in more detail.

- Some of the Groom brushes will paint colors on the hair as you work. If you're not ready to color hair, turn off the Rgb or Mrgb button on the top shelf. These buttons are enabled for some brushes and not for others.

- Experimentation is the key; try each of the grooming brushes and see which ones you like. Personally I find the GroomHairTips brush to be a huge benefit since it has a stronger effect on the tips of the hair. It makes it easier to create layering. The GroomHairToss brush is great for shaping the hair. Try different alphas and Z Intensity settings as you work. If you create a brush you like, save it!

- Once you have a decent style, start adding some color using the GroomHairColorizer brush. Brushes such as GroomRootColorize, GroomMidColorize, and GroomTipColorize allow you to add variations in hue to specific parts of the hair.

- Later in this chapter you'll learn how to render the hair realistically using the hair materials.

- There are many advanced capabilities within FiberMesh that can be used for more than just hair. Some advanced techniques allow you to use FiberMesh to place leaves on trees and create whiskers and eyebrows. For more information check out the free movies at the ZClassroom at www.pixologic.com.

Rendering Basics

In CG terms "rendering" refers to the process where software creates an image from the models, lights, and materials that you have put together. Many 3D software packages, such as Autodesk® Maya®, use very complex systems to create realistic images. ZBrush also has the capability to create compelling and realistic images from the models you sculpt on the canvas. However, in ZBrush, rendering is a bit simpler and faster than in other software packages.

Rendering, lighting, and materials are all areas that work together when creating an image. The examples in this section are designed to give an overview of how these elements work together and how you can use them creatively to express your own artistic vision. We'll start with an overview of the render modes available in ZBrush.

Render Modes

There are five render modes available in ZBrush: Flat, Fast, Preview, Best, and Best Preview Render (BPR). Each mode offers advantages and features ranging from improving performance while working to creating realistic or stylistic images. The following list gives a brief description of each mode:

Flat: Displays the model and colors painted on the surface, with no lighting or shadows. This mode is useful when you want to see the colors painted on the surface without the influence of materials or lighting. This is also good for creating a silhouette of the model.

Fast: Very basic lighting, with no shadows or materials. This displays the model and colors painted on the surface. This mode is great to use when sculpting dense models because the lack of lighting and materials improves performance.

Preview: By default, all models are rendered in Preview mode while you work in a typical ZBrush session. Throughout this book, you've been using Preview render mode without realizing it. Preview mode features preview shadows, reflection, basic lighting, and simplified materials.

Best: Renders accurate shadows, reflections, global illumination, and other effects. It takes more time than the other modes and is used most often for finalizing a completed composition in ZBrush.

BPR (Best Preview Render): This mode was introduced in ZBrush 4. This mode is the preferred method for rendering high-quality images because it has more features than the other modes (such as ambient occlusion, subsurface scattering, and realistic shadows) and is easier to use than Best render mode. This chapter focuses largely on using BPR.

Figure 9.15 shows a painted dragon model in each of the five modes.

Figure 9.15

The dragon model is shown in the five render modes from top to bottom: Flat, Fast, Preview, Best, and Best Preview Render (BPR).

Figure 9.16

To choose a render mode, select from the options at the top of the Render palette. To render using BPR, click the button at the top of the right shelf, which is circled in this image.

To switch renders using Flat, Fast, Preview, or Best, open the Render palette and choose one of the buttons at the top. To render using BPR, click the BPR button at the top of the right shelf, as shown in Figure 9.16, or press Shift+R. Both Best and BPR will take anywhere from a few seconds to a few minutes to render depending on the complexity of the model, the lighting, and the render features you have chosen.

When using Best quality to render an image, the render will update automatically each time you make a change. If you need to stop a render, just press the Esc key. To start it again, click the Render button in the Render palette.

To save you render time, ZBrush stores information about the previous render in a buffer. This means that, as long as you don't change the view of the model, the next time you render using BPR or Best mode, the render should be much quicker.

The Render palette contains myriad options to customize how the render will look. The examples in this chapter will cover the basics of some of these settings.

You can render any time while working on your models. It's a good idea to switch render modes often while sculpting to understand how the surface interacts with light and shadow.

Once you create a render, you can export the image by clicking the Export button in the Document palette. You can choose from many popular image formats including Photoshop (PSD). Later in the chapter you'll learn how to render individual passes that can be composited in Photoshop. This is a popular way to separate rendering elements such as shadow, diffuse light, depth, and other passes so they can be adjusted and recombined into a Photoshop composition.

The size (or resolution) of the exported document is determined by the current document size in ZBrush. You'll learn more about these techniques, as well as how to set up a ZBrush document for export to Photoshop, at the end of the chapter in the section titled "ZBrush and Photoshop." This section walks you through the process of setting up a high-quality render for export to Photoshop at a specific resolution. But before we get there, we need to cover the fundamentals of lighting and materials!

SAVE OFTEN WHILE RENDERING

When you shift your attention from modeling to rendering a high-quality image, remember to save your project often and save multiple versions. It is easy to accidentally create a setting that can crash ZBrush, causing you to lose your hard work.

Standard Lighting

Standard lighting in ZBrush is simple to use and yet very powerful. Using the controls at the top of the Light palette, you can change the direction of the light, add lights, and control light properties such as shadows, intensity, and ambience. The lights can be used to create a composition or as a sculpting aid. This section looks at how the standard light controls work and offers a few examples of how lighting can be used while sculpting and rendering in ZBrush.

The Light Palette

All elements pertaining to lighting are controlled through the Light palette. Unlike other 3D software programs such as Maya, you don't position representations of the lights in empty space; rather, you control the placement of lights using the sphere shown in the upper right of the Light palette. For this example, open a ZBrush project; you can use the DemonCar.ZPR project found in the Chapter 9 folder of the DVD or use one of your own.

BASIC LIGHTING AND MATERIALS

It's very important to choose a Standard material when working with the controls in the Light palette because these materials will react with the placement of the lights in real time while in Preview render mode. If you choose a MatCap material such as the default Red Wax material, changes on the canvas will not be visible when you move the lights around because MatCap materials have the lighting baked into the material. You'll learn more about MatCap materials later in this chapter. For this section, use the BasicMaterial2 material found in the bottom section of the material library. The Standard materials are highlighted by the rectangle in the following image.

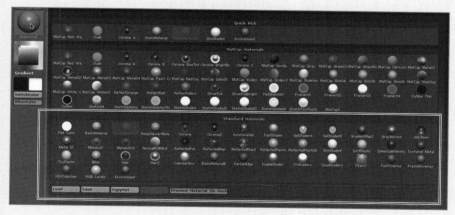

By default a single light is turned on in every ZBrush project; there is also a small amount of ambient light that affects everything on the canvas. To change the position of a light, drag on the small orange dot on the sphere in the Light palette. You'll see the lighting update as you drag the orange dot across the sphere (see Figure 9.17).

You can use the light position as a sculpting aid. Real-world sculptors constantly move

Figure 9.17

Drag the orange dot across the preview sphere in the Light palette to adjust the position of the light.

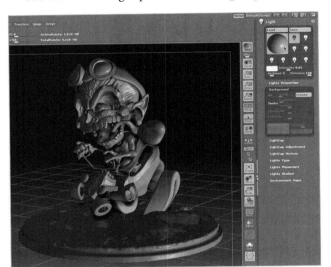

their lights around as they inspect their work. Different light angles reveal flaws in the surface that might not be noticeable otherwise. Press the Ctrl+P hotkey to activate interactive lighting while you work. As you move the brush over the canvas, the light updates automatically. Click on the canvas to stop moving the light. This saves you from going to the Light palette every time you reposition the light.

SEND THE LIGHT TO THE FRONT OR BEHIND

If the preview sphere in the Light palette goes dark, then the light has gone behind an object on the canvas. There is a trick you can use to toggle the position of the light to place it in front of or behind the 3D objects on the canvas. Placing a light behind the sphere can be a good way to create back lighting for the subject. Open the Light palette and click in the upper-right corner of the light position window. Clicking in this corner toggles the light position so that it acts as a front light or a back light. In the following graphic, the image on the left shows the light in front of the sphere; the image on the right shows the light behind the sphere.

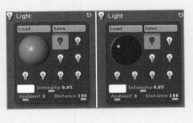

The area around the lighting control sphere is surrounded by light bulb icons. This area is the light switch panel, which lets you turn lights on and off. You can add up to eight standard lights in a ZBrush scene. If that's not enough, later in the chapter you'll learn how you can add as many lights as you like using LightCap.

To turn a light on, click one of the light bulb icons so it turns orange. Usually, you must click it twice—once to select the light and again to turn it on. When a light is selected, a gray border appears around the light icon. This means that when you drag on the sphere, you change the position of the selected light. Many of the sliders and controls in the Light palette affect the selected light. To turn a light off, click its icon until it is no longer highlighted in orange (see Figure 9.18).

Figure 9.18

An orange highlight on the light bulb icon indicates that the light is on. A gray border around a light bulb icon indicates that the light is selected.

LIGHT PALETTE PITFALLS

It is possible to adjust the settings for a light that is selected and turned off at the same time. When this happens, you won't see any change on the canvas as you change the position of the light until you turn the light on by clicking its icon until it turns orange.

Light Types

ZBrush uses four types of lights to illuminate the strokes and 3D tools on the canvas. By default, there is a single sun-type light that is turned on when you start a ZBrush session. Sun-type lights have no point source—all of their rays are cast in parallel to simulate light coming from a distant source. You place sun lights using the sphere icon in the light window.

The other three types of lights are point, spot, and glow. To change the type of light you are using, click one of the buttons in the Lights Type subpalette. This changes the type of light currently selected (see Figure 9.19). Remember that the lighting you see on the canvas may not be coming from the currently selected light. Make sure the currently selected light is turned on when you change the settings if you want to see the lighting update accordingly.

Figure 9.19

Change the light type for the selected light using the buttons in the Lights Type subpalette of the Light palette.

The Radial button at the bottom of the Light Types subpalette changes the behavior of the currently selected light so that the areas of the strokes or 3D tools that face away receive the light. This creates a good fill lighting effect. Fill lights simulate light coming from the sides of the subject. Any of the light types can be modified using the Radial button (see Figure 9.20).

Figure 9.20

**The Radial button
is a modifier that
makes the selected
light a fill light.**

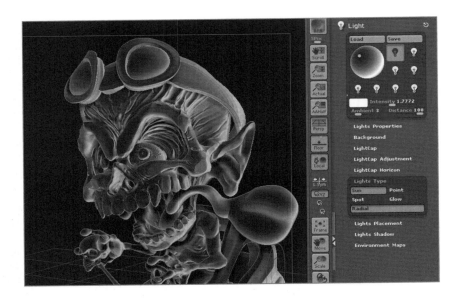

Sun Light

The following exercise will illustrate some of the differences between the types of lights:

1. Start a fresh ZBrush session.

2. Use the Open button in the File menu to open the DemonCar.ZPR project, or use one of your own models.

3. Choose the BasicMaterial2 from the materials inventory. The model should already have this material applied, but it never hurts to double-check!

4. Place the Light palette in a tray so the settings are easily accessible. Make sure only one light is on by clicking the orange highlighted light bulb icon in the Light palette (if it turns off, click the icon again to turn it on).

5. Drag across the sphere icon in the Light palette to change the position of the light. Set the position so that the demon is lit from the upper right.

6. Set Intensity to **1.5**.

7. Set the Ambient slider below the Intensity slider to **0**. This removes ambient light from the lighting on the canvas.

8. Click the second light bulb icon twice so that it is selected and highlighted in orange, indicating that it is on. This means you should have two orange highlighted light bulb icons in the Light palette.

9. Make sure the second light bulb icon is selected; there should be a gray border around the icon.

10. In the Lights Type subpalette, turn on Radial. This changes the second light into a fill light.

11. Click the color icon next to the Intensity slider to open the color picker. Choose a red color.

12. Drag on the sphere icon in the Light palette to change the position of the second light. A red band of light appears on the sphere. Position the light so that the red band illuminates the bottom of the preview sphere.

13. Set the Intensity slider to **0.8**.

14. Press Shift+R to create a Best Preview Render (see Figure 9.21).

This is a simple two-light rig, not earth-shattering by any means but a good example of how to use the standard lighting controls for sun-type lights in the Light palette. In the next section, you'll see how to use the point light type. Keep the same project open for the next section.

Figure 9.21

The demon is lit with a simple two-light rig and rendered using BPR render mode.

Point Light

The point light type works slightly differently than the sun-type light. To place the light, you'll use the settings in the Placement subpalette of the Light palette instead of the preview sphere. Keep in mind that the point light type is visible only when rendering in Best render quality mode.

1. In the Light palette, click the second light bulb icon to turn the second light off. Make sure the first light is still on.

3. Select the first light bulb icon in the Light palette, and set its Intensity value to **2**.

4. In the Type subpalette, click the Point button to set the light to the point type.

5. Expand the Placement subpalette. To change the position of a point light, drag from the P button in the Placement subpalette to a spot on the front of the demon's head.

6. In the Placement subpalette, set the radius to **2.5**.

The point light emits light in all directions from a single point in space, like a candle. The radius determines how far the light from the point light travels in the scene.

7. Click the Best button in the Render palette to create a render using the point light (see Figure 9.22).

Figure 9.22

The point type lights are positioned by dragging from the P button in the Placement subpalette to a location in the scene. Point lights render in Best mode and cast light in all directions.

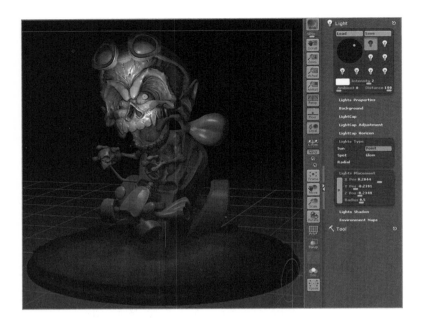

You can combine point lights with other light types as a way to accentuate parts of the model or create mood lighting in a ZBrush illustration. In the next section, you'll see how to use the spot light type. Keep the same project open for the next section.

RENDER WITH BPR AND BEST RENDER MODES

You can combine the features of Best and BPR rendering modes by first rendering using Best mode and then rendering a second time using BPR. Just make sure that you do not change the view of the model between renders. This allows you to incorporate features that only render in Best mode, such as point lights, into a BPR render.

Spot Light

The spot light type is positioned using both the preview sphere and the Placement subpalette. The preview sphere in the Light palette is used to position the light. The controls in the Placement subpalette are used to aim the light. Keep in mind that, like the point light type, the spot light type works only when rendering in Best mode.

1. In the Render palette, click the Preview button to switch to Preview mode.

2. In the Type subpalette of the Light palette, click the Spot button.

3. Drag from the P button in the Placement subpalette to the forehead of the demon to set the position where the spot light hits and illuminates the model, as shown in Figure 9.23.

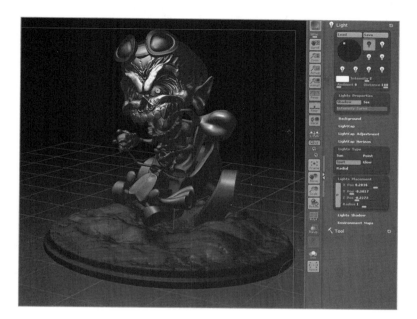

Figure 9.23

The spot light type is positioned by dragging from the P button in the Placement subpalette to a location in the scene. Spot lights render in Best mode and create a pool of light cast from a single direction.

4. Drag across the sphere icon in the Light palette to set the source of the spot light—the position where the light comes from. Drag it to the upper left of the preview sphere.

5. Change the Radius slider to change the cone size of the spot light. Set Radius to **1**.

6. Click the Best button in the Render palette to create a Best quality render.

The spot light is similar to the point light. The main difference is how the lights are positioned. In the next section, you'll see how to use the glow light type. Keep the same project open for the next section.

Glow Light

The glow light type adds ambient light that can tint parts of the model, adding an interesting look to the rendered image. Like point and spot type lights, glow type lights only render correctly using Best quality mode.

1. In the Render palette, click the Preview button to switch to Preview mode.

2. In the Type subpalette of the Light palette, click the Glow button.

3. Click on the color swatch next to the Intensity slider to open the color picker. Use the color picker to choose an orange color.

4. In the Placement subpalette, click the P button and drag from the button to the front of the demon character's head, as shown in Figure 9.24.

5. Set the Radius slider in the Placement subpalette to **0.5**.

6. Click the Best button in the Render palette to create a Best quality render.

Figure 9.24

The glow light type is positioned by dragging from the P button in the Placement subpalette to a location in the scene. Glow creates an ambient light that radiates from a point in space.

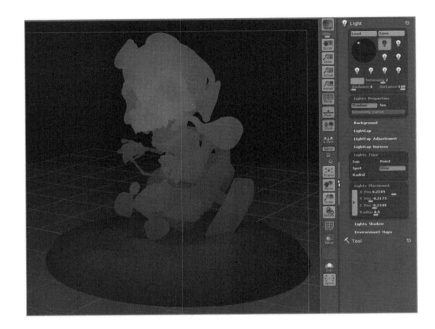

Spend some time experimenting with different light types. Mix sun, spot, point, and glow lights in different combinations and test the results using Best quality render mode. Later in this chapter you'll learn how to create an even wider variety of lighting effects using the advanced LightCap rendering system.

The Light Intensity Curve

The Light Intensity curve is an edit curve that works much like the curves you've used in other parts of ZBrush. This curve changes the intensity falloff of the light. By adjusting this curve you can design your own special light type. The following images show some effects you can easily achieve by playing with this curve (see Figure 9.25).

Figure 9.25

Use the Intensity curve in creative ways to create your own light types.

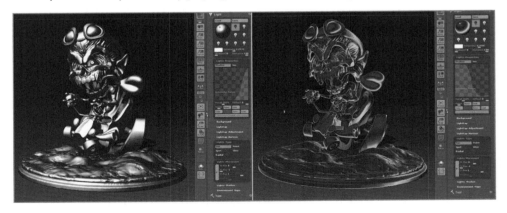

Shadows

You can render shadows using either BPR or Best quality rendering. To ensure that shadows render, turn the Shadows option on in the Render Properties subpalette of the Tool palette.

The settings for the type of shadows cast by a selected light in the Light palette are found in the Lights Shadow subpalette of the Light palette (see Figure 9.26, left image). To learn more about what each setting does, hold the Ctrl key and place the cursor over the setting.

The global controls for shadows when rendering with BPR are found in the BPR Shadow subpalette under Render Properties in the Render palette (see Figure 9.26, right image). To learn more about what each setting does, hold the Ctrl key and place the cursor over the setting.

If you want to cast shadows on the ground, activate the Floor button on the right shelf and then render using BPR. If the border of the grid clips the shadows, you can increase the size of the grid using the Grid S slider in the Draw palette.

Figure 9.26

The controls for an individual light's shadows are found in the Light palette (left). The controls for the global quality of BPR shadows are found in the Render palette (right image).

Shadows rendered using BPR are sharper by default than shadows rendered when using Best quality. However, you can create a sharp shadow using Best quality by adjusting the Aperture setting in the Shadows section of the Light palette.

Advanced Lighting with LightCap

LightCap is another ZBrush term invented by Pixologic to refer to their unique advanced lighting technology; LightCap is short for "light capture." LightCap works by creating a texture file that stores the lighting information that you create for the scene. This system is separate from the Standard lighting setup discussed in the previous section, but you can use the two together if you like.

The LightCap texture is mapped to a virtual sphere that surrounds the model. The color, position, and intensity of the lights are contained in this texture. The Details slider at the top of the Render Properties subpalette in the Render palette controls the resolution of the texture, so a higher setting creates more detailed lighting. You don't need to work with the texture file directly; instead you'll use the LightCap interface to add, edit, and remove lights from the scene. The interface and its controls are found within the LightCap subpalette.

The LightCap Interface

The LightCap interface is found in the Light palette. Expand the LightCap subpalette of the Light palette. This is where you add and position lights using LightCap. Follow these steps to create a basic LightCap lighting arrangement:

1. Load the DemonCar.ZPR project from the Chapter 9 folder on the DVD, or use your own model.

2. In the Light palette, click the orange light bulb icon to turn it off. Set the Ambient slider to **0**. Eliminate other lights in the scene so that you can focus on just the lights created in LightCap. This will help you better understand how the system works.

MATERIAL AMBIENCE

You'll notice some residual ambient light. The BasicMaterial2 material has an ambient light setting as well. To turn this off, expand the Modifiers subpalette of the Material palette and set the Ambient slider to **0,** as shown in the image at right.

Figure 9.27

A new light is added to the LightCap editor.

3. Click the New Light button below the preview window in the LightCap interface. A dim light appears on a sphere in the window, and a light appears on the model. The controls in the subpalette are also available now (see Figure 9.27).

4. Increase the Strength slider to raise the intensity of the light. It will become much brighter.

5. Drag on the sphere to position the light. You position lights by dragging on the sphere just like with standard lights.

6. Increase the Aperture of the light to change the size of the light on the sphere.

7. Adjust the Falloff to increase or decrease the fade at the edges of the light. Using a large Aperture with a Falloff of 0 creates a kind of graphic novel look.

8. To add another light, click the New Light button again.

9. Move this light to the bottom corner so that it is off the sphere. Increase the Aperture to create a fill light. Try setting the color to a deep hellish red, and press Shift+R to create a BPR render (see Figure 9.28).

Figure 9.28

Create a graphic novel look instantly by raising the Aperture of a light and setting its Falloff to 0.

You can add as many lights as you want using LightCap. You can select a light and adjust its settings by clicking the orange dots on the sphere. If it becomes difficult to select individual lights, use the Light Index slider to select a specific light. The Light Index is incremented by one each time you add a light. If you want to delete a light, just select it and click the Del Light button.

That's just a quick, fun example of how to add and adjust lights in LightCap. Of course, you can experiment to create many styles of lighting from stylistic to realistic. This will become more apparent as we delve deeper into the LightCap settings.

10. Select each light and click the Del Light button to return to the default black, unlit scene.

LightCap Settings

An interesting aspect of LightCap is that you can control the specular reflection of the light separately from the amount of diffuse lighting. To switch between Specular and Diffuse modes, click the buttons labeled Specular and Diffuse at the top of the interface.

The Opacity slider controls how much influence the light has in this particular mode. In other words, if you want to create a light that just appears as a reflected highlight on the surface, set the Opacity slider to **0** while in Diffuse mode; then click the Specular button to switch to Specular mode and increase the Exposure slider to make the light brighter. To get a feel for this, add a light and practice switching between Diffuse and Specular modes. Adjust the Opacity while in either mode and make a mental note of the effect.

SPECULAR REFLECTIONS

In computer graphics the term *specular highlight* or simply *specularity* refers to the reflection of a light source on a surface. It's that highlight that gives a surface its shiny or glossy quality. The term *diffuse* refers to the light that is reflected in all directions by a rough surface.

In Figure 9.29 two lights have been added to LightCap. The first light is only visible in Specular mode, since its Opacity has been set to 0 while in Diffuse mode. The second light is visible in both Diffuse and Specular modes. You can see the result on the model.

Figure 9.29

Two lights are added to LightCap. Opacity for Light 1 is set to 0 in Diffuse mode so it is only seen as a specular highlight on the model.

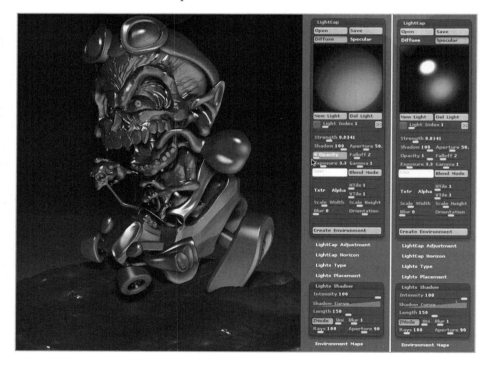

Strength, Opacity, and Exposure are different ways to control light intensity in LightCap. Strength is the overall presence of the light, Opacity controls the amount of specular or diffuse contribution the light makes in the scene, and Exposure has a multi-plying effect on the brightness of the light.

Gamma controls the contrast of the light, which can also affect how bright the light appears. To keep things simple you may want to stick to controlling light brightness using Strength and Opacity.

LightCap lights cast shadows just like standard lights. The Shadow slider controls the intensity of the shadow cast by the selected light.

The Create Environment button creates a background image that matches the LightCap light rig.

The Blend Modes menu lets you set a specific blending mode for the light. These modes are similar to the modes found in image-editing programs such as Adobe Photoshop.

LightCap Alphas

You can apply an alpha texture to a LightCap light to shape the look of the light on the surface. This is a great way to create a studio lighting effect, especially when rendering hard-surface objects such as cars and robots, as shown in Figure 9.30.

To add an alpha, select a light in LightCap and click the Alpha button. This opens the alpha library. Choose an alpha such as the white square. Alphas look best when they are applied only to the specularity of the light source, so try setting the Opacity in Diffuse mode to **0**. Use the HTile and VTile sliders to create a repeating pattern. The Orientation slider can be used to rotate the alpha, and the Scale Width and Scale Height sliders can be used to scale the alpha.

For an example of how this setup looks, load the thingy.ZPR project from the Chapter 9 folder on the DVD.

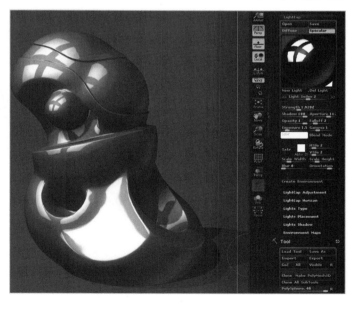

Figure 9.30

An alpha texture is applied to the Specular mode of a LightCap light to simulate a studio-style lighting effect.

Using a Background Image

One of the most interesting aspects of LightCap lighting is creating a lighting rig based on a panoramic image. This means that you can easily integrate one of your models into an image. The following exercise demonstrates how this can be done.

1. Load the thingy.ZPR project from the Chapter 9 folder on the DVD.

2. Expand LightBox and click the Textures link. Click the folder labeled Panoramas. This folder contains a number of panoramic images.

3. Double-click the last image in the row, the one labeled zBrush_2_Pulchri. This panorama is an image taken from inside an art gallery. It will take a few moments to load (see Figure 9.31). Once it is loaded you'll see it in the Textures palette.

4. In the Light palette, expand the Background subpalette. Click the Texture button and choose the image loaded in the previous step (see Figure 9.32). After a few moments you'll see the image appear in the background of the ZBrush canvas.

Figure 9.31

Load one of the images from the Panoramas folder in the Textures section of LightBox.

Figure 9.32

Select the texture by clicking the texture swatch in the Background subpalette of the Light palette.

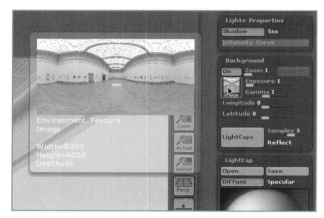

5. Scale the view of the thingy object so that you can see more of the background, and then turn on the Floor button on the right shelf.

6. Use the Longitude slider in the Background subpalette of the Tool palette to rotate the image. Set it to **224** so that the background is the corner of the room in the gallery.

7. Rotate and scale the view of the thingy object so that it matches the corner. Use the gridlines of the ZBrush floor to align the view with the background image. If the lines are hard to see, expand the Draw palette and click on the small color swatch to select a darker color for the gridlines. You can also use the Angle Of View slider in the Draw palette to make the perspective of the floor match the perspective of the room a little better (see Figure 9.33).

8. Once the grid is aligned with the background image, set the color in the Color palette to white, and choose the BasicMaterial2 material from the material library.

9. Expand the Light palette, and under Background click the Reflect button; this ensures that the image will be reflected on the object. Click the LightCaps button. ZBrush will take a few minutes to create a LightCap setup based on the image.

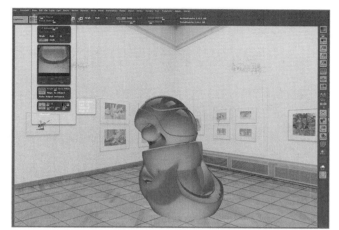

Figure 9.33

Use the gridlines to align the view with the corner of the room. You can make the lines darker using the settings in the Draw palette.

10. Once ZBrush is finished making the LightCap, press Shift+R to create a BPR render. The room is reflected on the surface, and the shadows cast on the floor appear to be integrated into the lighting.

You can further improve the realism of the render by turning on the Ambient Occlusion option in the Render Properties of the Render palette. This will cause the render to take much longer, though. If you use the Longitude and Latitude sliders in the Background subpalette of the Light palette, the lighting will rotate to match the background. Figure 9.34 shows the render with Ambient Occlusion activated. Figure 9.35 shows how the LightCap uses the lighting from the image in both the Diffuse and Specular modes. You can continue to add and edit lights after creating a LightCap from a panorama.

Figure 9.34

The image is rendered using BPR. The lighting and shadows help integrate the ZBrush model into the background image.

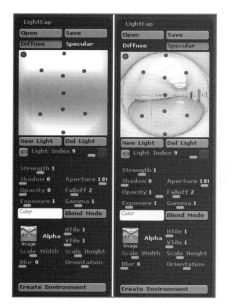

Figure 9.35

The LightCap is created by sampling the panorama in the background. You can see how the lights are placed in the Diffuse and Specular modes.

You can use panoramas in many creative ways. Many websites let you download panoramic images to be used as LightCaps. One of my favorite websites is the sIBL archive at `http://www.hdrlabs.com/sibl/archive.html`. You can use JPEG format panoramas or HDR panoramas, although JPEGs will render faster than HDR format images.

Saving LightCap Files

If you create a LightCap rig that you like and want to reuse for future modeling projects, use the Save button in the LightCap subpalette to save the rig in a special ZLD format. Use the Load button to load any LightCaps you may have saved. You'll also find examples of LightCap rigs in the `Project/LightCap Projects` folder in LightBox.

Material Basics

ZBrush materials determine the surface quality of your model. They are what make the model appear shiny, dull, waxy, or skinlike. There are many types of materials, but generally speaking the materials are divided into two major categories: Standard and MatCap. Standard materials are edited by adjusting sliders in the Modifiers subpalette of the Material palette. MatCap materials are based on a texture that includes light information that is baked into a texture and then applied to the surface.

Standard and MatCap materials can be mixed together to create some really interesting effects. This section will provide you with an overview of how to work with materials before diving into the details of how Standard and MatCap materials work.

Material Shaders

Materials are made up of shaders. A material can have from one to four shaders that are layered together. Each shader is just a list of properties that define how the surface reacts to light when rendered. The shaders occupy slots that are stacked together from left to right at the top of the Modifiers subpalette in the Material palette (see Figure 9.36). The slots are labeled S1, S2, S3, and S4. Each slot can contain different types of shaders or variations of the same shader in any combination. You switch from one shader to the next by clicking the slot buttons (S1, S2, S3, S4). Some materials have just a single slot available, while others have more. Shaders can be turned on and off by clicking the little circle in the slot button. If the slot button is highlighted, then the slot is selected, and all the modifier controls below affect that shader. If the circle is open, the shader is on; if it is closed, then it is off and will not affect the current material. As with lights, it is possible to modify a shader that has been turned off. If nothing happens when you adjust a shader's sliders, double-check to see if the shader has been turned off. If the shader slot button is grayed out, then the shader is unavailable for that material. Figure 9.36 shows the shader slot buttons for the TriShader material, which has three of the four shader slots available.

The ability to layer shader slots can lead to a near-infinite number of possibilities for creating material properties. The amount of influence one shader has on the material is determined by the settings in the Shader Mixer subpalette of the Material palette. But before we get into how shaders are mixed together, it's important to get a handle on working with individual shaders. You'll learn more about the Shader Mixer in the section titled "Paint Materials" later in this chapter.

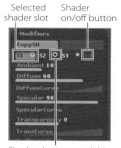

Selected shader slot   Shader on/off button

Shader slot is unavailable

Figure 9.36

The TriShader material has three of the four slots available. The highlighted button indicates the selected shader. The small circle turns the shader on or off.

Copying and Pasting Shaders

The process of creating and editing ZBrush materials is, like all things ZBrush, unique. You may have noticed that there is no button for creating a new shader. You can't add a shader to an existing material either. If you're used to working in a program such as Maya, this is a weird concept to wrap your head around. So how do you create a new shader? You actually copy and paste an existing shader from one material to another. As you've seen in previous chapters, ZBrush has a large number of presets. Some of these preset materials are set up to create a particular effect, such as metal, skin, or plastic. Other materials are simply generic presets available for you to edit. This example shows how you can create a new material preset by copying a shader from one material into another.

Figure 9.37

Select the ReflectedMap material from the material library.

1. Start a new session of ZBrush. Click on the border to the left of the canvas to expand the left tray. By default you'll find the Material palette is placed in this tray.

2. Click the Material icon in the upper left of the palette to access the material library. Find and select the ReflectedMap material (see Figure 9.37). When you select it, the modifiers for this material appear in the Modifier subpalette.

Figure 9.38

Switch to the S1 slot in the Modifiers subpalette of the Material palette.

3. The ReflectedMap material has two shader slots; click the S1 button to switch to the S1 slot. You'll notice that this shader has only a few controls (see Figure 9.38).

4. Click the CopySH button at the top of the Modifiers subpalette. This places a copy of the shader settings into ZBrush's clipboard.

5. Open the material library again and find the TriShaders material. Click its icon to switch to this material.

6. The TriShaders material has three shader slots. Click the S2 shader slot. Click the PasteSH button. You'll see the sliders and settings instantly replaced with the same sliders and settings you copied from the S1 slot of the ReflectedMap shader (see Figure 9.39).

The PasteSH button is available only when a shader has been copied to the clipboard. This is how you create a new material by copying and pasting shaders and settings from one material to another. It's an odd approach to building materials, but it's pretty simple once you get the hang of it.

You can also copy an entire material and paste it over another material. To do this, select a material from the library and click the CopyMat button in the Modifiers section of the Material palette. Then select another material and click the PasteMat button. The settings and shaders of the selected material will be replaced with the settings and shaders of the copied material. This is a good way to quickly create duplicate materials in case you want to make variations of one of your own custom presets.

Figure 9.39

Copy the settings from the S1 slot of the ReflectedMap shader and paste them into the S2 slot of the TriShaders material.

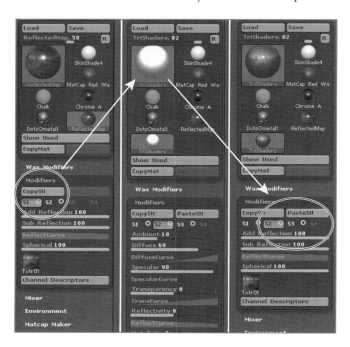

Saving Materials

So what do you do once you've created a new material that you like? Save it, of course! ZBrush uses its own ZMT file format to store material information. You can quickly build up your own library of materials for use on all your ZBrush models. Use the Save button at the top of the Material palette. This opens your computer's file browser. If you save the material file in the ZBrush 4R3/ZStartup/Materials folder, the file will appear in the material library the next time you start ZBrush. Alternatively, you can save the file in the ZBrush 4R3/ZMaterials folder; then the preset will appear in the Materials section of LightBox.

Downloading Materials

ZBrush artists love to create and share their own materials. Many artists use the forums at ZBrushCentral to share their materials and material-editing techniques. You can also find hundreds of free materials on the Pixologic home page; just point your browser to www.pixologic.com/zbrush/downloadcenter/library/ (see Figure 9.40). You can preview the materials on the Web; download the ones you like and load them into ZBrush.

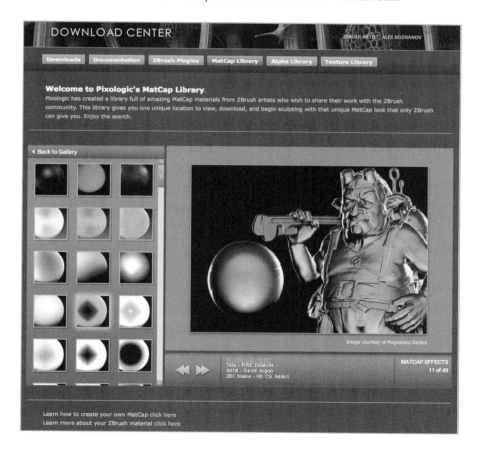

Figure 9.40

Hundreds of materials are available for free download at Pixologic's home page.

Designing Materials

By editing existing materials you can design your own presets. This section takes you through the process of designing some original materials.

Understanding MatCap Materials

MatCap stands for "Material Capture." This type of material captures lighting information and bakes it to a texture. It's very similar to the way LightCap works when designing lights. In fact, you can use the LightCap editor to create your own MatCap. This example shows you how to use LightCap to make a demonic cartoon-style shader for the demon character:

1. Use the Open button in the File menu to load the Demon.ZPR project from the DVD.

2. Place the Light palette and the Material palette into a tray.

3. Select the MatCap Red Wax material from the material library. When you choose a MatCap material, any changes you make in the LightCap editor automatically override the MatCap settings.

4. Expand the LightCap subpalette of the Tool palette and click the Add Light button. Immediately you'll see the preview of the MatCap Red Wax material instantly change to match the lighting in the LightCap editor.

5. We'll use the first light to create an overall greenish color for the demon. Click on the color swatch for the light, and pick a bright green color. Set the Aperture to **120** and the Strength to **1**.

6. Switch to Specular mode, and set Opacity to **0** so that the green color is only present in Diffuse mode.

7. Now let's create a hellish red glow that outlines the edges of the model. Switch back to Diffuse mode, and click the New Light button to add a second light to LightCap.

8. Drag the second light down to the bottom-right corner so that it is off the preview sphere. This creates a backlighting effect. Set the color to bright red.

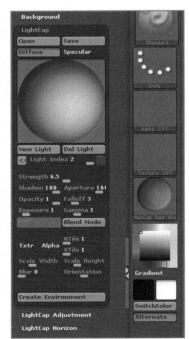

Figure 9.41

As lights are added to LightCap, the appearance of the MatCap Red Wax material is updated to match the lights.

9. Set the Strength of the second light to **6.5** and the Aperture to **160**. Set Falloff to **3** (see Figure 9.41). This creates a red rim light that adds a spooky outline to the character.

10. Finally, let's add a third light to create a bright yellow highlight. Click the New Light button again. Set the color of the new light to bright yellow and move it toward the upper right of the preview sphere.

11. While in Diffuse mode, set the Opacity of the third light to **0**. This means that the light appears as only a specular highlight.

12. Switch to Specular mode and set Aperture to **150** and Falloff to **2.5**. Set the Exposure to **2.2**. These settings were arrived at after some experimentation.

Now you have a rather stylistic LightCap arrangement that is just perfect for cartoons. If you look in the Material palette, you'll see that the MatCap Red Wax material has taken on an appearance very similar to the preview in the LightCap window except that the material shows both the Diffuse and Specular components at the same time (see Figure 9.42).

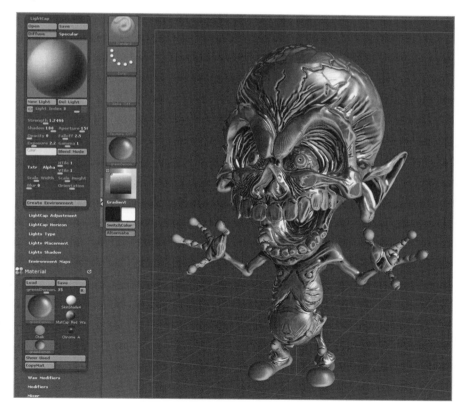

Figure 9.42

The MatCap material has been created via the LightCap interface.

13. To convert the LightCap to a material, just save the material. Click the Save button in the Material palette and save the file as **greenDemon.ZMT**. Save the file to the ZBrush 4 R3/ZMaterials folder so that it appears in the Materials section of LightBox.

14. Figure 9.43 shows the demon rendered using BPR.

Figure 9.43

The MatCap material has been created via the LightCap interface.

Editing a MatCap Material

You can continue to alter the properties of a MatCap material after you create it using the sliders in the Modifiers subpalette of the Material palette.

1. Continue with the project from the previous section. If you want to see an example of the material created in this chapter, use the Load button in the Material palette to open the greenDemon.ZMT file from the Chapter 9 folder on the DVD.

2. Expand the Modifiers subpalette of the Tool palette. There are a number of sliders here that allow you to alter the look of the material. But before you start moving them around, it's important to get a general idea of how the MatCap works.

3. Scroll to the bottom of the Modifiers subpalette of the Material palette, and hold your cursor over the small image. A pop-up window shows a larger preview. This texture is the basis of the MatCap material. All the lights you created earlier have been baked into this image.

Notice that the image has two circles. The circle on the left corresponds to the Diffuse channel of the LightCap, and the circle on the right corresponds to the Specular channel (see Figure 9.44). If you examine the properties of other MatCap materials, you'll see that some of them use two circles and some use just one.

If you take a look at the sliders in the Modifiers subpalette of the Material palette, you'll see that many of the properties are in pairs labeled A and B. For example, with Intensity A and Intensity B, the sliders labeled A control the influence of the left circle in the texture, and the sliders labeled B control the influence of the right circle. For those MatCap materials that have only a single circle, the B slider has no effect.

4. Spend a few moments experimenting with the sliders. You can change the colors of the materials using the Hue A and Hue B sliders.

You can also change the direction of the light by adjusting the Orientation A and Orientation B sliders. This can be very useful because, although the standard lights do not affect the appearance of surfaces that use the MatCap materials, the surface they are applied to does cast and receive shadows, and you'll want to make sure that the highlights and other lighting effects match the direction of the shadows. The Orientation sliders can help you do this (see Figure 9.45).

The colors you paint on the surface of the model are blended with the colors of the material. Currently, the color of the demon is white, but if you change the color in the color picker, the color of the surface is blended with the color of the material. You can control how much the material colors override the surface colors by increasing the OverwriteColor slider.

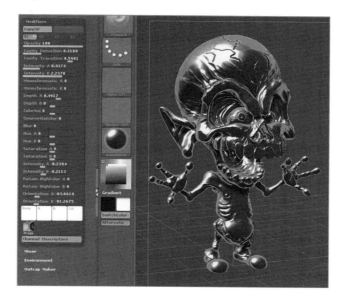

Figure 9.44

The MatCap material has been created via the LightCap interface.

Figure 9.45

Adjust the sliders in the Modifiers subpalette of the Material palette to create variations of the material.

CREATING A TOON MATERIAL WITH PHOTOSHOP

Using LightCap is not the only way to create a MatCap material. You can also create your own texture in Photoshop and use that as the basis for the MatCap material. For example, to create a scribbled toon-line effect, create a square image in Photoshop with a resolution of 512×512. Paint a scribbled circle like the one shown in the following image. Save the file in Photoshop format and import it into ZBrush using the Import button in the Texture palette. Then select a MatCap material, and open the Modifiers subpalette of the Material palette. Click on the preview image at the very bottom, and select the imported image to apply it to the material. Experiment with this technique to create some wild effects. The following image shows the demon rendered using a MatCap created this way. The original texture created in Photoshop is in the upper right of the image.

Painting Materials

So far you've been applying materials to the entire surface simply by selecting materials from the material library. You can also paint materials directly onto the polygons of a surface. In addition, you can use the Shader Mixer to determine how the shaders of the material are mixed together based on various surface properties. This section takes a look at some ways in which materials can be applied to your surface.

Polypainting Materials

The techniques for painting materials on a surface are very similar to the polypainting techniques you learned in Chapter 8. You can paint a material directly onto the polygons of a mesh using the sculpting brushes. There are a couple of tricks you can use to improve the look of the painted materials when rendering with BPR.

1. Open the DragonHeadSketch.ZPR project from the Chapter 9 folder of the DVD. This file contains the dragon head modeled in Chapter 3. I created a custom material using the LightCap interface and applied it to the surface. The material is called dragonSketch.ZMT, and it is also located in the Chapter 9 folder of the DVD.

CUSTOM MATERIALS ARE SAVED WITH PROJECTS—USUALLY

When you save a project, all the materials you edited are saved along with the models as part of the project. Well, most of the time anyway. Sometimes ZBrush will not load a material with your project, which is why it's always important to save your materials as separate ZMT files. If you load a project and you notice that some of the materials are missing, you can load the individual ZMT files, and this should correct the problem. If you don't save your materials, however, then you risk losing them forever if for some reason ZBrush forgets to save them with the project.

---

2. At the moment, if you switch from one material to another, the model will change materials as well. Before painting materials on the surface, you need to fill the surface with a base material. Select the dragonSketch material from the material library. On the top shelf, click the M button to switch to Material mode. In the Color palette, click the FillObject button (see Figure 9.46).

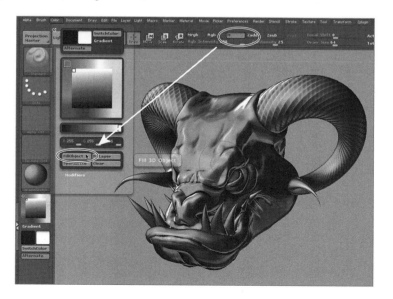

Figure 9.46

Click the M button on the top shelf to switch to Material mode; then use the FillObject button in the Color palette to fill the model with the current material.

You won't notice an immediate change, but if you switch materials in the material library, the surface should no longer update.

3. Select the MatCapMetal02 material from the library. You'll paint this on the eyes to make them nice and shiny.

4. Select the Standard brush from the brush library. Make sure that the Zadd and Zsub buttons on the top shelf are off. Make sure M is on.

5. Zoom in to the eyes and carefully paint the material on the eyeballs with the brush, as shown in Figure 9.47.

You'll notice that the material is applied to the entire polygon. Unlike polypainting, the materials are not blended across the surface, so the border edge where two materials meet looks very jagged. Don't worry though; that's an easy fix!

6. If you need to clean up stray brush strokes, you can switch back to the dragonSketch material, lower the Draw Size, and paint out any stray marks.

Figure 9.47

Use the Standard brush to paint the MatCapMetal02 material onto the eyeballs.

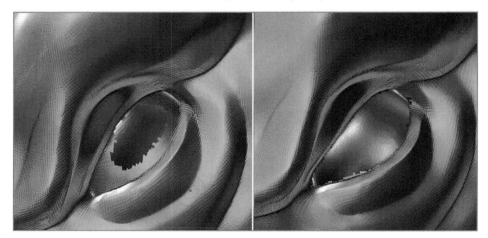

Figure 9.48

Set the Materials Blend-Radius in the Render palette to 3.

SAMPLE MATERIALS FROM THE SURFACE

You can sample a material from the surface by dragging from the materials library icon on the left shelf onto the part of the surface you want to sample. This is a quick way to switch materials without having to hunt through the materials library.

7. Once you have finished painting the eye, you'll probably still have a slightly rough edge. This can be fixed when you render the image with BPR. Open the Render palette and set the Materials Blend-Radius slider in the Render Properties subpalette to **3** (see Figure 9.48).

8. Zoom out from the eye so that you can see the whole model. Press Shift+R to render the image. This Materials Blend-Radius slider blurs the areas where two materials meet on the surface, which can remove the jagged edge (see Figure 9.49). The higher the value, the more blurred the edge will be.

This works well in most situations. There isn't a way to directly adjust the opacity of materials. However, there is a way to indirectly adjust the opacity of shaders, which can allow you to create much more subtle transitions between material properties. This is done using the Shader Mixer.

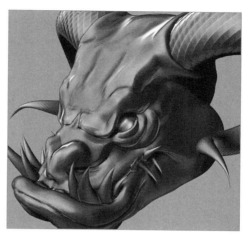

Figure 9.49

The border between the materials is blurred when rendered with BPR, resulting in a smooth transition.

The Shader Mixer

The Shader Mixer is a subpalette located below the Modifiers subpalette in the Material palette; see Figure 9.50. The sliders in the Mixer subpalette are active for any material that has more than one shader. The sliders determine how visible the shader is on the surface based on a variety of properties. For example, you can use the ByShadow slider to make a shader more prominent in the shadowed areas than in the lit areas. It is an amazingly powerful tool, especially when used in materials with three or more shaders. Each shader can have its own Mixer settings, leading to a wide variety of interesting material effects. In this section you'll get a sense of how to work with the Mixer on a simple example.

1. Open the femaleHeadHair.ZPR project from the Chapter 9 folder on the DVD.

2. In the SubTool subpalette of the Tool palette, select the Head subtool and turn off the visibility of the Hair subtool. We don't need the hair at the moment, and turning off this subtool will improve the performance of ZBrush while working.

3. Make sure the paintbrush icon next to the Head subtool is on so that Polypainting mode is active. You're going to paint colors onto the surface.

4. Open the material library and select the MatCapSkin06 material. In the Modifiers subpalette click the CopySH button to copy the settings in the shader slot.

Figure 9.50

The Shader Mixer controls are found in the Mixer subpalette of the Material palette.

5. Open the material library and select the DoubleShade material. Select the S1 slot and click the PasteSH button to paste the skin shader into the first slot of the DoubleShade material.

6. Click the little circle on the S1 button so it turns into a dot (see Figure 9.51). This turns the shader off. While working on Shader 2 (S2), it will be helpful to temporarily hide Shader 1 (S1).

7. Click the S2 button to select the second shader and use the following settings:

    Ambient: **0**

    Diffuse: **30**

    Specular: **100**

    Metallicity: **0**

    High Dynamic Range: **2.5**

The result is a dark, shiny, gray shader, as shown in Figure 9.52. Metallicity caused the highlight to be influenced by the hue of the underlying surface color. Setting this to **0** ensures that the specular highlights will be white, making them look very glossy. High Dynamic Range boosts the intensity of the colors.

8. Click on the dot on the S1 button to turn Shader 1 back on. The two shaders are combined, resulting in a shiny, overexposed material.

9. Make sure that the S2 button is highlighted. The Mixer settings will apply to the selected shader. You will set the Mixer options so that S2 appears only where you will paint dark, saturated colors. This way you can polypaint the lips so that they are shinier than the rest of the skin, as if the model is wearing lip gloss.

10. Expand the Mixer subpalette below the Material palette.

11. Click the Black button. This button composites the S2 shader as if the underlying shader was flat black. You'll see that the skin turns gray as if you had turned off S1.

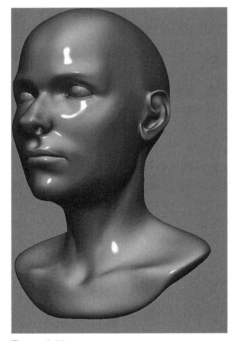

Figure 9.52

The S2 shader settings create a dark and shiny material.

12. Click the button labeled Replace(Normal) to the left of the Black button. This opens the Blend Mode menu. Choose the Screen blend mode. The pink returns. The shiny quality of S2 is still apparent, but now the material does not look as blown out. This is because with Screen mode activated, only the light colors of the S2 material appear composited on top on the S1 material (see Figure 9.53).

13. In the lower part of the Mixer subpalette, set the ByInt slider to **-100**. This is the ByIntensity setting. When this is set to a negative value, then the S2 material will only appear where the polypainted colors are dark. Since the model is currently painted white, the shininess of the S2 shader disappears.

14. Set the color picker to a dark red. Select the Standard brush. Make sure only the Rgb button is activated on the top shelf. Turn off Zadd, Zsub, M, and Mrgb. In this case you'll only paint colors on the surface, not materials.

15. Set the RGB Intensity slider to **1**. Paint the red color on the lips of the model using the Standard brush. Notice that the lips appear shiny (see Figure 9.54).

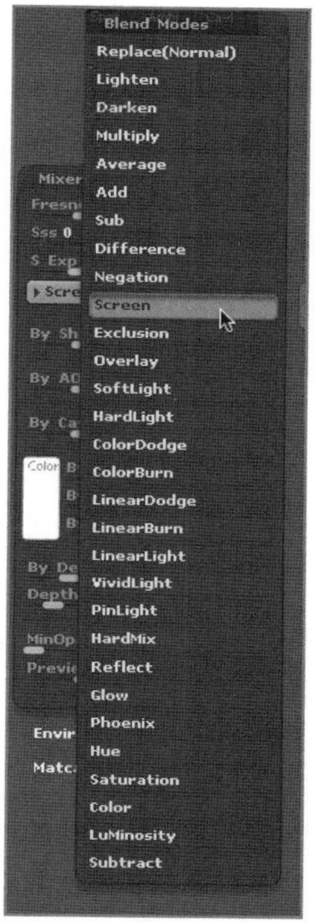

16. Experiment with some of the other settings. The Exp sliders are modifiers for the strength of the slider. Try an Int Exp of **0.01**. Then turn BySat to **100** and Sat Exp to **0.01**. I find this helps boost the presence of the S2 shader, but the BySat settings use saturation as a mask so that now only dark, saturated colors have the S2 shader applied.

Using this technique, the Rgb Opacity slider controls not only the opacity of the colors but also the opacity of the S2 shader. Try painting a light blue color fading to a dark blue color in the area above the eyes. The dark blue color should appear a little shinier than the

Figure 9.53

Choose the Screen blending mode from the Blend Modes menu in the Mixer subpalette.

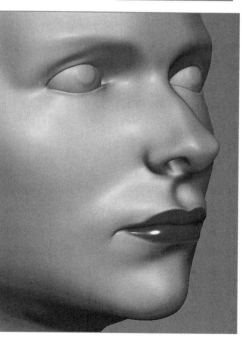

Figure 9.54

The Mixer settings tell ZBrush to make the shiny S2 shader appear only on the parts of the surface that have dark, saturated colors. This makes the lips appear glossy when they are painted dark red.

lighter blue colors. If you rotate the head and the light in the Light palette, this is easier to see (see Figure 9.55).

Figure 9.55

The intensity and opacity of the painted colors determine the intensity and opacity of Shader 2 so you can use color to blend areas, making them increasingly shiny as the color gets darker.

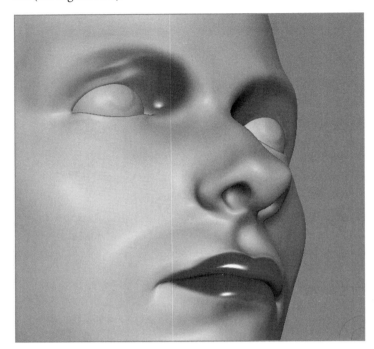

You can also use the Mixer to make a material appear only in shadowed areas, or just in cavities, or in areas where ambient light is occluded (AO). To see some of these effects you'll need to render using BPR. The options can be mixed and matched and varied in strength, allowing for infinite possibilities.

For additional practice you can experiment with one of the projects that comes with ZBrush. The TwoTone_Beetle.ZPR project found in the Projects section of LightBox is a simple PolySphere that has been set up so that as you paint light colors on the surface of the sphere, the materials appear dull, and as you paint dark colors on the surface it appears shiny.

BPR Rendering Techniques

This section demonstrates some of the more advanced features of the BPR rendering system. These techniques can be combined creatively in your ZBrush projects.

Subpixel Anti-Aliasing Quality

As discussed in Chapter 1, anti-aliasing refers to a trick used by graphics software packages to improve the quality of the edges of a digital image. All images created on a computer are made up of tiny colored squares known as pixels. Without anti-aliasing, these tiny squares are clearly visible along the edges of an object on a computer screen, which gives the image a jagged appearance. The process of anti-aliasing blends the colors of the edges together, creating a softer appearance for the edges.

When rendering with BPR you can control the amount of anti-aliasing using the SPix slider on the top of the right shelf (see Figure 9.56). To increase the quality of the anti-aliasing in the rendered image, increase the value of the SPix slider. Note that higher values will increase the time it takes to create the render.

Figure 9.56

The SPix slider on the right shelf controls the anti-aliasing quality when rendering with BPR.

Ambient Occlusion

Ambient occlusion is a popular way to simulate the look of diffuse lighting in computer graphics by using soft shadows in the cracks and crevices of 3D objects. The settings on the Bpr Ao subpalette of the Render palette allow you to balance the quality of the ambient occlusion shadows with the time it takes to render them.

To create ambient occlusion shadows, ZBrush creates an array of virtual lights in a sphere around the model. Each light casts a shadow, and the shadows are blended together. You don't actually see the lights in the scene, just their shadows. Models rendered with ambient occlusion tend to look solid and realistic. The settings in the Bpr Ao subpalette of the Render palette adjust the quality of the ambient occlusion shadows. To learn how each slider works, hold the Ctrl key and place the cursor over the name of the slider. These settings are similar to settings used to adjust the BPR shadow quality.

The following short exercise demonstrates a useful workflow for adding ambient occlusion to BPR renders:

1. Use the Open button in the File menu to load the demonCar.ZPR project from the Chapter 9 folder on the DVD.

2. In the materials fly-out library on the left shelf, choose the Chalk material. This material makes it easy to see how ambient occlusion looks when rendered; of course, in practice you can use any material you like.

3. Place the Render palette in a tray to access the controls.

4. In the Render palette, turn off the Shadows button. Turn on AOcclusion (Figure 9.57). This way you'll see only the ambient occlusion shadows.

5. Expand the Bpr Ao subpalette of the Render palette.

6. Press Shift+R to create a BPR render (see Figure 9.58).

Figure 9.57

In the Render palette turn off Shadows and turn on AOcclusion.

Figure 9.58

The model is rendered using ambient occlusion and the Chalk material.

You'll see the model with just the ambient occlusion shadowing. Try experimenting with the settings to see how you can change the look of the ambient occlusion shadowing. You can turn on the Spd button in the Bpr Ao subpalette of the Render palette to speed up render times while testing. Turning Spd off excludes ambient occlusion from the subpixel anti-aliasing calculations, resulting in a faster render. In addition, after the first time you render with ambient occlusion activated, ZBrush stores the calculations in temporary memory. If you do not change the view of the model, ZBrush will use this information so that it does not need to recalculate the ambient occlusion shadowing. This makes testing renders much faster. But if you change the view of the model, then the calculations will need to be recreated on the next render.

Subtool Transparency

When rendering with BPR, the Transparency controls in the material transparency don't work. Instead, you use the controls in the Tool palette to determine which subtools will render as transparent, and then the settings in the Render palette determine how the transparency works. This exercise walks you through the process for rendering transparent surfaces in ZBrush.

1. Open the spaceHelmet.ZPR project from the Chapter 9 folder on the DVD. This file contains a simple helmet model and a woman's head inside the helmet. At the moment you can't see her head because the chrome shield is opaque.

2. Before rendering transparency in ZBrush you need to activate the option in the Render palette. Expand the Render Properties subpalette of the Tool palette and turn on the Transparent option (see Figure 9.59, left image).

3. In the SubTool subpalette select the Shield subtool.

4. Scroll down to the bottom of the Tool palette and expand the Display Properties subpalette. Turn on the BPR Transparent Shading option (see Figure 9.59, right image).

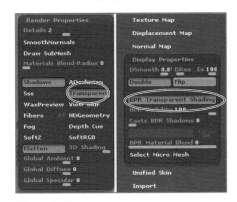

Figure 9.59

Turn on Transparent in the Render palette and then activate BPR Transparent Shading for the Shield subtool in the Tool palette.

5. Press Shift+R to render using BPR. When it finishes you'll be able to see the woman's head through the shield (see Figure 9.60).

Figure 9.60

The character's face is now visible through the transparent shield.

The reflections are not physically accurate; rather, they are baked into the material itself. If you want to reflect a specific image, you can use MatCap or LightCap lighting as demonstrated earlier in the chapter.

To control the transparency, use the BPR Visibility slider and lower the value to make the subtool render as less transparent. You can also use the settings in the BPR Transparency subpalette of the Render palette to set global properties for transparency (see Figure 9.61).

Figure 9.61

The quality of the transparency is defined using the controls in the BPR Transparency subpalette of the Render palette.

The Strength slider sets the overall strength of the Transparency.

The NFactor slider determines how the normal direction of the surface affects transparency. Low values mean the edges that face away from the viewing angle are less transparent than the areas of the surface that face the camera. A high value means that more of the surface is opaque.

The ByColor setting causes the transparency to be affected by the color intensity of the surface.

The CFactor setting determines how the color influences the transparency of the subtool. Think of it as a way to set a threshold value. When CFactor is at a low value, colors darker than white will make the surface appear transparent. When CFactor is at a high value, only the darkest colors will appear transparent.

The Refract slider creates the look of refraction, which is the distortion you see when looking at an object through thick glass. ZBrush refraction is not physically based, so it is limited in how realistic it can make refractions appear.

Wax Preview

Wax Preview creates a somewhat translucent effect in the surfaces you render with BPR. You can also preview the wax effect while you are sculpting your models in the Preview render mode. Each ZBrush material can have its own wax setting. Here's how you can use this feature.

1. Open the dragonHeadSketch.ZPR project or use your own model.

2. Open the material library and select a shiny shader such as SketchGummyShiney.

3. In the Render palette expand the Render Properties and turn on the WaxPreview button.

4. In the Material palette expand the Wax Modifiers subpalette. Set the Strength to **100**. The model takes on a warm glow that makes it look waxy and translucent (see Figure 9.62).

5. Create a BPR render. You'll see the effect appear in the render as well (see Figure 9.63).

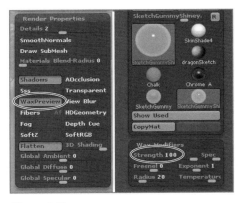

Figure 9.62

Activate WaxPreview in the Render palette and set the Wax Modifier Strength to 100 in the Material palette.

The sliders in the Wax Modifiers section affect how the wax effect appears in a BPR render; they do not affect the preview of the wax that you see while in Preview render mode. To learn more about how each slider affects the quality of the BPR render, hold the Ctrl key and place your cursor over the slider.

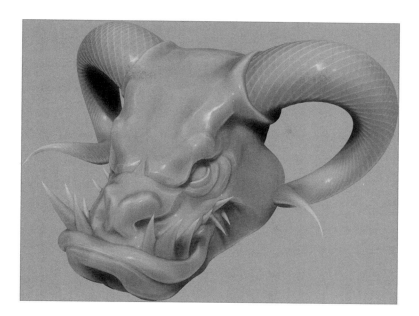

Figure 9.63

WaxPreview gives the model a slightly translucent effect.

Subsurface Scattering

The Subsurface Scattering option in ZBrush simulates the luminescent quality of the skin. As photons of light penetrate the layers of skin they bounce around, pick up the color of the deeper layers of tissue, and then exit the skin, giving it a kind of glow. This helps make the model look as though it is made up of living flesh. In many 3D packages this effect is simulated by more or less replicating the physical properties of light. In ZBrush the effect is created using a gradient of colors; this is a cheat rather than a physical simulation of light, but it's an effective one!

Working with subsurface scattering (SSS) in ZBrush is a little tricky since there are a few ways to create this effect and the interface is not terribly intuitive.

In this example you'll learn how to set up subsurface scattering on the female head model. This will add a hint of reddish color that is stronger on the thinner parts of the model, such as the ear.

1. Open the `femaleHeadHair2.ZPR` project from the `Chapter 9` folder of the DVD, or use one of your own models.

2. In the SubTool subpalette, select the Head subtool and turn off the visibility of the Hair subtool; this will make test renders much faster.

3. In the Render palette, enable the Sss button. If this button is not active, then the effect will not appear when you click the BPR button (see the left image in Figure 9.64).

4. From the Material palette select the FresnelOverlay material. This material contains two shaders—a basic shader and the Fresnel shader, which creates a gradient of colors used for subsurface effect.

5. In the Material modifiers make sure the S1 button at the top of the palette is selected. This is the first shader's slot. Click the little circle so that it turns into a dot. This is a switch that turns the basic shader off. You want to turn it off so you can focus on just the settings in the S2 slot.

6. Click the S2 button to switch to the FresnelOverlay shader. Make sure the circle is not a dot so that the shader is actually on (see Figure 9.64, right image). The model will turn black.

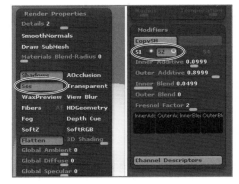

Figure 9.64

Activate Sss in the Render palette. Turn off the S1 shader and turn on the S2 shader for the FresnelOverlay material.

The color swatches at the bottom control the colors used in the gradient; the sliders at the top control the amount of influence of each color. The shader is essentially a way to mix the colors. The Fresnel Factor slider controls the strength of the gradient based on the viewing angle of the surface. You'll want to test render using BPR as you change these settings to get a sense of how they work.

7. Click on the Inner Additive color swatch and choose a deep red color. Set the Inner Additive slider to **0.5** and the Fresnel Factor to **1**. You'll see the surface appear red on the parts of the surface that face the front.

8. Click Outer Additive and set the color to orange; set Outer Additive to **0.25**. The edges that face away from the front pick up the orange color.

9. Click on the Inner Blend color swatch and set the color to a dark magenta; then set Inner Blend to **0.3**. You'll see that the Inner Blend color is overlaid on the Inner Additive color. As you increase the Inner Blend slider, the influence of the magenta slider becomes stronger.

10. Set the Outer Blend to a lighter magenta, and set the Outer Blend strength to **0.35**. This adds color to the Outer Additive modifier (see Figure 9.65).

The colors I'm suggesting and their values are fairly subjective and will change depending on the model. You'll most likely want to tweak them as you work. These warm colors are meant to give the impression of tissue beneath the skin. At the moment the gradient is applied to the entire surface. The Fresnel Factor slider is going to shift the gradient colors toward the edges when it's set to a positive value and toward the center when it's at a negative value. And you'll tweak many of these settings once you start putting the material together, but at least now you have a place to start.

Of course, this is just a gradient; it's not subsurface scattering just yet. To finish the basic effect you need to adjust some settings in the Mixer.

11. Expand the Mixer subpalette below the modifiers. Set the Sss slider to **100**. The surface will become very dark.

12. Set the S Exp slider to **0.8**. This controls how much of the Sss effect comes through. Lower values mean that more of the effect is visible, indicating a thinner surface.

13. Set the Blend mode to Add and turn on Black. The Black button means that the Sss shader will be composited on top of a black color, which means the other shader (the settings in the S1 slot) will not affect the quality. In general this speeds up the rendering of the effect (see Figure 9.65).

14. At the moment the effect may seem dark and subtle. Turn on the S1 shader by clicking the dot on the S1 button. Try a test render using BPR (Shift+R). You'll see the Sss effect created by the S2 shader mixed with the shiny quality of the S1 shader, giving it a slightly translucent effect (see Figure 9.65).

Many ZBrush artists will copy the FresnelOverlay shader into the S2 slot of the TriShader material and then use the S1 shader settings to control the diffuse properties and the S3 shader settings to create the specular properties of the material.

There are additional settings that control the quality of the subsurface scattering effect in the Bpr Sss subpalette of the Render palette. Most times you can leave these settings at their default values. The most important of these settings is SSS Across Subtools, which is off by default. If you are rendering subsurface scattering on multiple subtools at the same time, turn this option on (see Figure 9.66). Otherwise the subsurface scattering is calculated for each subtool individually, which does not look realistic.

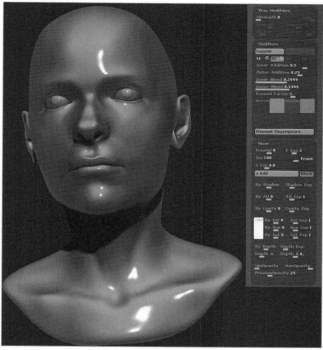

Figure 9.65

The settings for the FresnelOverlay shader are shown on the right. The left image shows the model rendered using BPU with both the S1 and S2 shaders turned on.

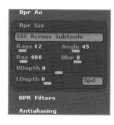

Figure 9.66

Turn on SSS Across Subtools when using subsurface scattering on multiple subtools.

Rendering Hair

Rendering hair created with FiberMesh is very easy; there are only a few settings you need to worry about to get a good result. These settings are found in the Tool palette at the bottom of the FiberMesh subpalette. There are also two Hair material presets that can help your hair look shiny and more realistic. Rendering hair can take a while, so it's a good idea to start with fairly low-quality settings in the FiberMesh subpalette and then gradually raise the settings and test while you go. This will save you some time because often you'll find that low-quality settings will still produce a very believable effect.

This example walks you through the basics of rendering hair created with FiberMesh.

1. Open the femaleHeadHair2.ZPR project from the Chapter 9 folder on the DVD.

2. First you'll apply the Hair material to the subtool that was generated from FiberMesh. Expand the SubTool subpalette of the Tool palette and select the Hair subtool.

3. Turn on the M button on the top shelf. You will fill the hair with the Hair material, so the M button needs to be on to activate Material mode (see Figure 9.67).

Figure 9.67

Activate the M button on the top shelf to switch to Material mode.

4. Open the material library and select the Hair material (see Figure 9.68, left image). The material will be temporarily applied to the head and eye as well, but you'll fix that in a moment. Expand the Color palette and click the FillObject button (see Figure 9.68, right image). This applies the Hair material to the FiberMesh.

5. Select the SkinShade04 material from the material library. The head and eyes will turn back to white, but since the FiberMesh hair has been filled with the Hair material, it will not change.

Figure 9.68

Select the Hair material from the material library (left). Click the FillObject button in the Color palette (right).

6. Expand the FiberMesh subpalette of the Tool palette. Since you are not sculpting the hair, turn off the Fast Preview button.

7. Set the Subdivisions slider to **1**. This controls how the polygons of the FiberMesh surface are subdivided. Increasing this slider will increase render time, and the hair may not need to be subdivided to look good. You can come back to this slider and increase it later on if the hair does not look smooth enough.

8. Set the Sides slider to **2**. This setting determines the number of sides each fiber has. Like the Subdivisions slider, it will increase render time, so start low and then raise only when needed.

9. Set the Radius slider to **0.3**. This slider controls the thickness of each fiber when rendered with BPR. Higher settings work well for grass or straw; lower settings work better for hair (see Figure 9.69).

10. Press Shift+R to create a BPR render (see Figure 9.70).

You can continue to adjust the settings to get the look you want to achieve. The Root and Tip Anisotropy sliders control the rotation of the specular highlights along the length of the hair. If you want to make the hair look more or less shiny, you can experiment with these settings as well as the specular strength of the Hair material. Figure 9.71 shows the hair with a Radius of 0.1 and Subdivision level of 3. Specularity has been increased in the Hair Material modifiers.

Figure 9.69

Adjust the settings at the bottom of the FiberMesh subpalette of the Tool palette.

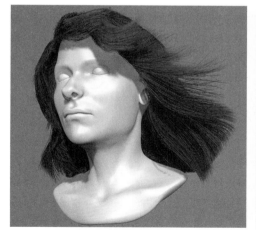

Figure 9.70

The hair is rendered at lower-quality settings using BPR.

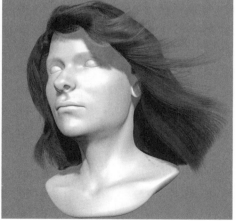

Figure 9.71

The hair is rendered at higher-quality settings using BPR.

FIBERMESH RENDERING TUTORIALS

There's a lot more you can do when rendering hair, including creating leaves for trees, swarms of butterflies, and other creative effects. For more information check out the free video tutorials posted to the ZClassroom at www.pixologic.com.

BPR Render Filters

BPR render filters are a great way to enhance your render after it has completed. The filters allow you to make adjustments and create effects without having to re-create the render or go to an external image-processing program such as Photoshop. BPR stores much of the information concerning depth, shadows, and ambient occlusion in memory after you create a render, so as long as you don't change the view or sculpt the model, you can apply the filters, make adjustments, and view the changes in real time. The following example demonstrates how to add depth-of-field blurring and other color adjustments to a render.

1. Open LightBox to the Projects section, scroll to the right, and select the Kotelnikoff_ Earthquake.ZPR project. Double-click the icon to load the project (see Figure 9.72). This project is also included in the Chapter 9 folder on the DVD.

Figure 9.72

Load the Kotelnikoff_ Earthquake.ZPR project from the Project section in ZBrush.

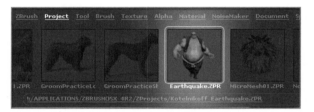

2. Rotate the view of the model so that the character's open right hand is in front of his body and his clenched left hand is behind him. This maximizes the depth in the composition, which will help you to see how the filters can be applied based on depth.

3. Open the Render palette; in the BPR Render Properties click the Ambient Occlusion button to activate Ambient Occlusion.

4. Press Shift+R to create a BPR render. This will take a while to calculate, so it's a good time for a break!

5. Once the render is complete, make sure you do not change the view or ZBrush will need to re-render the composition. Expand the BPR Filters subpalette of the Render palette (see Figure 9.73).

Figure 9.73

The BPR Filters subpalette of the Render palette

Each filter is stored in a channel slot. The buttons labeled F1 to F12 hold the settings for each filter, so you can apply up to 12 filters. Each filter is layered on top of the previous filter as you add it. The default F1 filter adds noise to the render. You can change this to get a different effect. Let's try adding some depth-of-field blurring to the render so that the parts of the character that are farther from the front appear blurry. I think it makes it easier to see how this works if you exaggerate the strength of the blurring, adjust the filter to set the depth, and then fine-tune the settings. Follow these steps to see what I mean.

Figure 9.74

Set the BPR render filter to Blur.

6. Click the F1 button so that the button turns orange. This indicates that the filter is selected. To turn the filter on, click the little dot icon in the upper right of the button so that it turns into a circle.

7. The noise effect is applied to the render, making it brighter and noisy.

8. Click the Filter button and set the Filter Type to Blur. Set the Strength slider to **1**. This adds an overall blurring effect to the render (see Figure 9.74).

9. Set the Blend mode to Replace and the Radius to **12**. This helps to make the filter's effect more obvious.

10. Find the Depth slider about halfway down the BPR Filters subpalette. Set the slider to **1**. This increases the strength of the filter based on the depth of the objects in the render.

11. Next you'll want to set the range of the depth so that you can determine which parts of the image receive less of the filter and which parts receive more. Click the Depth A slider and drag this onto the canvas to the character's belly button.

12. Click the Depth B slider and drag it to the character's clenched fist, as shown in Figure 9.75. The filter's strength is now set so that at the depth set by the Depth A slider the effect is at 0 percent and the depth set by the Depth B slider is at 100 percent. Between these values the strength of the filter increases. You can also use the Depth A and Depth B sliders to numerically enter these settings.

13. The Depth Exp slider adjusts the transition from 0 to 25. Very small values will make the effect more dramatic. Try 0.01 or even a negative value such as -0.02.

14. The Radius slider sets the size of the blurring in pixels. Set this slider to **5** so that the blurring is less dramatic. You should now have a nice depth-of-field effect that increases the sense of depth in the composition. And you don't have to re-render the image to see it! The amount of blurring is exaggerated in this image so that you get an idea of how it works. In your own compositions you'll probably want to lower the strength and the radius to create a more realistic effect.

Figure 9.75

Drag from the Depth A slider to the belly button, and drag from the Depth B slider to the character's fist. This will set the range of depth for the filter.

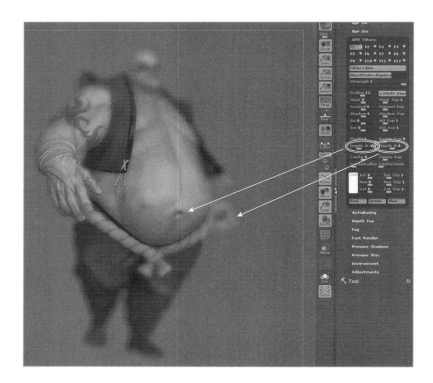

Figure 9.76

Edit the Blur settings once the depth has been established to create a more realistic depth-of-field–style blur.

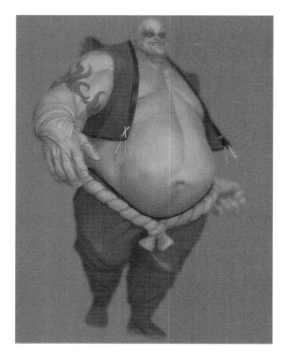

You can continue to add filters by clicking the F buttons in the palette. Layering filters opens up a wide number of possibilities for enhancing the look of your ZBrush compositions. Depth is only one of the ways in which filters can be applied. You can also use shadows, ambient occlusion, and subsurface scattering.

15. Turn on F2 and set the filter type to Intensity. Try the following settings to enhance the ambient occlusion shadowing in the render:

> Filter: Intensity
>
> Blend Mode: Multiply
>
> Strength: **1**
>
> Ao: **1**
>
> AO Exponent: **6**

Figure 9.77 shows the result.

The best way to understand how the filters work is to experiment with the settings. If you want to apply a filter based on ambient occlusion or subsurface scattering, you have to remember to first activate Ambient Occlusion and Subsurface Scattering in the Render Properties palette. The filter settings are saved with your project, and if you change the view and create another render, the filters will be applied automatically once the render finishes.

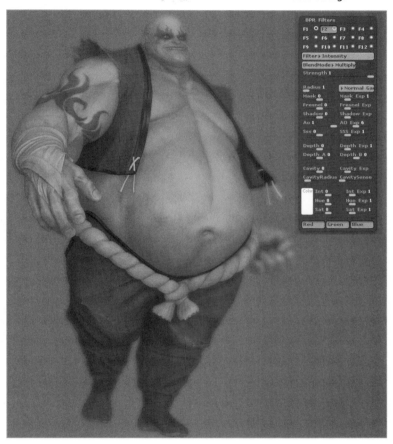

ZBrush and Photoshop

ZBrush and Photoshop make a perfect combination for creating amazing images. Many professional concept artists working within the video game and film industries use the two together to quickly produce many variations of character and creature designs within a short amount of time. Regardless of whether your goal is to be a professional designer or to make some cool images, you'll want to spend some time learning how the two programs can be used together. This section takes you through the process of setting up an image for a specific resolution, rendering in ZBrush, and then exporting passes to Photoshop for further processing. This is not meant to be a comprehensive Photoshop lesson.

If after reading this section you are hungry for more techniques, I recommend reading Scott Spencer's book *ZBrush Creature Design: Creating Dynamic Concept Imagery for Film and Games* (Sybex, 2012). In the book Scott includes detailed tutorials covering how he paints his ZBrush creature designs into compelling compositions using many of the techniques he uses at the Weta workshop in New Zealand.

Document Size and Background

If you want to set the document to a specific resolution, you can use the controls in the Document palette.

1. Load the DemonCar.ZPR project from the Chapter 9 folder on the DVD, or use one of your own projects.

2. Let's say you want to create a document to render at 800×1000. Open the Document palette and place it in a tray. Turn off the Pro button; this disables the Proportional resizing of the document so that you can enter specific values for width and height.

3. Set the Width slider to **800** and the Height slider to **1000** (see Figure 9.78). Click the Resize button. ZBrush will display a warning that lets you know that the tool will be dropped to the canvas. Click the Yes button to dismiss the warning.

Figure 9.78

Turn off the Pro button and adjust the Width and Height sliders in the Document palette.

4. The document will be scaled to the new size. The demon car will be dropped to the canvas and will appear distorted. Press Ctrl+N to clear the canvas, and drag down on the canvas to redraw the tool.

5. Press the T hotkey to turn on Edit mode. Rotate and scale the model on the canvas to find a good view.

6. To remove the gradient in the background, set the Range slider to **0**.

7. To change the background color, click the Back button and drag the cursor down to the color picker to choose the background color, as shown in Figure 9.79.

8. Save the project.

Figure 9.79

Drag from the Back color swatch to the color picker to set the background color for the document.

Render Passes

Whenever you render using BPR, ZBrush separates the render data into passes that can be exported and brought into Photoshop for compositing. The passes ZBrush creates depend on the render options you have activated in the Render palette.

1. Continue with the same project from the last section. Select the SketchGummy material from the material library. This will give the render a nice cartoony look.

2. In the Render Properties palette, turn on the AOcclusion option and the Sss option.

3. Set the SPix slider at the top of the right shelf to **4**. This increases the quality of the anti-aliasing, ensuring a nice smooth edge to the model. Press Shift+R to create a render using BPR.

4. When the render completes, you can export the image by clicking the Export button in the Render palette. Save the file using the Photoshop (PSD) format. The image will look like exactly what you see on the ZBrush canvas when you open it in Photoshop.

5. In the Render palette, expand the BPR RenderPass subpalette window. You'll see a number of small icons representing the render passes. Hold the cursor over the icons, and you'll see a preview of each pass (see Figure 9.80).

6. To export a pass, click one of the icons; this will open your computer's browser. Save the file to a directory on your local drive using the Photoshop format. The file is named after the type of render pass.

7. Click each icon to save the render pass.

8. Open Photoshop and load each of the passes.

9. Copy each of the passes into a single Photoshop document.

Here's a description of each pass with suggestions on how they can be used in Photoshop:

Shaded This pass is essentially what you see on the ZBrush canvas with colors, shadows, and material shading. This can be used as the basis for the Photoshop composite.

Depth This pass is a grayscale image representing the depth. This can be composited over the image using the Overlay blend mode and a low opacity to increase the sense of depth in the image. The

Figure 9.80

Hold your cursor over the icons in the BPR RenderPass subpalette of the Render palette to see a preview of the pass.

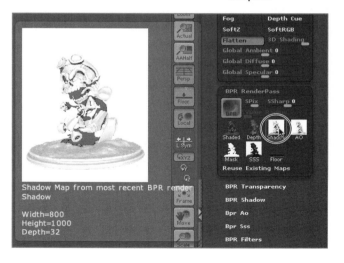

depth pass can also be used as the source for the Lens Blur filter to create depth-of-field blurring. To do this, copy the pass into a new alpha channel and apply Lens Blur to the image. In the Lens Blur options, set the source to the alpha channel with the pasted depth channel.

Shadow This pass is an image with just the shadows isolated. Composite this image over the render using Multiply mode to add shadows into the composition.

AO This pass has just the ambient occlusion shadows. This can be composited over the image using Multiply mode to accentuate the ambient occlusion shadowing.

Mask This is the alpha channel, which can be used to select the outline of the image so that it can be separated from the background.

SSS This is a grayscale image that contains the subsurface scattering information. Composite this over your image using Screen mode to add some translucency to the image. Lower the opacity and use the Hue/Saturation/Value adjustment in Colorize mode to add a little color.

Floor This image contains the floor. If you want to eliminate the visible edges of the floor, you can increase the Grid Size slider in the ZBrush Draw palette and render again.

Creating a Specular Pass

You may notice that the ZBrush does not offer an option for creating a specular pass, but it's very easy to do this using materials. This technique can be used to create any number of special passes based on material properties:

1. Continue with the project from the previous section.

2. In the SubTool subpalette turn off the paint brush icon for each of the subtools. This disables polypainting as well as material painting so that you can easily change colors and materials for all of the subtools at once.

3. Select the BasicMaterial2 material from the material library.

4. Open the Material palette and set the Ambient and Diffuse sliders to **0**. Set Specular to **100**.

5. In the Light palette, set the Ambient Lighting to **0**. In the Document palette set the Background color to black.

6. Press Ctrl+R to create a BPR render. The result will be a dark, shiny version of the render (see Figure 9.81).

7. Use the Export button in the Document palette to export the render using the Photoshop format.

8. Open the file in Photoshop, and copy and paste it into your document. Place the layer at the top of the composition.

9. Set the blend mode to Screen, and adjust the opacity to create the type of specular highlights you want on your model.

You can experiment with other materials to create additional types of passes. Try using LightCap to create a background panorama and export a render of the model for use as a background pass.

Figure 9.82 shows a composite created from render passes. The Photoshop file `Photoshop_composite_BPRPasses.psd` is included in the `Chapter 9` folder of the DVD. If you have Photoshop, you can open the file and take a look at how the passes are composited together.

Figure 9.81

Create a specular pass by rendering a version of the image with a dark, shiny material.

Figure 9.82

The exported passes are composited in Photoshop.

Summary

In this chapter you learned how to create hairstyles for your characters using FiberMesh. You learned how to generate a subtool from a FiberMesh preview and how to sculpt FiberMesh using the special hair brushes. You also learned how to set up basic lights in the Light palette and how to create advanced lighting rigs using LightCap. This chapter covered the basics of creating custom materials and how to render using BPR. Finally, you learned how to render passes from ZBrush and composite them in Photoshop.

CHAPTER 10

Surface Noise, Layers, and the ZBrush Timeline

The final chapter of this book introduces some advanced tools and techniques. At this point you should feel comfortable with the basics, and you probably appreciate the wide variety of options ZBrush offers you for bringing your creations to life. But of course, there's always more. The tools you'll encounter in this chapter build on everything you've learned to this point. They help you to add that final touch to your models that elevates your ideas to the level of artwork. These tools also increase flexibility in your sculpting workflow, which is especially important if your goal is to integrate ZBrush into an existing modeling and texturing pipeline.

This chapter includes the following topics:

- **Surface noise**
- **Using 3D layers**
- **Polypaint layers**
- **Using the Timeline**
- **Contact points**
- **Recording and playing movies**

Surface Noise

Surface noise is a special effect that ZBrush applies over the unmasked parts of a mesh. This is projected on top of sculpted geometry, which gives the look of super-fine detail even on a low-resolution mesh. You also have the option of "baking" the noise into the mesh so that it is incorporated into the details you sculpt on the surface.

There are many uses for surface noise, and applying it to the mesh is very easy. The noise is generated procedurally, meaning that it is the product of complex algorithms. ZBrush does the mathematical stuff and gives you an intuitive interface that lets you customize the overall look. The options for designing your noise have been expanded with the addition of the NoiseMaker plug-in, which is accessed through the Surface Noise interface.

The following exercises take you through the basics of creating surface noise and also demonstrate a few creative uses for this tool.

Making Some Noise

Let's take a quick tour of the Surface Noise interface using a simple PolySphere as an example mesh:

1. Start a new session of ZBrush. Load the DefaultSphere.ZPR project from the Projects section of LightBox.

2. Set the color to white in the color picker and choose the BasicMaterial2 material from the material library. This makes it very easy to see the effect of the noise on the sphere.

3. In the Tool palette, expand the Surface subpalette (Figure 10.1).

4. Click the Noise button, and a window appears. This is the Surface Noise interface, where you will establish the look of the noise.

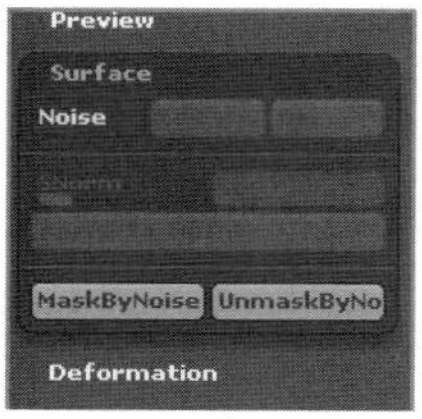

Figure 10.1

The Surface subpalette in the Tool palette

Take a look at Figure 10.2. The left side of the interface is dominated by a preview window that shows what the noise looks like on the mesh as you adjust the settings. You'll see the window update in real time while you adjust the controls.

You can rotate the view of the preview by dragging in the window. If you want to zoom in or out, drag left or right on the word *Zoom* in the upper right. If you want to move the view, drag on the word *Move* in the lower right. To frame the view, click on the word *Frame* in the upper left.

The Save button saves your settings as a .znm format file, and the Open button loads settings saved from other sessions. This is useful for creating your own library of noise settings for use on multiple projects.

The Copy button copies the settings to memory. This comes in handy when copying noise settings from one subtool or tool to another.

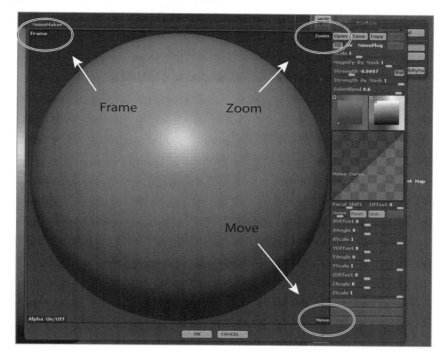

Figure 10.2

The Surface Noise interface

On the right side are a number of sliders and controls as well as the ubiquitous ZBrush edit curve. This is where the action is. Most of the work in editing noise involves playing around with these sliders until you come up with something you like.

The Scale slider adjusts the overall scale of the noise, and the Strength slider adjusts the amplitude of the noise. When Strength is set to a negative value, the noise is inverted so it pushes outward instead of inward (or vice versa depending on the how the noise is designed).

The Magnify By Mask slider adjusts the scale of the noise separately for those areas of the surface that have a mask applied.

The Strength By Mask slider adjusts the strength of the noise in the masked areas of the surface separately from the unmasked parts of the surface.

The ColorBlend slider gives the option of adding a tint to the noise. The two color pickers below the slider set the color of the tint. When the slider is pushed to the right, the color picker on the right is applied to the noise; when the slider is pushed to the left, the picker on the left sets the tint.

The edit curve customizes the intensity of the noise across the surface in a nonlinear fashion. When I use surface noise I find myself getting lost just playing with the edit curve graph for hours. The best way to understand the graph is just to play with it for a while. Try the following to create the look of a rocky asteroid.

5. Set the Scale slider to around **100** and the Strength slider to around **0.01.**

6. Click on the curve to add a point on the left side of the graph, and then move the point up and down; notice the change on the surface. In Figure 10.3, you can see how many different designs are possible just by playing with the graph.

Figure 10.3

Using the edit curve in the Surface Noise interface, you can quickly come up with a wide variety of looks for your noise effect.

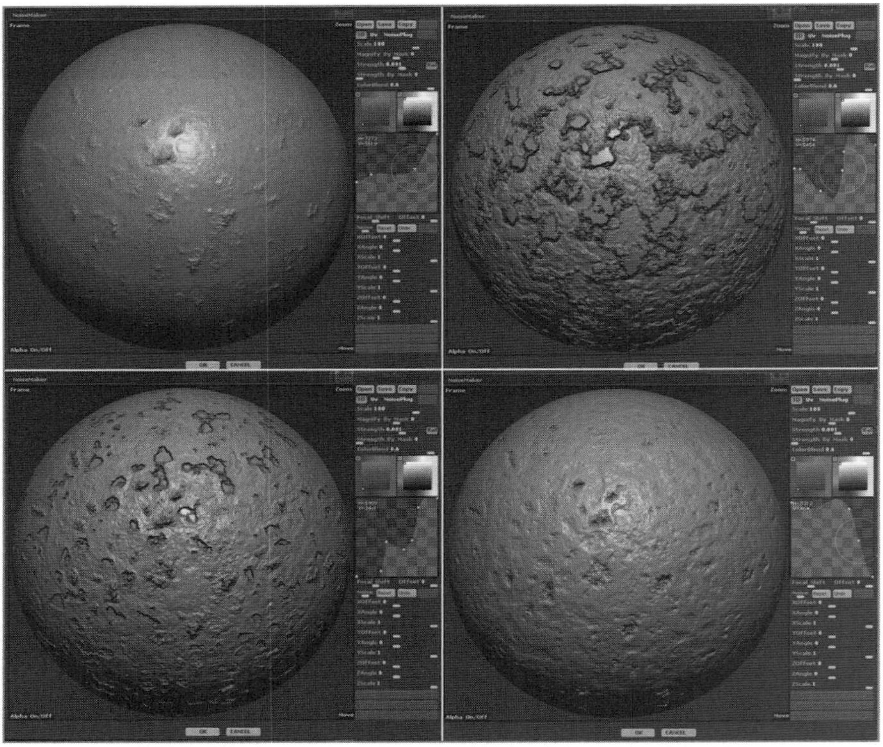

The offset, angle, and scale sliders below the preview window can be used to further refine the look of the noise. The sliders control the offset, angle, and scale along the indicated axis.

7. Once you have something you like, click the OK button at the bottom of the interface. The noise is then projected on top of the mesh.

It's important to understand that at this point the noise is just projected on the mesh but is not actually deforming the polygons of the mesh. It's like a bump map that creates the illusion that there is more detail sculpted into the mesh than is actually there. This is made obvious when you set the SDiv slider to a low setting. You can see the projected detail on top of the polygons of the surface.

SCULPT A NOISY SURFACE

When surface noise is projected onto a surface it does not slow ZBrush at all; you can still sculpt without affecting your work. Some traditional sculptors may find that a little surface noise applied to a mesh recaptures the organic look of traditional clay while sculpting in the digital world of ZBrush. Try it and see how you like it!

---

8. You may decide to change the look of the noise after leaving the Surface Noise editor. If so, click the Edit button in the Surface subpalette of the Tool palette.

You can use the Noise button in the Surface palette to toggle the visibility of the noise on or off; the Del button deletes the noise settings altogether.

Applying the Noise to Your Mesh

So what if you want to make the noise part of the mesh? This can be a useful trick for adding detail quickly. You can even use masking ahead of time to determine where the noise should be applied. This exercise shows how to apply noise to the unmasked parts of a surface to add a stony appearance to a model of a gargoyle.

1. Start a fresh session of ZBrush and load the gargoyle_start.ZPR project from the Chapter 10 folder on the DVD. This project contains a simple Notre Dame–style gargoyle model sculpted using Dynamesh.

2. In the Tool palette set the SDiv slider to **2**. At this level the model has around 2.5 million points. Since the noise will be baked into the mesh, it's a good idea to have as many points as you think will be needed to support the detail of the noise.

You can apply noise to the entire mesh, but to make the model more realistic it's a good idea to mask parts of the surface so that the noise is applied more or less unevenly across the surface. You need to mask the surface before applying the noise. I like to apply a mask based on the surface smoothness. This masks the hard edges, protecting them from the noise and making it look as though the hard edges of the stone are smoother than the rest of the surface. This effect will make the gargoyle appear more weathered and worn.

3. Expand the Masking subpalette of the Tool palette. Set the Range slider next to the Mask By Smooth button to **250** (see Figure 10.4). Set Falloff to **300**. These high Range and Falloff settings increase the spread and smoothness of the mask. Click the Mask By Smooth button. After a few moments you'll see the mask appear on the edges of the surface (see Figure 10.5).

Figure 10.4

Increase the Range slider next to the Mask By Smooth button to broaden the spread of the mask.

Figure 10.5

The mask is applied to the edges of the model.

4. Expand the Surface subpalette and click the Noise button to open the Surface Noise subpalette. Set Strength to **0.001**. Increase the Scale to around **30** to get a nice stony look. Set ColorBlend to **0** so only the deformation of the noise is visible and not the color effect.

5. Experiment with adjusting the graph. Zoom in on the preview window a little while adjusting the settings so you can see what is going on (see Figure 10.6).

Figure 10.6

Adjust the settings to create a subtle stony look.

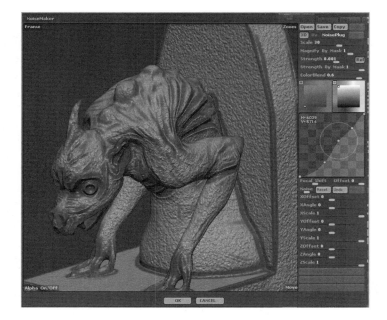

6. Try not to make the noise too strong; otherwise, when you apply it to the mesh the surface will balloon out in a weird way. Also, make sure the scale is not too small. If the noise is too fine, then the surface will look fuzzy. What you want is something more like stone.

7. When you have something you like, click the OK button. You'll see the noise on the surface on the canvas. At this point it's just being projected, and it has not been baked into the mesh.

8. Before applying the noise to the mesh, set the SNormal slider in the Surface sub-palette to **100**. This ensures that the surface normals are smooth when the noise is applied; it generally makes the noise look better. You can experiment with lower values if you want the noise to be crisper.

9. Now click the Apply To Mesh button. After a few moments you'll see that the noise has been baked into the mesh. If the surface is sufficiently high resolution and the noise strength is not too high, you should end up with a nice-looking noise, kind of like stone.

10. Ctrl+drag on the canvas to clear the mask. Notice that the areas that were masked are still smooth. Figure 10.7 shows the noise before and after it has been applied to the mesh.

Getting the perfect settings can take some work; however, there is a trick that will make applying surface noise much easier. You'll learn about this later in this chapter in the section titled "Using 3D Layers."

11. Save the project as `gargoyleNoise.ZPR`. We'll return to this model in the next few sections as we experiment with noise a little more.

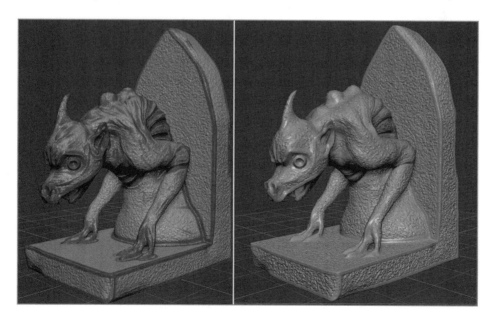

Figure 10.7

The noise is applied to the unmasked areas of the surface. Using masking with noise helps to create variation in the surface, which results in a more interesting effect.

Using an Image to Make Noise

You can use an image to determine the look of the noise on the surface. This opens up even more creative applications of noise. To get a really stony look for the gargoyle, let's see what happens when a rocky texture is used to control the design of the noise and how it appears when it's is layered on top of the noise created in the previous section.

Once again, start by applying a mask. It's not necessary to do this when using noise, but it makes for a more interesting look.

1. Continue with the same gargoyle model from the previous section.

2. In the Masking subpalette, set the Range slider next to the Mask By Smooth button to **30 and Falloff to 100**. Click Mask By Smooth to create the mask.

3. Then pick a nice rocky texture for the noise image. You can grab one from the Internet or use one of the many textures in LightBox. Open LightBox to the Textures section and scroll through the images. I like IMG_4959.jpg. Make a note of where this image is located on your hard drive. When the image is selected, you can see the path in the bottom of LightBox (see Figure 10.8).

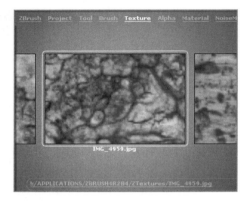

Figure 10.8

A large number of rocky textures can be found in LightBox and can be used for the Surface Noise effect.

4. Expand the Surface subpalette of the Tool palette and click the Noise button. This reapplies the last noise settings stored in memory, but of course we want to create new settings. Click the Edit button to open the Surface Noise interface.

5. To use an image for noise generation, click the Alpha On/Off button in the lower left (see Figure 10.9.)

6. When you click on this image, a browser window pops up. Use this to locate the image based on the file path shown in LightBox. The image I want to use is found in the ZBrush R3/ZTextures folder and is named IMG_4959.jpg (see Figure 10.10). You can use any image you like, of course, but this one seemed to create a nice effect.

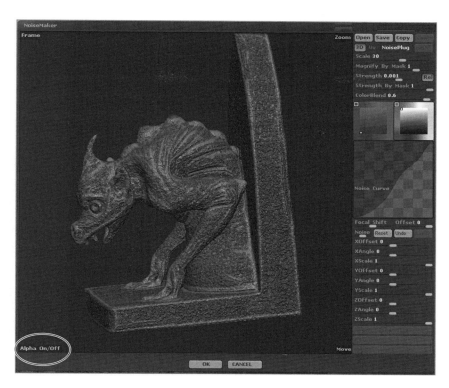

Figure 10.9

Click the Alpha On/Off button in the Surface Noise editor.

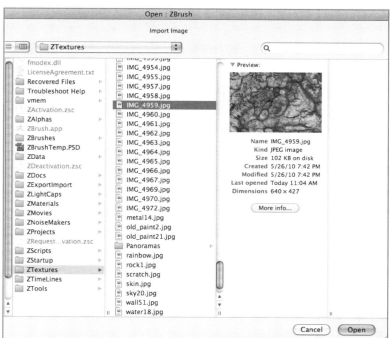

Figure 10.10

Load IMG_4959.jpg from the ZTextures folder.

7. The image is loaded, but it may be hard to see the effect, so adjust the settings a little. I achieved the best results by lowering the Scale to **1.625** and the Strength to **-0.0124**. Then I fine-tuned Strength by experimenting with the curve editor, as shown in Figure 10.11. Remember that you can create a sharp angle in the graph by dragging one of the points on the curve off the editor and then back on.

Figure 10.11

The settings are adjusted after the image has been selected.

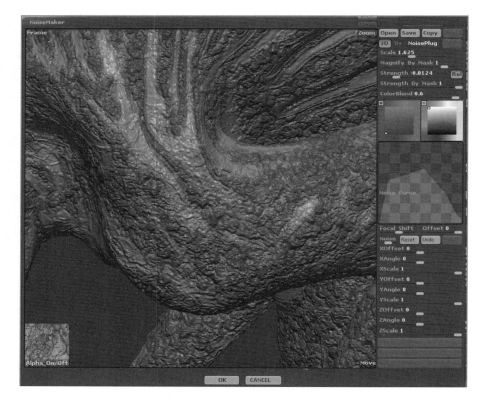

8. Once you have something you like, click the OK button to close the interface. Then increase the SNormal slider in the Surface subpalette to **100** and click Apply To Mesh.

9. Ctrl+drag on the canvas to clear the mask, and examine the results.

The gargoyle definitely looks much stonier.

Figure 10.12 shows the gargoyle with the stony texture applied. I spent a few minutes using the Smooth and hPolish brushes to sculpt the detail into something a little less extreme.

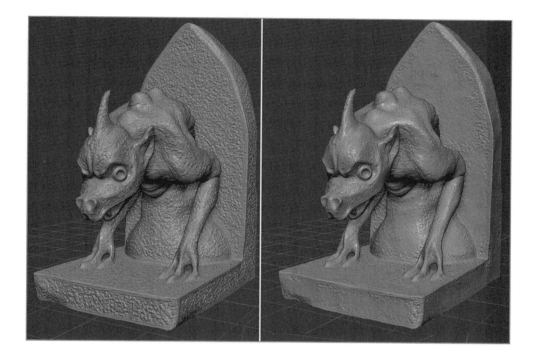

Figure 10.12
The texture-generated noise is applied to the mesh (left image). The hPolish and Smooth brushes are used to refine the look (right image).

Morph Targets

Morph targets are a familiar feature in many 3D animation programs. In Autodesk® Maya®, they are known as blend shapes. Many animators use morph targets to store the position of each vertex of a model in 3D space. By interpolating between the stored states, artists can create and animate facial expressions.

ZBrush allows you to store a single morph target for your 3D tool. If the tool is made up of multiple subtools, you have the option of storing a morph target for each subtool if you want.

Morph targets in ZBrush are easy to create and use. Their simplicity makes them ideal for testing facial expressions and other types of simple animation. They are also a good way to save the initial state of the model, which means you have a way to restore the model even after you run out of undos.

In Chapter 4 you had a brief introduction to morph targets when you learned how they can help when creating polygroups. But the usefulness of morph targets goes well beyond polygrouping. In this section you'll learn some additional practical applications for morph targets.

Storing a Morph Target

When you store a morph target, the position of each vertex in a model is stored in memory. This becomes part of the model. Until you delete a morph target, ZBrush keeps the state in memory. The morph target information is saved with the tool, so if you save the file, close ZBrush, and then open it again at a later time, the morph target information will still be intact. This means that morph targets can be used like a safety net. You can always return to the original state of the model at any point during the development of the model.

The controls for storing and using a morph target are found in the Morph Target subpalette of the Tool palette. Morph targets are stored for the current active subtool. Keep in mind that each tool can have only one morph target at a time. If you want to create a more complex arrangement that uses multiple variations of a model, then you need to use 3D layers, which are discussed later in the chapter.

This exercise demonstrates how to save a morph target:

1. Start ZBrush.

2. Use the Open button in the File menu to load the brainGuy.ZPR project from the Chapter 10 folder on the DVD.

The model is the head of a simple humanoid character created in ZBrush. The head should be on the canvas and Edit mode should be activated.

3. In the Tool palette, expand the Morph Target subpalette.

4. Make sure the Head subtool is the current active subtool. You can Alt+click on the head to select it (see Figure 10.13). On the canvas, the active subtool appears in a lighter color than the inactive subtools.

5. Click the StoreMT button (Figure 10.14, left image). This stores the current state of the model as a morph target.

When you click the StoreMT button, you'll see that the other buttons in the Morph Target subpalette become available, and the StoreMT button is grayed out (right image in Figure 10.14). This is how you know that the model has a morph target saved in memory.

When you store a morph target, you can still work on other subdivision levels. If you switch to another subdivision level after storing a target, all the buttons except the DelMT button become unavailable until you return to the subdivision level where the morph target was stored.

6. Continue with this same file for the next section.

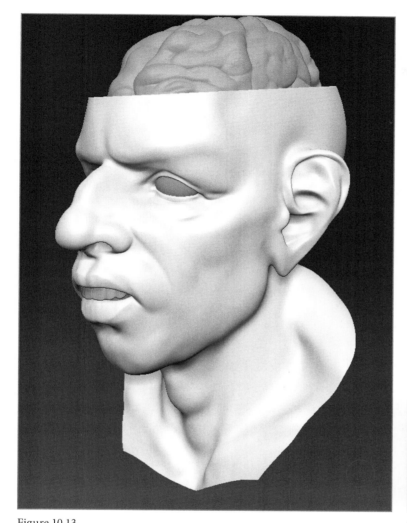

Figure 10.13

The Head subtool appears lighter than the other subtools, indicating that it is the active subtool.

Figure 10.14

Click the StoreMT button in the Morph Target subpalette of the Tool palette to store a morph target.

Switching Targets

Once a morph target has been saved, any changes you make after you store it will not be included in the stored information. You can switch between the changes you make and the stored morph target using the Switch button in the Morph Target subpalette of the Tool palette.

Here is how this works: in the previous section you stored a morph target for the Head subtool at the current subdivision level. The fact that the StoreMT button in the

Morph Target subpalette is grayed out is an indication that the model has a subtool stored already.

1. Open the sculpting brush library and select the Move brush.

2. Increase the Draw Size to **70**. Make some large-scale changes to the face. Use the brush to pull the eyebrows down.

3. In the Morph Target subpalette of the Tool palette, click the Switch button. The head returns to its original state.

4. Click the Switch button again. The brows go down again.

5. Drag the Morph slider to the right. The brows go up (center image in Figure 10.15). Drag the Morph slider to the left, and the brows go down even farther than their original state (right image in Figure 10.15).

Figure 10.15

The Morph slider lets you control the intensity of the morph.

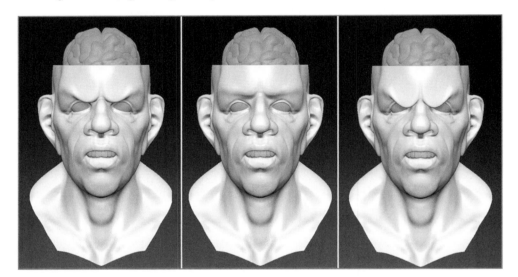

When using morph targets, try to keep in mind which state you are working on. The morph target saves two states: the stored state created when you clicked the StoreMT button and the altered state created by any changes made after you clicked the StoreMT button. If you switch back to the stored state and make changes, those changes will become part of the stored morph target.

The CreateDiff button creates a new mesh based on the difference between the stored state and the altered state. This mesh is stored in the Tool inventory with the prefix MorphDiff attached to the name.

The Project Morph button relaxes the mesh based on the stored morph target. This can help alleviate pinching and stretching problems while maintaining the detail of the surface.

6. Continue with this same file for the next section.

Deleting a Morph Target

You can delete a morph target at any time to make the changes permanent or to free up room for another morph target.

To delete a morph target, just click the DelMT button in the Morph Target subpalette of the Tool palette. This makes the current state of the model permanent, so if you have made changes to the model after storing a morph target, those changes are now permanent. If you switch back to the stored state and then delete the morph target, any changes you have made will be deleted.

1. Click the Switch button so that the model returns to its original state, before any changes to the brows were made.

2. Click the DelMT button.

The other buttons in the Morph Target subpalette of the Tool palette become grayed out, indicating that the model no longer has a stored morph target.

3. Continue with this same file for the next section.

Using the Morph Brush

The Morph brush is a special sculpting brush that can be used to restore specific parts of a model to the state that has been saved as a morph target. There are many creative possibilities for using the Morph brush. In addition, the brush can be used as the ultimate "Undo" brush. If you don't like the changes you've made on a part of the model, you can use the Morph brush to carefully paint out the changes you have made.

This exercise demonstrates how to use the Morph brush:

1. Make sure the head is the currently selected subtool.

2. In the Morph Target subpalette of the Tool palette, click the StoreMT button.

3. Use the Move tool to push the eyebrows upward. It's okay to be a little sloppy; the upper eyelids will probably be moved upward as well.

4. Open the sculpting brush library and select the Morph brush.

5. Lower the Draw Size to **20**. Set Z Intensity to **10**. The lower Draw Size and Z Intensity will make it easier to precisely paint the morph into specific areas.

6. Scale up the view of the model. Drag the brush over the stretched part of the eyelids (see Figure 10.16).

The upper eyelids move downward to their original state. Using the brush, you can fix problem areas that appear when you are sculpting facial expressions. It's a good idea to store a morph target when you begin editing your model so that you always have an easy way to fix problems such as stretched areas.

Figure 10.16

The Morph brush is used to fix the stretched areas of the upper eyelids after the brows have been moved upward.

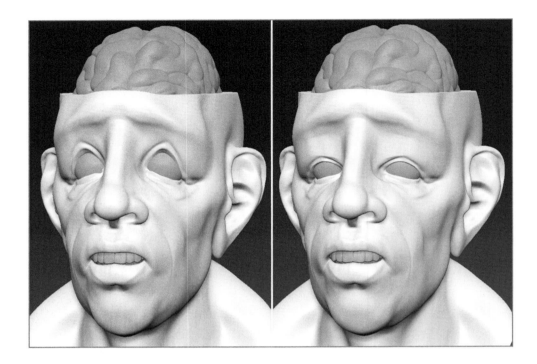

Using 3D Layers

Like morph targets, 3D layers store the position of the vertices in 3D space. But you can have as many layers as you like for each subtool, and the layers can contain different types of information. You can create different layers for different types of details. For example, you can store the wrinkles of a character's face on one layer, the pores on the skin on another layer, scars and bumps on a third, a facial expression on a fourth, and even the color of the skin on a fifth. The possibilities truly are endless.

In the following sections, you'll learn the basics of working with 3D layers.

The Layers Subpalette

The Layers subpalette of the Tool palette is where you'll find all the controls for working with layers (see Figure 10.17).

Figure 10.17

Use the Layers sub-palette of the Tool palette to create and manipulate 3D layers.

3D LAYERS VERSUS DOCUMENT LAYERS

Try not to confuse 3D layers with document layers. Document layers are very different and relate directly to illustrating in ZBrush and not to digital sculpting at all. Document layers are created using the Layer palette. For this chapter we will not be working with document layers, so avoid going into the Layer palette. Instead, stick to the controls found in the Layers subpalette of the Tool palette.

A layer can only be created when the model is set to the highest subdivision level; otherwise you'll see a warning. In this exercise, you'll learn how to create a 3D layer:

1. Start a new session of ZBrush.

2. Use the Open button in the File palette to load the BrainGuy.ZPR project from the Chapter 10 folder on the DVD.

3. Make sure the head is the currently selected subtool.

4. In the Layers subpalette, click the large box button to create a new layer (see Figure 10.18).

The top slot in the Layers subpalette is now highlighted. It is labeled Untitled Layer 1, and notice that the record button, labeled REC, is enabled.

5. Click the Name button in the Layers subpalette and enter the name Pores. This will create a custom name for the layer, which is now labeled Pores1 (see Figure 10.19).

It's always a good idea to name your layers because the Layers subpalette can quickly fill up with a lot of layers. If you don't name them, it will be difficult to tell what information is stored on a layer.

6. Use the Save button in the File palette to save the project as BrainGuyv01.ZPR.

7. Continue with this file in the next section.

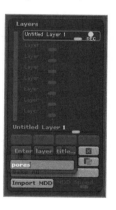

Figure 10.18
Click the large box button in the Layers subpalette of the Tool palette to create a new layer.

Figure 10.19
Use the Name button in the Layer subpalette to name the layer Pores.

Layer Record Mode

When you create a new layer, it is automatically set to Record mode. This is indicated by the REC label on the right side of the layer slot in the Layers subpalette of the Tool palette. Any changes you make to the model while the layer is in Record mode are stored in that layer. You can record in only a single layer at a time. If you create a new layer while an existing layer is in Record mode, the original layer will stop recording and the newly added layer will be in Record mode. Any changes you make to the model will be recorded in the new layer.

To turn off Record mode, click the REC button on the right side of the layer slot. The REC label will turn off and you'll see the eyeball icon instead. The eyeball icon controls the visibility of the layer.

You can turn off Record mode for all the layers and work on the model, but it's a good idea to use layers consistently. This will help you keep track of what changes are stored in which layers.

Layer Strength

You can record changes to a layer and then adjust the strength of the layer at any point afterward. This is an exceptionally useful feature for a wide variety of applications. One way I use this all the time is to modify the strength of surface noise after it has been baked into a surface. As you no doubt noticed from the previous section on surface noise, sometimes when you apply the noise to the surface the result is not what you would expect: the model balloons out or the noise is too intense or too subtle. Using layers in conjunction with surface noise, you can achieve a greater amount of control over the effect.

1. Continue using the BrainGuy_v01.ZPR project you saved in the previous section.

2. Currently there is one layer, named Pores. It should be in Record mode, indicated by the letters REC in the Layers subpalette of the Tool palette.

To create pores, you'll start by adding surface noise to the model. This creates a noise pattern all over the selected subtool.

3. Expand the Surface subpalette of the Tool palette, and turn on the Noise button.

4. Set Noise Scale to **0.5**. Set Strength to **0.025**.

5. Expand the Noise Curve and edit the shape of the curve so it resembles Figure 10.20.

Figure 10.20

Edit the Noise Curve to change the look of the noise on the surface.

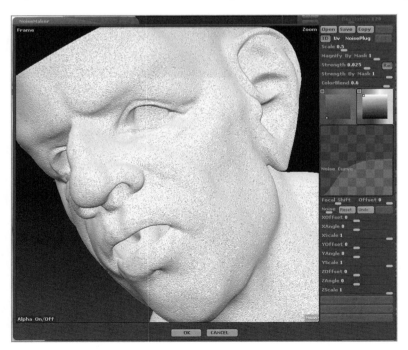

6. Click the Apply To Mesh button in the Surface subpalette of the Tool palette.

The noise pattern is now part of the mesh. Since the REC button in the Pores1 layer was activated, the noise that was applied to the surface is contained in this layer.

7. Click the eyeball icon. This disables the visibility of the pores. The noise pattern disappears.

8. Click the eyeball icon again to turn the Noise layer back on; the noise reappears. When the layer is invisible, the deformations stored on the layer are hidden but they are not deleted.

9. You can adjust the Pores slider in the Layers subpalette to change the strength of the layer. Set the Pores slider below the layer stack to **0.2**. The noise pattern is not as prominent when the slider is decreased.

Note that the slider in the layer stack next to the Pores1 layer can also be used to adjust the strength of the layer.

10. Set the Pores slider to **1.2**. The strength of the noise is much stronger.

You can set the slider strength above a value of 1 to make the changes recorded in the layer even stronger than when you origi-nally applied them. You can also invert the look of the layer by setting the slider to a negative value (see Figure 10.21).

11. Use the Save button in the File menu to save the project as **brainGuy_v02.ZPR**.

Baking Layers

The changes you create using layers can be made a permanent part of the model by baking the layers. In this example, you'll refine the look of the pores and then add wrinkles on another layer. Then these changes will be baked into the model, making them permanent.

1. Continue with the file from the previ-ous section.

The pores need a little smoothing to make them look more realistic. The SmoothPeaks brush works really well for creating realistic pores. This brush is not

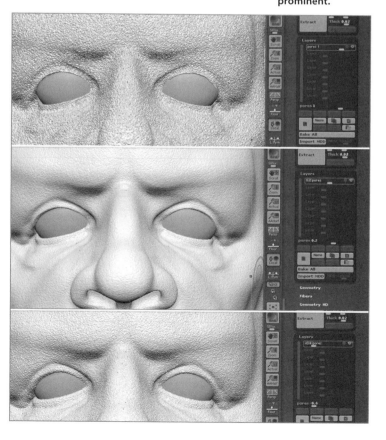

Figure 10.21

Adjust the value of the Pores slider to make the changes recorded in the layer more or less prominent.

in the standard sculpting brush library; it can be found in the Brush/Smooth section of LightBox.

2. Open LightBox to the Brush section and scroll to the left to find the Smooth folder. Double-click this folder to open it. Scroll to the left to find the SmoothPeaks brush (see Figure 10.22).

3. Double-click the SmoothPeaks brush. You'll see a warning reminding you that this brush will be mapped to the Shift key.

4. Select the Pores1 layer and set the Pores slider to **0.5**.

5. In the Layers subpalette of the Tool palette, click the new layer button, the large square button with the plus sign on it in the Layers subpalette of the Tool palette, to create a new layer.

6. Name the new layer SmoothPores.

If you try to smooth the model without creating the SmoothPores layer, a warning shows telling you that the model has active deformation layers and that sculpting is not possible unless you have a layer in Record mode. So you have a choice either to set the original Pores layer back to Record mode or to record the smoothing of the pores in a new layer. I prefer the flexibility of recording the smoothing in a new layer so I can adjust the strength later, which is why I recommend creating a new layer called SmoothPores. When you create the new layer, the Pores1 layer switches out of Record mode. Now the SmoothPores layer should be in Record mode.

7. Scale up the view of the mode. Set Draw Size to **60**; a large Draw Size smoothes more of the surface, making the work a little faster.

8. Hold the Shift key and set the Z Intensity slider on the top shelf to **40**. Use the brush to smooth the noise on the character's face. This Z Intensity setting should make the SmoothPeaks brush strong enough to even out the noise without erasing it completely. Hold the Shift key and brush over the surface. The pores start to look a little more realistic, thanks to the SmoothPeaks brush.

The Smooth Peaks brush smoothes only the parts of the surface that stick out. When it's used on a noisy surface, the effect can look a lot like skin pores (see Figure 10.23).

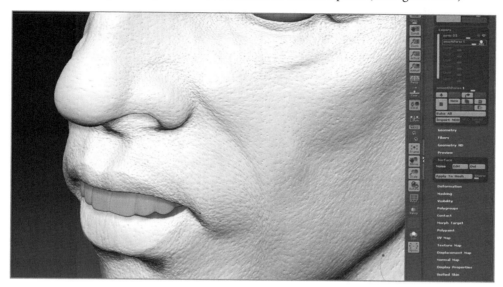

Figure 10.23

Smooth the noise to create realistic skin pores.

9. Brush over the entire surface of the head. You may want to vary the strength of the SmoothPeaks brush as you go to make some areas appear smoother than others. This adds variation to the overall look.

The pores may still look a little exaggerated but that's OK. You can still adjust the strength of the Pores layer to make the effect a little more subtle. In fact, you can experiment with the strength of both the Pores and the SmoothPores layers.

10. When you have finished smoothing the head, create a new layer in the Layers subpalette of the Tool palette. Click the Name button and name the new layer Wrinkles.

To create wrinkles, you can use the Dam_Standard brush (aka the Damian Standard Brush). It works well for creating fine lines, scratches, and wrinkles.

11. From the Brush palette select the Dam_Standard brush.

12. Use the brush to create wrinkles and fine lines below the eyes and in the folds of the skin (see Figure 10.24).

13. Once you have created enough wrinkles, go to the Layers subpalette of the Tool palette and click the REC button in the Wrinkles layer slot to turn off the layer's Record mode.

Figure 10.24

The Dam_Standard
brush is used to
create wrinkles on
the skin.

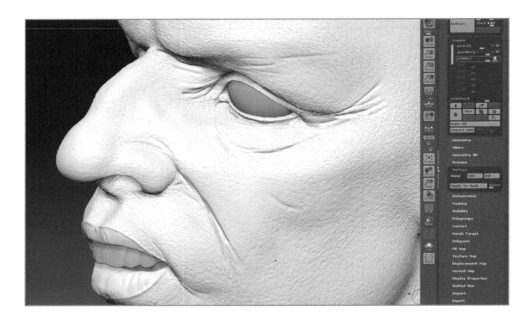

Figure 10.24

The Dam_Standard
brush is used to
create wrinkles on
the skin.

Figure 10.25

Try different values
for each of the lay-
ers in the Layers
subpalette.

14. Spend a few minutes experimenting with different values for the sliders on the Pores, SmoothPores, and Wrinkles layers (see Figure 10.25).

15. Before you bake layers, it's always a good idea to save your work! Use the Save button in the File palette and save the file as **brainGuy_v03.ZPR**.

16. In the Layers subpalette, click the Bake All button.

The Bake All button removes the layers from the Layers subpalette and makes the changes in each layer a permanent part of the sculpture. The values you have entered for each layer's slider determine the strength of the layer when it is baked.

If you want to remove the layer and all the recorded changes, click the Delete Layer button, the small button with an x on it in the Layers subpalette of the Tool palette, to delete the layer.

You may or may not want to bake your layers while working in ZBrush. It depends on what you're trying to do. Layers can be helpful as a way to test ideas while sculpting and also as a way to create variations of a model that you can present for director or client approval.

The other buttons in the Layers subpalette have the following functions:

The Up and Down Arrows (Shift+Page Up and Shift+Page Down) let you move up or down through the stack of layers (see Figure 10.26).

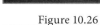

Figure 10.26

The up and down
arrows let you move
up and down in the
layers stack.

The Bent Up and Down Arrows (Ctrl+Page Up and Ctrl+Page Down) change the position of the selected layer in the stack, moving it up or down (see Figure 10.26).

Name Lets you rename the selected layer. Note that when you name a layer, a number is appended to the end of the layer, so Color becomes Color1 automatically. The number 1 indicates the intensity of the layer, which is set to 1 (or 100 percent) when you create the layer.

Duplicate Layer Creates a copy of the selected layer and adds it to the layer stack.

Merge Down Creates a new layer by merging the selected layer and the layer below it. For example, you could merge the Pores layer and the SmoothPores layer into a single layer.

Invert Reverses the depth of the strokes on the surface. For example, if you invert the Wrinkles layer, it would be like setting the Layer slider to -1. The wrinkles would push outward from the surface instead of inward.

Import MDD Can be used to import animation data as a layer. This is an advanced feature that is beyond the scope of this book.

Polypaint Layers

You can create a layer specifically for the color information painted on the model as a way to keep it separate from the sculpting details. You can use multiple layers that contain different versions of the colors and even use layers to blend between variations of the colors. If you are using ZBrush to paint texture maps for use in another 3D application, such as Maya, you can use layers to create multiple texture maps. One layer may contain the color of the model, another the reflectivity; another might be for ambient occlusion shadowing, another for cavity maps, and so on.

In the following sections, you'll paint texture maps for a human head model using different layers. Then you'll export each layer as a texture map.

Creating Polypaint Layers

To create a polypaint layer, all you need to do is create a layer for the active subtool and then start painting on it. ZBrush knows automatically that the layer is meant to contain the color information applied to your model. You can sculpt and paint on the same layer if you like, but it's a good idea to create separate layers for painting and sculpting. If you're not familiar with polypainting, read Chapter 8 to learn more.

This exercise demonstrates how to create polypainting layers:

1. Start a new session of ZBrush.
2. Continue using the version of the model that you started earlier in the chapter.
3. In the SubTool subpalette of the Tool palette, select the Head subtool.

When you start painting in a layer, make sure the tool is at the highest subdivision level. In the case of this model, the Head subtool should be at SDiv level 5.

4. Open the Layers subpalette of the Tool palette. Create a new layer and name it Color.

5. The REC button for the Color layer should be activated. Select the Standard brush and turn off Zadd on the top shelf. Turn on Rgb and use the brush to paint colors on the model.

You can use techniques similar to those discussed in Chapter 8 to paint the model (see Figure 10.27).

Figure 10.27

Colors are painted onto the skin while the Color layer is in Record mode.

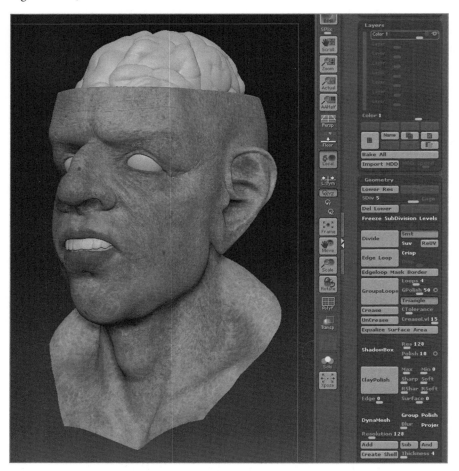

6. Once you are happy with the colors painted on the skin, use the Save button in the File menu to save the project as **brainGuyPolyPaint.ZPR**. It's always a good idea to save often while painting layers.

7. In the Layers subpalette of the Tool palette, click the eyeball icon to turn the layer visibility off. The head should turn white when you do this, indicating that the Color layer has been hidden.

8. Create a new layer and name it Specularity. The new layer should have the REC button on, indicating that it is in Record mode. The Color layer should be hidden.

Always double-check that the layer is in Record mode before you start painting!

A specular map is a grayscale texture that is connected to the specular or reflective channel of a shader network in another 3D program, such as Maya. The light parts of the map indicate a higher degree of reflectivity and shininess. Darker colors reflect less light and therefore look duller. When you create a specular map, you want light gray and white colors on the shiny parts of the face such as the nose, the cheekbones, the lips, and parts of the ear. Paint darker colors where you want the skin to be less shiny, like on the cheeks and the back of the head.

9. Paint an overall layer of gray on the head, and then use the Standard brush to add light areas for the shiny parts of the face and dark colors on the duller parts. Use the spray stroke and alpha textures to make sure the colors are spotted and uneven (see Figure 10.28). Too much evenness in the texture will make the head look like plastic in the final render.

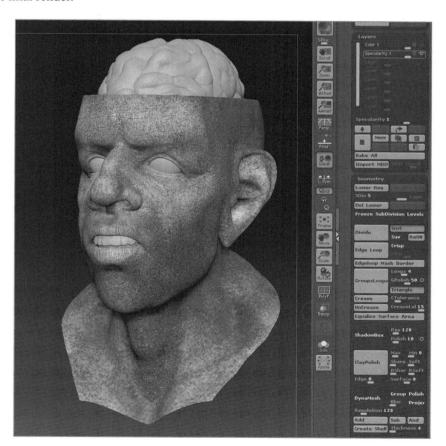

Figure 10.28

Dark and light areas are painted into a new layer named Specularity. The specular texture controls the reflectivity of the surface.

Figure 10.29

Create a new layer named Occlusion. Turn off the visibility of Color and Specularity.

Figure 10.30

Adjust intensity and scan distance in the Masking subpalette before you create the mask.

10. In the Layers subpalette of the Tool palette, click the eyeball icon to turn the layer visibility off. The head should turn white when you do this, indicating that the Specularity layer has been hidden.

11. Create a new layer and name it Occlusion. The new layer should have the REC button on, indicating that it is in Record mode. The Color and Specularity layers should be hidden (see Figure 10.29).

While the Occlusion layer is recording, you'll paint in some ambient occlusion shadowing. The texture map created from this layer can be added to a shader network in another 3D package to enhance the look of the surface while saving the time that it takes to calculate ambient occlusion shadowing.

12. In the Tool palette, open the Masking subpalette. Set Occlusion Intensity to **2** and AO Scan Distance to **0.2** (see Figure 10.30).

The Intensity control will make the masking more apparent, and increasing the scan distance increases the amount of shadowing on the surface. Calculating ambient occlusion can take a long time. To save time, you can set the model to a lower subdivision level before creating the mask.

13. In the Geometry subpalette of the Tool palette, set SDiv to **3**.

It's a good idea to lower the SDiv level when creating an ambient occlusion mask. This type of masking can take a long time to calculate on dense meshes. I like to lower the SDiv level, create the mask, and then set the SDiv level back to the highest value once the mask is applied. It's a great time saver.

14. In the Masking subpalette, click the Mask Ambient Occlusion button.

It will take a few moments to calculate the ambient occlusion shadowing. The result may seem fairly faint.

15. In the Geometry subpalette, set the SDiv slider back to **5**.

16. In the Layers subpalette, double-check and make sure REC is enabled for the Occlusion1 layer. Sometimes this will turn off automatically when you change subdivision levels.

17. Ctrl+click on a blank part of the canvas to invert the mask (or use the Ctrl+I hotkey).

18. Turn off the View Mask button.

19. Use the Standard brush to paint dark gray all over the face. The color should appear only in the unmasked parts of the surface (see Figure 10.31).

20. Use the Save button in the File palette to save the project as `brainGuyPolypaint2.ZPR`.

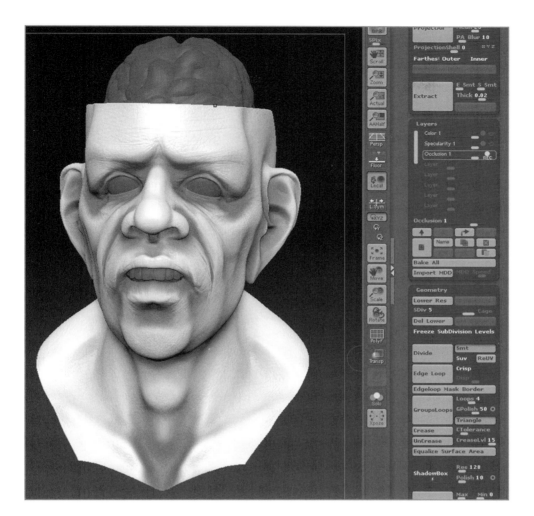

Figure 10.31

The unmasked area is painted gray, creating the look of shadows.

Creating Texture Maps

You can continue painting as many different layers of the model as you'd like. Some texture artists will paint separate texture maps for nearly every channel in a shader network. Using the layer Strength sliders, you can even blend the layers together by adjusting the slider setting on visible layers. Eventually you're going to want to export these texture maps so they can be used in other 3D programs. This is a simple process, but there are a few things you need to keep in mind.

UV TEXTURE COORDINATES

When you polypaint a model, your model does not need to have any UV texture coordinates since the color values are applied directly to the vertices of the object. However, if you want to convert the colors of the model into a texture that can be exported for use in other programs, you do need to create UVs. There are several ways to do this in ZBrush. For the example in this chapter, I have already created UV coordinates using the UV Master plug-in. Using UV Master is described in Bonus Content 2, "ZScripts and ZPlugins," on the DVD. You can also import UV coordinates created in another program. The techniques for using ZBrush with other programs are described in Bonus Content 1, "GoZ," on the DVD.

At this point, the example model already has UV coordinates, so you do not need to create any for this exercise.

The exercise in this section demonstrates how to convert and export each layer as a texture map.

1. Continue with the project from the last section or open the `brainGuyPolypaint2`.ZPR project from the `Chapter 10` folder on the DVD.

2. Turn on the visibility of the Colors layer. Turn off the visibility of the Occlusion and Specularity layers (see Figure 10.32).

Figure 10.32

Turn off the visibility of the Occlusion and Specularity layers. Turn on the visibility of the Color layer.

Before you create a texture from the colors recorded on a layer, you must make sure of two things: only the layer (or in some cases, layers) are visible, and any layer that you don't want to include in the texture is off. And make sure that none of the layers are in Record mode. The REC button should be off for all layers. If you see strange colors in your texture maps when you generate them, it's probably because the REC button is still on for one of the layers.

Figure 10.33

Set the UV Map Size slider to 2048 in the UV Map subpalette of the Tool palette.

3. Expand the UV Map subpalette of the Tool palette and set the size of the texture using the UV Map Size slider (see Figure 10.33). In this case, you can leave it at the default setting of 2048.

4. Expand the Texture Map subpalette of the Tool palette. Click the New From Polypaint button (see Figure 10.34).

A texture is created from the colors painted on the model. You won't notice any difference in the model, but you'll see a preview of the texture map in the Texture Map subpalette of the Tool palette.

Figure 10.34

Click the New From Polypaint button in the Texture Map subpalette of the Tool palette.

WHAT TO LOOK OUT FOR WHEN CREATING TEXTURES

When you apply a texture to a model, the texture covers the polypainted colors on the surface. Think of a texture as wrapping paper that is covering the entire surface of the model. When you create a texture from polypainting, the texture will look exactly like the colors painted on the model. Sometimes it's easy to forget that a texture has been applied to the model. If you paint on the surface of the model but you don't see any new colors painted on the surface, it may be because a texture is applied to the model. When this happens, just open the Texture Map subpalette of the Tool palette and turn off the Texture On button.

To export the texture, you'll need to clone it so that it appears as part of the texture library.

5. In the Texture Map subpalette of the Tool palette, click the Clone Txtr button. You'll see the texture appear in the texture library on the left shelf (see Figure 10.35).

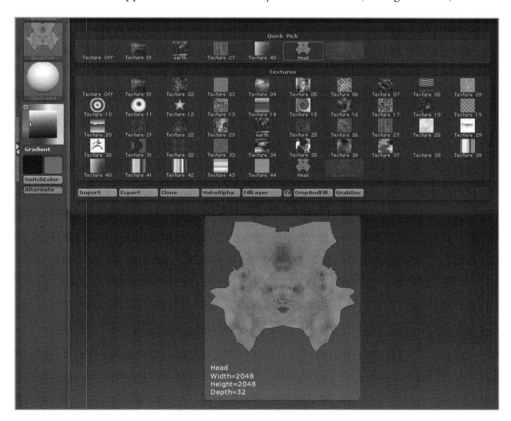

Figure 10.35

When you clone a texture, a copy appears in the texture library.

6. Open the texture library on the left shelf. Click the Export button. Save the texture to your local disk as **head_color.tif**.

7. In the Layers subpalette of the Tool palette, turn off the Colors layer and turn on the Specular layer.

8. Repeat steps 5, 6, and 7 to create the specular map. Save the file as **head_specular.tif**.

9. Repeat the process to create an ambient occlusion texture. Save the texture as **head_AO.tif**.

Once you have the textures saved to disk, you can import them into your favorite 3D program and add them to a shader network. Bonus Content 1, "GoZ," on this book's DVD goes into more detail about using ZBrush with other programs and includes information on how to create displacement and normal maps.

FLIPPED TEXTURES

Some 3D programs, such as Autodesk® Maya®, use a UV configuration that is inverted vertically relative to ZBrush. When you import a texture generated by ZBrush into Maya to apply it to the same model, you have to remember to flip the image vertically. One way to do this is to select the texture in the texture library and then click the FlipV button in the Texture palette before you export the file.

The ZBrush Timeline

ZBrush supports a limited amount of animation within the ZBrush interface. The animation capabilities of ZBrush are not intended to compete with sophisticated animation programs such as Maya. Rather, the ZBrush Timeline is a tool you can use as a way to record view positions of the model while sculpting, to present variations of a model in the form of a movie, and to test animation targets such as facial expressions for use in animation programs like Maya.

In the following sections, you'll see how the Timeline can be used to make a simple camera animation to show off variations of a model. You'll also learn how to create movies of your ZBrush sessions and turntables using the controls in the Movie palette.

The Movie Palette

ZBrush has the capability of recording everything you do on the canvas as a movie. This movie can be saved and exported to popular computer video formats such as QuickTime. The controls in the Movie palette are used to determine how the movie will be recorded and exported.

The Movie palette also has the controls for displaying and recording on the Timeline. Some buttons are only available once a movie has been recorded and is stored in the movie buffer. The Pause button is only available while a movie is being recorded.

Let's take a look at the buttons at the top of the palette (see Figure 10.36).

The **Load Movie** button is used to load movies that have been recorded and saved using ZBrush's special ZMV movie format. When you load a ZBrush movie, you can play it back and even add more using the record feature.

Play Movie plays back any recorded movie that has been loaded into the movie buffer.

Save As saves the movie that is loaded into the movie buffer to disk using the ZBrush ZMV movie format.

Export lets you save the movie that is loaded into the movie buffer as a QuickTime movie.

Record tells ZBrush to record everything that is going on in ZBrush, from the moment you click the button until you click the Pause button. The recorded movie is stored in a buffer while you are working in ZBrush. If you want to keep the movie, you must remember to save it or export it before closing ZBrush or it will be lost.

Turntable creates a movie of the 3D mesh that is currently on the canvas. The movie shows the active tool rotating around its axis. This is known as a turntable animation and is used to show off a digital sculpture from all angles. The turntable movie is appended to any movie that is currently loaded into the movie buffer.

Snapshot stores a still frame of the canvas and appends it to the movie currently loaded into the movie buffer.

TimeLapse creates a movie by taking a snapshot of the canvas each time the mouse is released or when you lift the stylus from the digital tablet. The resulting movie shows how the model has progressed over time using a time-lapse effect.

Pause stops the recording of the canvas.

Doc records only what is visible on the canvas.

Window records the entire ZBrush interface, including palettes.

Large, **Medium**, and **Small** set the size for the movie.

Delete clears the movie buffer of any recorded video that has been loaded into ZBrush.

Figure 10.37

**The Modifiers sec-
tion in the Movie
palette customizes
the way movies are
recorded.**

The Modifiers section contains a number of settings that determine exactly how the movie is recorded (see Figure 10.37). For a complete description of each control, just hold the mouse cursor over the label while holding the Ctrl key.

The Timeline

The controls for animating the camera views or the layers are found in the TimeLine subpalette of the Movie palette. To display the Timeline, click the Show button (see Figure 10.38).

The Timeline is displayed as a strip at the top of the canvas (see Figure 10.39). The tick marks on the Timeline represent the time in seconds. The label on the left of the Timeline displays the name of the selected layer in the Layers subpalette of the Tool palette. Or, if no layer is selected, the label Camera appears, indicating that the camera view is selected for the Timeline.

Figure 10.38

**Click the Show button
in the TimeLine sub-
palette of the Movie
palette to show the
Timeline.**

Figure 10.39

**The Timeline
appears above the
canvas in the ZBrush
interface.**

In this exercise, you'll see how you can create keyframes on the Timeline for the current camera view.

1. Use the Open button in the File palette to load the brainGuyPolypaint.ZPR project from the Chapter 10 folder on the DVD.

2. Place the Movie palette in a tray so that you can easily access its controls.

3. Click the Show button in the TimeLine subpalette of the Movie palette. The Timeline appears above the canvas.

4. Rotate, scale, and move the view of the model so that you are zoomed in on the face. Enable the Persp button on the right shelf to turn on perspective.

To the right of the Timeline you'll see the word *Camera*. This is letting you know that any keyframes you place on the Timeline will be applied to the current camera view.

5. Click the Timeline on the very left end. A large dot appears on the Timeline. This is a keyframe. The current view of the model is stored in the keyframe (see the left image in Figure 10.40).

6. Rotate the view and zoom away from the model. Click the Timeline about halfway across the Timeline (right image in Figure 10.40).

7. Drag the marker below the Timeline back and forth to scrub along the Timeline. You'll see the view of the model change over time.

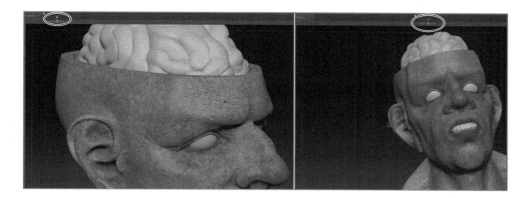

Figure 10.40

Click at different points on the Timeline to add keyframes for the camera view of the model.

To add more keyframes, just change the view again and click on the Timeline. To change a keyframe's position, just drag it left or right. To remove a keyframe, drag it upward off the Timeline. To change the length of the Timeline, change the Duration slider in the TimeLine subpalette of the Tool palette. The value shown is the time in seconds. The default is 30 seconds.

You can continue to manipulate the view of the model while you work. It won't affect the animation unless you add another keyframe on the Timeline. Camera animation can be a helpful sculpting aid. If you find yourself continually zooming in on one area or if you need to see the model from one particular view (perhaps if you need to match the model to a background), then you can create keyframes for the view. To return to a view, simply scrub along the Timeline to the point of the keyframe.

Animating Layers

The strength value of a 3D layer can be keyframed so that you can actually create animations based on the changes you sculpt into a character. This is a great way to display variations on a sculpture or test facial blend shape targets in ZBrush.

In this exercise, you'll learn how to animate a facial expression change in ZBrush using layers.

1. Continue with the project from the previous section.

2. In the Movie palette set Duration to **5**.

3. The Timeline should be visible above the canvas. If you don't see it, click the Show button in the TimeLine subpalette of the Tool palette.

4. By default, the camera is selected as the active tool on the Timeline. You can delete the keyframes on the camera by Shift+selecting the points on the Timeline and dragging upward. A warning message will ask you if you want to delete all points on the Timeline (see Figure 10.41). Click Yes.

5. In the Layers subpalette of the Tool palette, create a new layer and name it Smile.

Figure 10.41

Shift+select multiple points on the Timeline and drag upward to delete them. A warning message will appear.

6. The REC button on the Layers subpalette should be activated for the Smile layer (see Figure 10.42). To ensure that there are no masks on the model, hold the Ctrl key and drag a small selection on the canvas. When you release, all masks will be cleared.

7. In the sculpting brush library, select the Move brush.

8. Use the Move brush to shape the mouth into a smile. Pull the corners of the mouth back toward the ears, and shape the lower lip so that it is tucked under the front teeth.

9. Use the Move brush to pull the eyebrows up. The lower eyelids should move up as well (see Figure 10.43).

Figure 10.42

The REC button for the Smile layer should be activated.

Figure 10.43

Use the Move brush to shape the mouth into a smile. Move the eyebrows and lower eyelids up as well.

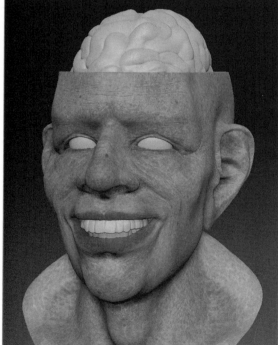

10. Set the slider for the Smile layer to **0**. The face returns to its original state, and the REC button automatically turns off when the value of the slider is changed.

11. Take a look at the Timeline. When a layer is selected in the Layers subpalette, its name appears to the left of the Timeline (see Figure 10.44). In this case the label should read "Smile" since the Smile layer is selected. If no layer is selected, then "Camera" is displayed. Make sure the layer you want to animate is selected before adding keyframes to the Timeline. This is why it's important to name the layers with a descriptive title. Click a point at the left end of the Timeline to create a keyframe.

12. In the Layers subpalette, set the slider for the Smile layer to **1**. Click a point midway through the Timeline to set a second keyframe.

13. Set the slider for the Smile layer to **-0.25**. This moves the points of the face in the opposite direction, causing the face to frown a little. Click a point at the right end of the Timeline to set a third keyframe (see Figure 10.45).

Figure 10.44

The name of the selected layer appears to the left of the Timeline.

14. Drag on the marker below the Timeline to test the change in the expressions. If you need to make a change to the smile, just set the slider for the Smile layer to **1**, turn on the REC button, and make the changes. This will be recorded into the layer.

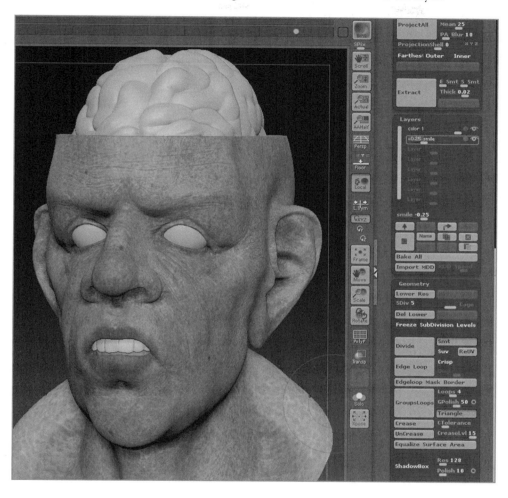

Figure 10.45

The slider for the Smile layer is set to -0.25, and a keyframe is added at the right end of the Timeline.

You can make even more sophisticated animation by adding additional layers. When you set a keyframe on a layer, you are recording the value of the layer's Strength slider. Animation is created by interpolating between different layer values. You can add additional layers and keyframe their strength values as well, creating overlapping movements. Keep in mind that each layer significantly increases the memory the project occupies on your hard drive, so try not to overdo it.

When more than one layer has been keyframed on the Timeline, you'll see black dots appear on the Timeline indicating the keyframes for unselected layers. Use this as a visual guide for timing the animation of multiple layers.

15. Use the Save button in the File palette to save the project.

Note that you can also animate the strength of polypaint layers so you can fade between different versions of colors painted on the model.

Recording and Exporting Movies

You can record a movie of the animation playing directly on the ZBrush canvas and using any render mode you like. To record a movie, you need to add at least two keyframes to the camera Timeline:

1. Continue with the project from the previous section.

2. The Timeline should be visible above the canvas. If you don't see it, click the Show button in the TimeLine subpalette of the Tool palette.

3. Make sure the word *Camera* appears to the left of the Timeline. This indicates that keyframes placed on the Timeline will be stored for the camera position.

4. Center the view of the character and rotate so that the character is facing the left side of the canvas.

5. Click the left side of the Timeline to create a keyframe.

6. Rotate the view of the model so that the character is facing the right side of the screen.

7. Click the right end of the Timeline to create another keyframe.

8. Shift+click the marker below the Timeline. This will cause ZBrush to play back the animation on the canvas starting from the point where you clicked the Timeline. The animation will continue to loop until you press the Esc key.

9. Ctrl+Shift-click the marker below the Timeline. ZBrush will play the animation again, but this time it records the animation and stores it in the movie buffer.

10. To stop the recording, press the Esc key.

11. To play the movie, click the Play button in the Movie palette. The animation is appended to any movies already loaded or recorded to the buffer.

12. To remove or change the fade-in text at the start of the movie, use the controls in the Title Image subpalette of the Movie palette (see Figure 10.46).

13. To save the movie to disk, click the Save As button. This will save the movie in ZBrush's special ZMV format.

14. To export the movie using the QuickTime format, click the Export button and choose the options in the Export dialog.

Figure 10.46

Change the duration of the fade in and fade out as well as text displayed for the movie title in the Title Image subpalette of the Movie palette.

If you want to render the movie using BPR, click the BPR button to create a render, then Ctrl+Shift-click the marker below the Timeline. Keep in mind that it could take ZBrush a long time to create an animation using this render mode.

The Timeline feature is quite powerful and offers a way to add real excitement to your sculpting portfolio reel.

To see a version of the movie created from this exercise, watch the `animatedFace.mov` movie in the `Chapter 10` folder on the DVD.

Contact Points

Figure 10.47

The babyDragon model is made up of four subtools.

Contact points allow you to easily animate subtools as single objects on the Timeline. This works best for simple animation and saves you the trouble of trying to create layers for each subtool and animate them to match the motion of the main tool.

In this example, you'll see how to create contact points so that the teeth of a dragon follow the movement of its mouth:

1. Use the Open button in the File menu to open the `babyDragon.ZPR` project from the `Chapter 10` folder on the DVD.

This model is made up of four subtools: Head, Eyes, UpperTeeth, and LowerTeeth (see Figure 10.47).

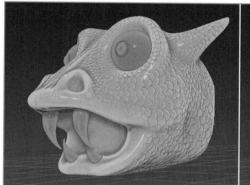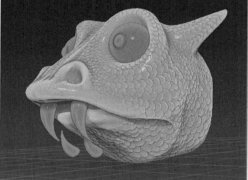

Figure 10.48

The mouth opens and closes when you move the marker below the Timeline.

Figure 10.49

The mouthClose layer has been animated on the Timeline.

2. Drag the marker below the Timeline from left to right. The dragon's mouth closes (see Figure 10.48). This action has been animated using a layer named mouthClose (see Figure 10.49).

Notice that the bottom teeth are left behind in the animation. To fix this, you'll create contact points between the head and the teeth.

3. Make sure the Head subtool is the currently selected subtool. In the Tool palette, expand the Contact subpalette.

Figure 10.50

The Contact subpalette of the Tool palette

The Contact subpalette has three main buttons labeled C1, C2, and C3 (see Figure 10.50). For contacts to work, you must establish three points between the animated surface and the subtool. To do this, you use the Transpose tool.

4. Click the Move button on the top shelf (hotkey = W). You can use Move, Scale, or Rotate—it doesn't matter. What does matter is that the Transpose handle is available.

5. Use the Transpose tool to draw a line from a point on the lower jaw to the base of one of the lower teeth. Rotate the view, and make sure the line goes to the tooth in all views (see Figure 10.51). Adjust the Transpose handle until it is clearly touching the surface of the jaw and the surface of the tooth.

Figure 10.51

The Transpose tool should connect the jaw to the tooth in all angles.

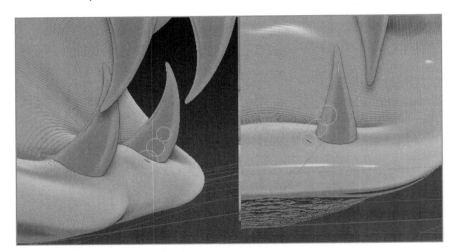

6. In the Contact subpalette of the Tool palette, click the C1 button. This stores the first contact point for the subtool, which lets ZBrush know how to move the lowerTeeth subtool in relation to the Head subtool. You need to make two more points to establish the contact.

7. Create another line from the jaw to the base of the other tooth, and click the C2 button.

8. Create a third line from the jaw to the base of either tooth, and click the C3 button.

9. Scrub the Timeline back and forth. Now the lower teeth move with the jaw (see Figure 10.52).

If the upper teeth move as well, then it's possible that the end of the Transpose handle was too close to the upperTeeth subtool. You can move the Timeline back to the start, adjust the Transpose handle, and restore the contact point by clicking the C1, C2, or C3 button in the Contact subpalette of the Tool palette. Also notice that the animation of the lower teeth occurs when you move the playhead on the Timeline. If you adjust the strength of the mouthClose subtool, the teeth do not move. Once you move the Timeline playhead, the teeth snap back into position.

10. To see a finished version of the project, use the Open button in the File palette to open the babyDragon_v02.ZPR file from the Chapter 10 folder on the DVD.

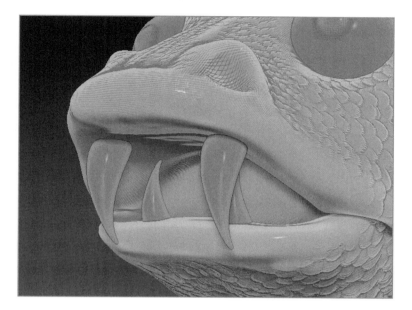

Figure 10.52

Now the teeth move with the jaw.

Summary

In this Chapter you learned how to add surface noise to an object. How to use morph targets and how to create 3D layers for storing various types of detail. You leaned how to use the ZBrush TimeLine to store and animate camera views. Finally you learned how record movies and how to animate facial expressions using the 3D Layers and the TimeLine.

About the Companion DVD

This appendix summarizes the content you'll find on the DVD. If you need help with copying the items provided on the DVD, refer to the installation instructions in the "Using the DVD" section of this appendix.

- **What you'll find on the DVD**

- **System requirements**

- **Using the DVD**

- **Troubleshooting**

What You'll Find on the DVD

The following sections are arranged by category and provide a summary of the content you'll find on the DVD. If you need help with installing the items provided on the DVD, refer to the installation instructions in the "Using the DVD" section of this appendix.

Chapter Files

In the Chapters directory you will find all the sample files for completing the tutorials and understanding concepts in this book.

The video files are stored in a Movies folder. The movies show how I sculpted some of the example files used in the book as well as demonstrations of specific ZBrush features and techniques.

You will also find two bonus chapters on GoZ and ZBrush plug-ins, as well as the sample files for these chapters on the DVD.

System Requirements

This DVD does not include the ZBrush software. You will need to have ZBrush 4R2b installed on your computer to complete the exercises in the book.

To complete the core exercises of this book, you need ZBrush version 4R2b or higher. Image-editing software, such as Adobe Photoshop or Corel Painter, will be helpful but not absolutely required for some sections. GoZ, which is explored in a bonus chapter found on the DVD, requires Autodesk Maya. However, you can also use Luxology modo, MAXON's CINEMA 4D, or Autodesk® 3ds Max®. Hardware requirements are a PC or Mac running ZBrush with a gigabyte or more of RAM. The more RAM you have, the better results you can get with ZBrush.

Make sure that your computer meets the minimum system requirements shown in the following list. If your computer doesn't match up to most of these requirements, you may have problems using the files on the companion DVD.

- A PC running Microsoft Windows XP, Windows Vista, or Windows 7 or an Intel-based Macintosh running OS X 10.5 or higher. The files on the DVD should be compatible with either operating system. The book was created using ZBrush 4R2b on an Apple Macintosh.

  - Your computer's processor should be a fast Pentium 4 or newer (or equivalent, such as AMD) with optional multithreading or hyperthreading capabilities. ZBrush requires at least a Pentium 3 processor.

- 2048 MB of RAM (4096 MB for working with multi-million-poly meshes)
- Monitor: 1280×1024 resolution or higher (32 bits)
- A Mac running Mac OS X 10.5 or newer
    - 1024 MB of RAM (2048 MB recommended for working with multi-million-polys)
    - Monitor: 1024×768 resolution set to millions of colors (recommended: 1280×1024 or higher)
- An Internet connection
- A DVD-ROM drive
- Apple QuickTime 7.0 or later (download from www.quicktime.com)

For the most up-to-date information, check www.pixologic.com/zbrush/system.

While it is possible to use a mouse with ZBrush, a Wacom or other digital tablet will enable you to paint and sculpt naturally. It is essential to use some form of Wacom tablet, be it a Cintiq or a standard Intuos, with ZBrush.

Using the DVD

For best results, you'll want to copy the files from the DVD to your computer. To copy the items from the DVD to your hard drive, follow these steps:

1. Insert the DVD into your computer's DVD-ROM drive. The license agreement appears.

Windows users: The interface won't launch if Autorun is disabled. In that case, choose Start → Run (for Windows Vista, choose Start → All Programs → Accessories → Run). In the dialog box that appears, type **D:\Start.exe**. (Replace D with the proper letter if your DVD drive uses a different letter. If you don't know the letter, see how your DVD drive is listed under My Computer.) Click OK.

2. Read through the license agreement, and then click the Accept button if you want to use the DVD.

The DVD interface appears. The interface allows you to access the content with just one or two clicks. Alternatively, you can access the files at the root directory of your hard drive.

Mac users: The DVD icon will appear on your desktop; double-click the icon to open the DVD, and then navigate to the files you want.

Troubleshooting

Wiley has attempted to provide programs that work on most computers with the minimum system requirements. Alas, your computer may differ, and some programs may not work properly for some reason.

The two likeliest problems are that you don't have enough memory (RAM) for the programs you want to use or that you have other programs running that are affecting the installation or running of a program. If you get an error message such as "Not enough memory" or "Setup cannot continue," try one or more of the following suggestions and then try using the software again:

Turn off any antivirus software running on your computer. Installation programs sometimes mimic virus activity and may make your computer incorrectly believe that it's being infected by a virus.

Close all running programs. The more programs you have running, the less memory is available to other programs. Installation programs typically update files and programs, so if you keep other programs running, installation may not work properly.

Add more RAM to your computer. This is, admittedly, a drastic and somewhat expensive step. However, adding more memory can really help the speed of your computer and allow more programs to run at the same time.

Customer Care

If you have trouble with the book's companion DVD, please call the Wiley Product Technical Support phone number at (800) 762-2974. Outside the United States, call +1 (317) 572-3994. You can also contact Wiley Product Technical Support at http://sybex .custhelp.com. John Wiley & Sons will provide technical support only for installation and other general quality control items. For technical support on the applications themselves, consult the program's vendor or author.

To place additional orders or to request information about other Wiley products, please call (877) 762-2974.

Please check the book's website at www.sybex.com/go/introducingzbrush3e, where we'll post additional content and updates that supplement this book, should the need arise.

Index

Note to reader: **Bolded** page numbers refer to main discussions of a topic. *Italicized* page numbers refer to illustrations.

Wiley Publishing, Inc.End-User License Agreement